Biology Workbook

NCEA Level 3

NEW EDITION

Martin Hanson | Penny Daddy | David Blaker

Australia • Brazil • Mexico • Singapore • United Kingdom • United States

Biology Workbook NCEA Level 3
2nd Edition
Martin Hanson
Penny Daddy
David Blaker

Cover designer: Cheryl Smith, Macarn Design
Text designer: Cheryl Smith, Macarn Design
Production controller: Siew Han Ong

Any URLs contained in this publication were checked for currency during the production process. Note, however, that the publisher cannot vouch for the ongoing currency of URLs.

First published in 2012 as Level 3 Biology Workbook by Cengage New House

For product information and technology assistance,
in Australia call **1300 790 853**;
in New Zealand call **0800 449 725**

For permission to use material from this text or product, please email
aust.permissions@cengage.com

National Library of New Zealand Cataloguing-in-Publication Data
A catalogue record for this book is available from the National Library of New Zealand.

9780170355582

Cengage Learning Australia
Level 7, 80 Dorcas Street
South Melbourne, Victoria Australia 3205

Cengage Learning New Zealand
Unit 4B Rosedale Office Park
331 Rosedale Road, Albany, North Shore 0632, NZ

For learning solutions, visit **cengage.co.nz**

Printed in Australia by Ligare Pty Limited.
5 6 7 8 9 10 11 21 20 19 18 17

Contents

Introduction

Using this resource

This workbook meets the needs of students doing NCEA Biology at Level 3. All seven standards are covered in detail, each consisting of several units.

Every unit has a group of review activities under the heading 'Check your understanding', with an overall total of over 270 questions. Answers are provided at the back of this book.

Internal

Each school has its own ways of dealing with internally-assessed standards 3.1, 3.2, 3.4 and 3.7. Some schools use individual student investigations and assignments, others use internal tests. This book provides enough information to help students with both types of assessment.

For each of the internal standards, dozens of different investigation topics are possible. It is not realistic to provide information for every possibility, but topics are suggested together with outline information.

External

Achievement standards 3.3, 3.5 and 3.6 are assessed through external exams, so information is provided in greater detail. In addition, each of these sections has ten 'exam-type' questions that require longer answers. Some of these questions are accompanied by 'scaffold' information to guide the answering process. The teacher CD contains answers to all 30 exam-type questions, together with model answers (exemplars) for some others.

A, M, E

This resource offers a depth of material for those aiming at any of the three grades: Achieved, Merit, Excellence. Research and technical information more appropriate to Excellence grade is enclosed in framed boxes marked by a big letter E. This differentiation means that students aiming for Achievement grade could save time by skipping E-box material for that particular standard. Students aiming for Merit grade could consider using these E-boxes.

Review activities and questions are not labelled A, M or E, because grades depend on answers, not on questions. However NCEA questions provide clues as to what grade could be earned. Most start with a verb; commonly *describe, explain, discuss*. Verbs like these give a clear indication of what a student needs to do to earn a particular grade.

Achievement: *describe, define, identify, list, match, name.*
Achievement with Merit: *explain, compare, classify, analyse, reason, summarise, sequence, apply.*
Achievement with Excellence: *discuss, evaluate, predict, design, plan, suggest, link, hypothesise.*

NCEA information is included at the end of each section.

3.1 Practical investigation

Unit 1 | Practical investigation

Achievement Standard 91601 offers three types of investigation:

A **Fair-test experiments.** Examples: investigating how much the growth of water plants is affected by fertiliser run-off.

B **A pattern-seeking investigation.** Example: looking for patterns in the distribution of plants or insects in a nearby natural habitat.

C **A modelling activity.** Example: developing an interactive computer program that mimics aspects of natural selection and/or genetic drift.

This unit introduces examples of the above three types, as well as revising key features of the scientific method. Details of NCEA requirements are at the end of 3.1.

Fig. 3.1.1 One example of a pattern-seeking investigation: the distribution of mangrove breathing roots in different kinds of substrate.

The nature of science

Biology is continually growing and changing, with new discoveries pouring in. How are things discovered in the first place, and why? It may help to see that any scientific investigation stands on three legs, each of which is essential to the process:

- questions — based on curiosity and a desire to find out
- ideas — including hypotheses and interpretations of evidence
- evidence — knowledge and information; some certain fact, some less certain.

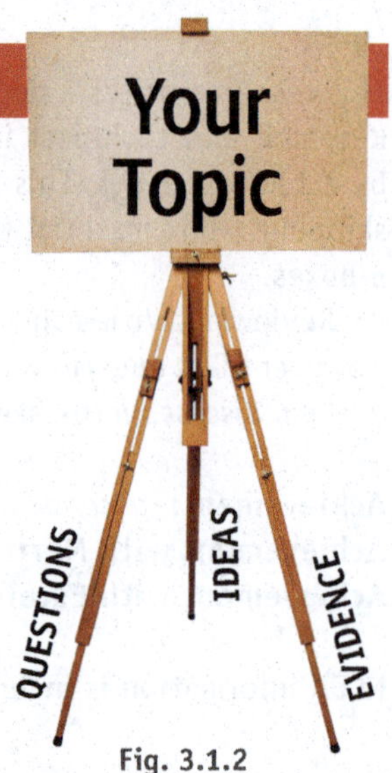

Fig. 3.1.2

Most evidence comes from scientists working in teams, their investigations guided by earlier knowledge and by scientific theories. Quite often theories are changed when new evidence is discovered.

The word *theory* has two different meanings.

1 In general, a theory is an opinion or a guess.

2 In science, maths and economics, a theory (aka 'theoretical model') is any big idea that helps explain many facts, e.g. atomic theory.

 ISBN: 9780170355582

Choosing a topic

Ideally your investigation should begin with a question arising from observation, from something you have noticed outdoors, or read about, or noticed in earlier experiments. Examples: How much effect does farm run-off have on plants in lakes and rivers? How successful are snails at finding their way home again?

Guidelines linked to AS 91601 state that the teacher will provide guidance, but that you have to come up with the ideas and design, and actually carry out the investigation yourself. In choosing a topic, you will also need to consider a number of realities, including:

- cause no harm. Anything involving animals will need ethical approval.
- limited time. Avoid slow-growing plants and complex investigations.

The activities in 'Check your understanding' 1–3 introduce a few possible topics. There are hundreds of possible topics for investigation, with choices and planning up to you.

Check your understanding

1 First, decide whether each of the investigations described below is a fair-test (ft) type or a pattern-seeking (ps) type. Next: most of the investigations could be suitable and meet the stated guidelines. Mark the suitable ones 'Y', the three unsuitable ones 'N'.

Investigation	ft/ps?	Y/N?
A Investigate the food preferences of slaters (woodlice/isopods) in captive conditions.		
B Compare the growth rates of young tomato plants at 20°C, 30°C and 40°C.		
C Mapping the distribution of barnacles from low-tide to high-tide mark.		
D Compare the growth rates of manuka trees in different soil conditions.		
E Find if the density of mangrove breathing roots depends on the type of mud or sand that mangrove trees are growing in.		
F Compare the effectiveness of several commercial disinfectants, using agar plates inoculated with bacteria.		
G Observe territorial and social behaviour of crickets that are being kept in captivity.		
H Compare the influence of different types of running shoe on sprint performance (or basketball boots on jump height).		

For the three above that you marked 'N', briefly explain why you made that decision; then suggest what modifications (if any) could make it a suitable topic for investigation.

1

Forming a hypothesis

Having decided on your topic and its central question, the next step is to come up with a hypothesis. A *hypothesis* is an 'idea under suggestion', or an 'intelligent guess'. Testable hypotheses are especially useful. Hypotheses can take the form of a *prediction* or an *if* … *then* … statement. Examples:

- If we experimentally increase the amount of fertiliser in water, then growth of plants should increase in proportion.
- If snails are moved about 10 m away from their home base, then most of them will probably find their way back.

hypo = under, *thesis* = idea
pre = before, *dict* = statement

Check your understanding

2 Suggest a hypothesis related to each of the following questions.

a How deep should corn seeds be planted?

If we try planting corn seeds at different depths, then we could …

b How effectively does citronella oil repel mosquitoes?

c How much does water pH affect plant growth?

d How much does watering frequency affect plant growth?

ISBN: 9780170355582

e What is the effect of temperature on CO_2 production by yeast?

____

____

____

Using variables

In most investigations, the scientific way to test a hypothesis is to compare situations that are the same in almost every way. To do this you need to understand about different variables.

The **independent variable** (IV) is the factor that you choose to change in an experiment, and thus know in advance. We say *independent* because the choice is yours. Your independent variable needs a range of at least four, which means at least four different situations or measured values.

The **dependent variable** (DV) is the factor likely to be influenced by the IV. We say *dependent* because it *depends* on the IV. The dependent variable gives your results (data). It is not correct to say that a DV is 'what is being measured', because in a good investigation all variables (IV, DV, CV) should be measured.

Controlled variables (CVs) are all the other variables that could possibly affect your results. Your CV list depends on what is being investigated, and can include variables such as temperature, light intensity, chemical concentration, etc. In order to make comparisons as fair as possible, CVs need to be kept as constant (controlled) as possible in your trials.

If these CVs are not the same for each trial, then the experiment may not be valid. Any kind of data could be:

- **qualitative**, meaning descriptions without measurements. Examples: warm and cold; five different colours; three size categories.
- **quantitative**, meaning that measurements are included. Examples: 17 grams; 0.1 mol/L. Use quantitative data wherever possible, but avoid falling into the trap of thinking that just because something can be measured, it must be important.

Example: A fair-test investigation in which the growth of duckweed is measured in solutions containing different amounts of dissolved fertiliser. In this plan, the number of individual green leaves in each of the containers below is to be recorded weekly over a period of three months.

Fig. 3.1.3 Floating duckweed is common on stagnant ponds. Each individual plant has only one or two leaves, and the plants reproduce rapidly by division (vegetative reproduction).

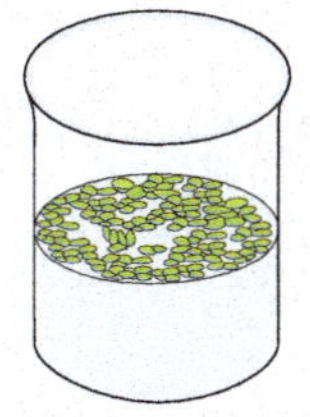

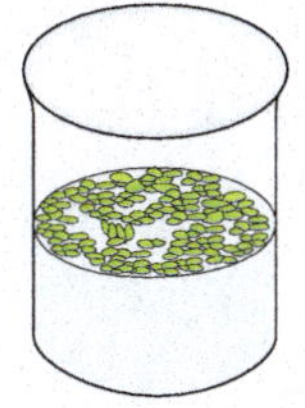

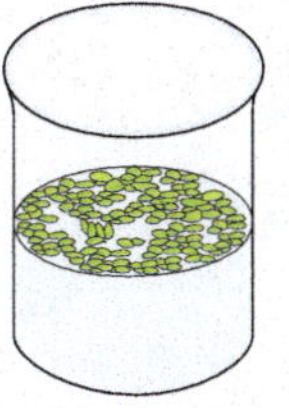

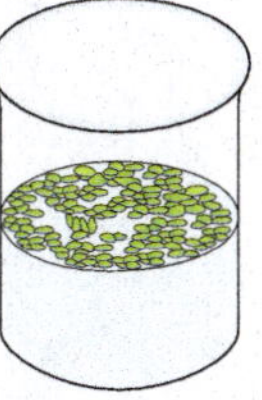

tap water only 1 g/L fertiliser 2 g/L fertiliser 3 g/L fertiliser 5 g/L fertiliser

Check your understanding

3 a Suggest a hypothesis this investigation was probably designed to test. Write your hypothesis in the form of a prediction.

b Suggest a suitable title for the investigation, in the form of a question.

c Identify the IV.

d Identify the DV.

e State the number and range of values for the IV in this particular investigation.

f List five or more controlled variables (CVs) that should be kept the same across all of the tests done in this investigation.

g Identify what is inadequate about the statement 'different amounts of dissolved fertiliser'. Suggest an improvement to this feature of the plan.

ISBN: 9780170355582

Planning your investigation

After you have chosen your central question and topic, use a logbook to record your plans and results, as suggested in the bullet list below. This record could be kept in digital form, but may be best in booklet form. Your teacher will need this logbook to provide guidance, and it must be handed in with your final report.

Suggested content of your logbook:

- your original hypothesis, plus any changes to it as you go along
- for fair test investigations, identify the DV, CVs, IV
- drawings and notes on your methods; how and why you intend to use any specialist equipment, how you plan to make measurements and record results
- do trial runs to check for problems. Note how well your experiments and data collection work, record any changes to your methods, and the reasons why they were made, and note the dates any changes were made.
- try to avoid bias, but be honest if you suspect bias in your own work. Example of bias: selecting results that show what you were hoping to find.
- write observations and results straight away in your logbook, not on scraps of paper. Use tables and photos and digital recordings where suitable.

Planning is one step in the overall process of your practical investigation. The full process involves the following steps:

1. **Planning**, as described above
2. **Carrying out** the investigation
3. **Processing** the information gained; which includes interpreting your data and relating this to relevant scientific principles and theories. Also relate this information to scientific research done by others.
4. **Reporting** on the investigation.

Since Achievement Standard 91601 is likely to take up less than one quarter of a school year (about 100 classroom hours per subject), it may be a good idea to create your own timetable to make sure that your investigation can be completed by hand-in date. Allocate a realistic number of days to each of stages 1, 2, 3 and 4.

After you have chosen an investigation topic, write your plans in a logbook. Include the following: the original observation and/or question you began with; your hypothesis; your IV; the range you intend to have for this variable; your DV, including a description of how you will measure it; a list of control variables: drawings and notes on your intended methods; an estimate of how long the investigation is likely to take; conditions under which you will keep live plants and animals (if any); a preliminary table in which you could record your first batch of results.

Final report

Your investigation needs to be written as a scientific report, to be handed in together with your logbook. Recommended seven subheadings:

- **Question or observation** that got your investigation started.
- **Aim:** what you set out to do. The aim could be to test a particular hypothesis.
- **Method:** what you actually did. Ideally this needs to be a step-by-step account. It does not need to give every detail (some information may appear only in your logbook), but needs to be in enough detail to enable anyone else to follow in your footsteps and repeat your investigations.
- **Results:** what you found. Results may be a mixture of description, tables, graphs, calculations. They do not need to show all the raw data, as this should be in your logbook.

- **Conclusion:** what the results tell you. A valid conclusion should link back to your original hypothesis. (A conclusion is not a summary of results.)
- **Discussion/evaluation:** your comments on possible sampling or measurement bias in your method. Also suggest how the method could be improved. Explain in what way your results link with other results, and with relevant scientific theories and principles.
- **References.** whether aiming for A, M or E, you should include a short list of all the resources you used, so that anyone reading your report can check the sources. This list could include science books, magazines, research literature. For both print and website information, identify the author, date, title, source.

Checklist

Tick each item to monitor your progress through the investigation.

- ☐ Hypothesis is clearly stated at the start.
- ☐ Topic approved by teacher before you start.
- ☐ Your investigation is feasible, given available resources and time.
- ☐ Ethics and animal welfare issues are taken into account.
- ☐ Reading research done before you actually start practical work.
- ☐ IV, DV, controls and measurement methods are all planned.
- ☐ Method of collecting data is consistent, and related to the study.
- ☐ Results being kept in a logbook, with back-up on computer.
- ☐ Presentation of data and statistics properly done (see Unit 2).
- ☐ Your report is arranged into sections, including a reference section.
- ☐ Draft report has been checked before the final version is printed out.

Computer modelling

This activity is only for those who already have skill in programming. It could be done in conjunction with Biology 3.5 (Achievement Standard 91605). The aim is to create a computer program that imitates one or other aspect of Biology 3.5. Whichever theoretical model is chosen, your computer-program model should ideally incorporate different scenarios. Some examples:

1. Natural selection, perhaps with different rates of mutation, or the arrival of a new predator.
2. Genetic drift, perhaps with different-sized gene pools.
3. Reproductive isolation, perhaps with different rates of gene flow.

ISBN: 9780170355582

Unit 2 | Graphs and statistics

For any investigation involving measurements, one common mistake is to write results on bits of paper that later become mixed up. For quantitative results it's best to enter data directly into a logbook, in a table that has been prepared in advance. Remember to include units. Having made the effort to collect data, the next steps are to make use of these results by presenting them in graphs, and also to use appropriate statistics.

Graphs

A graph provides a picture of information more clearly than any table can. If data are entered into a spreadsheet such as Microsoft Excel, the Chart Wizard function will draw graphs for you — but you still need to decide what kind of graph will best suit your purpose.

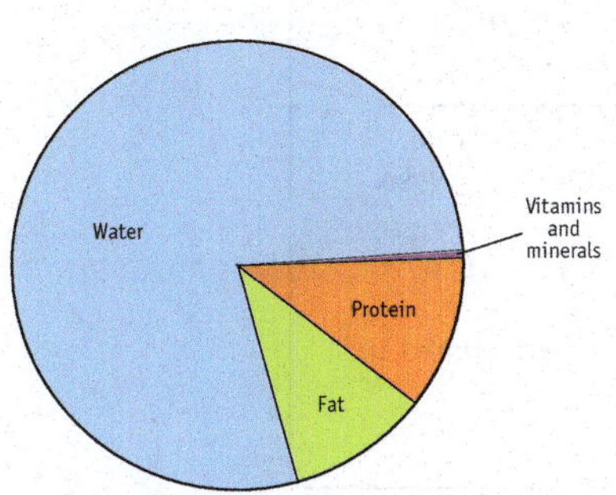

Pie chart Use this when one variable consists of separate qualitative categories and the other variable is a percentage.

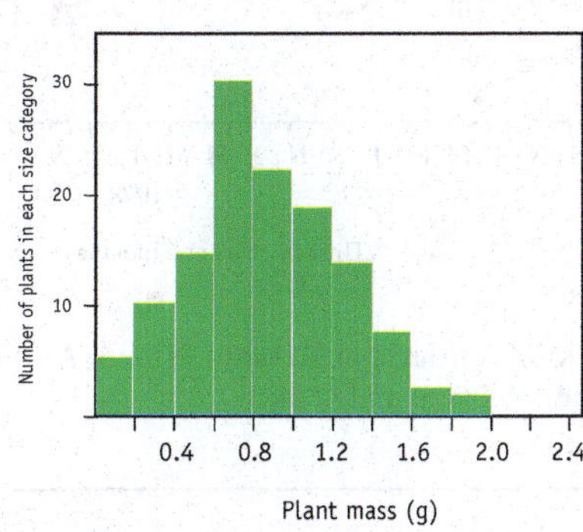

Bar graphs Can be used in much the same situations as a pie chart. Keep spaces between adjacent bars.

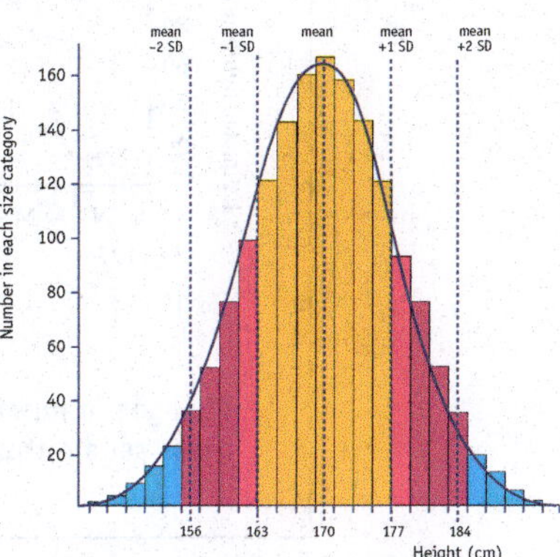

Histogram Use this where one variable has continuous data (or else measurements in categories) and the other variable is a count, usually a percentage.

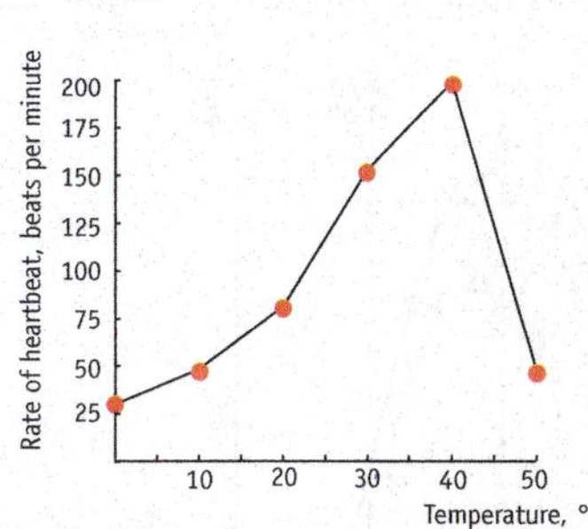

Line graph Use this in a situation where both variables — both the dependent variable and the independent variable are continuous.

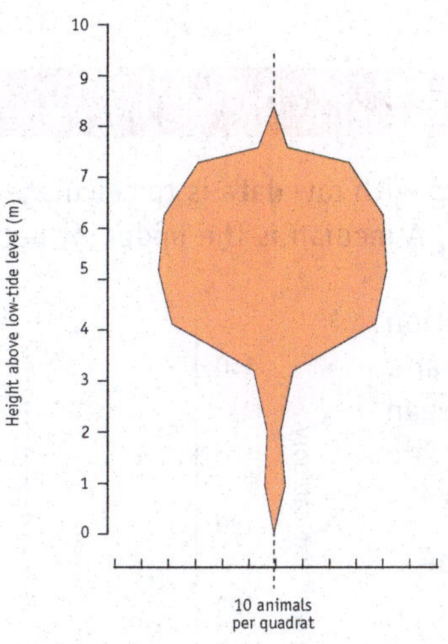

Kite diagram Sometimes used instead of a line graph. The kite axis can be horizontal or vertical.

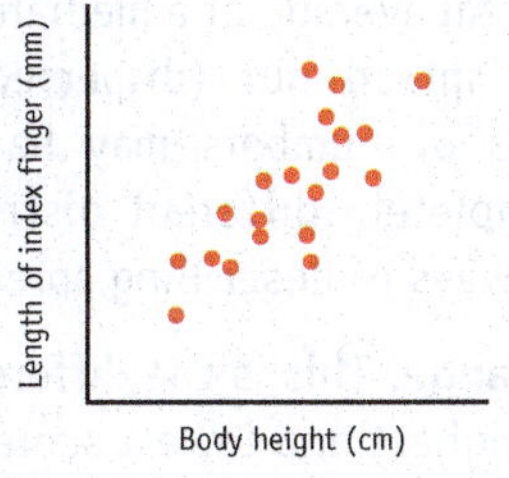

Scatter graph Can be used to find if there is a correlation between two variables.

Fig. 3.1.4

Whichever kind of graph you choose, present it in a way that anybody can understand at a glance. Six guidelines for line and scatter graphs are shown in this example.

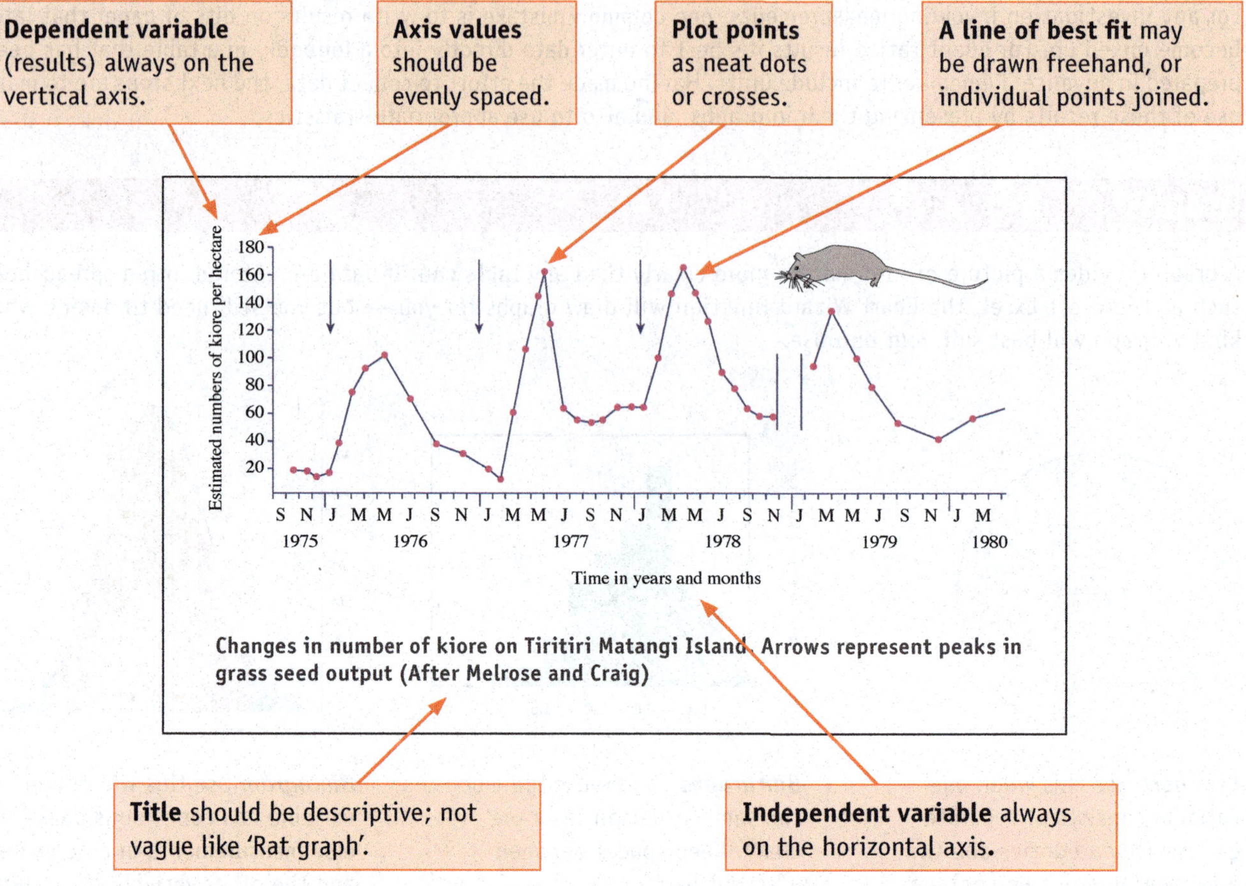

Changes in number of kiore on Tiritiri Matangi Island. Arrows represent peaks in grass seed output (After Melrose and Craig)

Fig. 3.1.5

Descriptive statistics

Averages and medians. The first step in dealing with raw data is to calculate a 'central' figure such as the average. An average is also known as a 'mean', symbol $\bar{x}$. A median is the midpoint between the highest and lowest figures.

Spread. An average or a median gives no indication of how spread out (dispersed) the results are. Two lots of numbers may have the same mean but completely different distributions. There are several ways of describing spread. Two of these:

- **range**. This is the difference between the highest and lowest scores.
  Example: 146 to 194, range 48.
  Problem: range figures do not show 'bunched' results.
- **standard deviation** (SD). Imagine a normal distribution for the heights of a hundred 17-year-old males. From one SD above the mean to one SD below will include 68% of them. Two SD above and below the mean will include 95%.

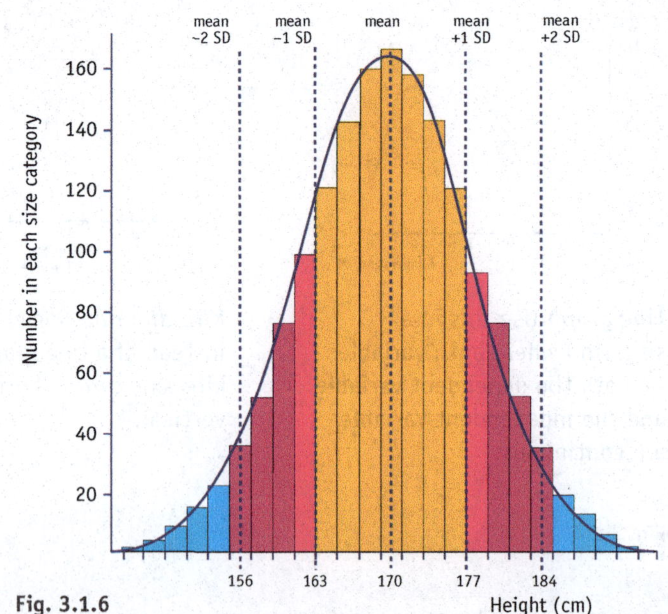

Fig. 3.1.6

ISBN: 9780170355582

Statistical difference

Often it is necessary to compare two sets of results. The question then arises: are the differences due to chance alone, or are the differences 'significant'? There are several kinds of tests to find out whether a difference is statistically significant or not. Two such tests are mentioned here. The 'Excellence' box below has details on how to do these tests.

t-test

This test is used to compare **continuous data** from two sets of results, usually two normal distributions. The t-test is most often used to find if the differences between the results are statistically significant, or due to chance alone.

Chi-squared test

The chi-squared test is used to compare **categories**; usually comparing actual observed results with expected results. It is often used in genetics and ecology. For example, if theory leads you to expect that a particular plant cross should produce a 3:1 ratio in the next generation, then out of 40 plants the expected result would in theory be 30 with red flowers, 10 with white flowers. An observed result of 29 red and 11 white is close to what was expected, the slight difference from the expected result probably due to chance. An observed result of 23 red and 17 white could mean that the expected 30-10 was based on a wrong assumption. A chi-squared test could decide whether this result was due to chance alone.

Null hypothesis and P

Both t-tests and chi-squared tests are used to evaluate the **null hypothesis.** A null hypothesis always assumes that 'any difference between the two sets of figures is due to chance alone'. Statistical difference tests may end up with the null hypothesis being rejected. The calculations involve finding the 'level of probability', **P.** If P is more than 0.1, the null hypothesis is probably correct. If P is less that 0.05, the null hypothesis is probably incorrect.

Calculated probability, P	Likelihood that the null hypothesis is correct	Reject the null hypothesis? Or not?	Is the difference significant?
P = 0.1	10%	not rejected	Not significant
P = 0.05	5%	not conclusive	Possibly significant
P = 0.01	1%	reject	Significant
P = 0.001	0.1%	reject	Highly significant

Calculations on statistical difference

A number of websites will do these calculations very quickly, but you first need to understand the language of statistics including: normal distribution, standard deviation, null hypothesis. You also need to select the right test for your purpose and make sense of the results in terms of P.

Two sites for online calculations: studentsttest.com *and* graphpad.com/quickcalcs.

t-test example

A t-test is used to compare two sets of continuous data, as in this example:

Group A measurements	27, 30, 36, 31, 28, 34, 31, 35, 33, 37, 35, 25, 26, 30, 33, 32 (n = 16, mean = 31.4375)
Group B measurements	34, 29, 38, 28, 32, 34, 26, 39, 32, 33, 34, 38, 27, 34, 39, 34 (n = 16, mean = 33.1875)

1

The averages for A and B are different. But are these differences 'real' (significant), or are they due to chance alone?

Step 1: Null hypothesis: The differences between A and B are due to chance alone.

Step 2: Enter the above data into an online t-test calculator, one result per line, then click 'calculate'. In this example, the result is P = 0.2.

Step 3: Interpret the results. P = 0.2 tells us there is a 20% probability that the difference between A's average and B's average is due to chance. 20% is quite high. In this case the null hypothesis cannot be rejected. In other words, the difference between A and B is not statistically significant.

Chi-squared (χ^2) example

Chi-squared results are used to compare data categories. In this example, two adjacent areas of mangrove swamp are surveyed, each exactly one square metre. Area X has a sandy surface, area Y has a muddy surface. The number of crab burrows is counted in each square. Raw data: 28 burrows in X, 52 burrows in Y. (Total 80 burrows.) If the surface (sand or mud) made no difference to these crabs, we would expect 40 in each area.

	Observed (O)	Expected (E)
Area X	28	40
Area Y	52	40

Step 1: Null hypothesis: The difference in burrow numbers between X and Y is due to chance alone.

Step 2: Enter the above four numbers into an online chi-squared calculator, then click 'calculate'. In this case, the answer is P = 0.007 at 1 degree of freedom.

Step 3: Interpret the results. 'Degrees of freedom' is defined as $n - 1$, where n is the number of categories, in this case 2 categories. P = 0.007 means there is a very low probability that the 28-52 difference at X and Y is due to chance. The null hypothesis is rejected. In other words, the difference in crab burrow numbers at X and Y is highly significant.

Check your understanding

1 Write the matching terms in the blank column. Choose from this list: *range, pie chart, mean, median, raw data, dispersion, dependent variable, standard deviation, normal distribution, histogram, line graph, skewed distribution, scatter graph.*

	Statistical term	Description
a		Another word for a calculated average.
b		A calculated measure of spread. Two of these cover 68% of a normal distribution.
c		Always placed on the vertical axis of a graph.
d		The difference between the highest score and the lowest score.
e		Another word for the 'spread' of results.
f		A spread of values bunched towards the high or the low end of a distribution.
g		Used where one variable consists of separate categories and the other variable is a percentage.

ISBN: 9780170355582

	Statistical term	Description
h		Used where one variable has continuous data and the other variable is a count or a percentage.
i		The midpoint between the highest score and the lowest score; sometimes used instead of an average.
j		A bell-shaped spread of values symmetrically bunched around the mean, with a long 'tail' at both ends.
k		Used to find if there is a correlation between two continuous variables.
l		Graph used in a situation where both variables are continuous.
m		Original measurements and results, before calculations have been done.

2 An experiment on plant transpiration under particular environmental conditions produced the following data: 26, 25, 22, 27, 23, 31, 28, 2330, 26. The units are milligrams water lost per minute.

a The 2330 result should be discarded because ______

______

b Calculate the mean from the above data.

______

c State the range for the above data. ______

d Calculate the median for the above data.

______

3 Supply the missing words.

When drawing most kinds of graph, the **a** ______ variable should be on the horizontal axis and the **b** ______ variable on the vertical axis. A **c** ______ graph is generally used where both variables are continuous. A **d** ______ graph is generally used when it not obvious at the start whether there is a correlation between two variables. A **e** ______ chart is useful for showing the proportions or percentages of different categories.

4 For a particular plant cross, genetics theory leads us to expect a 3:1 ratio in the next generation. Out of 40 plants, the expected result would be 30 with red flowers, 10 with white flowers. Use an online chi-squared calculator to find whether or not the following observed results are significantly different from the expected 30-10 results. In each case, give the value for P.

a 27 red, 13 white ______

b 25 red, 15 white ______

c 23 red, 17 white ______

d 21 red , 19 white ______

1

Biology 3.1 Practical investigation

NCEA Achievement Standard 91601: Carry out a practical investigation in a biological context, with guidance

Internally assessed, 4 credits

Achievement	Achievement with Merit	Achievement with Excellence
Carry out a practical investigation in a biological context, with guidance.	Carry out an in-depth practical investigation in a biological context, with guidance.	Carry out a comprehensive practical investigation in a biological context, with guidance.

Achievement

'Carry out a practical investigation ...' involves:

- developing a statement of the purpose, linked to a scientific concept or idea, and written as a hypothesis
- using a method that describes: (A) For a fair test: the independent variable and its range, the measurement of the dependent variable and the control of some of the key variables. (B and C) For a pattern-seeking or modelling activity: the data that will be collected, range of data/samples, and consideration of some other key factors.
- collecting, recording, and processing data relevant to the purpose of the investigation
- interpreting the processed data and reporting on the findings of the investigation
- identifying relevant findings from another source
- stating a conclusion based on interpretation of the process data which is relevant to the purpose of the investigation.

Achievement with Merit

'Carry out an in-depth practical investigation ...' involves:

- using a valid method that describes: (A) For a fair test: a valid range for the independent variable, the valid measurement of the dependent variable and the control of other key variables, with consideration of factors such as sampling bias and sources of errors. (B and C) For a pattern-seeking or modelling activity: a valid collection of data with consideration of factors such as sampling bias and sources of errors.
- collecting, recording, and processing reliable data to enable a trend or pattern (or absence) to be determined
- stating a valid conclusion based on the processed data in relation to the purpose
- explaining the biological ideas relating to the investigation. The explanation is based on both the findings from the investigation and those from other source(s).

Achievement with Excellence

'Carry out a comprehensive practical investigation ...' involves:

- justifying the choices made throughout the investigation by evaluating the validity of the method or the reliability of the data
- stating a conclusion that discusses the biological ideas relevant to the investigation and either the findings of others, scientific principles, theories, or models.

A *practical investigation* is an activity covering the complete process: planning, carrying out, processing, interpreting data, and reporting on the investigation. It will involve the collection of primary data. It is expected that the student will have opportunity to make changes to their initial method as they work through the investigation. The nature of the investigation could be the manipulation of variables (fair test), the investigation of a pattern, or relationship, or the use of models.

ISBN: 9780170355582

Socio-scientific issue

Unit 1 | Guidelines

Introduction

Biology-related concerns and dilemmas often appear in the media, or need to be dealt with in our everyday lives. One example: all parents need to decide about immunising their babies, and making these decisions means sorting out facts from myths, risks from benefits. Immunisation is a good example of a socio-scientific issue that has biological and social implications: ethical, economic, environmental and cultural.

Biology 3.2 (Achievement Standard 91602) requires students to develop an informed response to one socio-scientific issue. This unit offers general guidelines to a research project on whichever topic you choose, and Unit 2 contains case studies. A summary of NCEA requirements for AS 91602 appears on page 31, and the following list highlights some additional aspects.

For Biology 3.2 you are required to:

- choose a topic that has particular relevance to New Zealand and/or the South Pacific region
- research the biological and social aspects of your topic thoroughly, using a range of sources
- write a report that examines the issue from opposing sides and includes different viewpoints, considering whether or not they are biased
- compare the significance of the biological and social points raised
- evaluate the validity and bias of your resources
- develop a personal opinion and justify why you have taken this stance
- suggest a course of personal or societal action to address the concerns of the topic chosen
- suggest how effective the proposed actions are likely to be.

Selecting a topic

Your teacher may suggest a research topic, but if you wish to make your own choice the following page lists 15 more for you to consider. Choose a topic to which each of the following questions can be answered 'yes'.

☐ Has the topic got **strong biology concepts** that you could describe in depth? (For this project, avoid purely ethical dilemmas such as abortion.)

☐ Is the topic controversial, and does it offer the chance for you to describe and analyse **differing viewpoints**?

☐ Is the topic **current**? (Avoid issues that were important 10 or 20 years ago, but not at present.)

- [ ] Has the topic got a **mainly biological** basis? (For this project, avoid issues such as oil drilling that are mainly in the field of geology or chemistry.)
- [ ] Could you suggest **courses of action** that could bring about change?
- [ ] Does the topic have particular **relevance to New Zealand** and/or the South Pacific region?

2

Suggested topics

1. Immunisation such as MMR, plus facts and societal attitudes related to the pros and cons of immunising children.
2. Genetic screening for Down syndrome and genetic disorders such as cystic fibrosis and breast cancer.
3. Possum control and the various implications related to the use of 1080 compared with alternative control methods.
4. Global warming and how the greenhouse effect and climate change are impacting Pacific nations.
5. Xenotransplantation (animal-to-human transplants), together with issues of animal welfare and disease transmission.
6. Intensive fish farming and its implications for animal welfare, the local environment and food supplies.
7. Hormone growth regulators in the meat industry; their possible impacts on the health of farm animals and humans.
8. Stem cell research and its potential in medical treatments, also taking into account the ethical implications.
9. Reproductive technologies such as IVF and embryo selection, and their implications for society and health.
10. The recent use of 'vegetable oils' (from palm oil plantations) in a wide range of foods, and the implications for tropical rainforests and conservation.
11. The impact of whale- and dolphin-watching tourism on the wellbeing of whales and dolphins, as well as an analysis of the benefits for people.
12. Commercial fishing for southern bluefin and other tuna species in the Pacific: its effects on fish populations and food chains.
13. Intensive dairy farming, and the extent of its possible effects on rivers and water quality.
14. The proposal to tax soft drinks that contain high levels of sugar, as one way of combating the diabetes epidemic.
15. Keeping farm pigs in crates during farrowing and after, with its several implications: ethical, economic, and animal welfare.

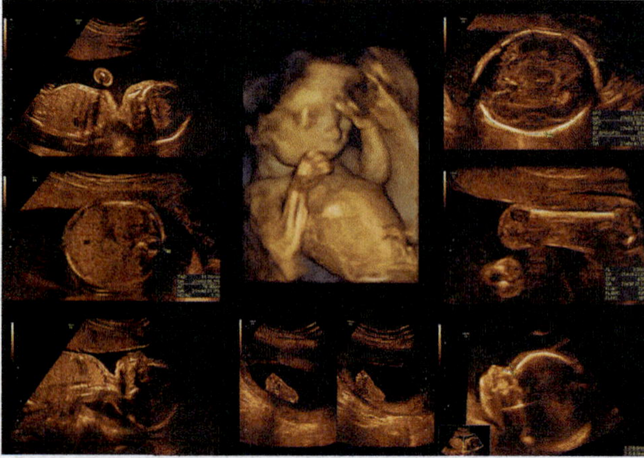

ISBN: 9780170355582

Topics related to genetic engineering and the use of GMOs are outlined in Section 3.7. Section 2.2 in *Biology Workbook 2* also has more research topic ideas.

Unlike the socio-scientific research project for Biology 2.2, teachers will not provide much input into your research and presentation for 3.2. Teachers may offer guidance to make sure that you are on the right track, but won't be making decisions every step of the way. Biology 3.2 requires that students do most research and decision-making themselves.

Fig. 3.2.1 Yellowfin are one of the less endangered tuna species.

Fig. 3.2.2 Intensive farming can affect water quality.

Fig. 3.2.3 Fish farming provides employment, but also has implications for water quality and for recreational uses.

Fig. 3.2.4 Whale watching.

Fig. 3.2.5 Possums and rats destroy wildlife as well as plants.

Guidelines

The main part of this unit is divided into three sections, related to three stages of progress through the research project and containing suggestions on how to:

- **collect** information
- **select** and organise information
- **present** the organised information.

To help you manage your time, write dates and estimated times needed into this table at the start, and tick each stage when accomplished.

Stage	Estimated days or hours allocated	Date to be finished
Collect information		
Select and organise		
Presentation		
Final hand-in date, with everything checked and revised		

2

Collect information

You will need to collect information from a wide range of sources. These could be from journals, radio, television documentaries, newspapers, websites, plus research papers in science journals — and could be found in electronic form or print media or interviews. A librarian or teacher may offer suggestions and guidance, but remember that each stage — collecting, selecting, presenting — is mainly up to you. Avoid the pitfall of spending too much time on the collecting stage, as this should be completed within a couple of days — a good reason to avoid any topic where information is hard to find.

Keep a log of all sources used. Start a document into which you copy and paste the exact source of information, including title, date of publication, author's name, exact source. This document can be titled 'Reference sources', with an edited version placed in your final presentation. Your teacher will give instructions on the type of referencing appropriate for the task. Although it may not be marked specifically, a reference list is part of research protocol.

Search for a range of opinions on **both** sides of your issue. This is needed for Excellence grade, and your discussion must consider both sides of the issue before you decide on your position. Some databases can do this search for you so it may be worth asking a librarian for advice.

Select and organise information

This stage involves organising your information into categories to make writing easier and also more logical for your teacher to read and therefore mark. For further assistance, look at the Achieved, Merit and Excellence part of this unit.

Achievement, Merit, Excellence

Page 31 has assessment details for the standard, some of which are repeated here.

To gain **Achievement** grade you need to integrate relevant biological knowledge to develop an informed response on your chosen issue by describing:

- the biological concepts and processes relating to the issue
- one biological and social implication of the issue
- two different viewpoints about the issue, for and against, ensuring you name the individuals, groups or organisations
- your personal opinion
- one proposed personal or societal action.

To gain **Merit** grade you need to develop a reasoned informed response by explaining your personal position and proposed personal or societal action, giving reasons and supporting evidence as to why you have chosen these.

To gain **Excellence** grade you need to develop a comprehensive informed response. This includes using analysis and evaluation of biological knowledge related to the issue to justify a personal position and proposed personal/societal action. This could be done by one of:

ISBN: 9780170355582

- comparing the significance of the biological and/or social implications
- considering the likely effectiveness of the proposed personal/societal action
- commenting on the sources of biological knowledge used by considering ideas such as validity or bias. Validity could include recent scientific papers that have peer review status. Bias could include attitudes, values and beliefs, or a vested interest by the group or person providing the information.

To help you select and organise information on your chosen topic, six aspects are suggested below. You do not have to give equal weight to all of them, but if aiming for Excellence grade, check to make sure your final presentation includes all six. Some of the aspects may be difficult to deal with adequately. For example, not all topics have an obvious positive and negative side. Also, some issues, such as genetic screening, will have little or no environmental impact.

Aspect 1: Biological processes

Provide detailed explanations on how the techniques related to your topic are actually carried out. For example, if your topic involves reproductive technologies such as IVF, you would outline how and why hormone treatment is given, how eggs are 'harvested', how they are fertilised, how and why they are stored before being implanted in the uterus. If genetic screening is involved, explain how genetic defects might be detected before implantation.

Aspect 2: Implications

Consider what positive or negative consequences the technique or process might have in the following areas. One example is given in each case.

Biological. Section 3.7 summarises some biological consequences related to crop plants that have been genetically modified to be resistant to glyphosate herbicides.
Social. Example: if couples are able to screen IVF embryos before they are implanted, what might the implications be for population sex ratios in the future?
Ethical. Example: in the case of IVF again, what should be done with surplus embryos? What should happen to the embryos if they are not destroyed? What happens when biological parents die before the embryos are needed? Who should decide? In matters such as this, there is no precedent in human history.
Economic. Some courses of action are very expensive, and healthcare budgets are limited. Example: is it better to spend $1 million on kidney dialysis for a few, or on primary health care for many diabetics?
Environmental. Example: using 1080 poison to control possum numbers may kill some native birds, but not using 1080 may result in the death of even more. Sometimes the choice is not between good and bad, but hard choices between bad and worse.

Aspect 3: Other opinions, your opinions

For all of these issues, people will take different standpoints depending on their education, experience and religious background. You will need to find examples of people or publications or websites who represent differing opinions on your issue. It is important the person or group is specifically named and their statements can be validated.

After careful consideration of all sides of the issue, you will no doubt have developed your own views on the subject. You will need to justify your opinion with logic and especially with reasons that are evidence-based. You may refer to other people's opinions to help explain your own.

Aspect 4: Compare significance

Discussing and comparing the significance of biological and/or social points points of fact is another aspect that distinguishes Excellence from Merit grades. Some items of information will be more important, others less important, some trivial, some irrelevant. It helps to recognise the differences.

Aspect 5: Validity and bias

Information is likely to be valid if backed up by peer-reviewed research reports, especially if recent. Your own report should state why the evidence you have chosen is valid.

Some information is biased, particularly when opinion is presented as fact. Bias is sometimes unintentional, and sometimes deliberate and disguised.

Five common indicators of bias: vested interests; ignoring alternative points of view; using emotive language and personal attack; promoting a conspiracy theory; being tricky in various ways such as quoting statements out of context. *Biology Workbook 2*, Section 2.2 has more on this.

Aspect 6: Action and effectiveness

For all grades — A, M and E — you are expected to suggest actions at a personal and/or societal level; actions that could help bring about change. What is appropriate and effective in one situation may be ineffective in another, but here is a short list of possibilities:

2

- Changing your own behaviour. Example: not buying oils derived from palm trees grown in areas where rainforests were destroyed
- Encouraging your friends to do the same
- Organising some action at school that will help widen the message
- Writing a letter on the subject to a local paper
- Writing a letter on the subject to a Member of Parliament
- Using social media to promote what you see as constructive change
- Creating and posting a short video to go on YouTube.

The effects of your proposed action(s) will depend very much on what you do, as well as the issue itself. Considering the likely effectiveness is, however, one of the requirements for Excellence grade.

Presentation

A printed report on several pages of A4 paper may be the most straightforward for most purposes at all grades A, M and E. A big poster is an attractive option in some cases, but it's unlikely that you could pack sufficient information into a poster to get beyond A grade. A PowerPoint presentation can convey more information than a poster can, but does not lend itself to integrating and discussing information thoroughly.

If you are producing a printed report, ask the teacher to tell you how long it should be. To give an idea of length, this unit is approximately 2700 words long.

Presentation alone is not enough, but do consider what font and style and spacing you choose. Print out your first draft, then use it to correct and streamline your writing. Say what needs to be said as clearly as possible. Run a spell check. Be concise. Avoid repetition. Make sure your essay or report is broken into paragraphs, each starting with each new idea or point of information.

Above all, avoid plagiarism. Copying and pasting large chunks of work from others and from the internet is dishonest. It will almost certainly be detected, and will cost you a grade. You will, of course, use many sources of information, but the final report needs to be put together in your own words. It is permissible to copy short pieces of text if you put them in *italics* to indicate it is directly taken from someone. This is often useful if the person quoted has a particularly colourful turn of phrase that would add interest to the report.

Remember to attach a printout of all the sources of information you used.

ISBN: 9780170355582

Check your understanding

1 Read the personal opinion below, then rewrite it to meet the requirements for Excellence grade.

'I think myxomatosis should not be released into the New Zealand population of rabbits, as in the long term it would not be successful and rabbit numbers would increase. Also, native flora and fauna could be adversely affected and this could be disastrous for our travel industry.'

2 Use a dictionary to find definitions of:

a validity (or valid)

b bias

3 For each of the five paragraphs in the presentation section above, write **one word** in the margin stating its main subject. You could use this 'one idea per paragraph' as a guide to your own writing.

Unit 2 | Case studies

Introduction

This unit presents three kinds of immunisation as outline case-study topics for Biology 3.2. The following pages definitely do not contain enough material for a full assignment. They provide only basic and limited information on immunisation, plus some guiding questions of the type you could use in an assignment.

Immunisation is also known as **vaccination**, a word originally used only for protection against smallpox. In 1796 Edward Jenner successfully tested the idea that giving people a dose of a mild infection known as cowpox could protect them against the deadly disease smallpox. He named his technique 'vaccination' from *vacca*, the Latin word for cow.

Immunisation generally works by giving a person a weak form of a disease or else dead viruses, in order to provoke an immune response in their body. In many cases this immune protection lasts lifelong. Smallpox has so far been the only disease to be eliminated worldwide, with the last known case occurring in Somalia in 1977. One current medical goal is to totally eliminate polio in the same way, through mass immunisation.

Significant numbers of parents object to having their children immunised, and the situation provides an example of an issue where people hold conflicting viewpoints. The following pages provide basic outline information on polio, MMR (measles, mumps and rubella) vaccination and HPV (human papillomavirus) vaccination.

Polio

Poliomyelitis is an infectious disease that causes part or complete paralysis in many who get it. Up until the 1950s, frequent epidemics caused widespread terror because polio apparently struck out of the blue; its cause unknown, with no prevention or cure. Polio affects mainly children, and tens of thousands of young people were paralysed or killed.

The first effective polio vaccine was developed in 1952 by Dr Jonas Salk, who gave his discovery to the world unpatented and for no financial reward. The Salk inactivated poliovirus vaccine (IPV) is usually administered orally as liquid drops. Since the 1950s almost all children in the developed world have received this, with near-total success. Rotary International has already vaccinated two billion children in 122 countries, mainly developing ones, and aims to eliminate it worldwide. Polio now occurs in only 10 countries and is endemic in only three: Nigeria, Afghanistan and Pakistan.

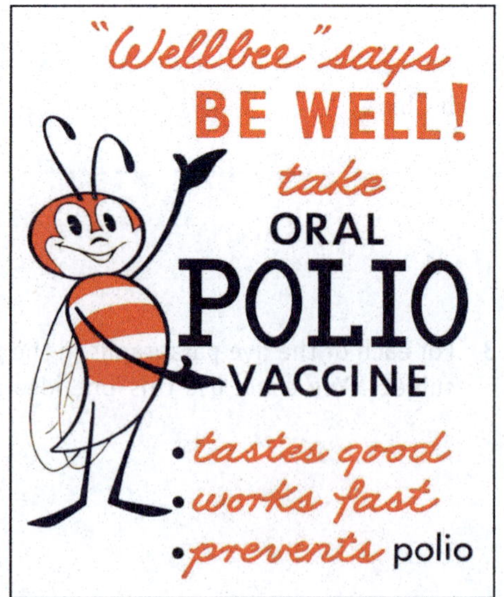

Attempts to wipe out polio in these three countries has run into problems. Political unrest in Pakistan has led to fierce opposition, and many local polio immunisation health workers have been murdered. The main reason was because the CIA successfully used a false immunisation campaign in their hunt for Osama bin Laden. Some in Pakistan now believe that any immunisation is part of a Western plot. The result is that polio incidence in the region is now rising.

Polio has disappeared from New Zealand and most other parts of the world as a result of immunisation, with the Western Pacific region being declared polio free in 2000. However, there is still a danger the virus could arrive with a traveller, and many infected people do not show any symptoms, so immunisation is still needed. Some parents believe that because the disease is now absent, there is no need to immunise their children.

ISBN: 9780170355582

Check your understanding

1 Salk polio vaccine is given by mouth, is completely painless, and side effects are extremely rare. Suggest why some people are opposed to their children receiving the Salk vaccine. List key points.

2 'Polio no longer exists in this country, so there's no point in immunising my child against it.' Write an answer to someone who holds this point of view. List key points.

3 Explain the biological concepts underlying the action of the Salk vaccine and other vaccinations in general.

9780170355582

MMR

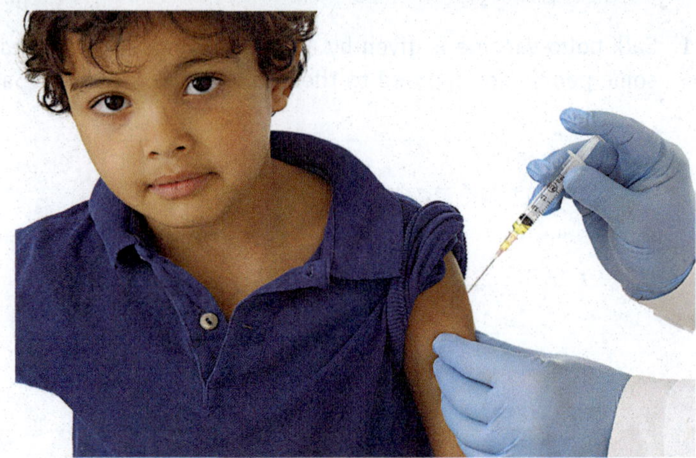

Most children in New Zealand receive MMR vaccine at age one and again at age three, giving them protection from three infectious diseases: measles, mumps and rubella.

Mumps in children is generally not very serious. Rubella is a minor childhood infection but if a pregnant woman has rubella there is a significant chance of permanent harm to the child: brain damaged, blind, deaf — which provides a strong reason for all girls to be immunised before puberty.

Measles is potentially serious, highly infectious and easily spread by coughing and sneezing. Measles is the most common vaccine-preventable cause of death among children worldwide, and has a particularly sad place in New Zealand's history. During the 1800s a series of measles and influenza epidemics swept the country, causing high death rates among Maori, who had little resistance to the new pathogens. It is estimated these epidemics halved the Maori population within less than a century.

MMR vaccination has become commonly used worldwide to protect children against measles, mumps and rubella. However, many parents believe that MMR is dangerous, and refuse to have their children immunised, putting them at considerable risk. In a 1998 report by Dr Andrew Wakefield, based on a study of 12 British children with autism, he stated there was a link between autism and MMR. This report was given huge publicity in the popular media. Soon after, larger-scale studies showed there was no connection at all between MMR and autism, and that Dr Wakefield's results were fraudulent.

However, the damage had been done. Although the original report has been discredited, there are now many websites supporting Dr Wakefield and opposing immunisation. One sample, from a natural health website:

> *These two cases, combined with numerous published studies out of the U.S., South America, and Europe, prove that the MMR vaccine is not the harmless vaccine that the conventional medical industry claims it is. In fact, everything that Dr. Wakefield found back in the late 1990s concerning the MMR vaccine — findings that cost him his career and reputation, by the way — are proving to be undeniably true.*
> *'There can be very little doubt that vaccines can and do cause autism,' Dr. Wakefield recently stated from his home in Austin, Texas. But the fact that these documents remain censored shows that the government is hiding something of importance from the public, which most definitely has to do with the connection between the MMR vaccine and autism. Concerned parents everywhere were right all along: MMR vaccine can cause autism.*

Doctors everywhere condemn statements such as these as highly misleading but many people remain uncertain and easily swayed by scaremongering. MMR vaccination rates have declined, and measles rates have increased.

Part of the problem is that for all vaccines, as with most medications, difficulties occur in a small number of cases. In the case of MMR the facts are:

- aseptic meningitis occurs about once in 800,000 doses
- anaphylactic shock occurs about one to three times per million doses
- encephalitis may develop in one per million recipients.

ISBN: 9780170355582

Check your understanding

4 List the basic facts about risks and benefits that accompany use of the MMR vaccine.

5 'I don't want my child to have even a one in a million risk of having a bad reaction to MMR vaccination, so I'm against it.' What kind of bias is revealed here? Suggest why this parent might be biased.

6 'I heard somewhere that some kinds of vaccination cause autism, so don't want my child to have any vaccinations at all.' Write an answer to someone who holds this point of view. List key points only.

2

HPV

The human papillomavirus (HPV) causes 99 per cent of all cervical cancers in women and is spread by sexual intercourse. The main risk factors are unprotected sexual activity with a number of partners, and smoking. HPV also causes genital warts in both girls and boys. There are 150 strains of HPV, with four of these linked to cancer and to warts (strains 16 and 18 cause 70 per cent of cervical cancers in women and another two cause genital warts).

Gardasil is a vaccine that protects against these four strains of HPV. Three doses of Gardasil give 95 per cent protection against these four strains of virus, and protection lasts at least eight years. However, not all HPV strains are covered by the vaccine, with about 30 per cent of cancers being caused by other strains. Using condoms helps prevent the spread of sexually transmitted infections, but may not completely eliminate the risk of HPV infection.

Cervical cancer is the third most common cancer in women. 'Smear tests' (aka 'pap tests') can detect this cancer at a moderately advanced stage of development. However, this cancer can take 10 or 20 years to appear after infection with the HPV virus, so doctors advise regular smears every three years. There is no medical cure. The usual treatment for cervical cancer is complete removal of the uterus, followed by courses of chemotherapy and radiation therapy. Long-term survival is not assured.

New Zealand has been vaccinating against HPV since 2006, with no charge for females aged 12 to 20. Side effects of the injections can include fainting, pain, numbness and, very occasionally, seizures. No deaths have been linked to Gardasil use.

The Ministry of Health website (www.health.govt.nz) encourages parents of young girls to discuss the subject of cervical cancer causes and immunisation with daughters from the age of 12, and consider giving permission for a course of Gardasil injections.

Check your understanding

7 List as many reasons as you can that parents might consider both for and against discussing the subject with their 12–14-year-old daughters and recommending a course of Gardasil immunisation. Consider ethical and social implications, as well as biological facts about the level of protection. List key points.

8 Suggest why some parents and daughters aged 12 to 14 might be unwilling to have the discussions suggested above.

ISBN: 9780170355582

9 In your opinion, what are the principal preventative measures that should be taken to reduce the rate of cervical cancer in the future? Your answer should include a course of action that you could implement to help your school or community deal with the issue. List key points.

Biology 3.2 Socio-scientific issue

NCEA Achievement Standard 91602: Integrate biological knowledge to develop an informed response to a socio-scientific issue

Internally assessed, 3 credits

Achievement	Achievement with Merit	Achievement with Excellence
Integrate biological knowledge to develop an informed response to a socio-scientific issue.	Integrate biological knowledge to develop a reasoned informed response to a socio-scientific issue.	Integrate biological knowledge to develop a comprehensive informed response to a socio-scientific issue.

Achievement

'Integrate biological knowledge to develop an informed response …' involves:

- presenting a personal position, developed using relevant biological knowledge
- proposing action(s) at a personal and/or societal level.

Achievement with Merit

'Integrate biological knowledge to develop a reasoned informed response …' involves:

- explaining why the position and the action(s) have been chosen.

Achievement with Excellence

'Integrate biological knowledge to develop a comprehensive informed response …' involves justifying the personal position and proposed action(s) by analysing and evaluating the biological knowledge related to the issue. This may include:

- comparing the significance of implications
- considering the likely effectiveness of the proposed action(s)
- commenting on sources and information, considering ideas such as
  - i validity — currency, peer review status, scientific acceptance
  - ii bias — attitudes, values, beliefs.

Integrate refers to selecting and collating relevant biological knowledge to develop an informed response.

A socio-scientific issue has both biological and social implications. The issue is one for which people hold different opinions or viewpoints. Social implications may be economic, ethical, cultural, or environmental.

Biological knowledge includes:

- biological concepts and processes relating to the issue
- biological and social implications of the issue
- differing opinions or viewpoints about the issue.

3.3 Plant and animal responses

Unit 1 | Biological clocks

Introduction

From bacteria to buffaloes, all living things need to survive long enough to pass on their genes. All face the same four basic problems:

- getting enough energy and raw materials for growth
- staying in places where environmental conditions are best
- avoiding being attacked or eaten
- reproducing; successfully rearing young.

Among the millions of species alive today there is a huge variety of different 'answers' to the same four problems. The ways in which any plant or animal achieves its 'answers' is characteristic of its species, and together make up its **niche**, its way of life. Niche is not the same as **habitat**, the kind of place where it lives.

Every animal and plant has a variety of adaptations, i.e. the ways it deals with its environment. Consider the specialised features of a dolphin. Its adaptations include streamlining, being born tail first, using sonar, having complex social interactions. Biology 3.3 deals with behavioural adaptations.

Every living thing has adaptations to these two broad categories of environmental influence:

- **Biotic** factors — other organisms including competitors, predators, prey, reproductive partners.
- **Abiotic** (non-living) factors, including temperature, wind, waves, chemicals, light intensity.

All environments change. Even in the near-constant physical conditions of deep oceans and deep underground caves, the biotic environment changes every time a predator approaches.

The ability to detect and respond to **stimuli** (environmental 'cues') is essential to survival. A migrating bird won't survive long if it can't navigate properly. In animals, stimuli are detected by **receptors** to light, gravity, chemicals, etc. Responses are brought about by **effectors** such as muscles, glands, in some cases individual cells.

 ISBN: 9780170355582

The study of behaviour — migrating, avoiding predators, etc. — raises two kinds of question:

- **Why?** Function? In what way does the behaviour contribute to reproductive success?
- **How?** How does it work? What are the mechanisms? What is the internal 'machinery' of nerves and chemicals that makes the behaviour happen?

Problems in studying behaviour
When studying behaviour, several pitfalls can occur.

- **Variation.** No two individuals are exactly alike, and this includes their behaviour. Differences in behaviour may be due to differences in genes, age, or previous experience.
- Difficulties of **observation**. It is not easy to observe behaviour in the wild, and we can't be sure that an animal or plant brought indoors will behave naturally.
- Try to avoid **anthropomorphism**, which means attributing human motives and emotions to an animal. Perhaps you think that the fish is 'worried' — but it may be better to say that it is avoiding you.
- Be careful with **teleology**. Teleology means attributing a sense of purpose to behaviour. Humans and perhaps other intelligent animals are aware of 'goals' in their behaviour; but it's hard to be certain that a homing pigeon has in mind a 'goal' of arriving. Possibly it does, or possibly it is simply motivated to keep flying in a particular direction until it finds home.

Circadian cycles

Most living things are affected by the daily cycle of light and dark. Many animals are **diurnal** (active during the day); others are **nocturnal** (active at night). Animals such as rabbits that are active at dawn and dusk are described as **crepuscular.** Even plants show daily rhythms. Examples: many flowers open and produce scent at particular times of the day, while moth-pollinated flowers produce scent at night.

In many cases these daily cycles continue when the animals are given artificial conditions with no clues about night and day. This kind of internal rhythm is described as **circadian**, which means 'about a day' — because the cycle is about 24 hours, not exactly 24.

Rhythmic behaviour is controlled in part by internal mechanisms (biological 'clocks'). We know this because in many cases when an animal or plant is kept under artificial constant conditions, its rhythmic behaviour continues. Fig. 3.3.2 shows an **actogram** (activity record) of a weta over 25 days. For the first 11 days the animal was maintained in alternating periods of 12 hours light and 12 hours dark. From day 12 to day 25 it was kept in constant darkness. For the first 11 days the animals became active at 'dusk', but in constant darkness its activity drifted out of synchrony with the external day-night rhythm. The weta's activity is said to be **free-running** — meaning behaviour without external time clues. This weta's rhythm continued independently of its external environment, which proves the behaviour is **endogenous** (has an internal origin). Such a rhythm is governed by an **internal pacemaker** (aka oscillator). An important feature of the oscillator is that it is hardly affected by temperature, so continues to be reliable in different weather conditions.

Fig. 3.3.1 A deep-sea angler fish lives in an unchanging physical environment. Only in deep caves and in the abyssal depths of the ocean are physical environments non-rhythmic.

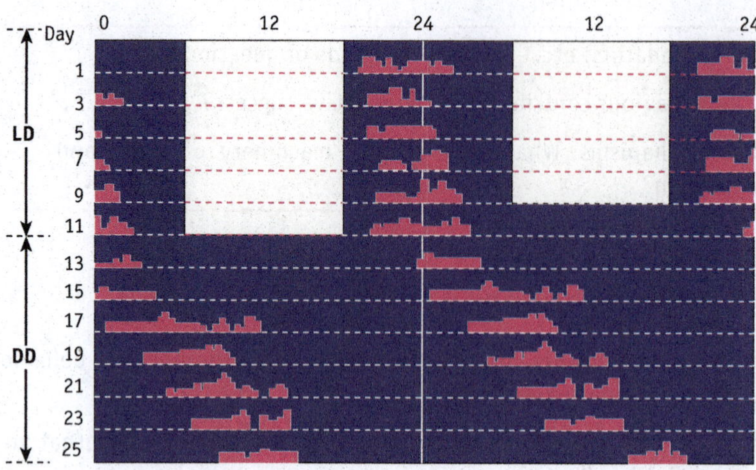

Fig. 3.3.2 Actogram of a weta kept for 11 days in artificial conditions with 12 hours light/12 hours dark, followed by 14 days constant darkness. This actogram shows a 48-hour timescale on the horizontal axis.

Fig. 3.3.3 shows an actogram of a hamster kept in constant light. By drawing a triangle on the graph from days 1 to 11, we see that after 10 days light, the animal's burst of activity begins about 4 hours later than it did on day 1, 10 days previously. In other words, the endogenous rhythm has become later each cycle. How much later?

4 hours/10 days = 0.4 hours later per day, on average

This means that the hamster circadian period under free-running conditions = 24.4 hours. Under normal conditions, the hamster's daily cycle is synchronised with environmental rhythms and its internal clock is slightly 'reset' each day. The word for this 'resetting' process is **entrainment.** Any environmental signal (such as sunset) that resets a biological clock is described as a **zeitgeber**, German for 'time-giver'. The time between the onset of activity between one day and the next — roughly 24 hours in this case — is known as the **period**. The duration of activity itself might only be a few hours.

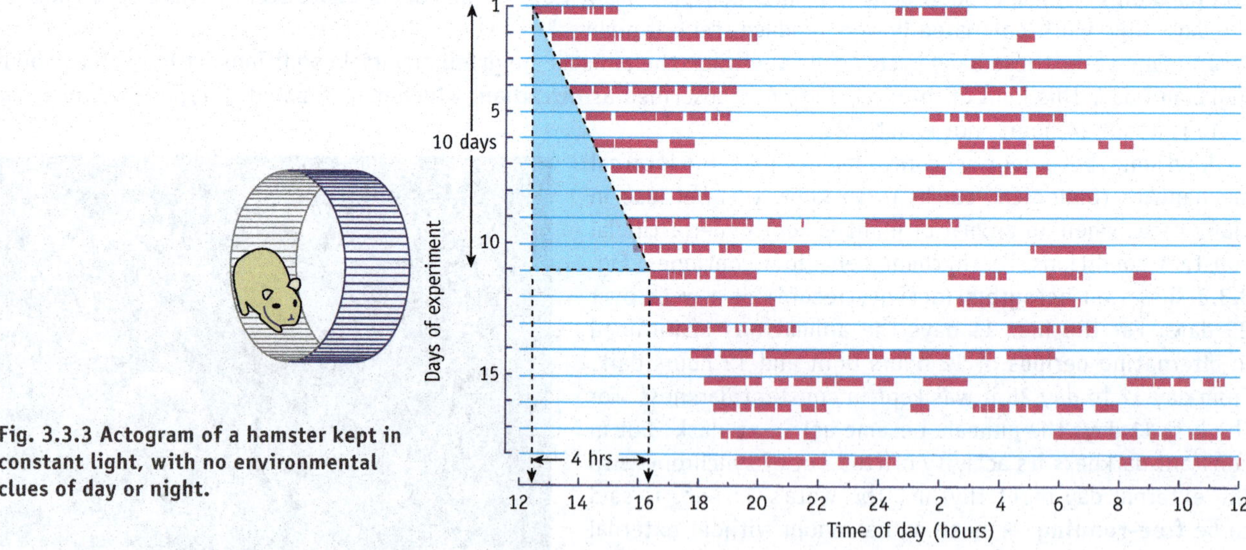

Fig. 3.3.3 Actogram of a hamster kept in constant light, with no environmental clues of day or night.

Under constant conditions, circadian rhythmic activities have been discovered in a wide variety of behaviours and physiological processes. A few examples of daily rhythms:

- cell division in human skin
- body temperature in humans
- urine output and composition in humans
- photosynthesis rate in constant light conditions
- stomatal movement in plants
- 'sleep' movements in leaves of clover and some other plants.

ISBN: 9780170355582

The period of the human circadian rhythm is about 25–26 hours under free-running conditions — such as experienced by people over-wintering at the South Pole where there is six months' total darkness.

Jetlag

The problem of jetlag applies to east–west air travel across multiple time zones. On arrival, the endogenous body clock is out of sync with local day and night times. Result: extreme tiredness. A similar situation arises with shift work. At the start of a night shift roster, the worker's body clock is out of step with their previous activity cycle.

It can take up to a week before entrainment resets the body clock to be in sync with local day/night conditions. Entrainment is faster if the traveller stays in well-lit conditions during daytime and sleeps at night, instead of only sleeping when tired. The way humans have evolved, blue light is the stimulus that tells our body and brain when to be awake, and dark tells them to go to sleep.

Tidal rhythms

Every creature living in the intertidal zone has to deal with the fact that about twice a day they are exposed to air. All organisms living in the upper part of the tidal zone then have to deal with problems of desiccation, greater temperature extremes, and sometimes rainwater replacing saltwater. As a result, most littoral (shore-living) creatures such as barnacles cease activity, and seal themselves inside their shells. Mobile animals such as rockfish seek shelter under stones.

Fig. 3.3.4 Animals inhabiting intertidal zones have circa-tidal rhythms that continue under free-running conditions if the animals are moved to a laboratory.

Fig. 3.3.5 shows the activity rhythm of the New Zealand cockle (tuaki), a mollusc living in sandy shores. When the tide is high, the two shells open and the animal filters plankton, extending two siphons. When the tide is low, the siphons are withdrawn and the shells close. In this experiment the animals were kept indoors submerged in constant conditions and the percentage of animals with siphons extended recorded. Even though continuously surrounded by seawater, the animals closed their shells when the tide would normally be out and opened them when the tide would be in. Cycles like this that approximately match tides are described as **circa-tidal**.

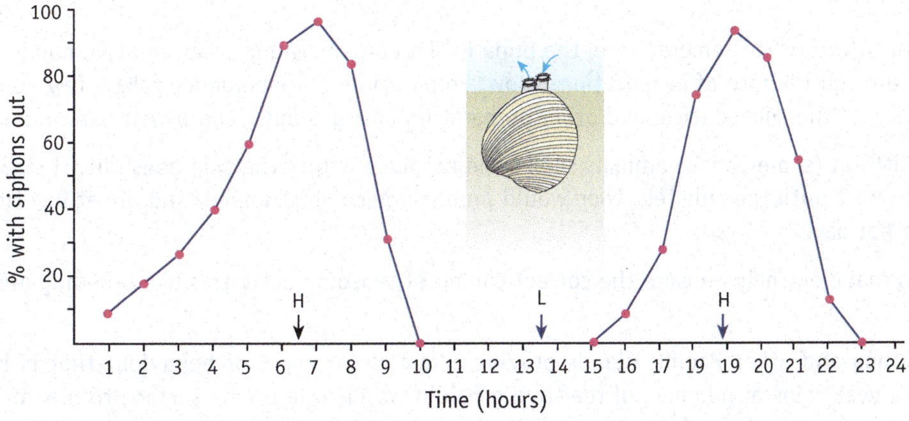

Fig. 3.3.5 The percentage of New Zealand cockles with shells open and siphons extended while kept in constant conditions.

E

Compound rhythms on the shore

Creatures living on the seashore have to cope with more than tidal rhythms. The tidal zone has complex rhythms with four different environmental cycles superimposed. First, there is a 24-hour cycle of day and night. Second, there is a regular tidal cycle, roughly 12.4 hours between one high tide and the next. Third, the 29.5-day lunar cycle results in especially high tides (spring tides, king tides) roughly every two weeks. Fourth, there are seasonal changes, with extremely high tides twice a year at the equinoxes in March and September. Biological rhythms are described as **circa-lunar** if they match the lunar cycle, when under free-running conditions.

Fig. 3.3.6 shows two rhythms in a European shore crab. When the tide is low the animals hide motionless under stones, and when the tide is high they come out to forage for food. There is also a daily rhythm in pigment cells in their epidermis. In the daytime the pigment cells expand and animals are darker, making them less conspicuous, while at night they become pale. Since the day/night cycle and the tidal cycle are not synchronous, the two rhythms 'drift' relative to each other.

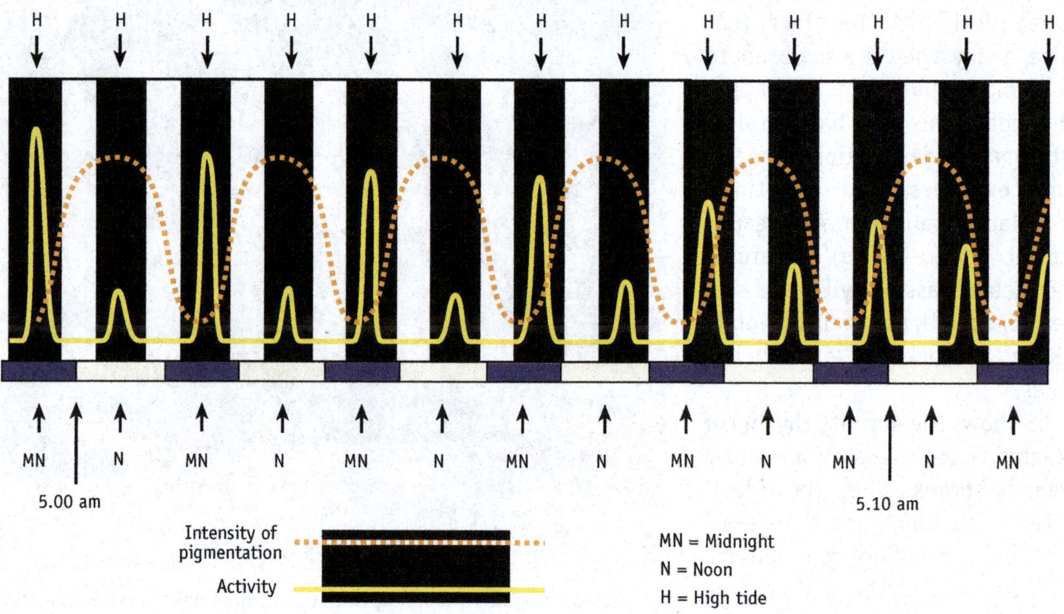

Fig. 3.3.6 Activity and degree of skin pigmentation in a European shore crab. Black columns represent high tide, blue bars represent night time.

How do biological clocks help survival?

Having an internal clock enables an organism to prepare for oncoming environmental change. Examples:

- Fruit flies (*Drosophila*) emerge from the pupa in the early morning, when relative humidity is at its maximum and the rate of evaporation is low. Preparations for emergence take a few hours, so the secretion of the adult cuticle and other preparatory changes must begin well before dawn.
- Many littoral (shore-living) animals seek a hiding place before the tide goes out. If slow-moving animals were to wait until the tide fell, they would probably become stranded, and die at low tide if it coincided with a hot day.
- An internal clock helps ensure the correct timing of seasonal activities like breeding and migration.

Samoa and Tonga and other Pacific islands provide a famous example of behaviour that is linked to biological clocks. Once a year colossal numbers of reef-living palolo worms rise to the surface to breed. This event happens around midnight, usually three days after the first new moon after the September equinox, and lasts only a few hours. The likely survival value of their synchronised behaviour? The number of worms is so great that predators can make little impact on them.

 ISBN: 9780170355582

Using internal clocks to tell the time

Many flowers secrete nectar at particular times of the day. Bees visit only those flower species that are actively secreting nectar at the time. Bees can be trained to visit several different sugar solutions at different times of the day, provided that each solution is presented at intervals of about 24 hours. In this mutualistic relationship, both species benefit from an internal clock:

- Bees don't waste time visiting flowers that don't offer food.
- Plants also benefit, because bees concentrate on a particular kind of flower at a given time; it increases the chances that pollen will be transferred to other flowers of the same species.

Many animals use their internal clock to navigate using the sun and stars (see Unit 3).

Where is the clock?

Experiments have shown that in mammals, the 'master clock' is located in the **suprachiasmatic nuclei** (**SCN**) in the hypothalamus region of the brain.

To be entrained, the SCN must be able to receive information from the outside world. In most mammals the *zeitgeber* is the light change at dawn or dusk. This is detected by certain cells in the retina of the eye, which communicate via neurons with the SCN.

How do the SCN communicate with the rest of the body? This is the role of the **pineal**, a tiny stalk-like structure on the roof of the brain. The pineal produces the hormone **melatonin** at night, promoting sleep and a nocturnal decrease in body temperature.

In birds, the clock is located in the pineal, which is directly sensitive to light that gets through the thin skull bone. In insects that have been investigated, the clock is located in the optic lobes of the brain.

Check your understanding

1 Matching pairs. Using the blank table below, write the letter of the term that matches the corresponding description.

1	Attributing human feelings and motives to an animal	A	abiotic factor
2	Attributing purpose to behaviour	B	anthropomorphism
3	An organism's way of life	C	biotic factor
4	Change in an organism's environment to which it can respond	D	effector
5	Factors in an organism's surroundings that affect it	E	environment
6	Influence due to other organisms, such as predation	F	habitat
7	Physical or non-living factor such as light, temperature	G	teleology
8	Place where an organism lives	H	niche
9	Structure that carries out a response to a stimulus	I	receptor
10	Structure that detects stimuli	J	stimulus

1	2	3	4	5	6	7	8	9	10

2 Matching pairs. Using the blank table below, write the letter of the term that matches the corresponding description.

1	Active around dawn and/or dusk	A	actogram
2	Active at night	B	circadian
3	Active during the day	C	circa-lunar
4	An activity-time graph	D	circa-tidal
5	Having a period of 12.4 hours	E	crepuscular
6	Having a period of 14.7 days	F	daily rhythm
7	Having a period of 24 hours	G	diurnal
8	Having a period of 29.5 days	H	endogenous
9	Having a period of *about* 12.4 hours	I	entrainment
10	Having a period of *about* 29 days	J	exogenous
11	Having a period of *about* a day	K	free-running
12	Having an external origin	L	lunar rhythm
13	Having an internal origin	M	nocturnal
14	A rhythm that continues without external rhythmic influences	N	SCN
15	Resetting of an internal clock by a rhythmic environmental cue	O	semi-lunar
16	Rhythmic environmental cue that resets an internal clock	P	tidal rhythm
17	Site of the internal clock in mammals	Q	*zeitgeber*

1	2	3	4	5	6	7	8	9	10	11	12	13	14	15	16	17

3 Name one example of each of these:

a a native nocturnal insect ______________________

b a native nocturnal bird ______________________

c a crepuscular mammal ______________________

d any diurnal animal ______________________

e any animal with compound rhythmic behaviour ______________________

4 Name two examples of plant activities that continue in rhythmic fashion under conditions of constant darkness.

____

____

5 Name three examples of human activities that continue rhythmically in constant environmental conditions.

____

____

____

ISBN: 9780170355582

6 Describe where the SCN are located, how they perceive light, and how they communicate with the rest of the body.

7 Complete the following sentences.

a The difference between 'entrainment' and 'endogenous' is

b We know that the human circadian period is about 25–26 hours, because

c The internal bodily cause of jetlag is

d The function of a *zeitgeber* is

8 The diagram below shows a recording of the activity of a captive weta over a 25-day period. For ease of visualisation the data are double plotted, each period of activity on the right being a duplicate of the left and shifted up one day.

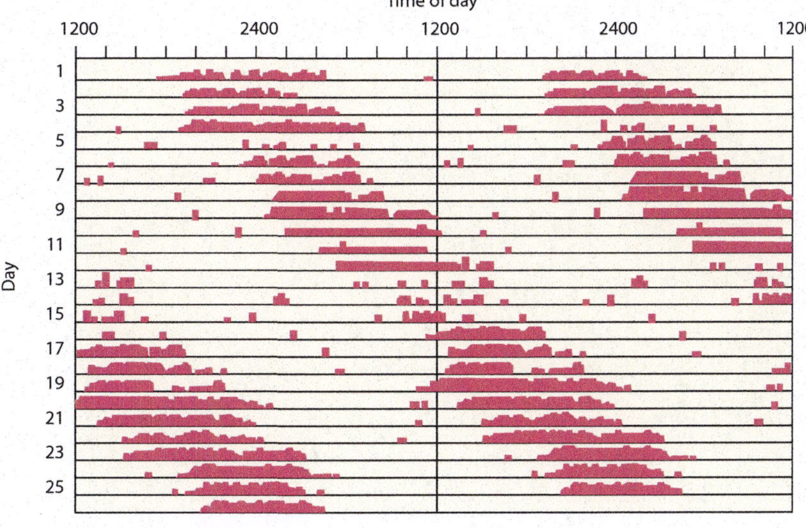

a State the technical name for this kind of diagram. ______________________________

b Suggest under what conditions the animal was kept.

____

____

c Calculate the period of the rhythm under these conditions.

____

____

d Explain the benefit to the animals of this behaviour being endogenous, instead of the animal just waiting until the evening and morning to arrive.

____

____

____

____

3

ISBN: 9780170355582

Unit 2 | Seasonal behaviour and photoperiodism

Anticipating seasonal change

All parts of the Earth have seasonal changes in climate: wet or dry, warm or cold. For living things to prepare for seasonal changes, they must somehow know in advance what time of year it is. The most reliable seasonal cue is day length, or **photoperiod** — although this does not apply in the tropics, where day length varies little. Most plants and animals living outside the tropics have evolved an ability to respond to changes in day length, an ability known as **photoperiodism.**

The breeding and migrating behaviour of many plants and animals depends on day length because it is so reliable. Weather is less reliable. If a few days of cold weather in December were the trigger causing kuaka (godwit) to set off on their annual migration northward from New Zealand, then they would arrive in Alaska in midwinter and freeze to death.

Many adaptations to seasonal change involve photoperiodism.

Examples:

- Flowering time in many plants.
- Production of winter buds in many temperate tree species.
- Production of tubers in potatoes.
- Migration in some birds.
- Laying down of fat prior to hibernation, in mammals such as polar bears.
- Production of winter coat in arctic foxes and other arctic mammals.

Fig. 3.3.7 Arctic fox in summer (top) and winter.

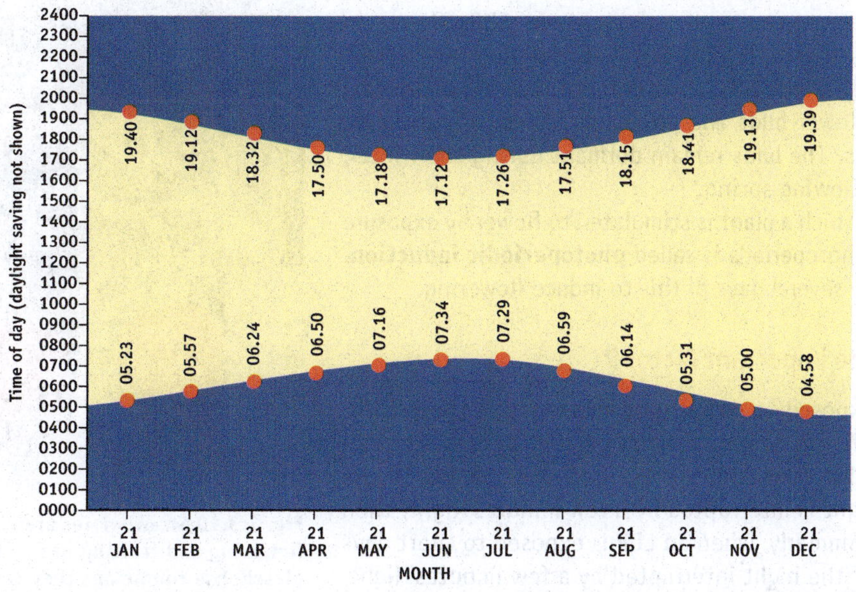

Fig. 3.3.8 Sunrise and sunset times for Auckland, latitude 37° South. Seasonal changes in day/night length are greater for places further from the equator.

Control of flowering and growth

Wheat, maize, rice: these three plant species provide most of humankind's food, and our survival depends on them. These plants and many others such as fruit trees can only produce food if they produce flowers. No flowers, no food. Flowering in many plants is dependent on the seasons, and in particular on day length. Much research has gone into finding why certain plants will flower in some months and not others. Early discovery: flowering does not depend only on the weather. In many cases the stimulus depends on the precise length of daytime.

After many experiments it was discovered that flowering plants could be grouped into three categories as regards to what triggers their flowering:

- **Short-day plants (SDP)**. These need a photoperiod less than a critical day length, CDL (Fig. 3.3.9). Examples: oat, ryegrass, clover, soybean, apples. CDL is not the same for all plants.
- **Long-day plants (LDP)**. These need a photoperiod greater than a critical value. Examples: strawberry, tobacco, and many other plants that flower in the summer months.
- **Day-neutral plants (DNP)**, in which flowering is not affected by photoperiod. DNPs tend to be opportunistic plants that will grow whenever soil and rainfall conditions are right.

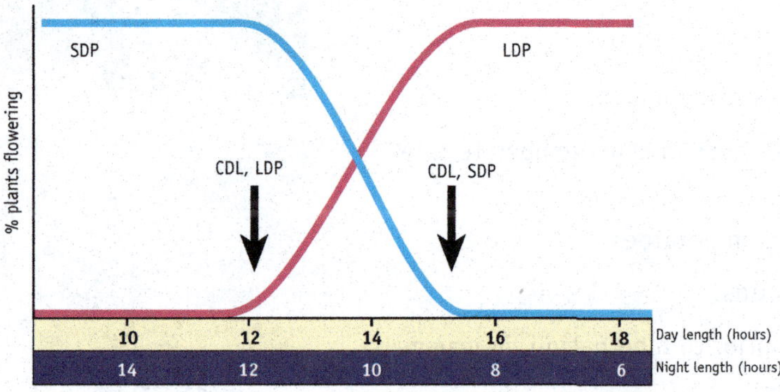

Fig. 3.3.9 Critical day length in short-day and long-day plants.

LDPs have their flowering process switched on when days are lengthening, in late spring and early summer. SDPs flower in autumn, when days are shortening. But flowering does not always happen immediately afterwards. Many spring-flowering perennials actually produce flower buds the previous autumn, for example tulips and daffodils. The buds remain dormant during the winter, and expand the following spring.

The process by which a plant is stimulated to flower by exposure to correct-length photoperiods is called **photoperiodic induction**. Most plants require several days of this to induce flowering.

Night length is the important factor

When an SDP is exposed to day length shorter than the critical day length (CDL), it will flower. If the same SDP is given artificial conditions with the same short days, and the middle of the artificially long night is interrupted by a few minutes' light, then it will not flower. Similarly, when an LDP is exposed to short days with the middle of the night interrupted by a few minutes' light, flowering is **induced** (triggered) (Fig. 3.3.11). Conclusion: when it comes to flowering, what matters is not the length of the day, but a certain minimum night length. Short-day plants should perhaps be called long-night plants.

Fig. 3.3.10 Strawberries are long-day plants, flowering and fruiting in summer. When grown in glasshouse conditions they can be 'tricked' into producing strawberries in winter, by giving them artificially long days, or else long winter nights interrupted by a short spell of bright light.

 ISBN: 9780170355582

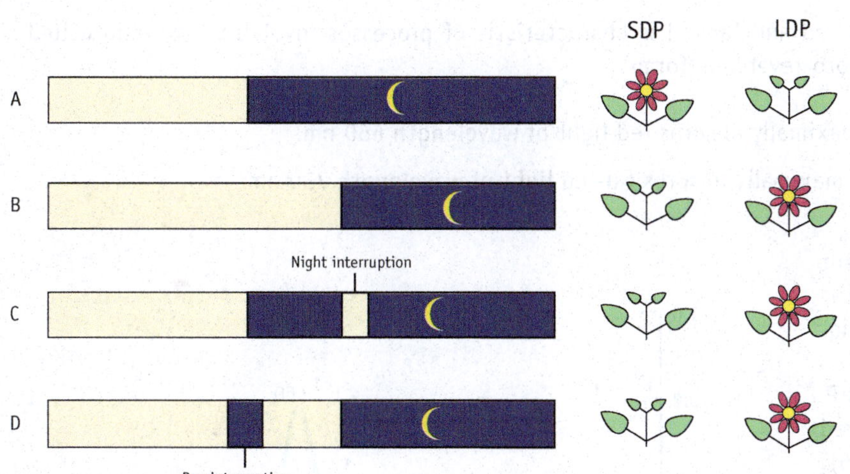

Fig. 3.3.11 Effect of a night interruption on flowering.

E

Measurement of photoperiod involves the pigment phytochrome

Further experiments showed that red light of wavelength 660 nm is the most effective in night interruption. An **action spectrum** is a graph of the effectiveness of different wavelengths of light in promoting a process (Fig. 3.3.12).

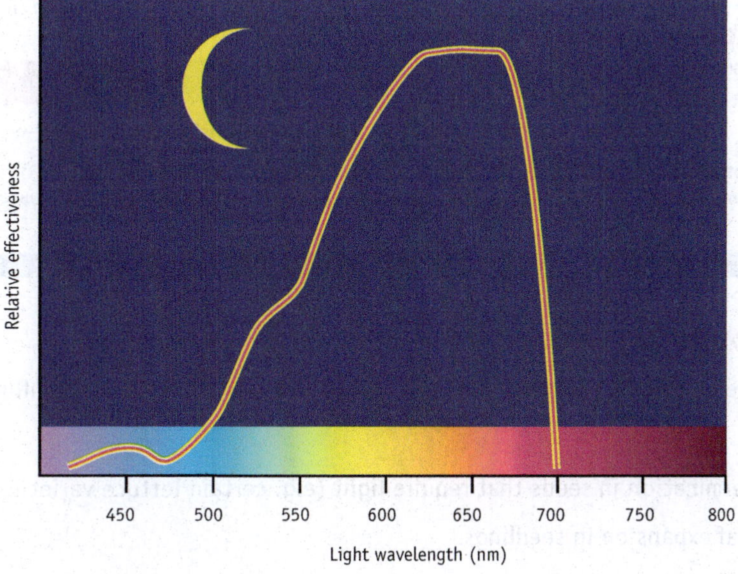

Fig. 3.3.12 Action spectrum for effectiveness of night interruption.

If a night interruption is followed by a few minutes' exposure to far-red light (730 nm), the effect of the red light is cancelled. If the far-red light is immediately followed by red, the effect of the far-red is cancelled. In fact, the last kind of light given is what determines the effect of a night interruption (Fig. 3.3.13).

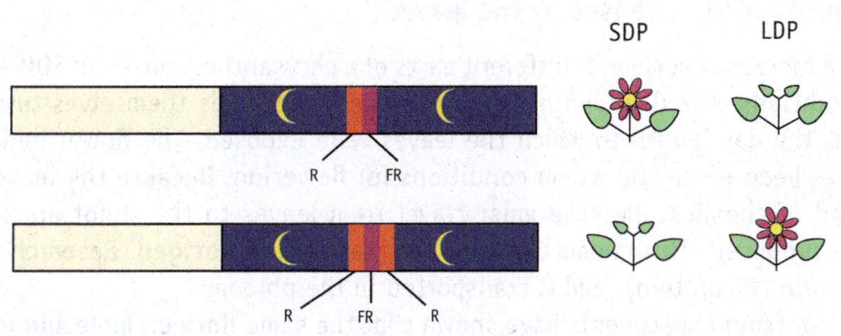

Fig. 3.3.13 Effect of red light is nullified if followed immediately by far-red light.

9780170355582

This reversibility of the effect of red and far-red is characteristic of processes involving a protein called **phytochrome**. It exists in two photo-reversible forms:

- P_r or P_{660} — 'r' because it maximally absorbs red light of wavelength 660 nm.
- P_{fr} or P_{730} — 'fr' because it maximally absorbs far-red light of wavelength 730 nm.

The relative absorption of different wavelengths of light by a pigment is called an **absorption spectrum** (Fig. 3.3.14).

Exposure to red light converts P_r to P_{fr}, and exposure of P_{fr} to far-red converts it back to P_r (Fig. 3.3.15). In addition, P_{fr} is slowly converted back to P_r in darkness. At one time, this dark-reversal was thought to be how plants measure the length of the night. The mechanism is now less clear.

Fig. 3.3.15 Interconversion of the two forms of phytochrome.

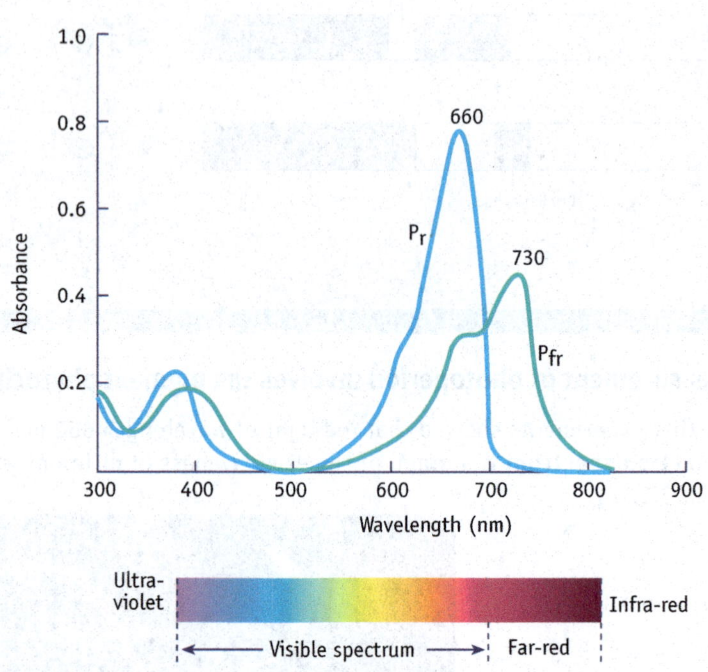

Fig. 3.3.14 Absorption spectra of the two forms of phytochrome.

Processes affected by phytochromes

There are actually several kinds of phytochrome, all involved in a variety of light-influenced processes besides flowering. Examples:

- Promotion of germination in seeds that require light (e.g. certain lettuce varieties).
- Promotion of leaf expansion in seedlings.
- Inhibition of stem elongation in the light.

Photoperiod is sensed by the leaves

In a famous experiment, different parts of a chrysanthemum — an SDP — were subjected to different photoperiodic conditions. The day length shining on the flower buds themselves turned out to be unimportant; what mattered was the day length to which the leaves were exposed. The flower buds of the plant on the left (see Fig. 3.3.16) have been given the wrong conditions for flowering. Because the leaves below it are receiving long nights, some kind of chemical message must travel from leaves to the shoot apex (apical meristem), where the flower buds are produced. This chemical messenger was named **florigen**. Research has shown that florigen is a small globular protein (FT protein), and is transported in the phloem.

Grafting experiments have shown that the same florigen molecule is the signal in both LDPs and SDPs. How can we be sure of this? When an SDP is grafted onto an LDP, the plant flowers regardless of whether it is given short or long photoperiods (Fig. 3.3.17).

 ISBN: 9780170355582

Fig. 3.3.16 Evidence that photoperiod is perceived by the leaves. The width of the purple and yellow bands represents the length of artificial days and nights.

Fig. 3.3.17 Evidence from grafting experiments showing that the internal flowering signal is the same in SDP and LDP.

Vernalisation

Many plants will only flower if they have had several weeks' exposure to cold in the previous winter. Example: most apple and apricots varieties and many other plants adapted to cooler climates. This cold requirement for flowering is called **vernalisation.** It differs from photoperiodic induction of flowering in that low temperature acts directly on apical meristem tissue (in buds at branch tips), and is not detected by the leaves. Vernalisation is an additional requirement for flowering, as well as day length.

Photoperiodism in animals

Seasonal changes in temperature can affect animals directly or indirectly. Ectotherms ('cold-blooded' animals, such as reptiles) become sluggish in cooler temperatures because of the effect of temperature on enzyme activity. In many endotherms ('warm-blooded' animals, namely birds and mammals), metabolic rate rises in colder conditions as a way of maintaining body temperature. In some mammals, the onset of colder conditions sets in train changes leading to hibernation, which involves a reduction in metabolic rate.

Hibernation is one way of avoiding adverse conditions. Another is migration, dealt with in Unit 3. Among insects, a common adaptation is **diapause.** This is a period of suspended development in the life cycle, which for many insects is adult-eggs-larva-pupa-adult. Example: the common white butterfly has several breeding generations every year. For any larva that happens to be growing in autumn, the pupa stops development and does not resume the cycle until spring. The stimulus that triggers diapause is a decrease in day length at the last larval stage.

Check your understanding

1 Write matching words in the blank column. Choose from this list: *hibernation, vernalisation, diapause, photoperiod, endotherm, florigen, phytochrome, strawberry, metabolism, absorption spectrum.*

a	Day length	
b	Flowering hormone	
c	Induction of flowering by cold	
d	Light-sensitive pigment involved in plant photoperiodism	
e	Period of arrested development in the life of an insect	
f	Graph showing effectiveness of light against wavelength	
g	One example of a long-day plant	
h	State of slow metabolism in some mammals	
i	A word for animals with a high body temperature setting	
j	A general word covering chemical activity in any living thing	

2 Using the graph showing day and night length in Auckland on page 41, find the following:

The date and day length of the summer solstice, the longest day.

The date and day length of the winter solstice, the shortest day.

The two equinox dates when day and night are (almost) exactly equal in length.

3 Complete the following sentences.

a We know that plants perceive day and night length in their leaves and not their flowers because

b We know that flowering in short-day plants is actually triggered by long nights because

c To switch off flowering in *Chrysanthemum* (a short-day plant, CDL 11 hours), plants being grown indoors should be given

ISBN: 9780170355582

d Plants (and also animals) use day length as an indicator of time of year, and do not rely on seasonal factors such as temperature, because

____

____

____

e The term 'long-day plant' is misleading because

____

____

4 A particular short-day plant species with a critical day length of 11 hours can be induced to flower by a single suitable 24-hour photoperiodic cycle. A grower gave a collection of these plants — grown indoors under artificial conditions — 10 hours' light followed by 14 hours' dark, and checked on the plants in the middle of the dark period. The plant failed to flower. Suggest why they failed, and suggest what the grower should have done in order to induce flowering.

____

____

____

____

5 Three species of plant, X, Y and Z, have different photoperiodic requirements for flowering. One is a long-day plant, another is a short-day plant, and the third is a day-neutral plant. A number of plants of each of the three species were subjected to light-dark cycles of various kinds as shown in the diagram below. A blue bar represents darkness and a yellow bar represents light.

For each of X, Y and Z, state whether it is an SDP, LDP or DNP.

X = ____________ Y = ____________ Z = ____________

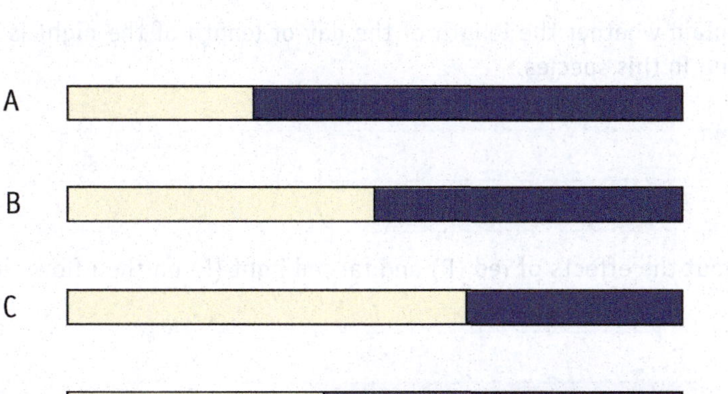

6 Plants of a certain species were subjected to a range of seven different light and dark treatments (I–VII in the diagram). Blue bars indicate darkness, yellow bars indicate light periods. The letters indicate the kind of light treatment (L = normal light, R = red light, F = far-red light). The effect of each treatment on flowering is given on the right.

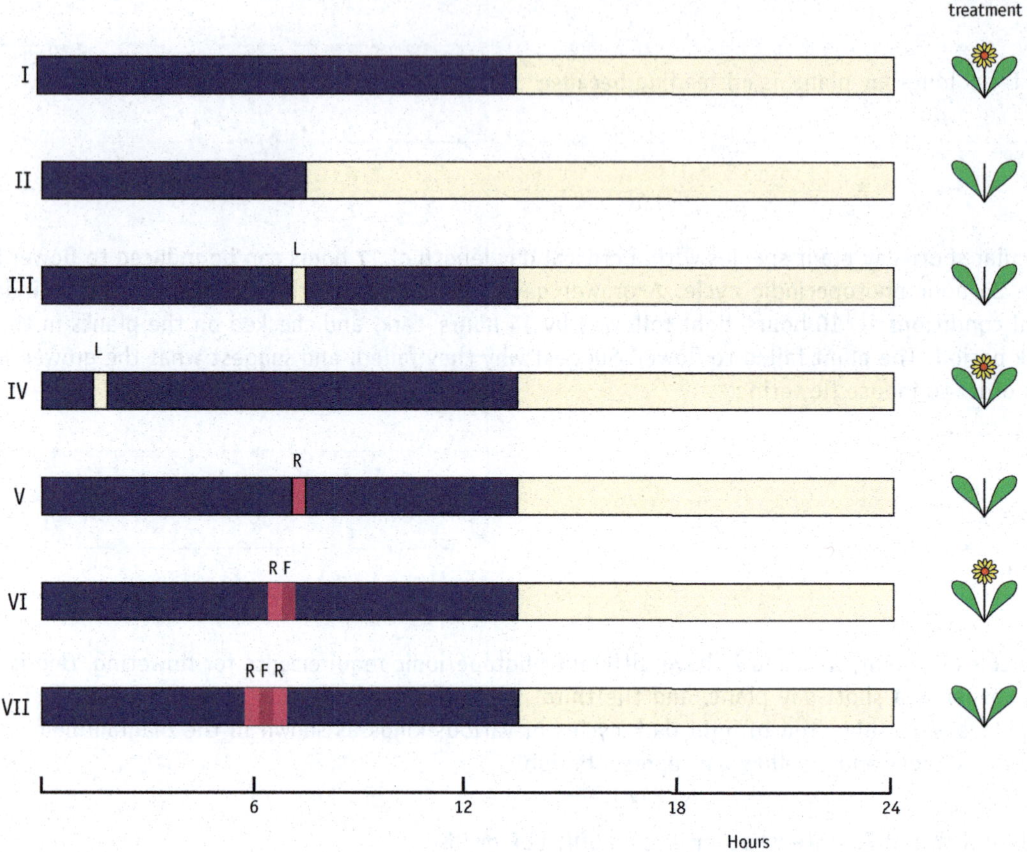

a Using the results from I and II, state the photoperiodic group (SDP, LDP, DNP) to which this species belongs.

b Refer to the results from I to IV, and explain whether the length of the day or length of the night is the critical factor in the induction of flowering in this species.

c From V, VI and VII, write a conclusion about the effects of red (R) and far-red light (F) on their flowering.

d Describe how these factors could be used to induce this species to flower out of season.

ISBN: 9780170355582

Unit 3 | Animals: finding the way

Most animals are able to move away from danger and towards more favourable conditions. Birds migrate, sharks find food, snails avoid sunlight. Different kinds of 'directional' movements:

- **Taxes and kineses**: simple orientation responses to changes that have already occurred.
- **Migration**: long-distance movements, in anticipation of changes that have not yet occurred.
- **Homing**: direction-finding partly based on landmarks.

Taxis

A taxis is a simple response in which an animal moves either towards a stimulus (a positive taxis) or away from it (a negative taxis). This kind of response is common in animals such as snails and slaters, which are active at night when it is cool and damp and hide in sheltered places during the day. Taxes (the plural of taxis) are named according to the kind of stimulus and the direction of the response. Examples:

- Negative gravitaxis: movement away from gravity, as when snails crawl upwards after being disturbed. In some books, gravitaxis responses are named 'geo-taxis' (an older term).
- Negative phototaxis: movement away from light, for example earthworms or slaters.
- Positive chemotaxis: movement towards a chemical, as when a mosquito moves towards CO_2 produced by a potential host.

E

Kinesis

In kinesis behaviour the direction of movement is random, but the rate changes when the animal encounters different conditions. The stimulus could be temperature (thermokinesis), light (photokinesis), touch (thigmokinesis). There are two general kinds of kinesis:

- Orthokinesis (*ortho* means 'straight'). The speed of forward movement becomes faster when the animal is in unfavourable conditions. The animal slows down when conditions are right.
- Klinokinesis (*klino* means 'turning'). The frequency of turning decreases when the animal is in less favourable conditions. The rate of turning increases as the animal encounters favourable conditions, making it more likely to stay in the area.

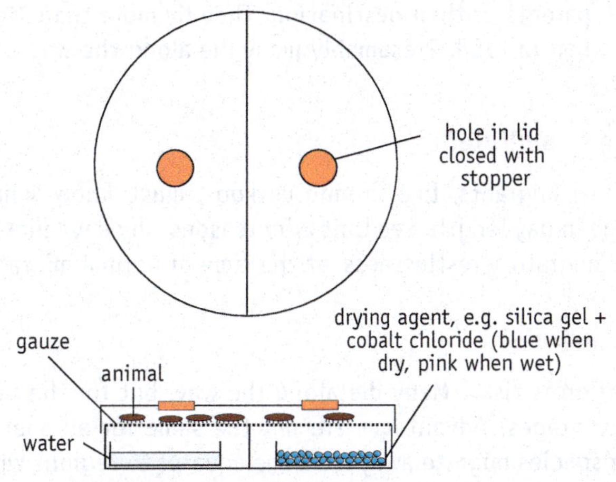

Fig. 3.3.18 A 'choice chamber' experiment for investigating the responses of animals such as woodlice to different humidities.

Migration

Migration is complex behaviour and differs from kineses and taxes in important ways:

- Migration anticipates the environmental change the animal is to take advantage of, or avoid. Example: a polar bear begins to store fat weeks before conditions become harsh.
- Most migrations occur over long distances, out of any contact with the destination. Example: titi (muttonbirds) migrate from the northern Pacific to New Zealand in September, and return in March.
- Migration in most cases occurs regularly at a particular time of the year.

Examples of migration

- Salmon mate and lay their eggs in freshwater streams, and the young later migrate downstream to the sea where they spend the next few years. As mature adults they migrate back to the stream in which they were hatched, guided by a memory of its smell.
- Longfin eels begin life in deep Pacific waters, migrate to New Zealand rivers where they spend most of their life, then as mature adults return to their breeding grounds to lay eggs and die.
- Humpback whales spend the summer feeding on abundant plankton in polar seas, then migrate to tropical waters each year in winter to give birth.

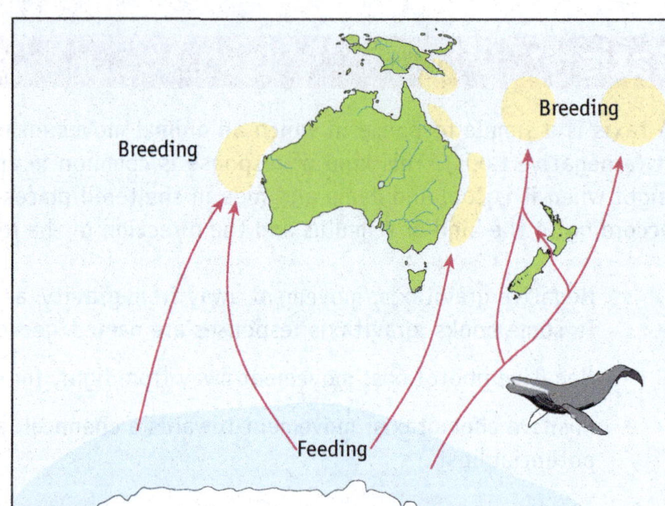

Fig. 3.3.19 Migration routes of humpback whales.

- Turtles migrate across the Atlantic towards tiny Ascension Island where they lay their eggs.
- Shining cuckoos (pipiwharauroa) lay their eggs in the nests of grey warblers in New Zealand. A few months later the young cuckoos migrate to the Solomon Islands alone, having never experienced either their parents or their destination. They fly more than 2000 km of open ocean, which means several days without rest or food. Presumably many die along the way.

When to migrate?

Seasonal migrants, like shining cuckoos, must 'know' what time of year it is. In most cases studied, the cue is change in day length. See Unit 2 for reasons why day length and not weather is the trigger. When caged, many birds show 'migratory restlessness' at the time of normal migration.

Why migrate?

Migration is risky. Many die along the way, but for the behaviour to continue its advantages must outweigh the disadvantages. Advantages are not the same for all species. In some cases, it is to avoid snowy winters, while other species migrate away from the equator to regions where longer days give more feeding time each day. In the case of humpback whales, the polar food chain shuts down in the winter; also newborn calves won't die of cold in warm tropical waters.

Finding the way

Many species of migratory birds have been studied in detail, with discoveries of astonishing endurance and direction-finding ability. Godwit (kuaka) fly nonstop from Alaska to New Zealand each September, a journey of many days. Individuals that make even a small error in navigation will miss their target and die — so there must be strong selection pressure favouring individuals that are excellent navigators.

ISBN: 9780170355582

Navigation can only succeed if the animal has a sense of:

- direction (a 'compass')
- time (an accurate internal clock)
- position (a 'map'), which tells the animal where it is in relation to where it should be.

Many birds use navigation and also use pilotage landmarks when they get closer to home. Some species use more than one type of compass, so there are 'back-ups' in case one type fails. *Excellence in Biology NCEA Level 3* gives details of some experimental evidence.

Fig. 3.3.20 Kuaka (bar-tailed godwit), which migrate between New Zealand and Alaska. The southward journey is made non-stop.

Solar and star compasses

The sun's position can be used as a compass, but only if the animal knows the time. This is where an internal clock comes in; to compensate for the apparent movement of sun and moon across the sky. The same clock is needed when navigating by star patterns at night. Experiments on caged birds have shown that if the sun's position is changed 90° (by using mirrors), the direction of 'migration restlessness' also changes by 90°.

Polarised light

When light from the sun meets the atmosphere, its waves are oriented in all directions, but by the time it reaches the ground, it has become polarised, meaning that its waves are in a particular plane. Bees can detect the plane of polarisation of sunlight. This can be used to tell the direction of the sun as long as any small part of the sky is clear.

Earth's magnetic field

Turtles, trout, many birds and insects (e.g. bees) are all known to use the earth's magnetic field as a compass. In trout, tiny crystals of magnetite (iron oxide, Fe_2O_3) have been found in the anterior (front) end of the body, and are thought to be part of the magneto-receptor system. Similar crystals have also been found in pigeons and dolphins.

Pilotage

Some animals find their way by 'pilotage': using landmarks or scent marks they have encountered before. Examples: homing pigeons over shorter distances; ants following a trail. True navigation is different — it is the ability to find the way even when in unfamiliar territory.

Check your understanding

1 Write the matching terms in the blank column. Choose from this list: *compass, kinesis, positive gravitaxis, navigation, orthokinesis, taxis, klinokinesis, negative phototaxis, pilotage, thigmokinesis, migration.*

a	Animal moves in a direction that depends on direction of stimulus	
b	Downward movement in response to gravity	
c	Movement away from the direction of light	
d	Any regular seasonal movement of a whole population	
e	Sense system that provides clues about the direction of north/south/east/west	

f	Rate of movement depends on strength of stimulus	
g	A form of direction-finding based on landmarks	
h	Complex direction-finding that relies on a sense of position	
i	Frequency of turning depends on strength of the stimulus	
j	Any form of orientation in which the rate of movement changes	
k	Movement in response to contact	

3

2 Describe two probable advantages of long-distance north–south migration of humpback whales, which feed in seas around Antarctica in summer and give birth in tropical seas in the southern winter.

3 Kuaka spend March to September in Alaska where they breed, and the rest of the year in New Zealand. Their southern migration is a nonstop journey taking several days.

a Suggest two disadvantages of this long-distance migration, compared with those bird species that travel shorter distances to warmer climates.

b The advantages must outweigh disadvantages, or else the behaviour would have been selected against. Suggest one advantage of kuaka migratory behaviour.

4 Complete the following sentences.

a Three kinds of compass used by migrating birds are

b When navigating by star or sun, birds need an internal clock in order to

c Bees are able to navigate using sunlight on a cloudy day, but only if

5 Describe how migrating salmon find the exact river in which they were hatched.

ISBN: 9780170355582

6 The diagram below shows the results of a series of experiments on the use of magnetic cues in homing pigeons. Birds were released individually, 27–50 km from home. As each bird disappeared from sight its direction ('vanishing bearing') was recorded. In each illustration, *a* = the mean vanishing bearing and *r* is a measure of their dispersion, also represented by the length of the arrow. In each experiment, birds were divided into two groups. One group had bar magnets (pink circles) on their backs and the other had brass rods (yellow circles as controls). Carrying a magnet will distort a magnetic sense of direction.

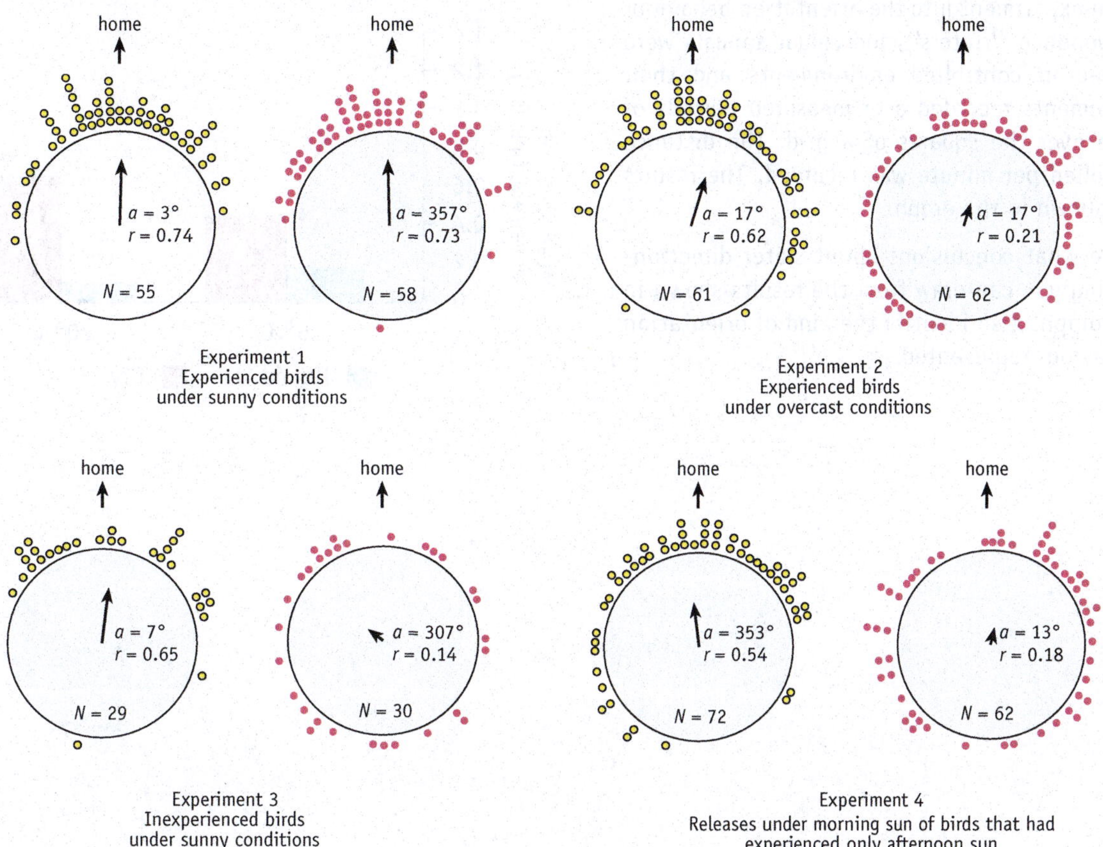

Experiment 1. Experienced birds were released on a sunny day.

Experiment 2. Experienced birds were released on an overcast day.

Experiment 3. Birds that had been raised in an aviary without ever seeing the sun were released on a sunny day.

Experiment 4. Birds that had been allowed to experience only the afternoon sun were released in the morning on a sunny day.

Using these results, suggest conclusions about the cues by which pigeons find their way home.

7 Explain how is it possible for homing pigeons to find their way home from a distant area they've never been to before.

8 In an experiment into the orientation behaviour of woodlice ('slaters'), individual animals were placed in controlled environments and their movements recorded over measured periods of time over the squares of a grid. The distance travelled per minute was recorded. The results are shown in the graph.

State what conclusions about slater direction-finding you can draw from the results shown in the graph. Also identify the kind of orientation behaviour represented.

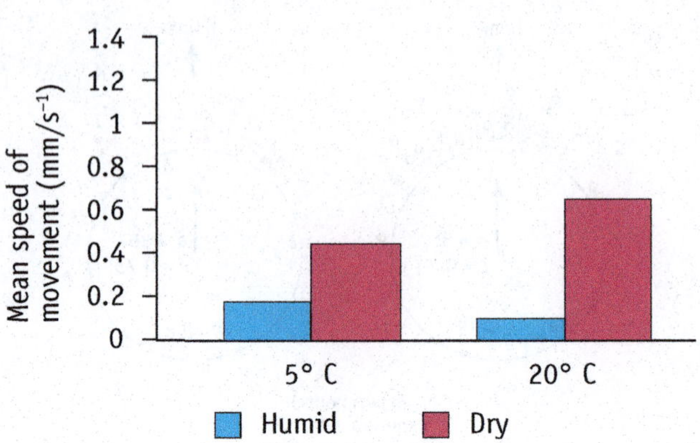

3

ISBN: 9780170355582

Unit 4 | Plants, orientation, tropisms

Since plants can't move around they have to make do with conditions wherever they happen to start growing. They do, however, have two kinds of limited movement: **tropisms** and **nastic movements** (also known as 'nasties').

Tropisms

A tropism is a growth movement in response to a directional stimulus. (*Trope* means 'to turn'.) A tropism can be positive (towards a stimulus) or negative (away from a stimulus). Tropism movements are not reversible. Examples:

- Positive phototropism — growth towards light
- Positive gravitropism — growth towards gravity (i.e. downwards)
- Negative gravitropism — growth away from gravity. Example: seedling stems.
- Positive chemotropism — growth towards a chemical. Example: root systems towards a nutrient source.
- Positive hydrotropism — growth towards water. Example: in root systems; a special case of chemotropism.
- Thigmotropism — growth movement in response to touch. Example: grapevine tendril.

When a stem bends, this is the result of cells on one side elongating faster than on the other. This only happens in parts that are still growing in length, which generally means young stems, roots and petioles (leaf stalks).

Phototropism

Phototropism is a growth movement that depends on the direction the light is coming from. Young stems are generally positively phototropic. The ability of stems and leaves to orient themselves towards light enables them to make maximum use of available light for photosynthesis.

Experiments using coleoptiles

A coleoptile is a spear-like sheath that protects the young leaves of a grass seedling as it grows up through the soil. Growth in length is entirely by cell enlargement, cell division having ceased at an earlier stager.

Coleoptiles are highly sensitive to light. Fig. 3.3.21 shows a number of simple experiments involving coleoptiles and one-sided light. From these experiments we can make the following conclusions:

- The phototropic stimulus is detected by the tip.
- The region that bends is some distance away from the tip.
- Therefore some kind of 'influence' or signal must be transmitted away from the tip.

Later experiments showed that the 'message' was a water-soluble chemical that stimulated the cells to elongate. The chemical was given the name **auxin**, later chemically identified as **indole-3-acetic acid**, IAA. The effect of auxin is to make the cell wall more easily stretchable, thus promoting cell enlargement (Fig. 3.3.23).

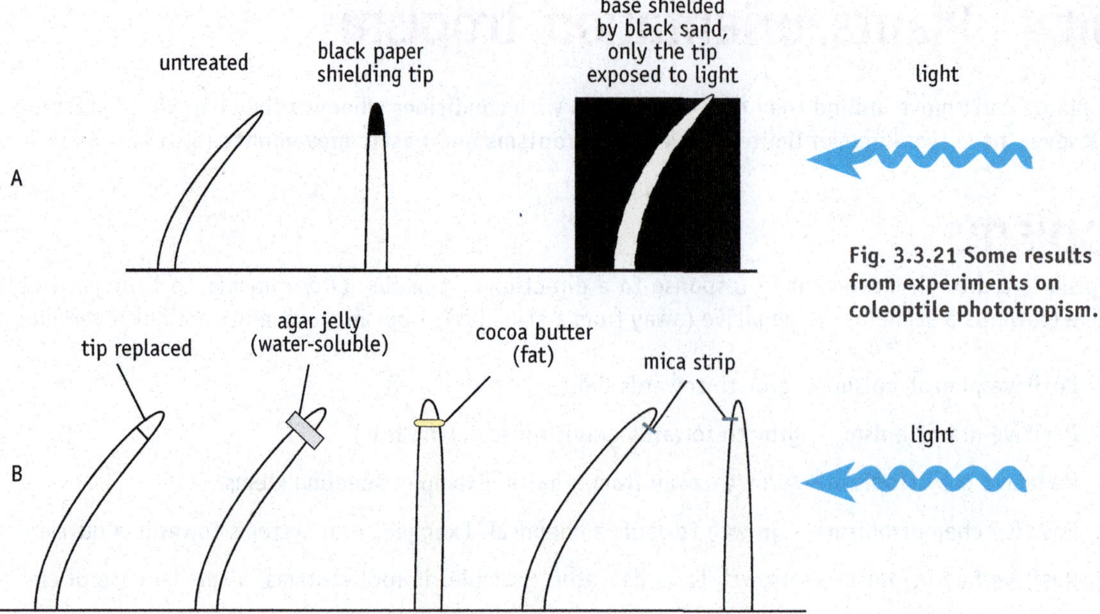

Fig. 3.3.21 Some results from experiments on coleoptile phototropism.

3

IAA can be transferred from coleoptile tips into blocks of agar, a water-soluble jelly. When an agar block containing IAA is placed on one side of a decapitated coleoptile, the stump curved away from the side on which the block had been placed (Fig. 3.3.22).

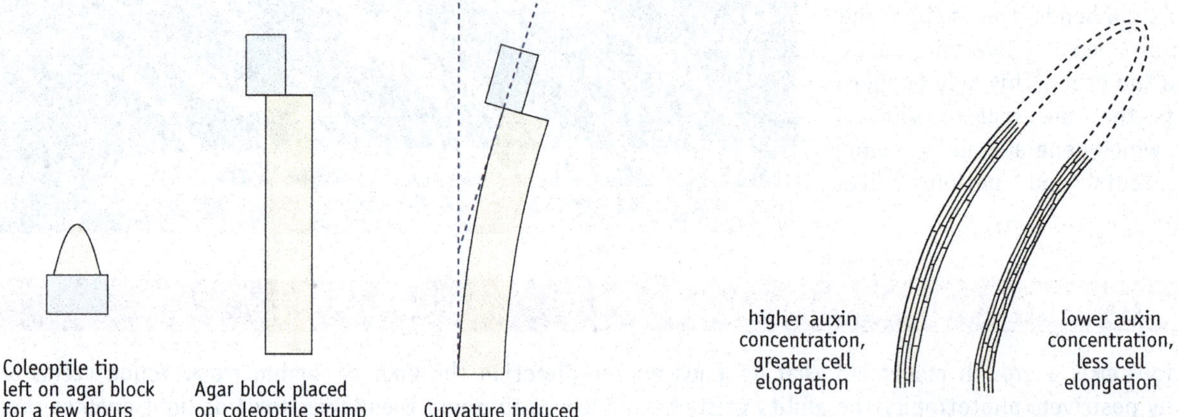

Fig. 3.3.22 Using an agar block to collect auxin.

Fig. 3.3.23 In a coleoptile, auxin stimulates cell extension on the shaded side.

Measuring auxin

Experiments showed how relative amounts of auxin could be measured. When an agar block containing auxin is placed off-centre on a coleoptile stump, the degree of curvature is proportional to the amount of auxin in the block. This means that auxin concentration can be expressed in terms of its biological activity: the amount of curvature. Using this method, it was shown that when a coleoptile tip is unilaterally illuminated, auxin is transported to the shaded side (Fig. 3.3.24).

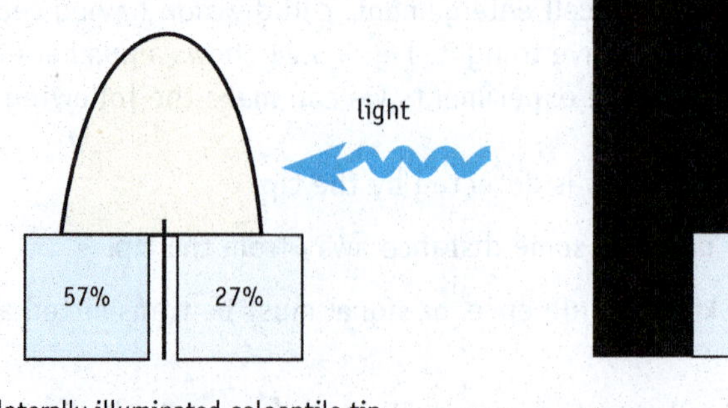

Fig. 3.3.24 Experiment on lateral transport of auxin.

ISBN: 9780170355582

Auxin transport

To exert its effect, auxin is transported away from the tip of a coleoptile to regions of cell elongation. Experiments have shown that auxin transport is **active**, since it requires energy from respiration; much **faster** than diffusion; always in a **tip-to-base** direction.

Auxin production in a coleoptile does not depend on light; it continues in darkness. In unidirectional light it is transported from the illuminated side of a coleoptile tip to the shaded side, before being transported down to the elongating region.

Phototropism in leafy shoots

Coleoptiles are not typical shoots, and the mechanism of phototropism is slightly different (Fig. 3.3.25). The young leaves that receive most light export the most auxin, as a result of which the shaded side of the stem receives most auxin and elongates the most.

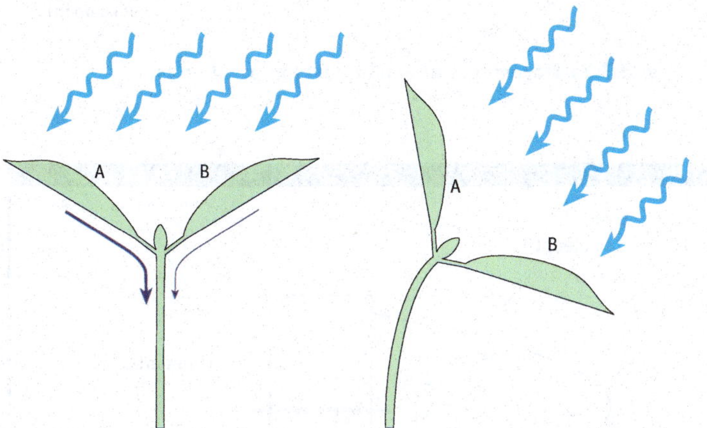

Fig. 3.3.25 Phototropism in a leafy shoot

Fig. 3.3.26 Thigmotropism: the growth movements of a tendril in response to touch. When the tendril grows stronger, it helps to hold the plant upright and obtain more light.

> **shoot**: the above-ground parts of a young plant (stem, leaves, etc.).
> **radicle**: embryo root that emerges from a germinating seed.
> **plumule**: embryo shoot and leaves that emerge from a germinating seed.

Gravitropism

Gravitropism is growth movement in response to the direction of gravity. The most gravity-sensitive plant regions are the radicle and plumule of seedlings:

- Radicles are positively gravitropic. By growing downward, the root reaches a more reliable water supply and gains better anchorage.
- Plumules are negatively gravitropic. This moves a young stem towards light even though to begin with it is in darkness underground.

Fig. 3.3.27 Norfolk Island pines remain vertical throughout life, regardless of the direction of wind or light. This shows they are dominated by a strong negative gravitropic response.

Klinostats

A difficulty with studying gravitropism is that gravity can't be turned on and off. A solution is to use a klinostat (Fig. 3.3.28). This has a slowly rotating wheel with a plant fixed to it. The wheel rotates about once every 15 minutes, so the direction of gravity changes faster than the plant can respond.

By stopping a klinostat for varying times, it can be shown that for a radicle to respond, it must be exposed to a gravity stimulus for at least 10 seconds to about 3 minutes. The mechanism for detecting gravity involves starch-storing organelles called **amyloplasts.** These are slightly denser than the rest of the cytoplasm and thus tend to sink (Fig. 3.3.29).

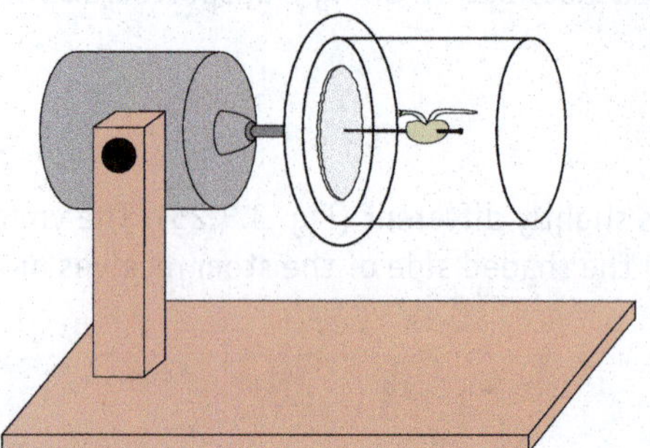

Fig. 3.3.28 A klinostat.

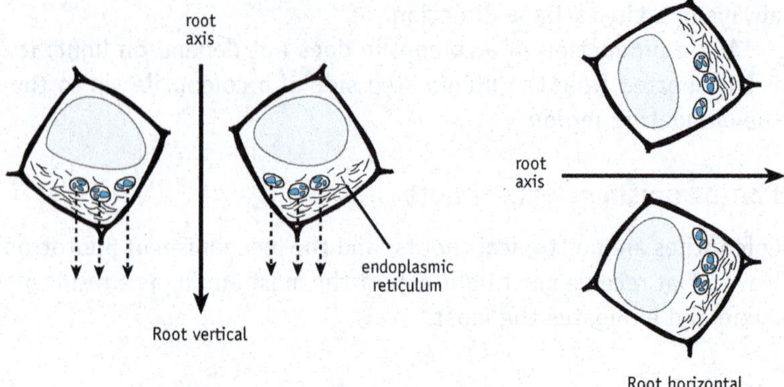

Fig. 3.3.29 Movements of amyloplasts in plant cells.

E

Transmission of the signal

The force of gravity pressing the amyloplasts on the cytoplasm must in some way send a message to the zone of elongation. As in phototropism, the messenger in coleoptiles is auxin. This was shown by using agar blocks to absorb auxin from the upper and lower halves of a horizontal coleoptile tip (Fig. 3.3.30). Result: more auxin entered the lower block than the upper one.

In shoots, auxin stimulates cell elongation. In roots, auxin inhibits cell elongation. Auxin synthesised in the shoot is translocated to the root tip, from where it is transported to the elongating region behind. Unless the root is vertical, auxin is translocated more along the lower side, thus causing downward bending. The difference in sensitivity of different regions to auxin is seen in the graph in Fig. 3.3.31. In root tips, a low concentration of auxin will inhibit cell extension; an extremely low auxin concentration will stimulate cell extension. Both of these effects combine to cause the root to curve downwards.

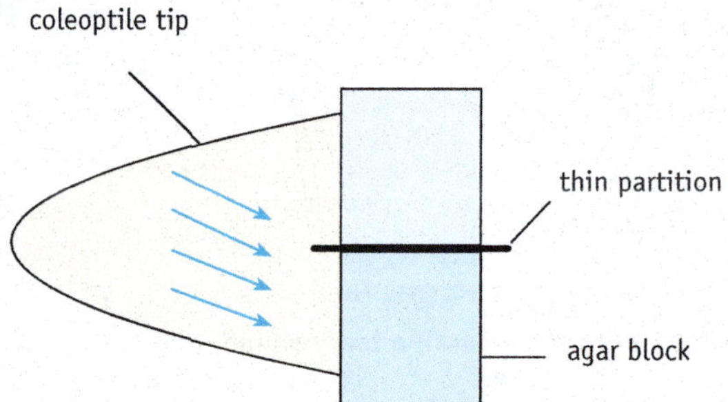

Fig. 3.3.30 In a horizontal coleoptile tip, most auxin moves downwards.

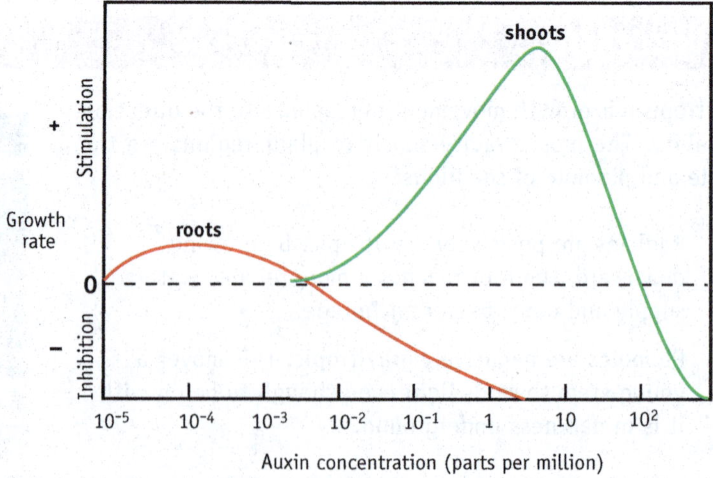

Fig. 3.3.31 Different growing regions vary in their response to auxin. At most concentrations, auxin stimulates cell enlargement in stems, and inhibits cell enlargement in root tissues.

 ISBN: 9780170355582

Nastic movements ('nasties')

Nastic movements are comparatively quick movements that involve changes in pressure inside plant cells. Examples: the sleep movements of some flowers; the leaves of a Venus flytrap. Nasties differ from tropic movements in several ways:

- they are not affected by the direction of the stimulus
- they are reversible
- they are comparatively quick.

Nasties are named according to the kind of stimulus. Photonasty is a movement in response to a change in light intensity, e.g. the opening of many flowers in the light. Thermonasty is movement in response to a change in temperature. Thigmonasty is a response to touch.

Thigmonasty

Thigmonasty is a plant movement that occurs in response to contact. A famous example is the Venus flytrap, an insect-eating plant native to North America. Like other insectivorous plants it grows in boggy ground in which nitrates are in short supply, so makes up for the lack by feeding on insects to get amino acids from them.

The plant attracts insects by its leaves, which are conspicuously tinged with red and which secrete nectar at the margins. When an insect touches one of six sensory hairs more than once in about 35 seconds, cells at the midrib of the leaf suddenly lose turgor (water pressure), closing the trap. Gland cells on the epidermis of the leaf then secrete enzymes that digest the insect, and the amino acids and other products are absorbed.

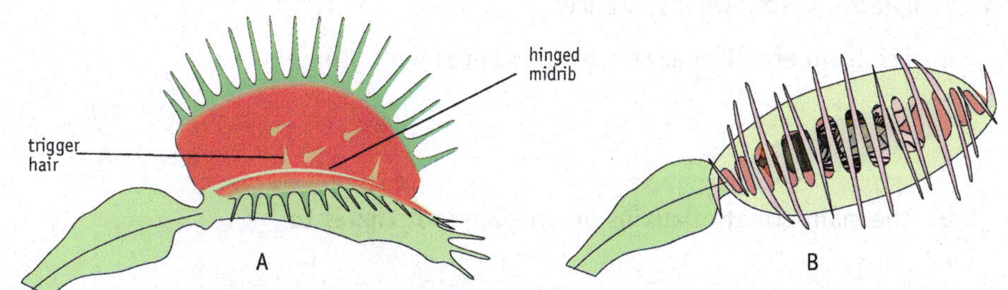

Fig. 3.3.32 A Venus flytrap leaf before and after capture of a fly. Touching the sensory hairs on the leaf trigger a touch response.

Check your understanding

1 Write matching words in the blank column. Choose from this list: *auxin, phototropism, thigmotropism, thigmonasty, plumule, tropism, gravitropism, coleoptile, nasty, radicle.*

a	Any growth movement that depends on the direction of a stimulus	
b	Growth movement in response to contact	
c	Growth movement in response to gravity	
d	Growth movement in response to light	
e	Root of an embryo plant	
f	Plant growth substance involved in phototropism and gravitropism	
g	Any comparatively quick turgor movement in plants	
h	A rapid plant response to touch	
i	Stem and leaves of embryo plant	
j	A covering over the leaves of a young growing grass	

2 During germination, the radicle (root) shows positive gravitropism. Complete the following sentences.

a 'Positive gravitropism' is one way of saying that

b Two advantages this positive gravitropism gives the plant are

c The main effect that auxin has on cells close to the root tip is to

d During germination, the plumule shows negative gravitropism, which benefits the young plant by

3 State the chemical name for auxin. ______________________

4 Complete the following sentences.

a The main effect of auxins on growing stems is to

b The main effect of auxins on growing root tips is to

c Three differences between a tropic and a nastic response are

d We know that adult Norfolk pines do not have any phototropic response because

5 Five different coleoptile tips were treated in different ways as illustrated below, and kept in darkness.

Which of the following pairs would you expect to show the *least* growth in length?

A 1 and 2

B 1 and 4

C 2 and 4

D 4 and 5

E 3 and 5

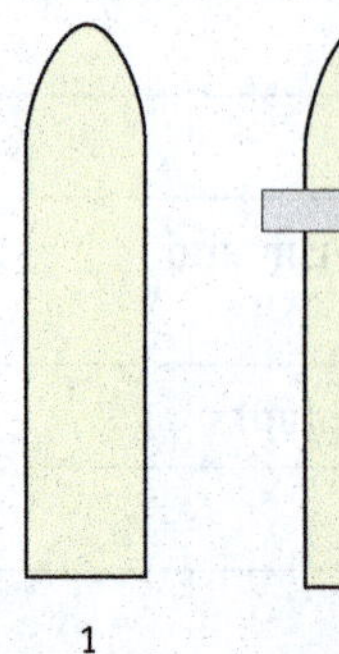

1
Untreated coleoptile

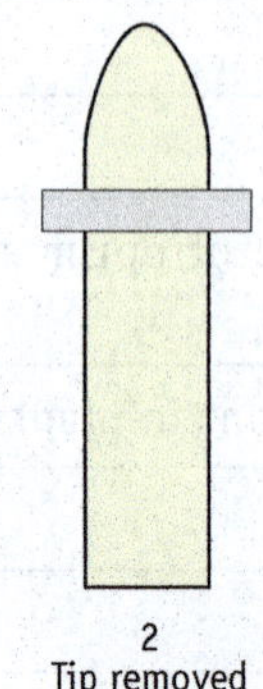

2
Tip removed and replaced on agar

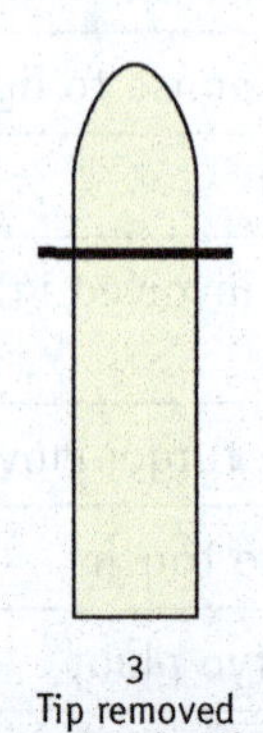

3
Tip removed and replaced on Al foil

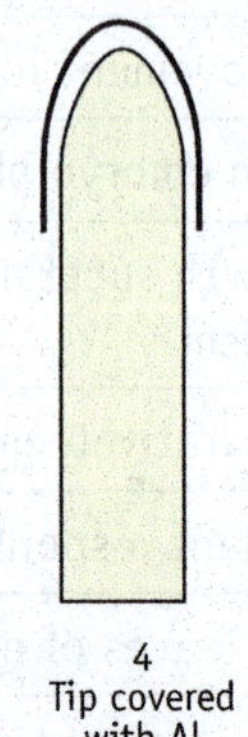

4
Tip covered with Al foil

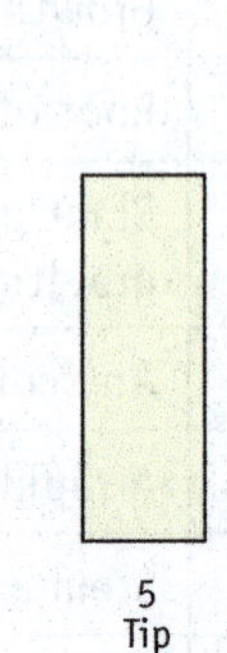

5
Tip removed

ISBN: 9780170355582

6 Different numbers of coleoptile tips were placed on four equal-sized blocks of agar (A to D) for different periods of time, as indicated in the table below. The blocks were then placed off-centre on freshly decapitated coleoptiles, which were then kept for two hours in darkness. Which block would cause the greatest angle of curvature in the coleoptile? Justify your answer.

Number of coleoptiles on agar block	Time left standing on agar block	
	2 hours	4 hours
1	A	C
2	B	D

7 Segments of coleoptiles were cut from just behind the tips. In each segment, a block of agar containing IAA (shaded) was placed against one end, and an agar block containing no IAA (unshaded) was placed against the other end, as shown in the diagram. The end that had been nearest the tip is indicated by 'T' and the end nearest the base by 'B'.

After two hours, in which of the arrangements 1 to 4 would you expect IAA to be present in the previously 'empty' agar block? Circle the letter of your choice.

A 2 and 4

B 2 and 3

C 1 and 4

D 1 and 3

E 1 and 2

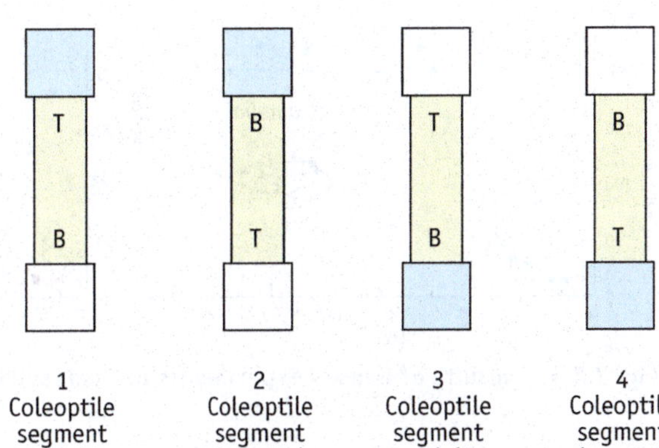

8 Referring to the diagram at right, explain in detail the auxin-related mechanism for the shoot growing upwards and the root growing downwards.

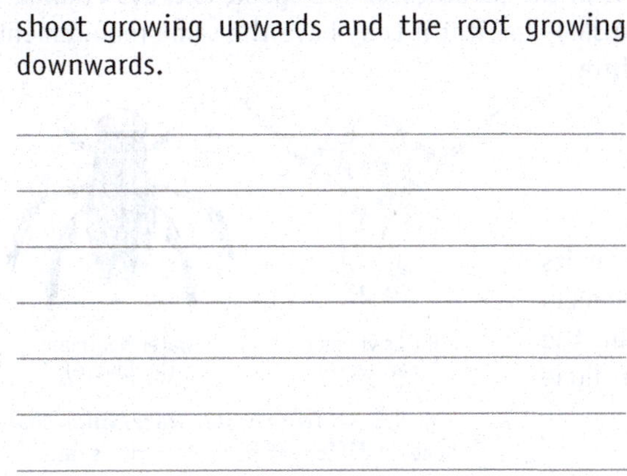

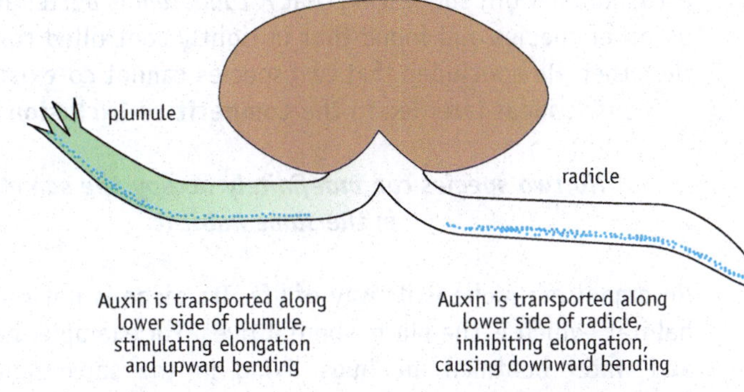

Gravitropism in a germinating bean seed.

Unit 5 | Competition and cooperation

Species relationships cover a wide range of behaviour, from predation to parental care. Within this range, behaviour can be grouped in two broad categories:

- **intraspecific behaviour** — between members of the same species (*intra* means 'within')
- **interspecific behaviour** — between members of different species (*inter* means 'between').

Interspecific competition

3

Competition for resources happens whenever demand is greater than supply. Except in times of sudden abundance, resources such as food are always limited, which restricts how many organisms can live in a particular area.

Interspecific competition is difficult to study in nature because conditions are constantly changing, so it is easier to study it in a laboratory where conditions can be controlled. Laboratory experiments on competition were carried out by G.F. Gause, using two different species of *Paramecium*: *P. caudatum* and *P. aurelia*. In some containers he had a single species, and in others he kept both. Some of his results are shown in Fig. 3.3.35.

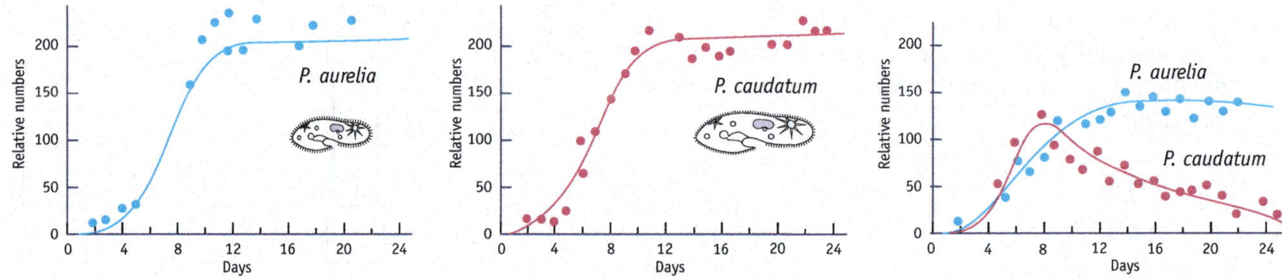

Fig. 3.3.33 Results of Gause's experiments on competition between two species of *Paramecium*.

In competition, *P. aurelia* usually eliminated the larger *P. caudatum*. However, if Gause changed the water regularly, *P. caudatum* 'won', suggesting that *P. caudatum* is better able to tolerate wastes. Gause then did similar experiments on other species and found that in tightly controlled conditions in the laboratory, one species always eliminated the other. He concluded that two species cannot co-exist in the same habitat if they have the same requirements.

Gause's ideas later led to the **Competitive Exclusion Principle**:

No two species can indefinitely occupy the same niche in the same habitat.

An organism's niche is its way of life. Its niche is not the same as its habitat, which is the place where it lives. For example, backswimmers and water boatmen are bugs living in the same ponds, but the backswimmer is a predator, and the water boatman feeds on algae (Fig. 3.3.34).

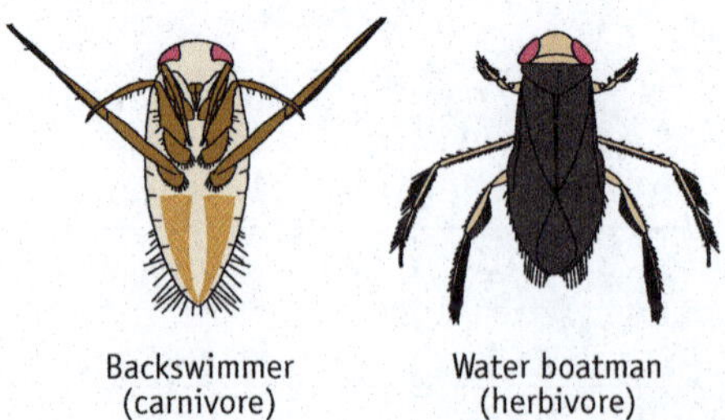

Fig. 3.3.34 Two similar water bugs that occupy different niches in the same habitat.

Niche specialisation

In nature there are many examples of closely related species that avoid competing with one another by having highly specialised niches. Example: the robin and the tomtit occur together in forests over much of New Zealand. Both feed on small insects and other invertebrates, but have different feeding habits. The tomtit searches for food among the branches of trees; the robin looks for insects on the ground.

 ISBN: 9780170355582

Fig. 3.3.35 New Zealand robin (toutouwai) and tomtit (miromiro) have slightly different niches.

Ecological patterns of distribution

Natural communities have structures that reduce the amount of competition between species. The following situations were studied in Level 2 Biology.

Fig. 3.3.36 These beetles have an odd niche: their larvae feed exclusively on elephant dung. There are many species of similar beetles, each specialising in dung from different mammals.

Stratification: vertical layering of plants in a forest, with shrub layer, sub-canopy, canopy, etc.

Zonation: horizontal bands of different species, such as in a tidal zone. Competition for space within each species may be intense, however.

Succession: a slow process of change that happens over time in habitats that are barren or else damaged. Succession happens in stages and can take centuries to complete.

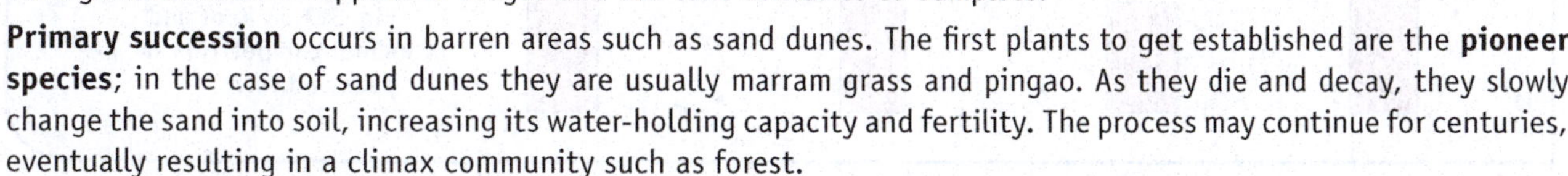

Primary succession occurs in barren areas such as sand dunes. The first plants to get established are the **pioneer species**; in the case of sand dunes they are usually marram grass and pingao. As they die and decay, they slowly change the sand into soil, increasing its water-holding capacity and fertility. The process may continue for centuries, eventually resulting in a climax community such as forest.

Secondary succession occurs in habitats that have been damaged or disturbed, such as by fire or overgrazing. The first plants to get established are 'weeds'; plants well-adapted to grow fast in exposed sunny situations. Example: manuka. These pioneer trees improve the soil and create conditions unsuitable for themselves but suitable for other trees that eventually overshadow the pioneers.

Fig. 3.3.37 Zonation of seaweeds and oysters and barnacles on a harbour wall.

Allelopathy

Some plants reduce competition from other species by producing chemicals that inhibit 'rival' growth. Example: walnut trees, which produce these chemicals in their roots. This is called **allelopathy**, and is similar to **antibiosis**, where a microorganism secretes a substance (antibiotic) that inhibits the growth of competitors. Example: *Penicillium* gives off a substance (penicillin) that discourages the growth of nearby bacteria.

9780170355582

E

Experiments on competition in plants

Land plants may compete above ground for light or below ground for water and minerals. To separate these two influences, experiments on competition between peas and corn were conducted under four types of conditions:

- Peas alone (no competition).
- In same pots as corn with shoots intermingled (root and shoot competition).
- In same pots as corn but with shoots separated (root competition).
- In separate pots but with shoots intermingled (shoot competition).

Growth of the peas under different conditions was calculated as dry mass they produced compared with dry mass when grown alone. As Fig. 3.3.38 shows, root competition was much more severe than shoot competition since it had the greatest effect on growth.

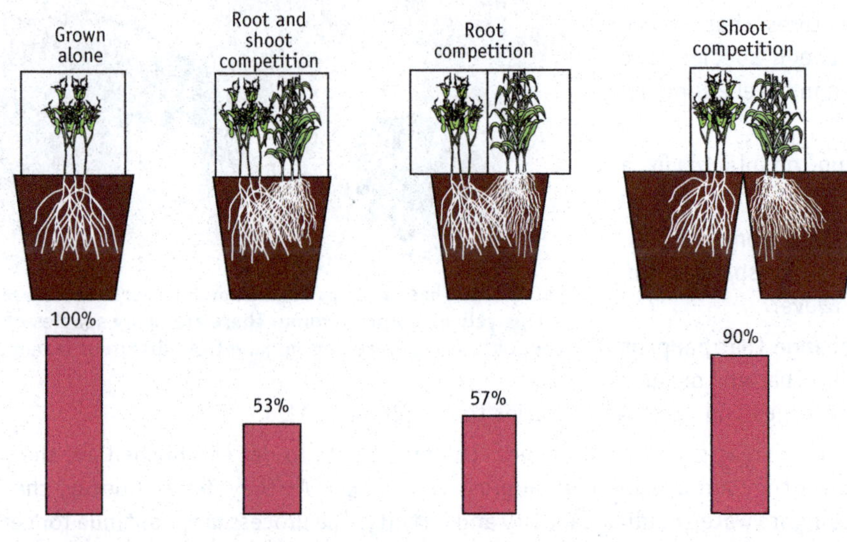

Fig. 3.3.38 Root and shoot competition in peas and corn.

Intraspecific competition

Intraspecific competition can be for any combination of food, living space, dominance, territory, breeding partners.

Competition for territory

In some species a territory can provide a complete food supply, so the owner need never leave. In other species the territory is a small defended area, with most food being obtained from a much wider home range area. At the small-territory extreme, gannets defend an area less than 1 m radius around the nest. In some social animals, territorial defence is the responsibility of the whole group, which means that a bigger group can defend a bigger area. Example: pukeko, which live in extended families ranging from five to 15 individuals.

Fig. 3.3.39 A male tui's breeding success depends on defending a suitable territory big enough to attract a female.

territory: an area that an animal defends against others of the same species.
home range: a wide area of occupation that is not defended, but is used as a food source.

 ISBN: 9780170355582

Rituals in agonistic behaviour

Fig. 3.3.40 Two ritual behaviour patterns can be seen in these monkeys. A low-ranked individual is grooming a dominant one, which is threatening the photographer.

Intraspecific competition can in some cases lead to direct combat. Example: zebras fight by aiming kicks at a rival's head. However, in most situations combat does not lead to serious injury, because combat is to some extent replaced by rituals.

Animals equipped with lethal weapons such as claws can cause great damage, and even a winner could later die of injuries. Instead, competitive encounters usually take the form of **ritual signals**, which are understood by both sides. A gives **threat** signals to B, then B may respond with **submission**, and retreat. **Agonistic behaviour** is a term used to cover the whole range of ritual threat displays and ritual submission.

Agonistic behaviour varies from one species to another. Example 1: a thrush uses song to advertise his territory and warn other males to stay away. Example 2: competing dogs will snarl and growl and shoulder-charge each other. When one dog lowers its tail or rolls on its back, this ritual is normally understood as submission, and the contest de-escalates. Example 3: a cat territorial defence ritual usually starts with a staring threat. If the other cat signals its submission, the dispute is over. If the staring contest produces no result, then the conflict may escalate.

Interspecific cooperation

Fig. 3.3.41 Lichen.

Fig. 3.3.42 Ant 'milking' an aphid for honeydew, a sugary secretion.

Fig. 3.3.43 Many kinds of flowers and butterfly are closely dependent on each other.

Mutualism is any form of cooperation in which different species benefit from living in association with each other. Mutualistic relationships vary in the degree of closeness. At one extreme individuals come into contact only occasionally, and do not depend completely on each other. At the other extreme, two species live in a physiological relationship that is so close that it is essential for the survival of both. Some examples:

- **Pollination** of flowers by insects.
- **Ants and aphids**, which some ants 'farm' as sources of honeydew. The ants protect the aphids from predators.
- **Ants and fungi**. Some tropical ants cut leaves and bring the pieces back to the nest as food for fungi, which the ants then farm and eat. The fungi cannot live independently of the ants, and vice versa: an example of **co-evolution**.
- **Cleaner fish**. Get their food by picking parasites from the mouths and gills of larger reef fish, which in turn open their mouths when the cleaner fish approach, and are then cleaned of irritating parasites.
- **Cellulose digestion** in herbivores. Animals like cows and sheep can't produce enzymes to break down the cellulose in their food; they rely on enzymes produced by microorganisms that live in their guts. These microorganisms get food and a suitable environment, and the cow gets sugar from cellulose breakdown.
- **Mycorrhiza**. This is a relationship between a plant and a fungus. The fungus lives in the roots of the plant but its hyphae extend into the soil and absorb minerals more effectively than the plant can. The fungus, on the other hand, obtains carbohydrate from the plant.
- **Lichens**. A lichen is a mutualistic association between a fungus and an alga. There are many different kinds of lichen, but in each case the alga is photosynthetic and makes glucose; while the fungus provides a tough outer covering and a sheltered micro-environment for the alga cells to grow in.

Intraspecific cooperation

In many animals, individuals may benefit from living close to others. Besides benefits to predators and prey (Unit 6), there are a number situations where group life brings benefits, sometimes with arrangements such as hierarchies which make group life more harmonious. As well as the cooperative situations described below, breeding and parental care are dealt with in Unit 7.

Social insects

Some types of insects have highly cooperative social systems, with a whole 'colony' behaving in some ways like a single organism. Main examples: many kinds of ants, bees, wasps, and all termites. These all have elaborate caste systems with different individuals specialised for different tasks.

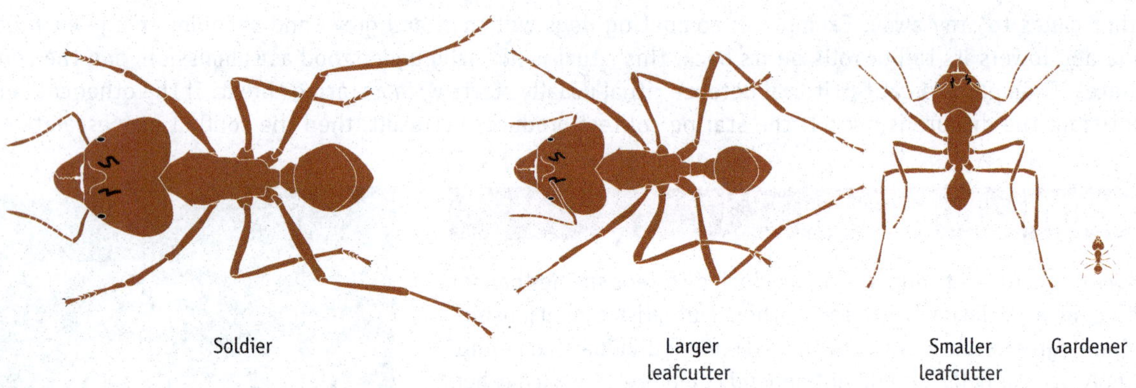

Fig. 3.3.44 These worker leafcutter ants are all sisters, specialised for different tasks in their colony. The queen is much bigger and is the only reproductive female in the colony.

Reducing heat loss

Some animals deal with cold conditions by huddling together in groups. Example 1: male emperor penguins cluster together to incubate the eggs, enabling them to survive temperatures of −60°C in gale-force winds. Example 2: honeybees overwinter in tight clusters, trapping the heat produced by their metabolism and raising the temperature inside their hive.

Fig. 3.3.45 Monkeys clumped together for warmth in near-freezing conditions.

Social hierarchy

In some social animals all individuals have equal status — as in a shoal of fish. Other species have a structured system in which each individual dominates some in the group and gives way to others — except for the top-ranking individual that dominates all others in the group. Also known as a pecking order, **hierarchy** arrangements occur in hens, monkeys, dogs and many others. See question 9 on page 68.

Once each individual 'knows its place', conflict is reduced. In this sense a hierarchy is cooperative as well as competitive. High-ranking individuals get first access to food and more mating rights in some cases. Those at the bottom may get less food, but maybe not so little as would be the case if they lived alone, and there is always a chance of promotion when a more dominant individual dies.

ISBN: 9780170355582

Check your understanding

1 Write the matching terms in the blank column. Choose from this list: *niche, intraspecific, allelopathy, Gause, hierarchy, interspecific, antibiosis, agonistic, pioneers, ritual.*

a	Competition between species	
b	Discovered the Competitive Exclusion Principle	
c	Any formalised behaviour containing social signals	
d	Competition within a species	
e	Sum total of an organism's requirements	
f	First plants to live in an area not previously colonised	
g	Inhibition of plant competitors by chemicals	
h	Inhibition of bacterial competitors by chemicals	
i	Threat and submission behaviour	
j	A system of social organisation with ranking	

2 Explain what is meant by competition.

3 State Gause's Principle.

4 Classify relationship types by writing associated words in the appropriate boxes below. Choose from: *territory, mutualism, parental care, dominance hierarchy, niche differentiation, social insects, allelopathy.*

Interspecific behaviour	**Intraspecific behaviour**
Competition:	Competition:
Cooperation:	Cooperation:

5 Complete the following sentences.

a The main difference between territory and home range is

b Intraspecific competition is generally much more intense than interspecific competition because

c One big advantage of social animals having ritual threat and submission behaviour compared with settling disputes by fighting is that

____

____

6 Pukekos are social animals, mostly living in groups of five to 15 individuals. Some individuals are submissive to dominant individuals, and only feed after all the dominant individuals have eaten. A submissive individual on balance benefits from staying with the group because

____

____

____

7 In many social animals such as monkeys, individuals groom each other. Explain the assumed benefits to the whole group of this kind of behaviour.

____

____

3

8 Complete the following sentences in a way that makes it clear which species gains what benefits.

a In the case of cleaner fish, the advantage to each species is ____

____

____

b In a mycorrhizal mutualism arrangement, the advantage to each species is ____

____

____

c In the case of leafcutter ants, the advantage to each species is ____

____

____

9 A group of monkeys was studied in captivity, and the number of times each monkey threatened another one was noted. The monkeys were given names. Results were recorded in a table (below), which shows, for example, that Red threatened Black a total of 26 times.

Monkey threatened by another	Monkey who threatened another									
	Red	Orange	Yellow	Green	Blue	Indigo	Violet	White	Black	Grey
Red	-	13	5	0	14	0	25	9	0	0
Orange	0	-	8	0	22	0	0	17	0	0
Yellow	0	0	-	0	0	0	0	0	0	0
Green	14	4	2	-	1	0	6	3	27	0
Blue	0	0	10	0	-	0	0	18	0	0
Indigo	8	1	2	32	0	-	4	2	20	0
Violet	0	22	8	0	15	0	-	15	0	0
White	0	0	13	0	3	0	0	-	0	0
Black	26	8	4	0	10	0	17	7	-	0
Grey	7	1	2	24	1	41	2	1	12	-

 ISBN: 9780170355582

a How many times did Blue threaten Violet? ______

b How many times did Indigo threaten Grey? ______

c Which monkey threatened all the others at least once? ______

d Which monkey never threatened any of the others? ______

e Which was the highest ranked monkey? ______

f Which was the lowest ranked monkey? ______

g Arrange all 10 monkey names in sequence from highest to lowest rank, based on the above results.

______

______

h Which were the only two monkeys that threatened each other? This is probably evidence of a challenge for ranking.

______

i Suggest a reason why the highest ranking monkey threatened the lowest ranking monkey only twice.

______

______

j Suggest how a hierarchy arrangement like this reduces conflict in social animals.

______

______

10 Nitrogen-fixing bacteria such as *Rhizobium* are the only organisms that can convert elemental nitrogen (N_2, in the air) to a chemical form that plants can use. Some of these nitrogen-fixing bacteria live freely, but many live in mutualistic association with plants, especially those of the legume family. The bar chart shows the result of an experiment involving soybean (a legume) and a grass (*Paspalum*). The plants were grown in pots, each pot containing two *Paspalum* and four soybean plants. Plants were grown with (+N) or without (–N) nitrate fertiliser, and with (+R) or without (–R) *Rhizobium*. Four pots, four different treatments, as represented on the horizontal axis of the graph. After six months' growth the plants were harvested and the dry mass of each was measured, as shown in the bar graphs. ('Dry mass' is the amount of completely dried plant material, which gives an accurate measure of growth.)

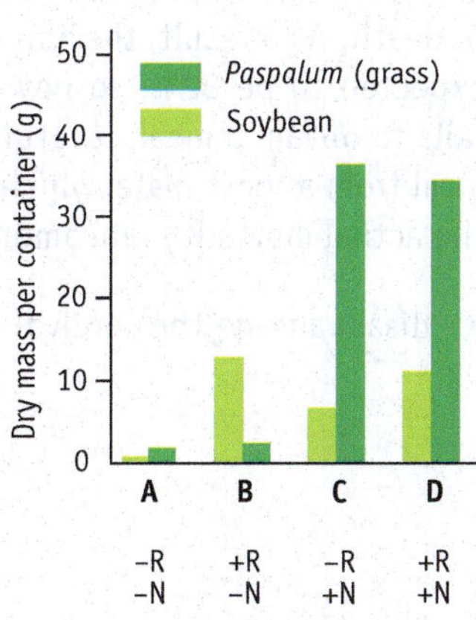

a Explain the difference in results between pots A and B. ______

______

______

b Explain the difference in results between pots B and C. ______

______

______

c Explain the difference in results between pots C and D. ______

______

______

d Explain what benefit *Rhizobium* gains from its relationship with the legume.

e Explain what benefit the legume gains from its relationship with *Rhizobium*.

f Predict in what soil conditions legumes such as clover would be at a competitive advantage over grasses.

3

11 Vampire bats in South America feed on the blood of large mammals such as cattle and horses. The bats spend the day in roosts consisting of a few unrelated males and a dozen or so related females and their young. Obtaining blood without the host swatting the bat with its tail is not easy. The bats use heat-receptors in the nose to find a warm area of skin where blood vessels are near the surface. The bat then scoops out a small area of skin, an anticoagulant in the saliva preventing the blood from clotting. Feeding skills improve with age; on average, young bats fail to obtain a meal one night in three, but 93% of adults are successful on a given night. If a bat goes without food for two consecutive nights, it starves to death. As a result, the annual mortality rate would be expected to be 82%, so how do they survive? If a bat fails to obtain a meal, it returns to the roost and begs a meal from a roost mate, which usually responds by regurgitating some blood. As a result of this sharing of food, the actual mortality rate among adults is only 24% per year. Suggest how the act of feeding a 'roostmate' could:

a disadvantage the survival and reproductive success of the individual that gives food away

b help the survival and reproductive success of the individual that gives food away.

ISBN: 9780170355582

Unit 6 | Exploitation: predation, parasitism

Exploitation is any interspecific relationship where one species obtains food from another, which is always harmed to some extent. There are three main categories of +/ – interspecific exploitation:

- **Predation**: where an individual of one species (the predator) kills an individual of another species (the prey)
- **Parasitism**: where an individual (the parasite) feeds off an individual of another species (the host), usually without killing it
- **Grazing** (aka **herbivory**): where an individual eats parts of many plants without killing any individual.

Different strategies: costs and rewards

The word 'strategy' is used in Biology to mean a whole combination of adaptive features that equip an animal (or plant) for its particular niche. In this context, 'strategy' does not mean a conscious plan as it does in human decision-making.

Tigers and wolves are effective predators but their strategies are very different. Tigers are solitary hunters, using a stalk-and-pounce method. Wolves are pack hunters, using teamwork and steady running to exhaust their prey. Tigers and wolves did not plan to be like this; natural selection has equipped them with these different strategies in response to their different natural habitats; tigers in forest, wolves in open country.

One way of analysing strategy is to look at energy costs and energy rewards. If a young tiger gains energy rewards (food) greater than its energy costs, it will have a good chance of living long enough to breed. If its energy rewards are less than the costs, it will starve. The balance can be a delicate one, and many wild animals are chronically lean and hungry. Energy costs can take different forms; such as energetic movement, or else allocating food to build body parts.

energy costs

energy rewards

Predator strategies

Predators have a wide range of strategies for catching and killing prey. In all cases selection has acted to maximise energy gained (the reward) for energy invested (the cost).

Traps

Predators that trap their prey tend to sit motionless until the prey blunders into the trap. Example: spiderweb. In this case the predator expends energy in building the web, and little energy on moving around. Wolf spiders and jumping spiders have a different strategy, catching their prey by active pursuit but spending little energy on building webs.

Mimicry

Some predators deceive the prey by mimicking a harmless species, for example the sabretooth blenny mimics a harmless 'cleaner' fish to get close to the prey's gills, and then bites chunks off the gills. Since the 'prey' is injured but not usually killed, these blenny fish could perhaps be described as parasites.

To deceive the victim, the mimic must be relatively uncommon, or the victim will learn not to open its gill covers.

Group membership

Belonging to a group enables larger prey to be killed. A single lion cannot take on an adult buffalo — twice the weight of a lion and with massive horns — but a pride of lions will sometimes attempt prey this big. In one study it was found that any lioness hunting alone had a 15% chance of success, but in a group the success rate jumped to 40%. Of course this also incurs the cost of having to share food. Another difference of belonging to a group: this can make it easier to find food, as when sparrows forage in flocks.

Prey strategies

Safety in numbers

For prey animals, living in a group can be safer for several reasons:

- Predator detection: a large group means more eyes and ears to detect predators
- Dilution effect: an individual is less likely to be captured if it is one of a large group
- Confusion effect: predators find it harder to concentrate on an individual prey if others are dashing to and fro.

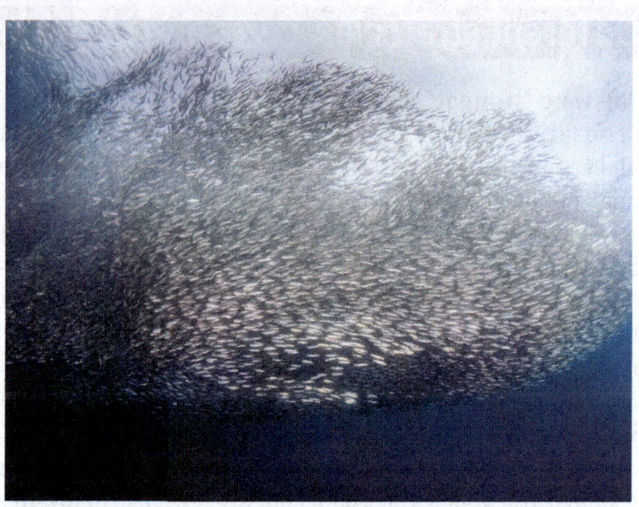

Fig. 3.3.46 In a large school of fish like this, predators have difficulty in singling out individual prey.

Deception

Deceiving predators is another defence strategy. There are several kinds of deception, for example:

- **Crypsis** (camouflage)
- **Batesian mimicry**, in which a tasty species closely resembles a distasteful and often toxic species. For example the tasty and non-toxic viceroy butterfly (the mimic) closely resembles the distasteful and toxic monarch butterfly (the model). This kind of defence works best if the mimic is rare compared with the species it imitates. (This deception is named after the naturalist Henry Bates.)
- **Mullerian mimicry** — two or more toxic or dangerous species resemble each other, thereby gaining more protection (see Fig. 3.3.47).
- **Autotomy** — the shedding of parts when attacked. Tuatara and all New Zealand lizards can shed their tails when attacked, which gives them an improved chance of escape. Many crabs can shed their chelae (pincers). Autotomised parts can usually grow again, but there is an energy cost in this.

Synchronised breeding

In many colony-nesting birds, individuals start breeding almost simultaneously each year, and as a result the eggs are laid within a short period of each other. Though predators eat many eggs and young, they eat a smaller proportion than they could if the eggs were laid over a longer period. In a similar strategy used by palolo worms in Samoa, millions of animals release their eggs on the same night of the year in such colossal numbers that predators can only eat a tiny fraction of the sudden abundance of food.

 ISBN: 9780170355582

Defence by chemicals

Plants have a wide variety of chemical defences. Many produce poisons such as cyanogenic glycosides that release hydrogen cyanide when their leaves are damaged by predators. The leaves and flowers of tutu, a native shrub, contain a deadly alkaloid poison.

Some herbivores can tolerate plant poisons. Example: caterpillars of the monarch butterfly store the poison in their food, the leaves of swan plant, so they become poisonous to predators.

Bees and wasps have stings that inject painful chemicals — a strong deterrent to predators. A bee dies after stinging a person or animal who is raiding their hive, but this strategy has a genetic reward because the breeding queen carries copies of the worker's genes.

Fig. 3.3.47 Monarch butterfly caterpillars are poisonous to birds, and rely on their colours as a warning display. Throughout the animal kingdom, bright combinations of yellow and black are common warning signals.

Warning colouration

For an animal that defends itself with chemicals, it pays to warn potential predators of the danger so that no attack is attempted. Many such animals have **aposematic** (warning) colouration, making them very conspicuous. Examples: wasps, garter snakes, monarch butterfly.

E

Predator numbers are influenced by their prey numbers

One would expect predator numbers to be influenced by the abundance of their food supply, and this is backed up by observation, as the following examples show.

Kiore

Until they were eliminated from Tiritiri Matangi Island in 1993, the numbers of kiore (Polynesian rat) fluctuated with their summer food supply of grass seeds (Fig. 3.3.48).

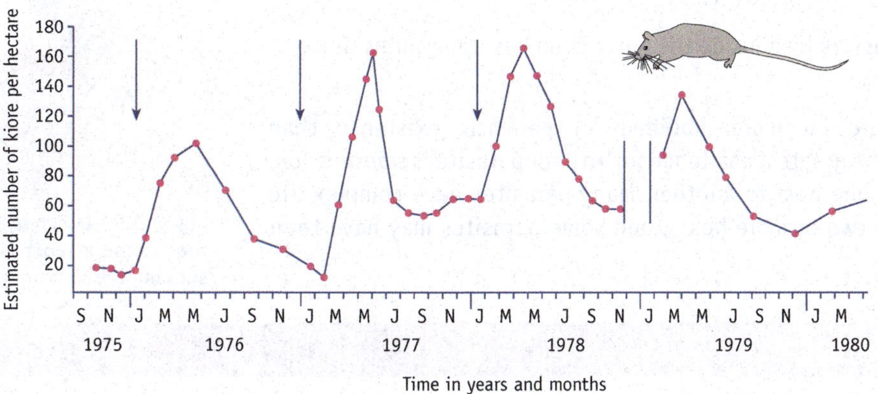

Fig. 3.3.48 Numbers of kiore on Tiritiri Matangi Island over several years. Arrows represent peaks in grass seed output.

Canadian lynx and snowshoe hare

Records of pelts traded by the Hudson's Bay Company of Canada over many years show cyclic fluctuations in the numbers of lynx and their principal prey, the snowshoe hare (Fig. 3.3.49). The graph shows that the rises and falls in the numbers of snowshoe hares were followed by peaks and troughs in the numbers of lynx.

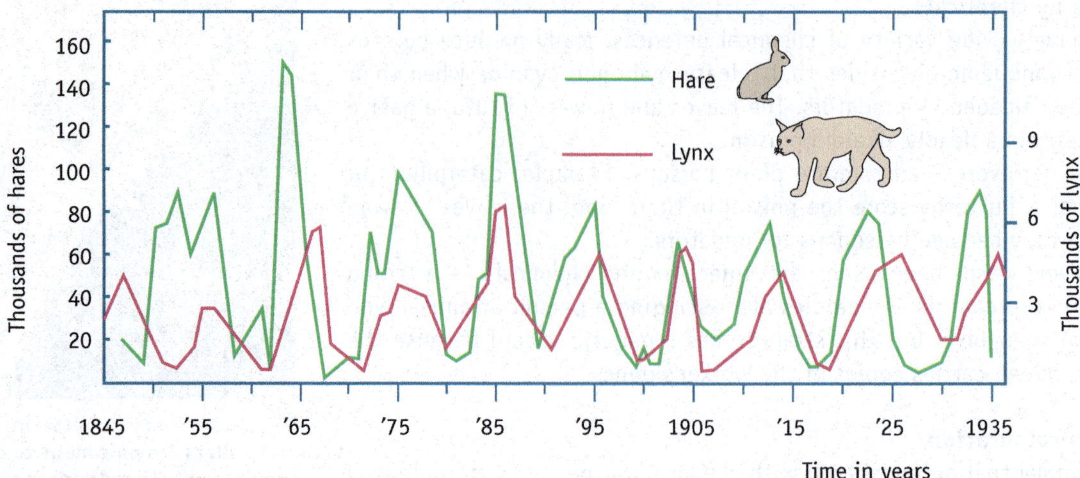

Fig. 3.3.49 Numbers of lynx and snowshoe hares.

Some predators exert a powerful influence on the numbers of their prey. For example, the introduced cabbage white butterfly was a serious pest in New Zealand until a wasp was introduced. It lays its eggs inside the pupae and the larvae feed on the pupae, killing them. Wasps like these are known as *parasitoids*.

3

Parasitism

Parasitism differs from predation in that the victim (the host) is not normally killed. A predator has to keep finding new prey, but most parasites depend on a single host's ability to provide food on a long-term basis. It is not in the 'interests' of the parasite to harm its host, and the best-adapted parasites do little damage. A predator can be compared to a hacker who steals someone's entire life savings; a parasite can be compared to a hacker who steals a little money daily over a long period.

Animal parasites can be divided into two main groups:

- **Ectoparasites** feed on the outside of the host. Examples: fleas, lice, adult mosquitoes, ticks.
- **Endoparasites** feed inside the host. Examples: tapeworms, flukes.

Endoparasites are far more modified for parasitic existence than ectoparasites. The greatest challenge for an endoparasite is *transmission*, or getting from one host to another. Many parasites have complex life cycles involving two or more hosts, and some parasites may have their own parasites.

Fig. 3.3.50 Leeches are ectoparasites that spend a short part of their life cycle sucking blood from a host.

Social parasites

Social parasites exploit their hosts in unusual ways. **Brood parasites** use a member of another species to raise their young. Example: most species of cuckoo. **Kleptoparasites** steal other animals' food by harassing them. Example: skuas; birds which rob smaller seabirds. **Slave-making** ants kidnap the larvae of other ants and rear them as their own workers.

Plant parasites

A few flowering plants are parasitic. Some are **partial parasites** that obtain water and minerals from their host plants but not energy, as they have chlorophyll and can photosynthesise. Example: mistletoe plants, which parasitise trees. Some are **total parasites** that have no chlorophyll, relying on their hosts for organic matter as well as water and minerals.

ISBN: 9780170355582

Check your understanding

1 Write the matching terms in the blank column. Choose from this list: *predator, exploitation, aposematic, endoparasite, alkaloid, Batesian mimicry, brood parasite, crypsis, autotomy, ectoparasite.*

a	Blending with the background	
b	Distasteful and toxic chemical produced by plants	
c	Feeds at the expense of another organism, killing it in the process	
d	Colour combinations that warn a potential predator	
e	Palatable animal resembles a dangerous or unpalatable one	
f	Lives on the outside of its host	
g	Any win/lose relationship between different species	
h	Uses animal of another species as foster parent	
i	Shedding a body part to distract a predator	
j	Lives inside its host	

2 Complete the following sentences.

a One important difference between a parasite and a predator is that

b The word 'strategy' as applied to animals in the wild means

c One important difference between a predator and a grazing animal is that

d Compared with free-living animals, most endoparasites put a much larger proportion of their energy into reproduction because

e Batesian mimicry is the term for any situation in which

3 Name an example of:

a a partial plant parasite and its host

b a social parasite and its host.

4 Suggest one behavioural characteristic that is usually associated with crypsis.

3

5 Identify whether each of the following exploitation relationships is predation, parasitism, or grazing.

a Caterpillars eating oak tree leaves

b Birds eating these caterpillars

c A mosquito sucking blood from one of these birds

d Zebras eating grass

e A vampire bat feeding from a horse

6 A turtle's main defence against predators is having a thick shell.

a Suggest one kind of 'energy cost' involved in this defence strategy.

b Suggest one kind of 'energy saving' involved in this defence strategy.

7 Lizards sometimes shed their tails as a means of escaping a predator. This does not always work, but when it does work, suggest one energy cost of this strategy.

8 Suggest why 'domesticated' leaf vegetables are so prone to slug attack compared with their wild relatives.

9 Many kinds of birds (gannets, for example) collect in large colonies for the breeding season, then disperse over wide areas during the non-breeding season. Discuss this as a strategy, explaining the advantages and disadvantages, **a** to individuals, and **b** to the whole group.

10 Some predators such as lions hunt in groups; others such as tigers and leopards are solitary hunters. Discuss the advantages and disadvantages of group hunting strategy compared with hunting solo.

 ISBN: 9780170355582

Unit 7 | Breeding behaviour

In nature even the most successful individual — no matter how strong or fit — becomes a genetic dead-end if it does not reproduce and pass on its genes.

Generally, reproductive behaviour requires success at two stages: (1) successful fertilisation, and (2) offspring successfully reaching adulthood, with an average at least two adult offspring per two parents, over a lifetime.(Note that reproductive behaviour here refers to sexual reproduction, not vegetative reproduction.)

For many aquatic animals and plants, sexual reproduction presents few problems. They simply pour eggs and sperm into the water, and as long as both are present near each other and the timing is right, many of the eggs will be fertilised. Examples of animals that behave like this: kina (sea urchins), oysters, many kinds of fish. For animals that have fertilisation inside the female body, breeding behaviour includes courtship.

Courtship behaviour

The term **courtship** describes behaviour patterns and rituals that lead up to mating. These rituals have two main roles:

1 Courtship helps ensure that male and female are the **same species**. A greenfinch courting a goldfinch is wasting its time.

2 Courtship helps **synchronise** male and female behaviour — which is especially important in the case of predators like spiders, where the larger female could easily eat the male.

Courtship display rituals are in many cases a series of exchanges between the sexes. These rituals are different for every species, and occur even in individuals that pair for life and have been together for years, such as swans, geese and penguins. Courtship displays and signals can be any combination of:

- **olfactory** (smell) signals — **pheromones**, especially in insects and mammals (not important in primates)
- **auditory** — for example bird songs and calls
- **visual** — postures and displays in many kinds of fish, birds, lizards, insects
- **tactile** (touch) — for example a male spider touching the female's web in just the right way.

Fig. 3.3.51 Courtship displays in these albatrosses involves a series of display rituals. Continued for days, these reinforce the pair bond and stimulate hormone changes that are necessary for rearing their young.

Competition for partners

In many animals, males compete for females. This can take the form of fighting between males in some species, or courtship songs and displays in others. As far as we know, in most cases the female decides on the basis of which partner is potentially the best parent. Example: emperor penguins are monogamous and mate for life; females tend to choose larger males because they are the ones best able to keep eggs warm.

Leks

A lek is a collection of males, gathered in one place for competitive displays to entice females seeking prospective mating partners. Leks occur in a few kinds of birds and mammals, such as topi antelope. The place is not a territory and is not used after the lek is over.

Parental care

When it comes to caring for eggs and young after the moment of fertilisation, there are two kinds of reproductive strategy. There are plenty of examples of animals and plants in each category, and many others that tend towards one or the other extreme.

r-strategy: produce large numbers of eggs or young, and the survival rate is low.
K-strategy: produce few eggs or young, and the survival rate is high.

r-strategy	**K-strategy**
Many eggs or young	Produce few eggs or young
Little or no nutrition provided	Provided with abundant nutrition
Little or no parental care	Lengthy period of parental care
Low survival rates	High survival rates

End result: 

Number of offspring

End result: 

Number of offspring

Oysters are extreme r-strategists, releasing up to 60 million microscopic eggs a time into the sea. Elephants are extreme K-strategists. Mothers have 22 months' gestation, produce one calf at a time at an advanced stage of development, feed them milk for at least two years, and care for them very well. Since an elephant can produce at most four or five calves in her lifetime, each calf represents a massive 'investment' in time and energy by the mother.

It is not reasonable to compare elephants with oysters; better to compare closely related animals such as rats and guinea pigs. Both are rodents, and both tend towards the 'K' end of the spectrum:

- Rats: three weeks' gestation, up to 14 young at a time, born naked, blind and helpless
- Guinea pigs: 10 weeks' gestation, one to four young at a time, born large, active and covered with hair.

Two technical words apply to mammals and birds born in these states:
Altricial: born or hatched naked, blind and helpless. (See swallow photograph on the next page.)
Precocial: born or hatched well-covered, active, and rapidly independent.

Fig. 3.3.52 Corals have simple r-strategy reproduction, and are seen here pouring millions of eggs and sperm into the water. A very low proportion of fertilised eggs survive.

Fig. 3.3.53 Newborn precocial guinea pigs with mother.

ISBN: 9780170355582

We cannot apply moral judgment to r- and K-strategies. Animals do not choose a particular strategy; natural selection has shaped them in response to a variety of factors. Both strategies work. A wild animal or plant only has a limited amount of food resources to invest, and in the case of r-strategy this 'investment' is allocated to quantity and not quality. Many animals have a K-strategy and some level of parental care, with a high level in all mammals and most birds. Many kinds of spider, fish, crayfish and even scorpions take care of their eggs or young or both.

K- and r-strategies also exist among plants. Example: avocado trees produce one seed in each fruit, with an abundant food supply. This is a common feature of trees adapted to life in shady forests, where young plants need a big food supply to start them off and have a chance of getting towards the light. At the other extreme, pohutukawa trees produce millions of tiny seeds, very few of which survive. Pohutukawa are adapted to life along coastlines and rely on wind to spread their seeds.

Monogamy, polygyny, polygynandry

Some species have **monogamy**, with a pair bond enduring as long as they both live. Some species have **polygyny** (polygamy), with each breeding male having a harem of females and taking little or no part in the care of his offspring. A few species have paternal care, in which young are looked after mainly by the father. Examples: kiwi and seahorses. A few others have **polyandry**, where one female has many males. Example: emu. About 3% of bird species have **polygynandry**, where the young are reared by several adults. Example: pukeko.

Nature is diverse, and different species have evolved different reproductive strategies. In each case, natural selection has led to the evolution of one of the above strategies, probably because in particular conditions it had the highest success rate.

Fig. 3.3.54 Most small birds — like these swallows — live only two or three years, and may have only one chance to breed, so invest much time and effort into caring for their young. Parent birds, even if near-starving, will feed their offspring first.

Fig. 3.3.55 Frog reproduction is intermediate between K- and r-strategy. Breeding adults produce hundreds of eggs (not millions), each with some food supply, and guard their eggs for a while.

Fig. 3.3.56 Pukeko are cooperative breeders, with most young birds cared for by adults other than their parents.

Kin selection

Some animal behaviour appears to be **altruistic**, with individuals making an effort to benefit others of their species, even when they are not closely related. **Kin selection** is a type of altruistic behaviour towards close relatives, and probably happens in most cases of polygynandry. New Zealand examples: pukeko and whitehead. By helping care for young relatives and increasing their survival chances, the carer also increases the likely success of its own genes — since they are all related. Carers also gain useful experience. Individual carers probably do not know this — their behaviour has been shaped by natural selection.

3

Check your understanding

1 Write the matching word in the blank column. Choose from this list: *pheromone, precocial, tactile, courtship, r-strategy, synchronisation, altricial, olfactory, pukeko, K-strategy.*

a	Young born or hatch at an advanced stage	
b	Young born or hatch in helpless state	
c	Intraspecific signalling chemical	
d	Breeding behaviour that can lead to mating	
e	An example of a polygynandrous breeder	
f	One function of courtship behaviour	
g	Produces a small number of well-protected young	
h	Produces many young with little protection	
i	Refers to a sense of touch	
j	Refers to a sense of smell	

2 Name three quite different animals that provide little or no parental care.

3 Name three quite different animals that provide a high level of parental care.

4 Identify two roles of courtship behaviour.

5 Complete the following sentences.

a R-strategy animals do not care for their young, and compensate for this by

b In species that have plenty of parental care, the life expectancy of parents can be reduced (compared with non-breeders) because

ISBN: 9780170355582

c Two ways in which a young bird benefits from having a high level of parental care are

d Rainforest trees generally produce large seeds with a generous food supply because

6 Some bird species are cooperative breeders. One of the most studied species is the Florida scrub jay. These birds pair for life and live in year-round territories containing one breeding pair and anywhere from zero to six non-breeding helpers. Helpers assist in feeding the young and in defending the nest. Almost all helpers are related to the breeders. The graph shows breeding success at different stages, in relation to the number of helpers.

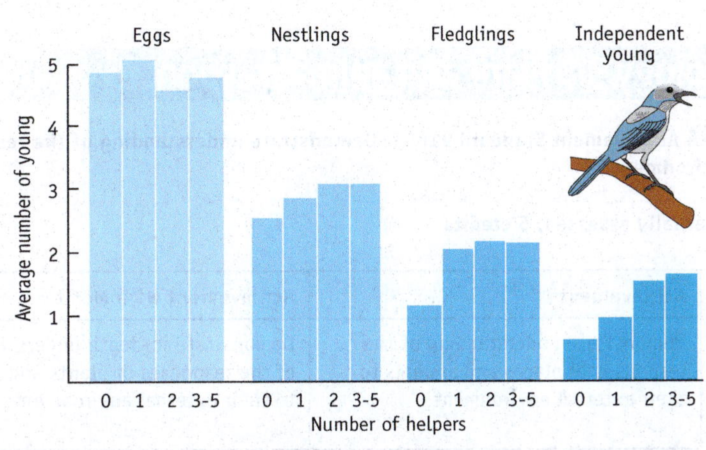

Effect of Florida scrub jay helpers on breeding success (After Wolfenden)

a Explain what effect helpers have on egg production.

b Explain what effect helpers have on offspring survival.

c Explain the significance of the fact that almost all helpers are related to the breeders.

7 Pukeko are communal breeders, and siblings help raise each other's young. Discuss the advantages and disadvantages of such a system: **a** to parents, and **b** to older offspring.

8 Some bird species have camouflaged females and highly ornate males that perform elaborate courtship rituals. The birds of paradise from New Guinea are an extreme example. Suggest what advantages the female might get from choosing a male with bright colours and vigorous display rituals.

3

Biology 3.3 Plant and animal responses

NCEA Achievement Standard 91603: Demonstrate understanding of the responses of plants and animals to the external environment

Externally assessed, 5 credits

Achievement	Achievement with Merit	Achievement with Excellence
Demonstrate understanding of the responses of plants and animals to their external environment.	Demonstrate in-depth understanding of the responses of plants and animals to their external environment.	Demonstrate comprehensive understanding of the responses of plants and animals to their external environment.

Achievement
'Demonstrate understanding ...' involves describing plant and animal responses to their external environment. The description includes the process(es) within each response and/or the adaptive advantage provided for the organism in relation to its ecological niche.

Achievement with Merit
'Demonstrate in-depth understanding ...' involves using biological ideas to explain: how the responses occur; and also why the responses provide an adaptive advantage for the organism in relation to its ecological niche.

Achievement with Excellence
'Demonstrate comprehensive understanding ...' involves linking biological ideas to explain why the responses provide an adaptive advantage for the organism in relation to its ecological niche. The linking of ideas may involve justifying, relating, evaluating, comparing and contrasting, and analysing.

Responses are selected from those relating to:

- orientation in space (tropisms, nastic responses, taxes, kineses, homing, migration)
- orientation in time (annual, daily, lunar, tidal rhythms)
- interspecific relationships (competition for resources, mutualism, exploitation including herbivory, predation, and parasitism)
- intraspecific relationships (competition for resources, territoriality, hierarchical behaviour, cooperative interactions, reproductive behaviours).

External environment will include both biotic and abiotic factors.

ISBN: 9780170355582

Exam-type questions

QUESTION ONE

The diagram is an actogram representing the movements of a cockroach kept in laboratory conditions for 20 days. For the first 10 days the animal was given normal day-night lighting, but after day 10 it was kept in constant darkness. (Redrawn from Brady: *Biological Clocks*.) Study the information and answer the questions that follow.

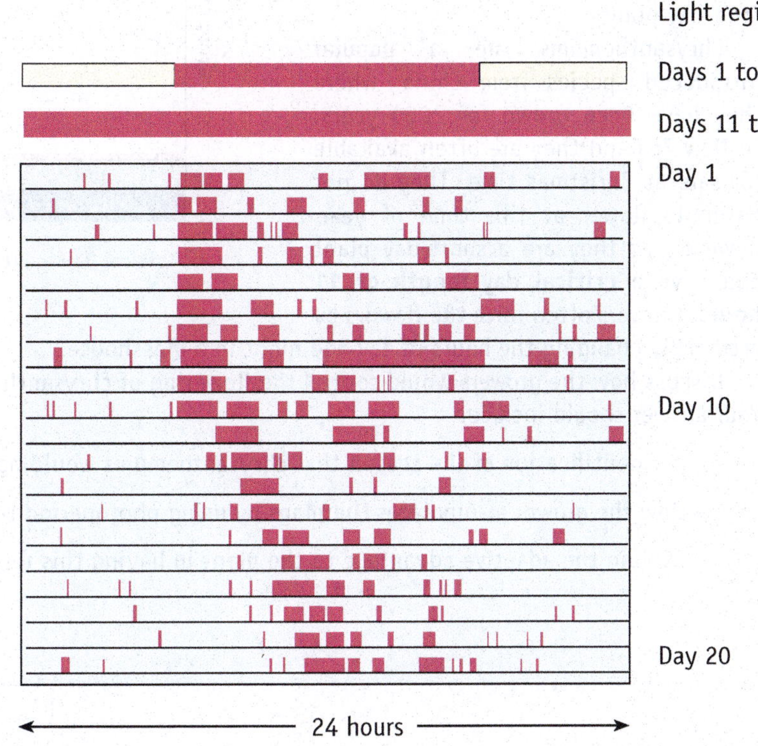

The results show that the cockroach's rhythm is due to an endogenous biological clock. Discuss the experiment and its results, making sure to address the following points.

- The specific name for the type of them shown.
- Explain why the experimenter used two different light regimes.
- Explain how these results lead to the conclusion that the cockroach has an internal body clock.
- Explain the advantage this type of behaviour gives the animal in its natural environment.

– Name the rhythm …

– The first light regime days 1-10 shows …

– The second light regime days 10-20 shows …

– It was necessary to have two different light regimes because …

– We can tell from the actogram that the cockroach has an internal body clock because …

– Explain here why it is an advantage for the animal to anticipate nightfall …

– Consider its nocturnal habits, predators, and risk of desiccation …

Use this page to create a key points plan that could form the basis for a longer answer to be done on your own paper.

QUESTION TWO

Many seasonal activities such as flowering are controlled by photoperiod (day length). The graph below shows the critical day length for short-day and long-day plants.

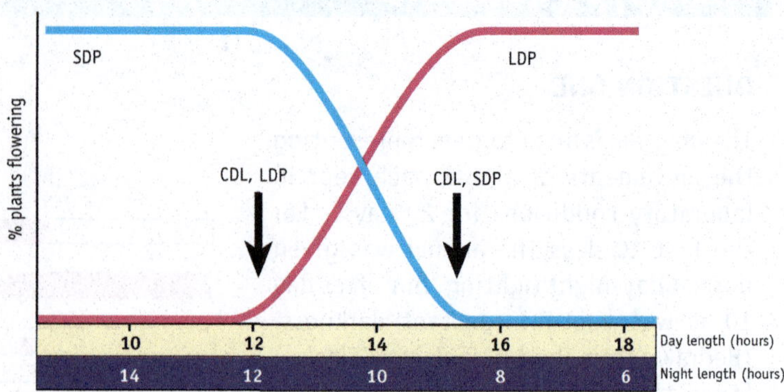

Critical day length in short-day and long-day plants.

Chrysanthemums are a popular introduced species from China, where they have been grown for 2000 years. In New Zealand they are often available for sale at Christmas time. They do not naturally flower at this time of year, however, as they are a short-day plant and have **a critical day length of 11 hours.** Growers often force the flowers by artificially changing the hours of day and night in a glasshouse.

Discuss how the growers would control the flowering of chrysanthemums in time for Christmas in New Zealand. Your answer should include:

- An identification of the season that chrysanthemums would normally flower.
- How the grower manipulates the plant by using photoperiod to trigger flowering.
- Explain the adaptive advantage to the plant in having this response to photoperiod.

Use this page to create a key points plan or a mind map that could form the basis for a longer answer to be done on your own paper.

3

ISBN: 9780170355582

QUESTION THREE

The diagram below can be used to explain how the phytochrome system controls flowering in long-day plants, e.g. *Cyclamen*.

Referring to the diagram, explain how the system enables plants to synchronise flowering. In your answer you should include:

- The names of any hormones involved.
- Where the stimulus is perceived in the plant.
- The specific type of stimulus involved.
- How flowering is triggered in the plant.
- The adaptive value of this response.

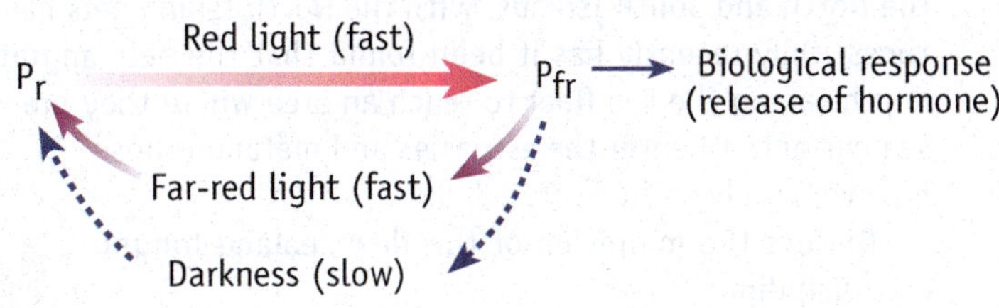

Use this page to create a key points plan or a mind map that could form the basis for a longer answer to be done on your own paper.

QUESTION FOUR

Longfin eel migration

The New Zealand longfin eel (*Anguilla dieffenbachii*) is a very long-lived fish — there are records of females reaching 106 years old and weighing up to 24 kg. Longfin eels are catadromous: they grow and mature into fertile adults in freshwater systems and then migrate to the sea to breed. The average age of eels before migration varies between the North and South Islands, with the North Island eels having younger migration ages and thus faster generation times. Only recently has it been found that the eels migrate to the Pacific Ocean near Tonga, swimming at great depths along the sea floor to reach an area where they breed and spawn. The young larvae float and swim back on sea currents to enter the estuaries and metamorphose into young elvers in rivers.

Discuss the migration of the New Zealand longfin eel, including:

- The advantages and disadvantages of making such a long journey to breed.
- Methods of navigation the eels would probably use.
- The problems of moving from salt water to fresh water and then back to salt water.
- A possible reason why North Island eels migrate at an earlier age than their South Island relatives.

- Define migration.
- Suggest at least two possible advantages in this eel migration (must be more than one: refer to question).
- Suggest at least two probable disadvantages on the way.
- Suggest possible navigation methods. Consider the depth that the eels travel at.
- Explain osmotic problems linked to living in sea compared to fresh water.
- Explain how specified differences between North and South island habitats may affect eel development.

Use this page to create a key points plan that could form the basis for a longer answer to be done on your own paper.

ISBN: 9780170355582

QUESTION FIVE

Plants respond to environmental stimuli. Some early experiments were carried out to try to discover an explanation for the mechanism of their response to a unidirectional light source.

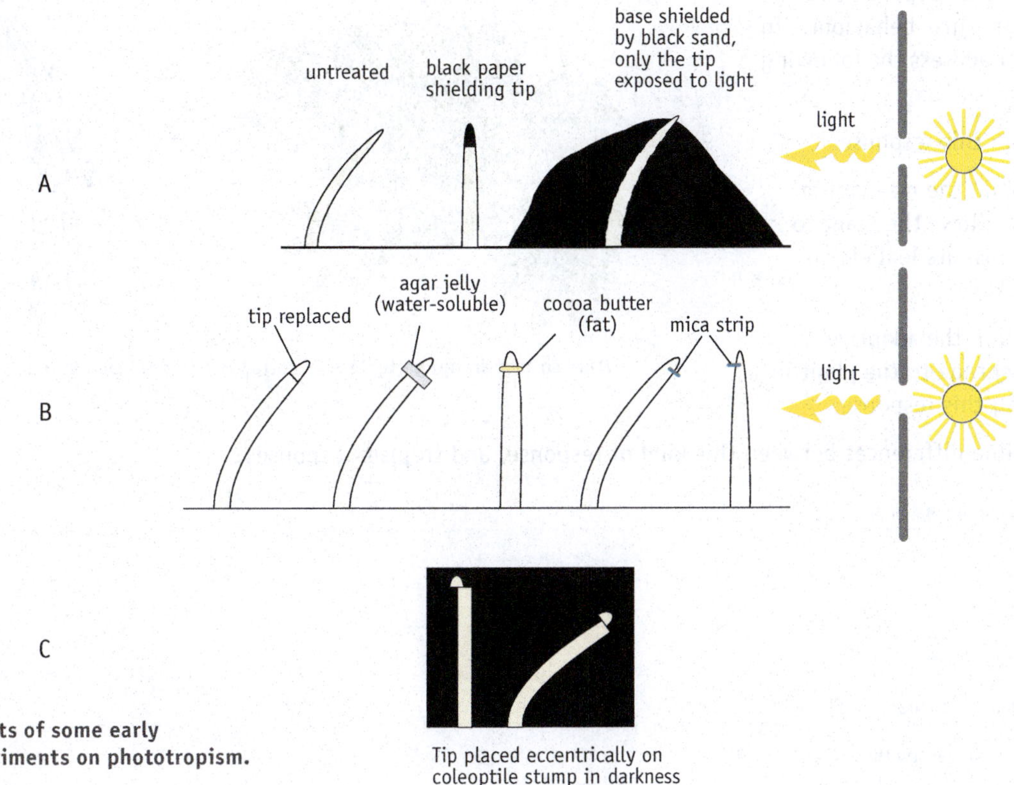

Results of some early experiments on phototropism.

a Study the results above and use this information to explain the mechanism involved. You will need to address the following in your answer:

- The specific name given to this plant response.
- What the experiments A, B and C suggest about the nature of the chemical involved.
- Explain how the response provides an adaptive advantage for the organism.

Use this page to create a key points plan or a mind map that could form the basis for a longer answer to be done on your own paper.

QUESTION SIX

The sensitive plant *Mimosa pudica* is indigenous to Indonesia. When brushed against or when it senses vibrations near it, the plant responds by collapsing its leaflets.

Discuss this response and the reasons for this behaviour. In your answer address the following points:

- Name this response.
- Explain the mechanism that allows the plant to collapse its leaflets so quickly.
- Explain the adaptive advantage to the plant in using this response.

Mimosa leaf in open (left) and collapsed (right) positions

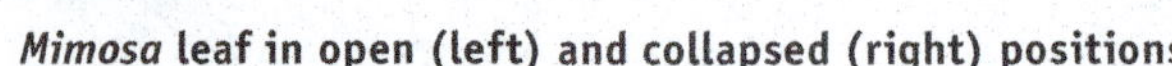

- Outline differences between this kind of response, and tropism responses.

– Name this kind of behaviour
of mimosa.

– Explain in detail how the plant
causes its leaflets to drop.
You will need to identify the
part of the leaf, the term
turgor, salt movement,
and osmosis.

– Suggest possible advantages
of leaf collapse:
1. in relation to immediate survival
2. in relation to long term survival
of species.

– Explain at least two differences
between tropisms and nastic
responses, e.g. by writing
tropisms are ...., and
.... however nasties
involve ....
and ....

Use this page to create a key points plan that could form the basis for a longer answer to be done on your own paper.

ISBN: 9780170355582

QUESTION SEVEN

New Zealand fur seals (*Arctocephalus forsteri*) breed on the coast of the South Island. They are sexually dimorphic, with the big males often having bloody fights to maintain sole mating rights to a harem of females. In these fights young pups that get in the way are often crushed and killed. The males typically only maintain the harem for two or three years and the females all come into season (fertility) at the same time, so the male must impregnate the females while defending the whole herd from aggressive competitors. Females nurse pups for 10 months. They routinely leave their pups for 2–12 days to feed, then return to nurse the pup for 2–7 days. The male and female breeding strategies are thus very different.

Discuss the reproductive behaviour of the New Zealand fur seal. In your answer be sure to consider the following:

- The name given to this type of breeding behaviour.
- The benefits and costs to both the male **and** female of this kind of breeding.
- Why a male only defends his territory for two or three seasons.
- Why female seals are better off living in a harem than in a monogamous relationship.

Fur seals.

Use this page to create a key points plan or a mind map that could form the basis for a longer answer to be done on your own paper.

QUESTION EIGHT

Kokako are endemic endangered birds belonging to the same family as saddleback and the extinct huia. North Island kokako were once common in lowland forest, but now number only about 2000 birds in scattered patches of forest and regenerating bush. The South Island subspecies is thought to be extinct.

Kokako are medium-sized birds with a beautiful song that is inherited genetically. They are highly territorial. Male and female look similar, and have to be identified by DNA testing. They have short rounded wings and can fly only short distances of up to 100 m between trees, mostly using the powerful legs to jump between branches. They have evolved behaviour to avoid detection by hawks, usually building their nests in treetops with good canopy cover.

They live up to 25 years and have stable pair bonds. The female lays up to three eggs, and incubates the eggs for 55 days until they hatch. The chicks fledge (fly) 30–35 days later. The male contributes by feeding the female on the nest, and both birds feed the chicks. Kokako eat fruits, insects and leaves.

Use this information to help you answer the following questions on the territorial behaviour of the kokako.

- Explain the difference between territory and home range.
- Suggest what resources the territory may provide for the kokako.
- Explain why territory size varies with different types of forest and bush.
- List some benefits and costs of a pair of kokako defending a territory.
- Suggest how the birds signal and defend their territory.

Kokako.

3

Use this page to create a key points plan or a mind map that could form the basis for a longer answer to be done on your own paper.

ISBN: 9780170355582

QUESTION NINE

Northern rata (*Metrosideros robusta*) usually begins life as an epiphyte. It sends aerial roots downwards to the ground and lateral roots to surround the 'host' trunk, finally enclosing the 'host' tree and sometimes growing into a huge mature rata up to 25 metres high with a trunk of 2.5 metres wide. Eventually the 'host' tree rots, leaving the rata with a hollow trunk. When the rata reaches the canopy it forms a mass of branches containing small pale fleshy leaves quite different from the small darker leaves it had at the juvenile stage.

Once the roots are well established, profuse orange flowers are borne and can be seen from many kilometres away, as rata is often taller than surrounding trees. It is capable of growing by itself without a 'host' if gaps in the canopy appear. However, it then only achieves a stunted low growth habit. As seen in the photograph, mature rata often host epiphytes of their own.

Discuss the adaptive strategies of rata. You will need to consider the following points in your answer:

- Name the relationship it has with its 'host' tree.
- Explain why the structure of the tree is different in the epiphyte, mature tree and ground-based varieties.
- Explain the advantages to rata of employing an epiphytic growth habit if it can grow from the ground and reach a flowering stage sooner.

Use this page to create a key points plan or a mind map that could form the basis for a longer answer to be done on your own paper.

QUESTION TEN

Leafcutter ants (*Atta cephalotes*) have powerful jaws that vibrate a thousand times a second to slice off pieces of leaf. Size for size, their bodies are amazingly powerful, able to carry pieces of leaf that weigh at least 20 times their own body weight (the same as a human carrying a one-tonne load). Their colonies contain different sorts of workers. Soldier leafcutters have huge jaws strong enough to cut through leather, and small gardener leafcutters work below ground and process the pieces of the leaf that the harvesters bring back for the fungi to digest. The nest also contains a single queen, laying all the eggs needed to keep the colony supplied with new workers. There can be 3–8 million ants in a single colony, which can measure 15 m across and 5 m deep.

Leafcutting ants cannot eat leaves. Instead, they carry the cut pieces back to the nest and use them as compost to cultivate a particular fungus from which they harvest sugar. This fungus cannot survive outside the nest or reproduce without help by the ants. If the ants collect plant material that is toxic to the fungus, the fungus seems to release a chemical signal that stops the ants collecting that particular plant material.

Discuss the leafcutter ants' niche. Be sure to include:

- The type of relationships the leafcutter ant has with the trees and the fungi.
- The relationship that exists between the fungi and the leaves.
- The advantage to the worker ants in living in a colony in which only the queen and fertile males can breed.
- The significance to the rainforest of 20% of leaf material produced by the trees annually being cut and deposited underground.

Use this page to create a key points plan or a mind map that could form the basis for a longer answer to be done on your own paper.

ISBN: 9780170355582

Internal environmental control

Unit 1 | Homeostasis basics

Every active cell has thousands of chemical reactions going on. This biochemical activity — aka **metabolism** — depends on having the correct conditions such as pH, dissolved substances, temperature, oxygen supply. How are cells provided with 'correct conditions' when outside environments keep changing?

Internal environment and control

In larger animals — including humans — very few cells are in contact with an outside environment. Most cells are surrounded by an **internal environment** consisting of **tissue fluid** that fills the spaces between them, as shown in Fig 3.4.1. Blood cells have plasma as their internal environment. Whether tissue fluid or plasma, this internal environment is chemically regulated to keep it as constant as possible. In addition, mammals and birds regulate their whole body temperature.

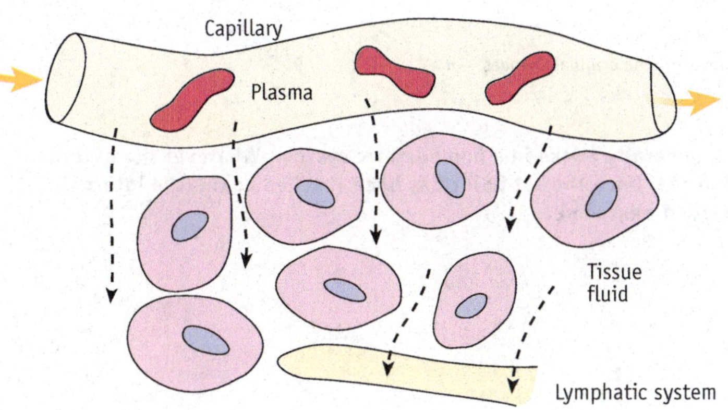

Fig. 3.4.1 Most body cells are surrounded by tissue fluid, which makes up an internal environment. Blood plasma, tissue fluid and lymph fluid: all three are linked and are chemically much the same.

Fig. 3.4.2 Human body temperature is regulated to remain close to a set point of 37 °C. If for any reason it rises above 42 °C, then protein breakdown begins, followed by brain damage and death.

Biology 3.4 enables students to study any of five different control systems:

- body temperature
- blood pressure
- osmotic balance
- level of blood glucose
- levels and balance of respiratory gases in tissues.

> **homeostasis:** regulation of blood and tissue fluid to keep conditions the same, so that processes can occur at optimal rates. (Greek *homeo* = the same.)
> **negative feedback:** any process in which the output is used to reduce the input, in order to bring about equilibrium (stability).

These control systems are covered in Units 2 to 6. Some schools may choose to study two of these, some more. Details of NCEA requirements are given on page 134.

The internal environment of mammals is regulated very precisely, with concentrations of oxygen, salts and sugars all being kept within narrow limits. Any such process of control or regulation is known as **homeostasis**. All homeostasis processes involve **negative feedback** mechanisms.

All control systems — including both biological and human-made ones — have three main components:

- the **sensor** (aka receptor) that monitors external or internal changes
- the **controller** that switches the effector on and off
- the **effector(s)** that respond with an output to reverse the original change.

4

In some cases, the sensor and controller components are in the same place. A flow diagram such as this one can be used to show how these three components link up.

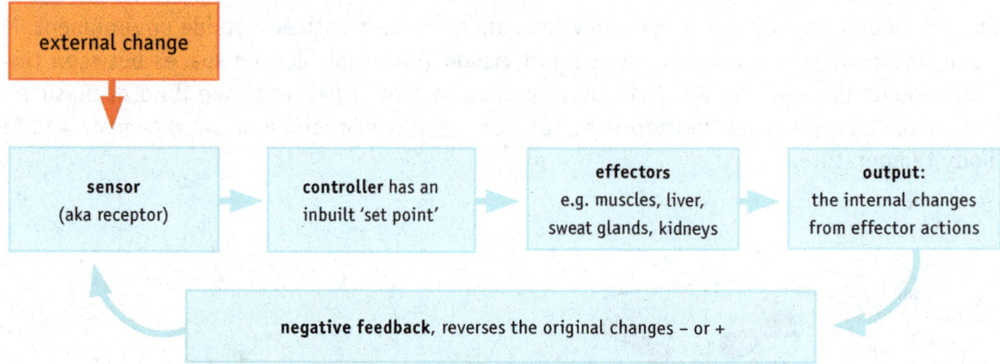

Fig. 3.4.3 Flow diagram showing how negative feedback generally works in a homeostatic system. Whatever the external change, the internal mechanism acts to achieve the opposite. Once the set point has been reached again, the internal controller mechanisms switch off the effectors until needed next time.

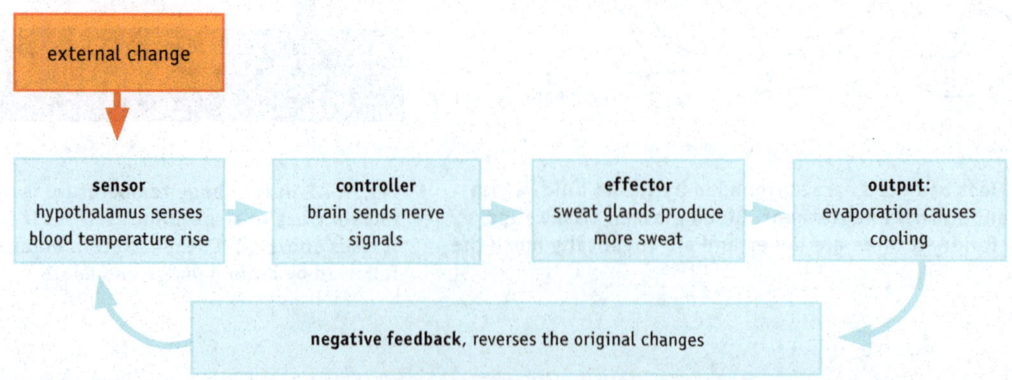

Fig. 3.4.4 The control of your body temperature during a game of sport provides an example of a negative feedback loop. The components sensor, controller and effector are features of almost all homeostatic systems, whether electronic or natural.

ISBN: 9780170355582

Thermostats use negative feedback principles to electronically control temperature. If the set point for room temperature is 20 °C, and if cold air is allowed to enter the room, then the thermostat sensor detects the change, the controller switches on heaters (the effectors), so that room temperature eventually rises. When sensors detect that temperature has reached the set point again, the heaters are automatically switched off.

Equilibrium

Feedback systems result in equilibrium (stability, balance). There are two different types of equilibrium:

- **Static equilibrium**, where there is no movement.
- **Dynamic equilibrium**, where there is a continual adjustment and movement, such as inflow being balanced by outflow. All control and feedback systems in the body involve some kind of active dynamic equilibrium.

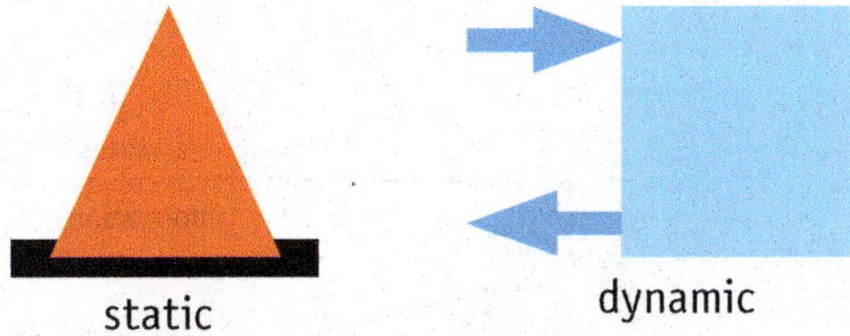

Sensors and signals

Sensors and controllers are located in different parts of the body, such as the hypothalamus in the brain and the islets of Langerhans in the pancreas (see Unit 5). Communication from sensors (and controllers) to effectors happens in one of two ways:

- **the nerve system**; high-speed one-way communication. Specialised nerve cells (**neurons**) carry impulses of about 70 millivolts at speeds of up to 100 metres per second.
- **hormones.** Hormones are chemical messengers that travel in the blood, taking up to a minute to reach the effector. Example: insulin. Some hormones are protein molecules; most have very specific effects. Hormone-secreting glands are collectively known as the **endocrine system**. Further details are in Units 4 and 5.

4

The nerve system

The human nervous system is enormously complex, but can be simplified into two main components:

- **central nervous system** (CNS); the brain and spinal cord.
- **peripheral nerves.** These nerves consist of long **sensory neurons** carrying impulses to the CNS, and **motor neurons** carrying impulses from the CNS to effectors such as muscles.

The **hypothalamus** is a small region of the brain with vital receptor and controller functions in homeostatic systems. It senses changes in body temperature, blood sugar and carbon dioxide. It has nerve connections with the nearby **pituitary gland**, a pea-sized endocrine gland at the base of the brain, and secretes a number of different hormones.

Autonomic nerves are part of the peripheral system. They are not under voluntary control, and have involuntary control over many body functions such as heart rate, breathing and sweating.

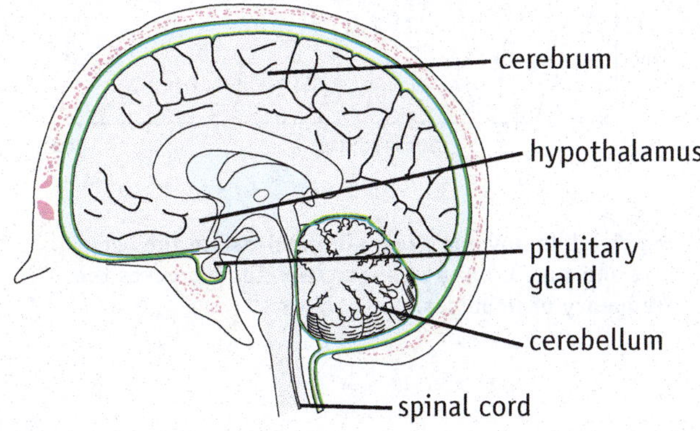

Fig. 3.4.5 Cross-section view of a human brain showing the protective membranes (in green), the pituitary gland, and the hypothalamus region.

E

Despite variation in neuron type, all nerve signals are the same: an electrical spike of about 70 millivolts that travels at about 100 metres per second. At every point where each neuron almost makes contact with another there is a **synapse**, a microscopic gap that briefly delays the spread of impulse 'excitation'. Every second, single neurons transmit huge numbers of impulses and receive huge numbers from others. Integration of this information is somehow achieved through the behaviour of synapses, in ways we are only beginning to understand.

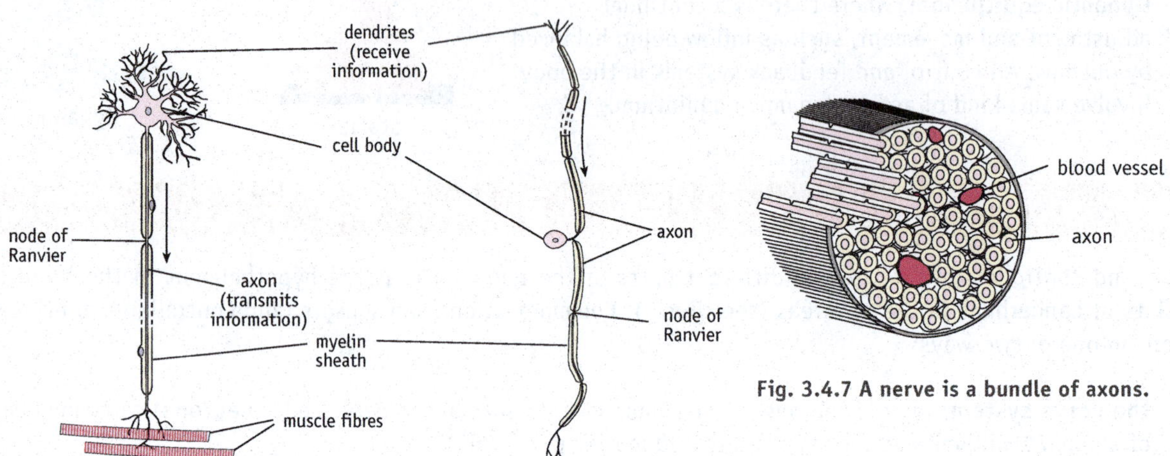

Fig. 3.4.6 Nerve cells (neurons) are highly specialised for carrying signals. Two types are shown here. Each axon is capable of carrying signals in one direction only.

Fig. 3.4.7 A nerve is a bundle of axons.

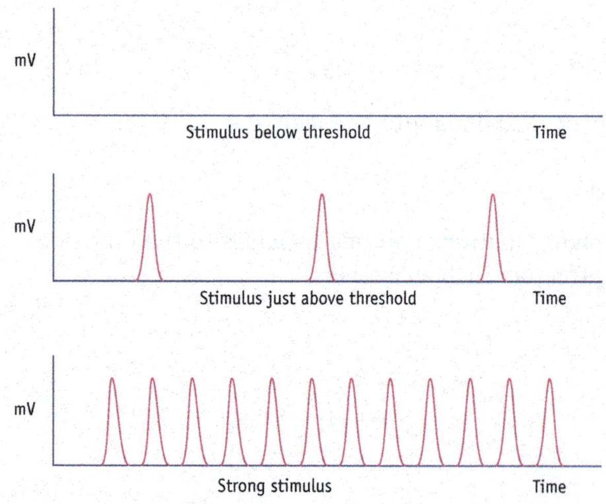

Fig. 3.4.8 In any one axon, all impulses are the same size and speed, but a stronger stimulus increases the frequency of impulses.

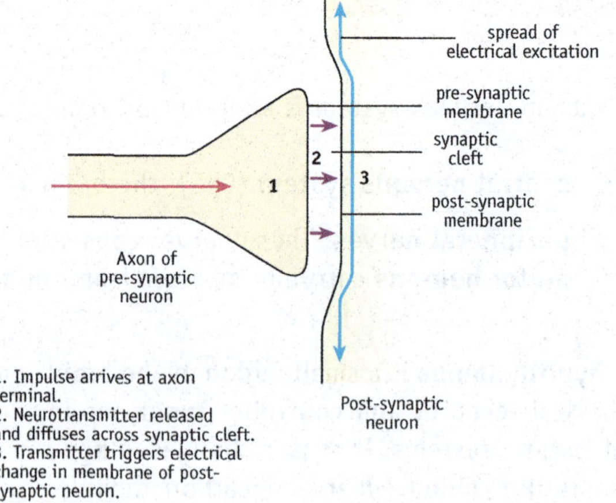

Fig. 3.4.9 A simple view of events at a synapse. Transmitter chemicals can in some cases stimulate the post-synaptic neuron, in other cases inhibit it and act as an 'off switch'. In reality each neuron may be receiving input from hundreds of other neurons.

4

ISBN: 9780170355582

Check your understanding

1 Write matching terms in the blank column. Choose from this list: *insulin, hypothalamus, plasma, neuron, pituitary, CNS, synapse, peripheral, endocrine, tissue fluid.*

a	Technical word for nerve cell	
b	Junction gap between two nerve cells	
c	Fluid around and between almost all body cells	
d	Includes both brain and spinal cord	
e	Brain region that senses temperature change	
f	Any gland or cell that produces hormones	
g	Hormone involved in sugar control	
h	Liquid component of the blood	
i	Endocrine gland at the base of the brain	
j	Nerves other than those in brain and spinal cord	

2 Explain the biological meaning of 'set point', and give one example.

3 Describe the general biological role of negative feedback. Name two examples.

4 Complete these sentences.

a By 'internal environment' we mean

b By 'negative feedback' we mean

c In temperature control systems, the purpose of a thermostat is to

d The main difference between a static and a dynamic equilibrium is

4

5 Using the thermostat description, draw a flow diagram to represent its working. Your diagram can be modelled on those used in this unit.

6 Explain what is meant by 'effectors', and give two human body examples.

7 Imagine a situation where a thermostat has been wrongly wired, so the heater automatically switches on when the room warms to a certain temperature. Predict what the result would be. (This would be an example of positive feedback or 'vicious circle'.)

4

8 Column A shows the general process involved in negative feedback; column B represents one aspect of body temperature control in humans. Complete B by writing in these five statements in the correct spaces: *Hypothalamus region in brain senses a temperature rise; Body temperature falls slightly; Sweat glands become more active; Evaporation causes cooling; Hard game of sport on a warm day.*

A General process or stage	**B** Temperature regulation in humans
External change (usually caused by environmental changes)	
Sensor (detects the change)	
Controller	Hypothalamus
Effector(s) (the part(s) that brings about action)	
Output (the change brought about by the effector)	
Result of this change	

ISBN: 9780170355582

Unit 2 | Temperature control

Keeping balanced

All living things generate heat from metabolism — even plants and insects produce some heat. However, only birds and mammals are able to balance heat gain and heat loss in a way that keeps body temperature almost constant. We describe these two groups as **homeotherms** (also known as endotherms). All other living things are **poikilotherms**, because their body temperature is always close to surrounding air or water temperature. (In Greek, *homeo* = the same; *therm* = heat; *poikilo* = various or different.)

Describing reptiles as 'cold-blooded' is misleading, because a lizard can reach a very warm 40 °C when it is sunbasking. We use the word **ectotherm** to describe animals that can to some extent control their body temperature using external heat sources in this way (*ecto* = outside).

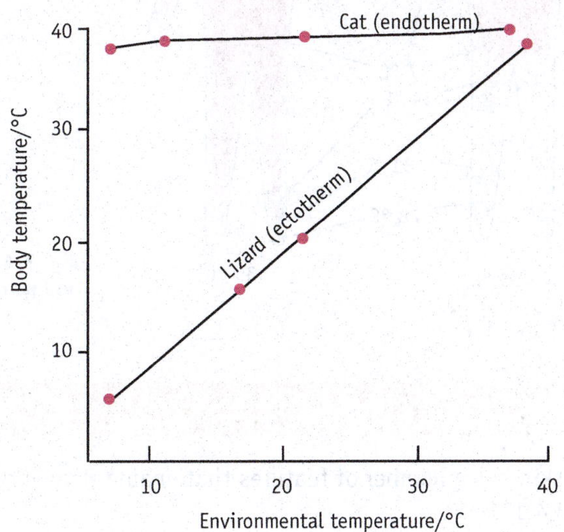

Fig. 3.4.10 Effect of external temperature on body temperature in a cat and a lizard. At low temperatures, a cat can hunt and be active, but a lizard can only move slowly — because enzyme activity slows at lower temperatures, as it does in any animal.

Most mammals keep their body temperature set point at 37 °C or 38 °C; birds are in the range 40–42 °C. These homeotherms achieve temperature stability by having two general abilities:

- able to balance heat gain and heat loss, as shown in shown in Fig. 3.4.11
- have internal feedback mechanisms to achieve this balance.

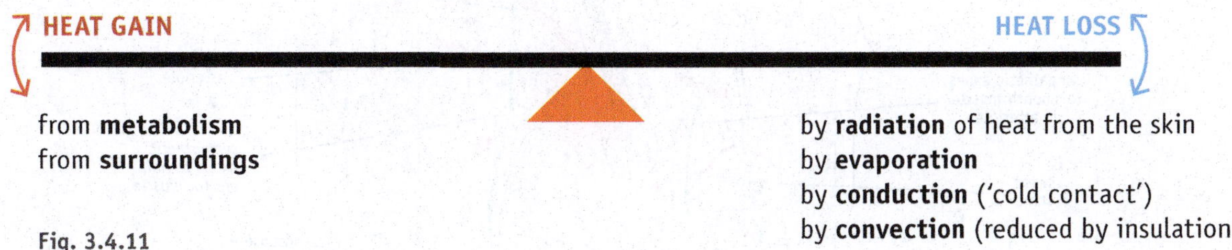

Fig. 3.4.11

The internal feedback mechanisms have the usual components of homeostatic systems:

- **sensors**; in this case the hypothalamus (also see Unit 4)
- **controllers**; in this case in the hypothalamus and also the thyroid gland
- **effectors**; in this case sweat glands, skin arterioles, skeletal muscles.

Although humans are homeotherms, body temperature remains constant only in the body core and brain. As Fig. 3.4.12 shows, even in mild 20 °C conditions, skin and hands and feet temperatures can easily drop below 28 °C. Under near-freezing conditions, our fingers and toes can get as cold as 10 °C, which is uncomfortable but does reduce further heat loss and helps to conserve core temperature close to 37 °C.

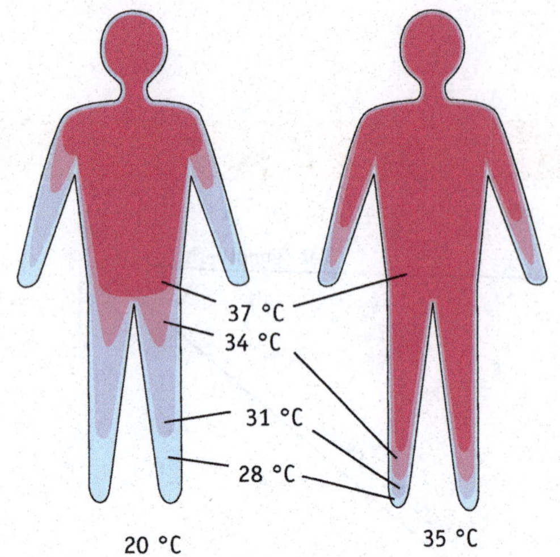

Heat and temperature are not the same. Temperature is measured in °C. Heat is a total quantity of energy and depends on temperature, type of substance, and mass of substance. It is calculated in joules (J) or in kilojoules (kJ).

Fig. 3.4.12 Core and outer temperatures under cooler and warmer conditions.

Heat loss from the skin

Human skin has a number of features that enable it to vary the rate of heat loss. Some of these features are shown in Fig. 3.4.13.

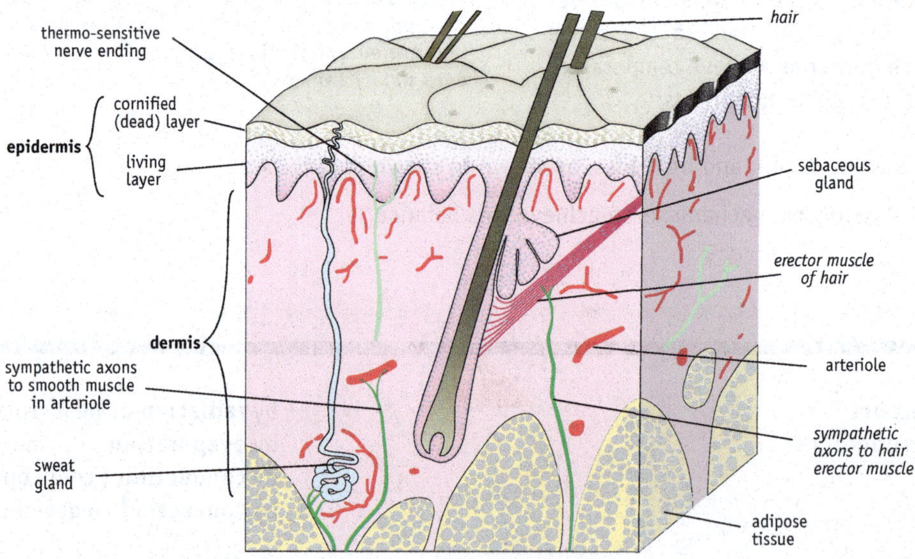

Fig. 3.4.13 Cross-section of the human skin. Autonomic motor nerves are shown in dark green. Sensory nerves are shown in pale green. ('Sympathetic' refers to one type of autonomic nerve.) Structures involving temperature control in non-human mammals are labelled in *italic*.

Sweat glands and evaporation

Humans are sweaty animals. We have more sweat glands per square centimetre than any other mammal, and our rate of sweating can be changed from almost zero to more than one litre per hour in extremely hot conditions. It takes 2.2 kilojoules of heat energy to evaporate just one gram of water — and this evaporation cools the skin. Blood returning from cool skin will, after a short delay, begin to lower the inner core temperature.

 ISBN: 9780170355582

Vasodilation and radiant heat

Bare skin radiates heat whenever it is warmer than the surroundings. When arterioles supplying the skin dilate (open wider), more blood flows to the skin, which then becomes flushed and warms up (Fig. 3.4.14). Under cold conditions, the opposite occurs: there is constriction (narrowing) of the same arterioles, blood flow is reduced and the skin becomes cooler and pale, even bluish. Having cold skin may feel unpleasant, but it reduces heat loss. Vasodilation (widening of blood vessels) happens not only in response to heating; it also happens in response to embarrassment — and results in blushing.

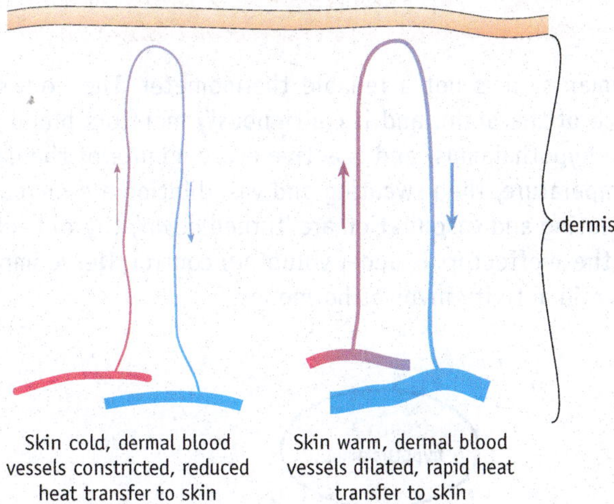

Fig. 3.4.14 When blood flow to the skin is increased (right), the skin becomes flushed and warm, so that more heat is lost. The opposite happens under cold conditions (left).

Convection and insulation

Any kind of insulation will cut down convective heat loss. Most mammals and birds have superb natural insulation and are able to fluff their fur or feathers in extra-cold conditions, which increases the thickness of the insulating layer, which reduces heat loss even further. Humans, of course, rely on clothing instead. Human hair is almost useless for insulation purposes, but in cold conditions we can see an evolutionary leftover — our microscopic hair-raising muscles still attempt to fluff what little body hair we have, hence goosebumps.

Not all hair exists for insulation purposes. As well as its sensory whiskers, a cat has long coarse 'guard hairs', beneath which is a shorter finer undercoat where most insulation happens.

Conduction

Lying on a cold surface or in cool water are quick ways of cooling down. Wallowing by elephants and rhinos are examples of behavioural temperature regulation — and have little to do with skin structure.

All of the above — sweating, vasodilation, hair fluffing — are continually being adjusted by signals from autonomic nerves.

Heat production

Most of the chemical energy in our food is eventually lost as heat produced in metabolism. The biggest heat producers (per kilogram) are kidneys, heart, brain and muscles. Blood produces almost no heat, but it does carry heat from warmer areas of the body to cooler ones.

Muscles

Because an average adult has over 20 kg muscle, this is where most heat can be generated: over 10 kJ per minute when muscles are working hard. Moving around or jogging on the spot generates a great deal of heat compared with sitting down. When core body temperature drops below a certain level (about 35°C), uncontrollable shivering takes over, major muscles trembling violently and with the eventual result of raising body temperature.

Thyroid hormone

The thyroid gland in your neck produces the hormone **thyroxine**. Unlike other hormones, its target is 'everywhere' in that it speeds up the metabolism of all body cells.

thyroid gland stimulated → more thyroxine → faster metabolism → increased heat production

Thyroxine production is itself stimulated by **TSH** secreted by the pituitary gland, which in turn is part of a continuous chain of action, as shown in Fig. 3.4.15.

Sensor and control centre

Human skin is not a reliable thermometer. The body's main temperature sensor is in the hypothalamus at the base of the brain, and it continuously monitors blood temperature. The control centre is located nearby, also in the hypothalamus, and is active every minute of the day. When the sensor detects even a small increase in blood temperature, then sweating and vasodilation are increased. When it detects a decrease in body temperature, then sweating and vasodilation are 'turned down', thyroid activity is increased, and shivering may be triggered. Not one of these effectors is under voluntary control. Nerve impulses travel to the skin through the autonomic nerves, and thyroid activity involves hormones.

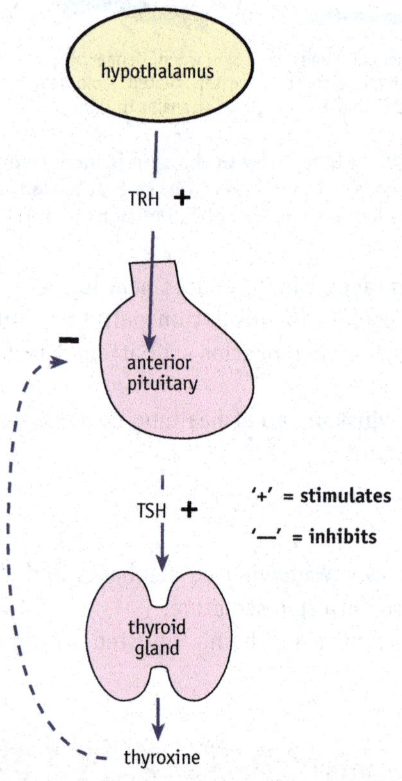

Fig. 3.4.15 Regulation of thyroid activity. Increased levels of thyroxine inhibit TSH production, which acts as a negative feedback loop. TSH = thyroid-stimulating hormone, TRH = thyrotropin-releasing hormone.

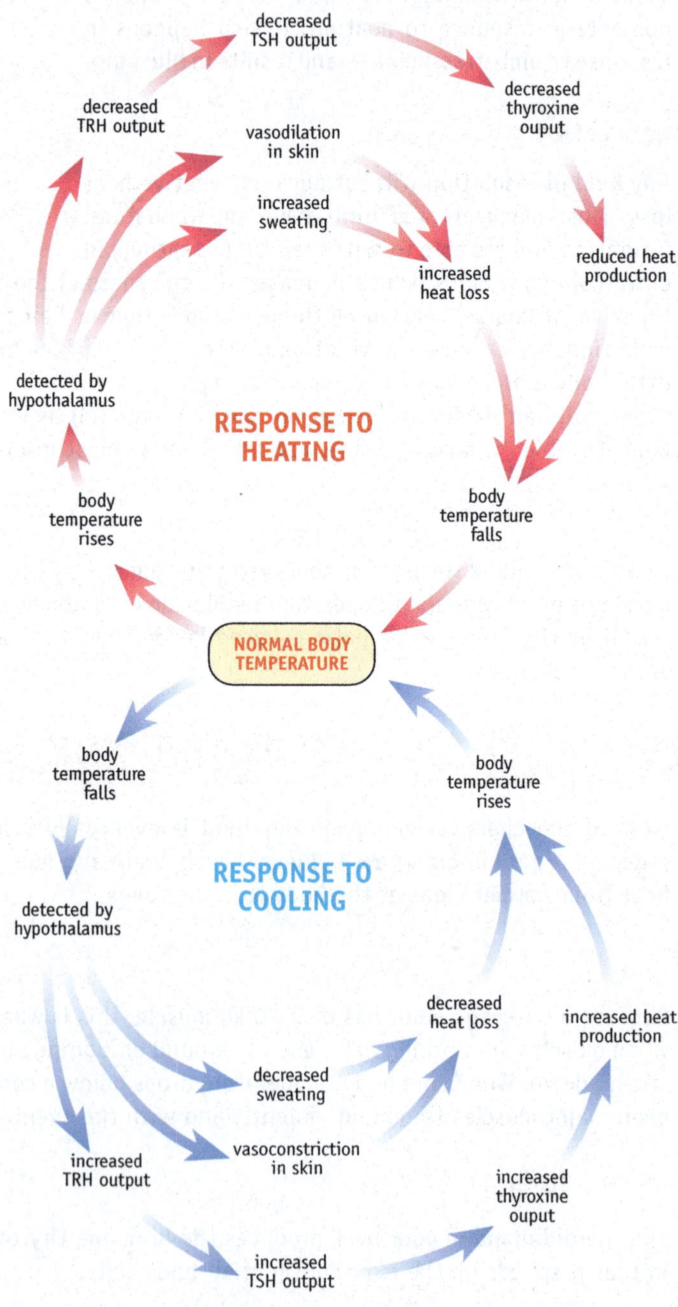

Fig. 3.4.16 Homeostatic feedback loops in temperature control.

Fig. 3.4.17 Under sunny conditions lizards are able to regulate their body temperature and keep it close to 35°C by moving from shade to sun-warmed rock every few minutes — an example of behavioural temperature regulation.

ISBN: 9780170355582

When things go wrong

The temperature control system seldom breaks down but can be pushed to the limits of normal functioning, resulting in hypothermia (*hypo* = under) or hyperthermia (*hyper* = above).

Hyperthermia

This can happen when a person has a fever and is 'running a temperature' because of an infection, and also in very hot conditions. Small children are particularly at risk. Whatever the cause, when core body temperature reaches 40 °C, a person feels very sick; and at 42 °C they could die. At this temperature, irreversible protein breakdown begins. Normal body temperature of 37 °C is very close to the upper lethal limit. Explanation: enzymes work better when warmer, and evolution has produced a situation that leaves only a small safety margin.

Hypothermia

Hypothermia can occur under very cold conditions or after even one hour in cold water, when the body cannot generate enough heat to compensate for the rate at which heat is being lost. Severity is progressive. Mild hypothermia: awake and shivering, core temperature 35 °C to 32 °C. Moderate hypothermia: confused, not shivering, core temperature 32 °C to 28 °C. Severe hypothermia: unconscious, core temperature 28 °C to 20 °C. Below 20 °C is fatal.

A tradition of giving alcohol to a hypothermic person makes the situation worse, not better, because alcohol causes blood vessels in the skin to dilate, so body heat is lost even faster. First-aid treatment for severe hypothermia involves rewarming slowly and carefully to avoid a potentially fatal fall in blood pressure.

Frostbite is not the same as hypothermia. In frostbite, the circulation to hands and feet is shut off to reduce overall heat loss in subzero conditions. If circulation stops for too long, toe and finger tissues will die and amputation is the only option. Chilblains — skin ulcers caused by repeated chilling — are a lesser condition.

E

Heat exchangers

Penguins have a problem: they are warm-bodied and swim in icy water. Their chunky body shape and thick waterproof feathers help reduce heat loss, but their flippers are thin and not insulated. Flippers have to be that shape and do need a blood supply, which means that blood returning from the flippers is very cold. So why does this blood not fatally chill a penguin?

Penguins have a **counter-current heat exchanger**, a device in which arteries supplying the flipper are closely wrapped around veins returning blood from the flipper. Result: outgoing blood is pre-chilled, incoming blood is pre-warmed, and very little heat is lost (Fig. 3.4.18).

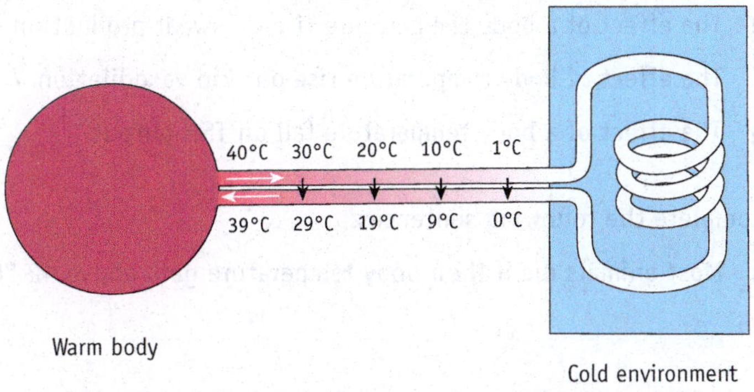

Fig. 3.4.18 Model of a counter-current heat exchange system. The red circle represents a penguin's warm body, the blue rectangle represents the flipper immersed in icy water, and the tubes that join them represent the heat-exchange mechanism.

Similar heat exchangers exist in other animals, such as in seagull legs, seal flippers and whale flippers. Many human technologies imitate these systems as a way of reducing heat loss.

Check your understanding

1 Write the matching terms in the blank column. Choose from this list: *thyroxine, hypothalamus, hyperthermia, vasodilation, autonomic, homeotherms, hypothermia, ectotherms, TSH, poikilotherms.*

a	Location of the temperature sensor	
b	Animals that keep warm using external heat sources	
c	Animals that are able to regulate body temperatures	
d	The opening up of blood vessels	
e	Hormone that stimulates thyroid activity	
f	Hormone secreted by the thyroid gland	
g	Body temperature too low	
h	Body temperature too high	
i	Body temperature changes with that of the environment	
j	Nerves supplying sweat glands	

2 Predict the effect in each of the following situations by writing *increases* or *decreases* or *no effect*.

a The effect of increased TSH on thyroxine output. ______

b The effect of increased thyroxine on metabolism. ______

c The effect of increased thyroxine on TSH output. ______

d The effect of thyroxine on sweat secretion. ______

e The effect of a body temperature rise on sweat production. ______

f The effect of body temperature rise on skin vasodilation. ______

g The effect of a body temperature fall on TSH output. ______

4

3 Complete the following sentences.

a Most animals die if their body temperature gets above 42 °C because

______

b Animals like lizards move slowly when their body temperature is low because

______

c As regards temperature regulation, the main role of the hypothalamus is

______

4 Explain the advantage of having body temperature maintained close to 37 °C and not 27 °C, which would require less energy to maintain.

______

ISBN: 9780170355582

5 Describe the general function of blood in temperature regulation.

6 Name five main body regions where heat is generated.

7 Explain the internal cause of goosebumps.

8 Explain how an insulating layer of fur reduces heat loss through convection.

9 Counter-current heat exchangers (as in penguins) and vaso-constriction in the skin (as in humans) are different ways of reducing heat loss. Compare these two systems to highlight the essential difference between them.

10 Complete this diagram by writing a few words in each box. The 'effector' box has been done for you to indicate what is needed in the others.

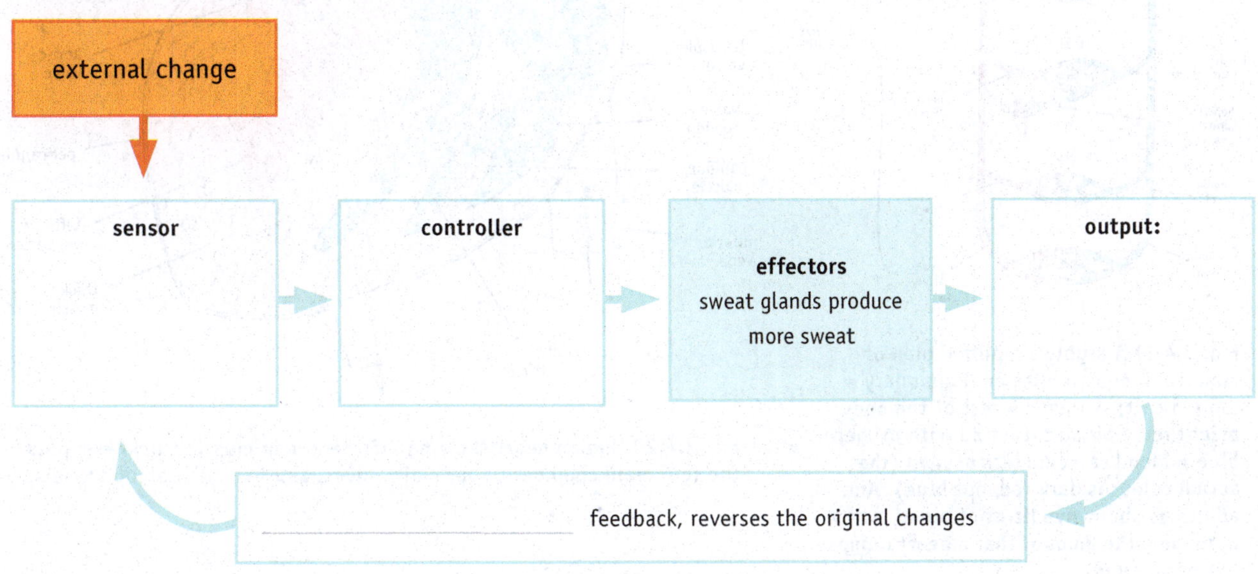

Unit 3 | Blood pressure control

Is blood pressure 130/80 good or bad? What causes high blood pressure? How is it regulated? To answer these and other questions, we first need to understand the circulatory system and how it works.

Circulation and heart

Like all other mammals, humans have a **double circulation**. The right side of the heart pumps blood to the lungs to be oxygenated, and the left side pumps blood at even higher pressure to the rest of the body. Fig. 3.4.19 shows a simplified version of this arrangement.

The two sides of the heart seem to be in parallel, but are actually in series. Blood that is pumped from the left side eventually finds its way to the right side, which means that the two sides must pump equal volumes of blood at each beat. Compared with the left, the right side of the heart pumps blood under lower pressure in order to avoid the risk of tissue fluid leaking into the alveoli.

The left and right sides of the heart beat in synchrony. When the two ventricles are contracting, the two atria are relaxing, and vice versa. The contraction and relaxation phases are shown in Fig. 3.4.21. Between each atrium and ventricle is a valve which allows blood to flow in only one direction. Also, one semi-lunar valve is located in the aorta, and another in the pulmonary artery. Heart valves cannot move by themselves: they are pushed open or closed by blood pressure.

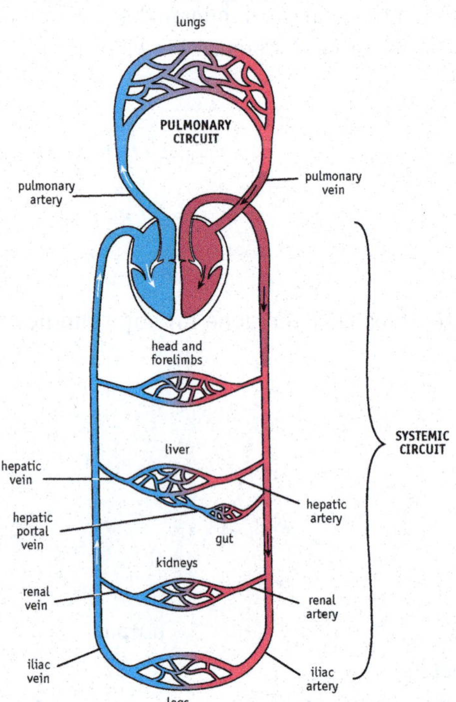

Fig. 3.4.19 A highly simplified plan of mammal blood circulation. Pulmonary = lung circuit; systemic = rest of the body; bright red = blood saturated with oxygen; blue = blood carrying less oxygen (the actual colour is dark red, not blue). An adult has about five litres of blood, which is roughly the amount that a heart pumps out each minute.

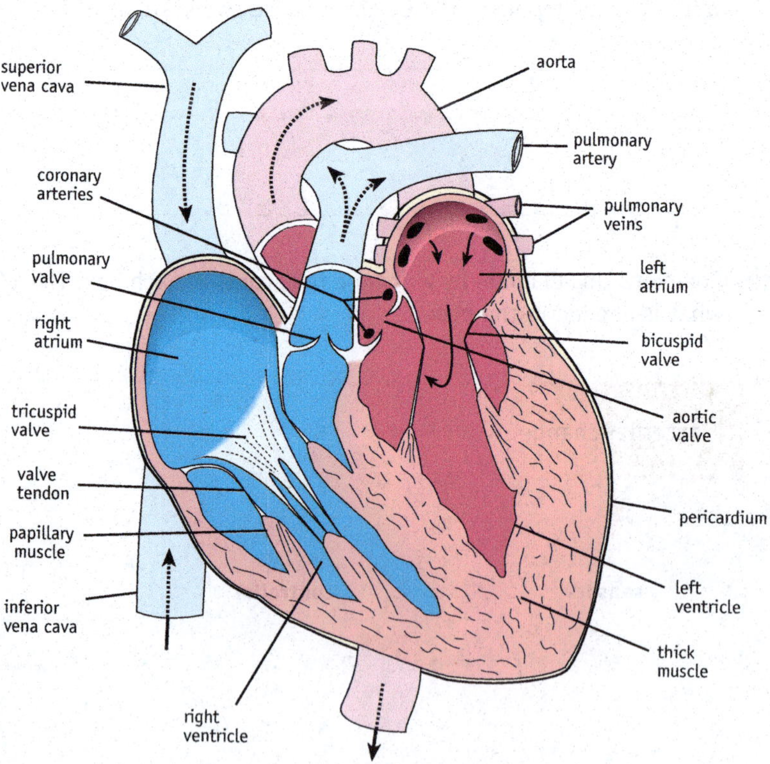

Fig. 3.4.20 Human heart showing differences in muscle thickness, plus the four main chambers, four main valves, and five main blood vessels.

ISBN: 9780170355582

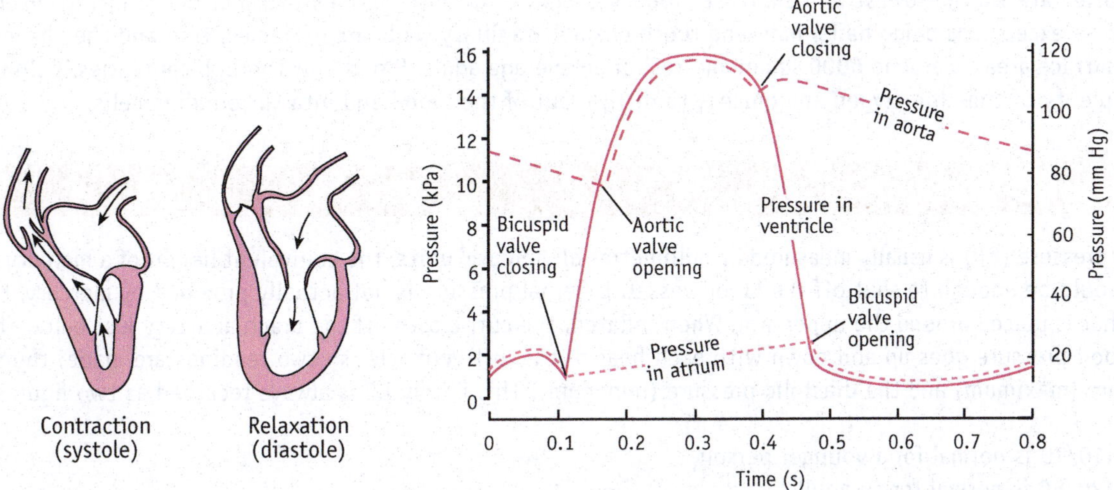

Fig. 3.4.21 Left ventricle shown at contraction and relaxation stages (systole and diastole). The graph shows events of the cardiac cycle, with a pulse at each heartbeat. The red dashed line shows pressure in the aorta; in this case a 120 mm peak at systole, about 80 mm at diastole.

Blood vessels

Arteries take blood away from the heart, at high pressure. **Veins** return blood to the heart, at lower pressure.

Because of the artery/vein pressure difference, veins have a large diameter with thin walls, while arteries carrying an equivalent amount of blood are smaller in diameter with much thicker, more muscular walls.

Both veins and arteries have a muscle type known as **smooth muscle**, because it lacks the bands visible in other muscle types. Smooth muscle contracts slowly and is not under voluntary control — it is controlled by the autonomic nerve system.

The smallest arteries, with an internal diameter of 1 mm or less, are known as **arterioles**. Their walls have a thick layer of smooth muscle. When this contracts, it narrows the diameter of the arteriole, reducing the amount of blood flowing to that region.

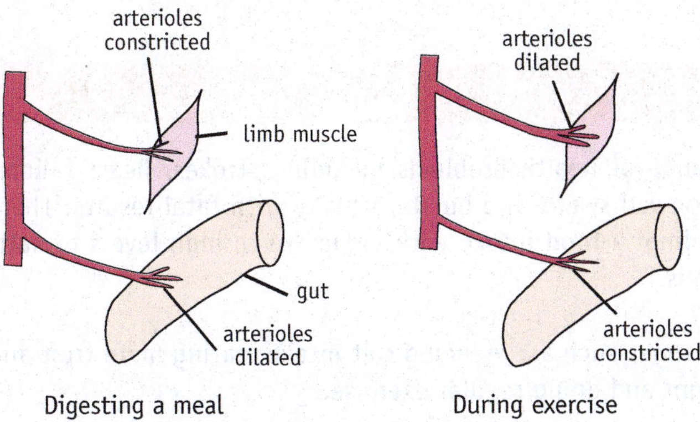

Fig. 3.4.22 Arteriole muscle layers can constrict (reduce their diameter), but when relaxed this increases the distribution of blood to a particular body region.

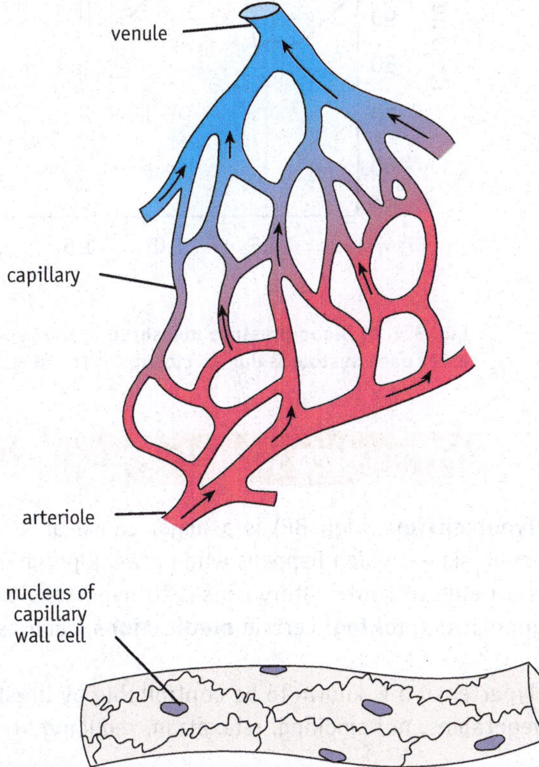

Fig. 3.4.23 A 'capillary bed', with a single capillary in side view, shown at greater magnification.

Capillaries are the narrowest and shortest blood vessels of all, with billions of them reaching into every body region — exceptions being nails, hair, and tooth enamel. Capillary walls are extremely thin and they have a large total surface area — around 6000 square metres for an average adult. Blood flow through capillaries is slow, which gives plenty of time for oxygen and glucose to diffuse out of the blood and into surrounding cells.

Measuring blood pressure

Blood pressure (BP) is usually measured in 'millimetres of mercury' units; the equivalent height of a mercury column that would be enough to shut off the blood vessel. External pressure is not actually provided by mercury, but by a cuff that is placed around the upper arm. When inflated, the cuff closes off the brachial artery just below the skin.

Blood pressure goes up and down with each beat of the left ventricle, so two readings are made: the systolic pressure (maximum) and the diastolic pressure (minimum). This is why BP is always recorded as two figures.

110/70 is normal for a younger person
120/80 is normal for an adult
140/100 is high for an adult (hypertension)
90/50 is very low (hypotension)

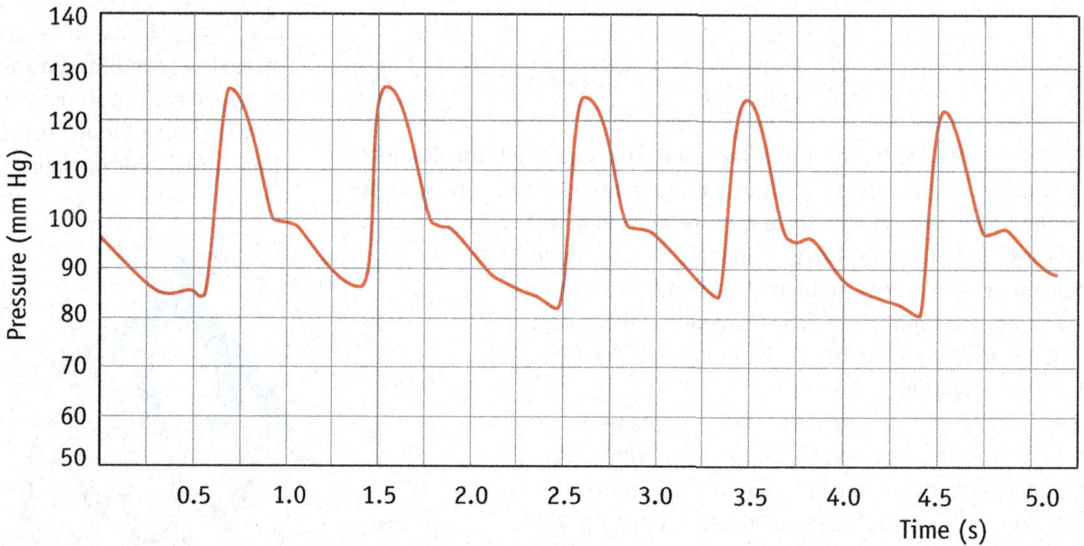

Fig. 3.4.24 Blood pressure measured in the radial artery in the wrist. The small plateau in pressure about 0.2 s after each systole is due to closing of the semi-lunar valve in the aorta.

When things go wrong

Hypertension (high BP) is a major cause of a wide range of health problems including strokes, heart failure, aneurysm — which happens when a weak patch of artery wall swells and bursts, usually with fatal results. There is a range of contributory causes to hypertension including: a food intake with moderate to high levels of **salt**; **genetics**; **smoking**; certain **medications**, such as steroids.

Hypertension is known to be controllable by lifestyle changes such as: reducing salt intake, eating more fruit and vegetables, not smoking, relaxation, reducing body weight and doing regular exercise.

In the case of **hypotension**, BP is at times so low that insufficient blood may be pumped to extremities and to the brain. A person with low BP may feel faint, particularly when standing up from a lying position. Minor hypotension is a common result of people giving blood: a loss of half a litre out of five litres total causes a temporary drop in pressure, but the body soon compensates for this.

 ISBN: 9780170355582

Control of blood pressure

Blood pressure is regulated by the autonomic nervous system, with several homeostatic feedback loops that act to either lower or raise pressure. Control mechanisms lead to the diameter of arteries being dilated or narrowed, and also to changing the total volume of blood circulating around the body.

Blood pressure sensors — **baroreceptors** that are sensitive to stretch — are located in the walls of the carotid artery that supplies the brain. The **control centre** is located in the medulla — the upper spinal cord. **Parasympathetic neurons** in the autonomic nervous system are the links between the sensors and control centre and the heart. If BP gets above normal, the feedback loop results in heart activity being inhibited, which in turn reduces BP.

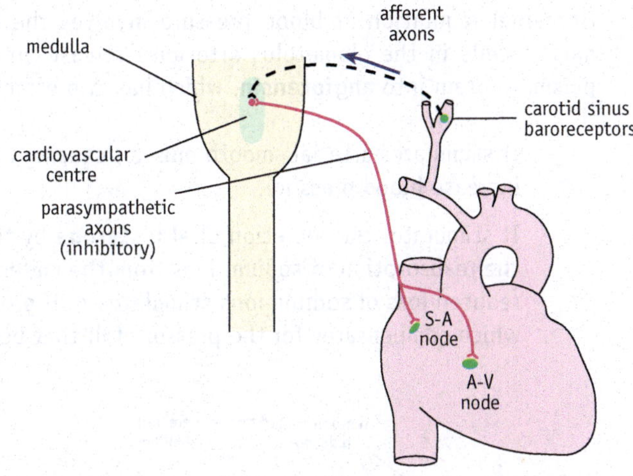

Fig. 3.4.25 Location of some structures involved in blood pressure regulation. S-A = sinu-atrial node, A-V = atrio-ventricular node. Each of these is a small area of cells that generate electrical signals, the S-A node being the heart's inbuilt pacemaker. The pacemaker can be overridden by information from the control centre.

Adrenaline also influences blood pressure. In emergencies, the autonomic system stimulates the adrenal glands to release more adrenaline. This hormone has a number of bodily effects that help equip the body for rapid action, including a sudden increased heart rate, and blood being diverted to the muscles — which causes the skin to go pale. The heart rate increase and the constricted arteries both act to raise BP. **Aldosterone** is another hormone that influences blood pressure.

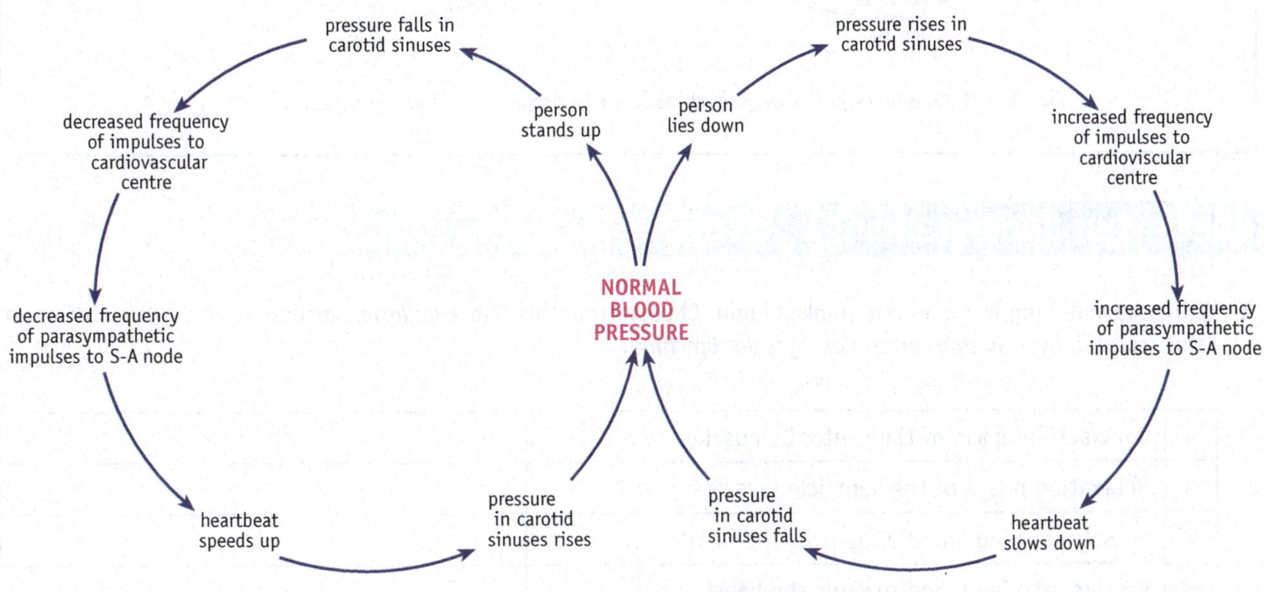

Fig. 3.4.26 How blood pressure is regulated following changes in posture. The response takes a few seconds, which is why some people briefly feel faint when suddenly going from lying down to standing up.

E

Aldosterone, sodium, and blood pressure

Hormonal regulation of blood pressure involves the kidneys. Following a slight fall in blood pressure, muscle cells in the glomerulus arterioles release an enzyme called **renin**. This converts an interactive plasma protein into **angiotensin**, which has two effects:

- It stimulates arterial smooth muscle, causing a generalised vasoconstriction and helping to increase blood pressure.
- It stimulates the secretion of **aldosterone** by the adrenal gland. This steroid hormone promotes the reabsorption of sodium ions from the collecting ducts in exchange for potassium ions. The reduced loss of sodium ions stimulates ADH production, therefore causing a rise in blood pressure, which compensates for the pressure fall that began the process.

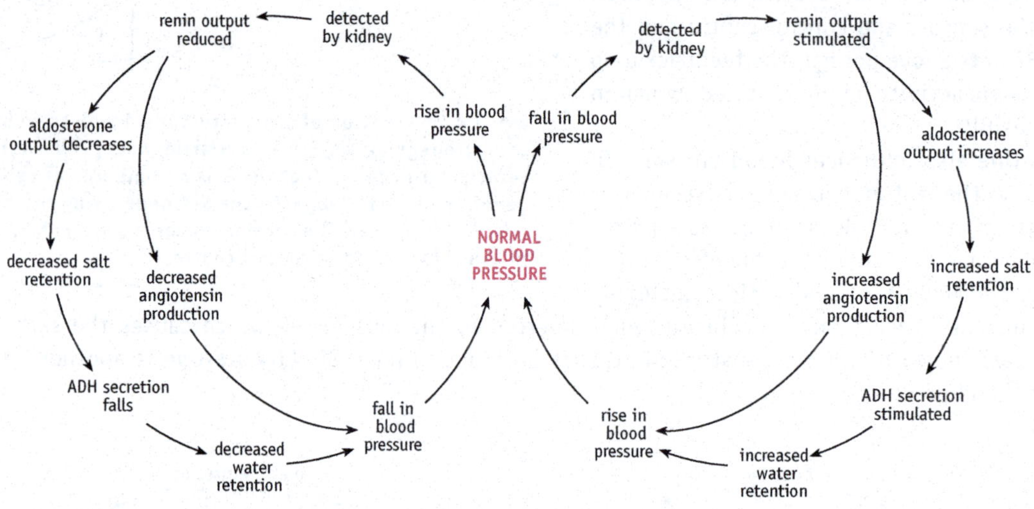

Fig. 3.4.27 Kidney hormone-mediated responses to changes in blood pressure.

Check your understanding

1 Write the matching words in the blank column. Choose from this list: *capillaries, arteries, hypertension, diastole, veins, carotid, hypotension, arterioles, systole, brachial.*

a	Contraction phase of the ventricle muscles	
b	Relaxation phase of the ventricle muscles	
c	Vessels carrying blood away from the heart	
d	Vessels carrying blood towards the heart	
e	Arteries with narrow diameter and thick walls	
f	The smallest diameter blood vessels of all	
g	Artery usually used to measure blood pressure	
h	Artery carrying blood to the head	
i	Another word for high blood pressure	
j	Another word for low blood pressure	

ISBN: 9780170355582

2 Complete the following sentences.

a Compared with the right ventricle, the left ventricle is more muscular because

b When arteries become less elastic, this can increase blood pressure because

3 Explain how arterioles are able to direct blood away from one body region and towards another.

4 The 'stroke volume' is the amount of blood pumped into the aorta by each beat of the aorta. Calculate to the nearest litre the amount of blood pumped:

a per minute, at 60 beats a minute, stroke volume 80 mL.

b per minute, at 150 beats a minute, stroke volume 100 mL.

c per hour, at 60 beats a minute, stroke volume, 80 mL.

5 Explain the difference between systole and diastole.

6 Explain what a blood pressure of 110/70 refers to.

7 Describe where the main baroceptors are, what their function is, and how they work.

8 Explain how a person can develop hypertension. Describe what steps can be taken to control this, and why.

Unit 4 | Water control

Living things are mostly water — around 65 per cent in the case of humans, although this varies with age and health. The water content of your tissue fluid and blood plasma is, however, kept close to 92 per cent, and is constantly regulated to compensate for any water uptake and also minute-by-minute variations in water loss — for example from sweating in hot conditions.

Water balance

Blood water gain and water loss are kept in balance, as shown in the diagram. Each type of gain and loss is variable, so the percentages shown are approximate. Adjusting urine output is a key part of the regulatory process.

water gain	water in blood	water loss
food	→ →	35% in evaporation from skin and lungs
drink	→ →	5% in faeces
metabolism	→ →	65% in urine output by kidneys

Blood plasma water balance is continually being fine-tuned to within 0.1 per cent, and if plasma water content falls even 10 per cent it can result in death by dehydration. The processes around water balance are known as **osmotic regulation** (aka osmoregulation). Kidneys have a key role in this. Someone with kidney failure can only survive with daily dialysis — a high-tech intervention that replaces some but not all kidney function.

Kidney structure

People normally have two kidneys, though a few have three. Each kidney is about 12 cm long and well protected in the upper abdominal cavity, close to the muscles that support the spine. Human kidneys are bean-shaped, but look different in some other mammals.

Each kidney receives aortic blood from the **renal artery**, with blood exiting by a **renal vein**. Between them, the two kidneys take about a quarter of the heart's output, around one litre of blood each minute, which is a major blood supply considering their small size. Internal structure is complex, and only microscopic study can explain how blood enters and urine exits and what happens in between. The urine flows from each kidney along a tube called the **ureter**, both ureters emptying into the bladder, whose exit is the **urethra**.

Inside each kidney are about one million **nephrons**, or 'kidney tubes'. One end of each nephron has a microscopic cup-shaped **Bowman's capsule**, the other end empties its contents into a collecting duct. Fig. 3.4.29 shows a highly enlarged picture of one single nephron and its blood supply.

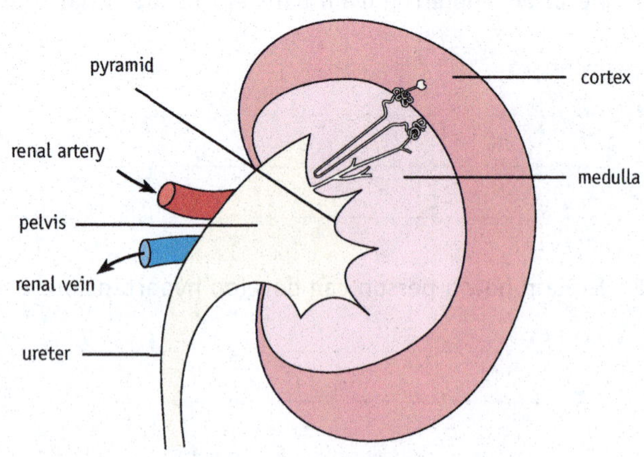

Fig. 3.4.28 Main regions of a human kidney.

ISBN: 9780170355582

Pressure filtration

Inside each Bowman's capsule is a collection of capillaries known as the **glomerulus**. Blood pressure forces some water and its dissolved substances out of the blood and into Bowman's capsule. This process is called **pressure filtration**, and about one tenth of the water in the blood entering the kidneys is filtered in this way; a combined total of around 100 mL a minute for all two million nephrons.

Fig. 3.4.30 shows glomerulus structure and the filtering process. Fig. 3.4.31 shows finer detail, including how water is forced through sub-microscopic holes in the blood vessels. These holes allow water and smaller molecules to exit, but blood cells and most protein molecules are too big to go through the filter. If blood or proteins ever appear in the urine, this can be a sign of kidney damage.

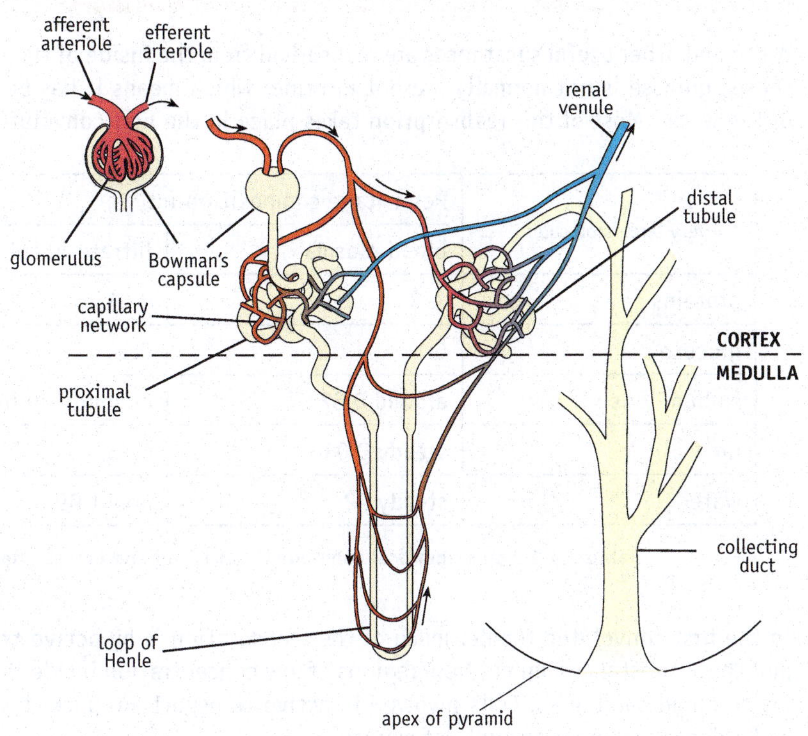

Fig. 3.4.29 A nephron and its blood supply and collecting ducts (*proximal* = nearer; *distal* = further).

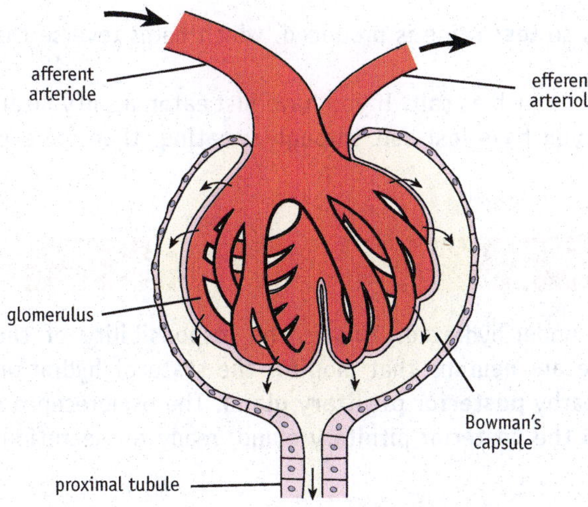

Fig. 3.4.30 A glomerulus inside Bowman's capsule. Blood pressure forces water and smaller molecules to filter into Bowman's capsule. The total surface area of these blood vessels is about half a square metre in each kidney.

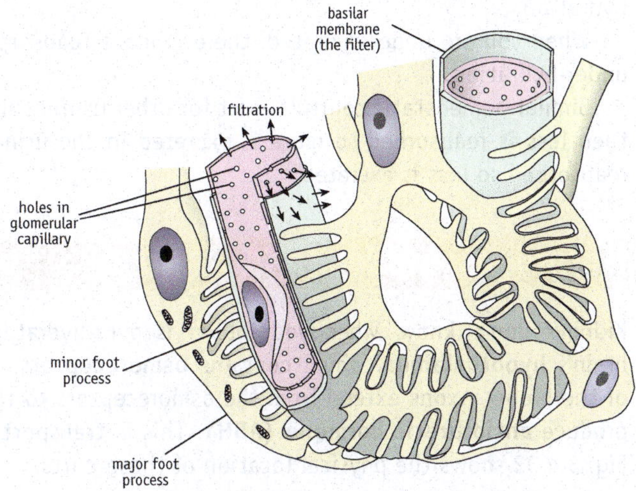

Fig. 3.4.31 The surface of glomerular capillaries are surrounded by starfish-shaped cells known as 'podocytes', which extend from the surface of Bowman's capsule and receive the filtered fluid.

Blood pressure forces smaller molecules out of the blood and into Bowman's capsule. This includes nitrogenous waste substances like urea, but also vital substances like water, glucose sodium, chloride and vitamins. At normal rates of filtration, any young person filters about 100 mL of water a minute, around 6 L per hour, a rate of loss that would rapidly be fatal. For this reason, most water is reabsorbed back into the blood.

Reabsorption

Water and other useful substances are reabsorbed from the inside of the nephron back into the blood. As Table 3.4.1 shows, glucose is not normally present in urine, which means it has been totally reabsorbed, together with most of the water. Most of this reabsorption takes place in the first convoluted tubule.

* = very large molecules	Percentage composition in:		
	blood plasma	filtrate in tube	urine
proteins *	7–8	0.01	0
glucose	0.1	0.1	0
sodium ions	around 0.32	depends on food	depends on food
urea	steady 0.03	0.03	about 2
water	steady 92	about 99.5	variable, 92–98

Table 3.4.1 Some chemical components of blood and urine. (Many others are not shown here.)

In the first convoluted tubule, much of the reabsorption is by **active transport**, meaning that it needs energy to pull these substances 'uphill' from regions of low concentration inside the tubes to regions of higher concentration inside blood capillaries. Cells involved in active transport are packed with mitochondria that supply this energy, and kidneys use great amounts of oxygen.

The amount of water reabsorbed in the collecting ducts and in the loop of Henle varies according to circumstances — and this is where homeostasis is at work.

When you are over-hydrated, there is **less** reabsorption, so **more** urine is produced, which reverses the over-hydration.

When you are under-hydrated, there is **more** reabsorption, so **less** urine is produced, which helps reverse the under-hydration.

4

Similar homeostatic controls exist for other useful substances such as salt. If you have just eaten a salty meal, then less is reabsorbed so more is excreted in the urine. If you have lost salt through sweating, then more is reabsorbed so less is excreted.

Hormones and feedback control

Kidneys don't 'know' when your blood is over-hydrated or under-hydrated. This is the responsibility of the brain's **hypothalamus**, which contains **osmoreceptors**. These are neurons that monitor the state of hydration of the blood. Axons extend from the osmoreceptors to the nearby **posterior pituitary gland**. The osmoreceptors produce **antidiuretic hormone (ADH)**. This is transported to the posterior pituitary gland, ready for secretion. Fig. 3.4.32 shows the physical location of these parts.

- The effect of ADH is to increase the rate at which water is absorbed from the collecting ducts back into the blood — which has the effect of making urine less watery and more concentrated.
- When the body is over-hydrated, less ADH is produced, so less water is reabsorbed — which has the effect of making urine less concentrated.

Fig. 3.4.33 sums up these automatic feedback processes that are part of the homeostatic control of water in blood plasma.

ISBN: 9780170355582

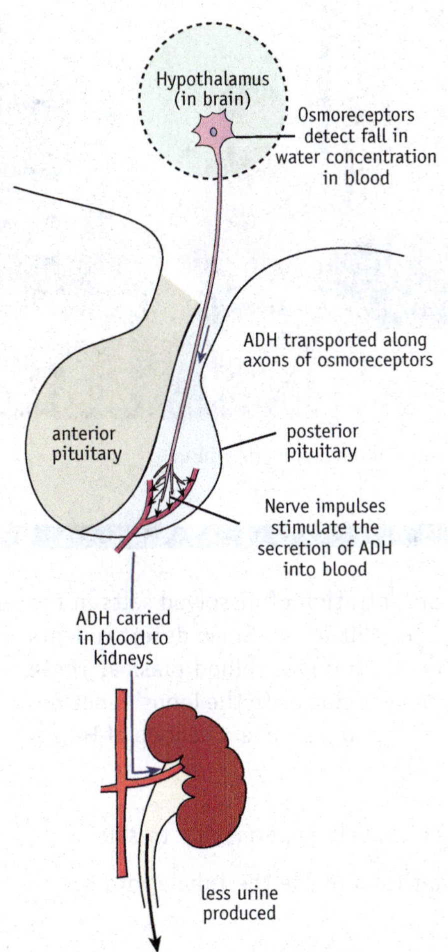

Fig. 3.4.32 Production of ADH in the hypothalamus, and its transport to the pituitary gland and then the kidneys. (Not to scale: pituitary gland is 1 cm diameter, kidney 12 cm long.)

When things go wrong

Some medical conditions and medications affect the kidneys.

1 **Kidney stones.** As well as water and about 2 per cent of the waste compound urea, urine contains other compounds including phosphates and uric acid. Under some conditions, these can crystallise, usually in the ureter. These crystals can grow into 'kidney stones' several millimetres in diameter, and are excruciatingly painful. Kidney stones are more likely to develop if someone is chronically dehydrated.

2 **Diabetes.** Diabetes has many serious effects, some of them affecting kidneys. Normally all glucose is reabsorbed into the blood, but in diabetes the blood glucose level can become so high that glucose is lost in the urine. Also, less water is reabsorbed, causing abnormally high volumes of urine to be excreted.

3 **Diuretics.** Several kinds of drug have a diuretic effect, which means increase urine flow. These drugs cause less ADH to be produced, with the result that more urine is produced an hour or so later. Alcohol and caffeine and some kinds of weight-loss pills are well-known diuretics.

4 **Dialysis.** A number of medical conditions can cause kidney failure, but a sufferer can be helped by being put on a dialysis machine. The treated person's blood is diverted through a dialysis machine for a few hours each day, with the machine imitating the pressure-filtration stage of kidney function. However, it cannot imitate the reabsorption phase, and loss of water and glucose and other substances has to be compensated for.

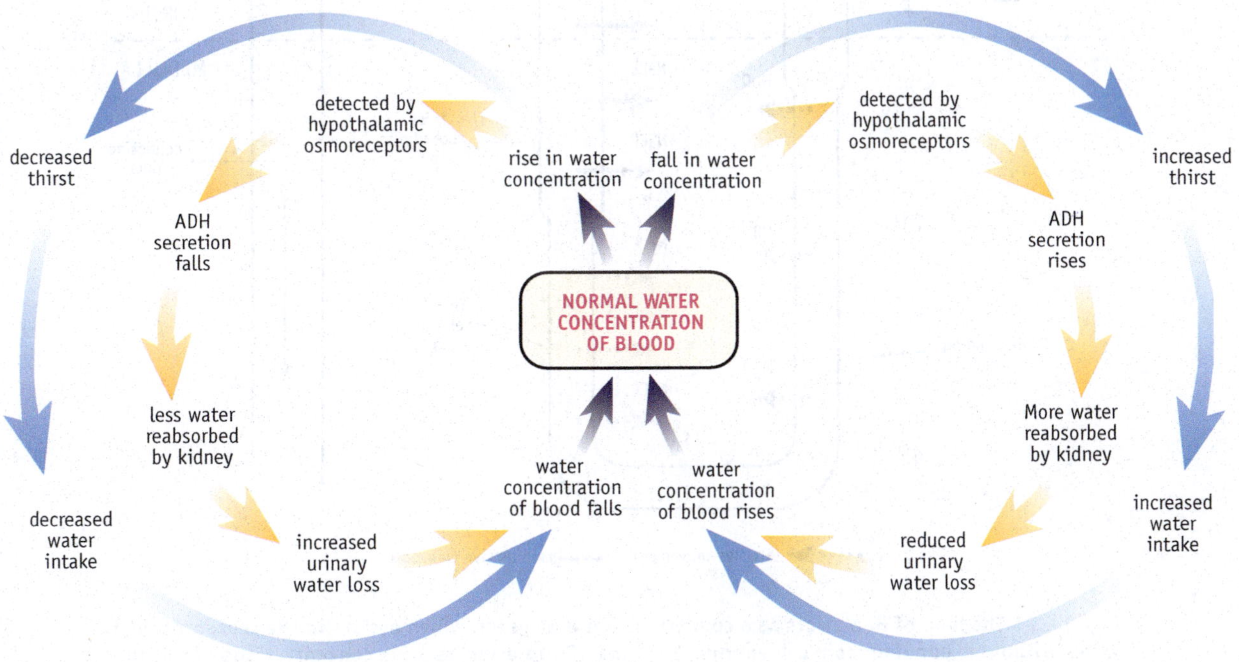

Fig. 3.4.33 Negative feedback control of body water concentration. Blue = control of water uptake; orange = control of water loss.

5 **Party pills.** Ecstasy users may have been told that they need to drink enough water to avoid dehydration, but some users encounter the problem of over-hydration, which causes hyponatremia (literally 'low salt'). The human body normally maintains a blood equilibrium of electrolytes, including salt. Sweating causes the body to lose salt. The primary cause of hyponatremia in Ecstasy users is drinking excessive amounts of water, which dilutes the salt in the body to a dangerous level. Unfortunately, as the electrolytes get out of balance, body systems start to fail and the sufferer begins to exhibit signs of crisis such as diarrhoea, over-salivation, stupor, vomiting, muscle tremors, confusion, frequent urination, and their brain begins to swell. This swelling (aka cerebral oedema) can and does lead to brain damage, paralysis and death.

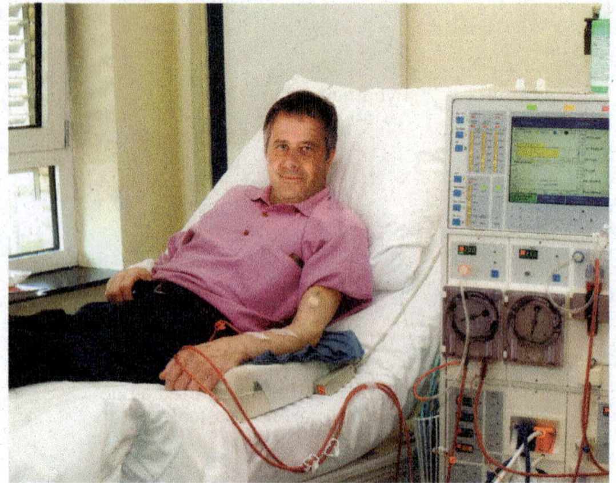

Fig. 3.4.34 Dialysis machine in use.

E

Humans are able to produce urine with up to four times the plasma concentration of dissolved salts in the plasma. This is achieved by reabsorbing most of the water lost in pressure filtration. Some desert rodents can conserve water even better, producing urine up to 25 times as concentrated as blood plasma. These animals have loops of Henle many times longer than in humans, which gives a clue as to the loops' function.

In humans, the final and variable amounts of water absorption occur in and just after the loop of Henle. The loop consists of two parts:

- the **descending limb**, whose walls are permeable to water but relatively impermeable to salt
- the **ascending limb**, whose function is to actively transport salt from inside the tubule into the fluid around the tubules.

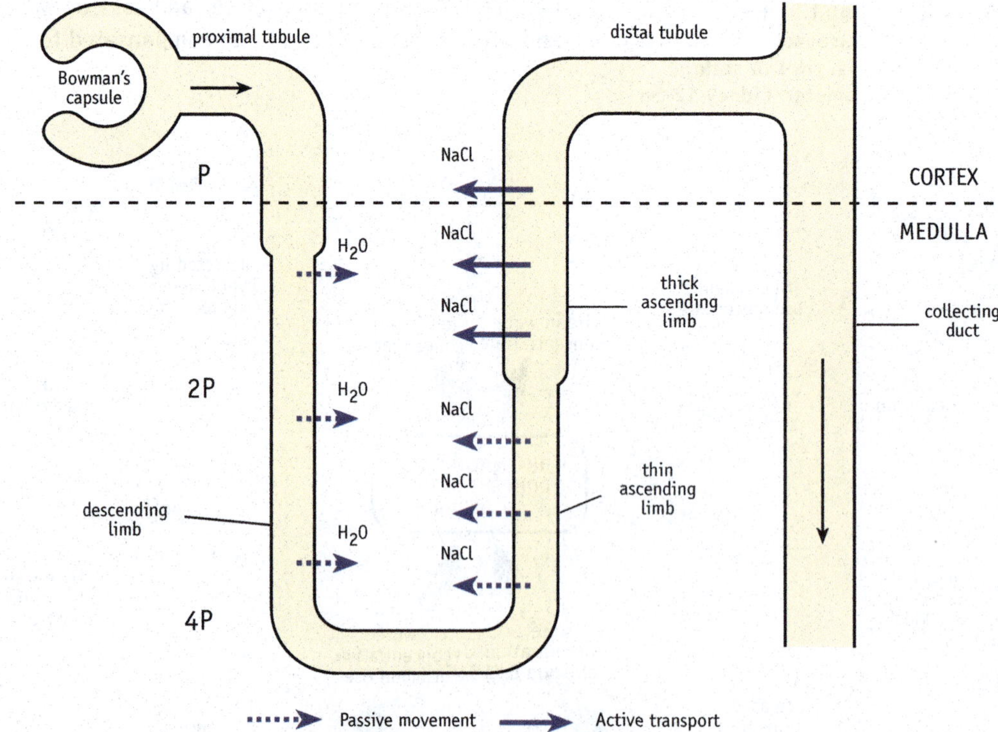

Fig. 3.4.35 The loop of Henle acts as a countercurrent multiplier, which assists in the reabsorption of water without expending too much energy. P, 2P and 4P represent relative concentrations of salt in tissue fluids surrounding the loop.

ISBN: 9780170355582

The ascending limb pumps salt into the fluid around it. This raises the salt concentration around the descending limb, causing osmotic removal of water from it. The liquid delivered to the ascending limb now has a higher salt concentration than it did a few moments before. This enables the ascending limb to raise the salt concentration outside it to a higher level than would otherwise be possible. This arrangement is called a **countercurrent multiplier**, 'countercurrent' referring to the fact that the liquid flows in opposite directions in the two limbs of the loop, 'multiplier' referring to the fact that small concentration differences developed at each level then become greater towards the 'U' end of the loop.

The permeability of the collecting ducts to water depends on the concentration of ADH in the blood. When ADH is relatively high, the collecting ducts are more permeable to water so more water is reabsorbed from the urine, resulting in more concentrated urine.

Check your understanding

1 Write matching terms in the blank column. Choose from this list: *mitochondria, glomerulus, renal artery, dialysis, hypothalamus, ureter, urea, renal vein, ADH, osmoregulation.*

a	Major blood vessel taking blood to kidneys	
b	Major blood vessel taking blood from kidneys	
c	Another term for water regulation	
d	Capillary network inside Bowman's capsule	
e	A hormone involved in water regulation	
f	These are associated with active transport	
g	Medical process in place of some kidney function	
h	Brain region sensitive to plasma water levels	
i	Nitrogenous waste compound	
j	Tube leading from kidney to bladder	

2 Complete the following sentences:

a Very few protein molecules enter Bowman's capsule because

____

____

b The main direct effect of ADH is to

____

____

c The function of osmoregulation is to

____

____

d The region of the nephrons where most reabsorption takes place is

____

9780170355582

3 Complete the following sentence by writing the word *increase* or *decrease* in each space.

If you lose a lot of water by sweating, this causes your blood water concentration to

a ____________________, which in turn causes production of ADH to **b** ____________________,

which then results in **c** ____________________ amount of water reabsorption, which causes a slight

d ____________________ in blood water content, and also **e** ____________________ urine production.

4 Look at Table 3.4.1 on page 114 before answering **a** to **c**.

a Suggest the mechanism causing the difference between the protein percentage in blood plasma compared with filtrate.

b Explain the 'how' reason behind the difference in glucose percentage in filtrate and in urine.

c Describe the 'how' mechanism causing the difference in glucose percentage in filtrate and in urine.

5 Complete this feedback diagram by writing in the responses in each white box.

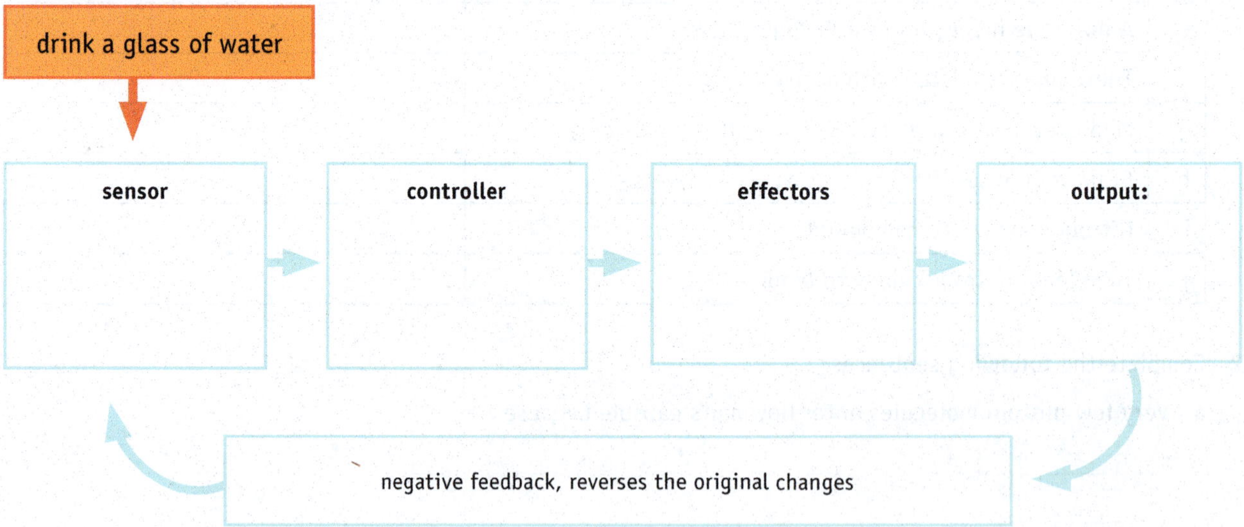

drink a glass of water

sensor → controller → effectors → output:

negative feedback, reverses the original changes

6 Explain some possible causes of kidney failure. Describe measures that can be taken to remedy the situation.

 ISBN: 9780170355582

Unit 5 | Blood glucose control

Why glucose?

Glucose is the main fuel for every energy-releasing process in your body. Its ultimate destination: cell cytoplasm and mitochondria, where the energy contained in glucose is used to manufacture ATP, which in turn supplies energy for movement, chemical synthesis and nerve activity. Glucose is particularly important to the brain, which uses no other fuel — except in times of starvation. (Note that in all active cells, glucose molecules are first converted to pyruvic acid molecules, which then enter the mitochondria where the main energy-release processes occur.)

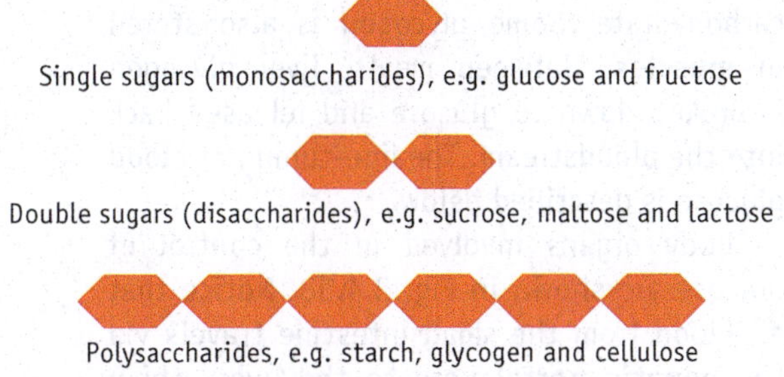

Fig. 3.4.36 Carbohydrate categories

As Fig. 3.4.36 shows, glucose is a six-carbon 'single sugar' (**monosaccharide**). Monosaccharides are part of a wider family of substances known as **carbohydrates**, which includes **polysaccharides** (like starch and glycogen) and **disaccharides** (like sucrose; ordinary kitchen sugar).

After a starchy or sugary meal, your blood glucose level begins to rise sharply, and during every burst of activity it falls again — but the body normally keeps blood glucose close to 0.1 per cent. Failure to regulate glucose leads to serious health consequences, including diabetes. For most people, blood glucose is regulated within the limits shown in Table 3.4.2.

Different units of measurement	Blood glucose normal range		
	Low normal	Mid-range	High normal
mmol/L	4.5	5	6.5
per cent, by weight	0.08	0.09	0.117
mg/100 mL	80	90	117

Table 3.4.2 The normal range of blood glucose levels. In most countries this is measured in mmol/L (millimoles per litre) of blood. A 'fasting' glucose level above 8 mmol/L may indicate diabetes.

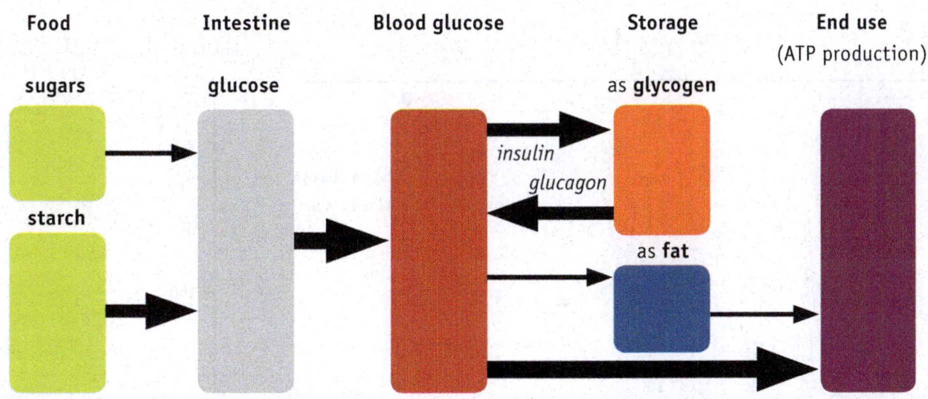

Fig. 3.4.37 Simplified diagram showing the movements of glucose from food to its eventual destination in cells. Glucose is used 24/7, but we eat only three times a day. Blood glucose level is regulated within limits, mainly by moving it in and out of temporary storage in the form of glycogen. Names of controlling hormones are shown in *italic*.

How glucose enters the blood

You don't need to eat glucose to have it in your blood. Soon after eating any carbohydrate meal, bigger molecules are digested, then small-molecule breakdown products are absorbed from the small intestine. This always increases the amount of glucose in the blood. In a healthy diet, most glucose comes from the digestion of **starch**, a polysaccharide. Unfortunately, many processed foods and drinks now have a high proportion of **sucrose**, a disaccharide (double sugar). Sucrose is digested and absorbed very quickly, and over many years this may eventually trigger diabetes. Smaller amounts of glucose are also derived from the breakdown of surplus amino acids, which occurs in the liver.

How glucose leaves the blood

After a meal, glucose is in surplus. The **liver** stores this in the form of **glycogen**, a polysaccharide similar to starch. After a carbohydrate-rich meal, the liver can store up to about 10 per cent of its mass as glycogen, enough to last two days if you ate no more carbohydrate. Some glycogen is also stored in **muscles**. Between meals, liver glycogen is broken down to glucose and released back into the bloodstream. The fine-tuning of blood glucose is described below.

Body organs involved in the control of glucose are shown in Fig. 3.4.38. Notice that all blood from the small intestine travels via the **hepatic portal vein** to the liver, which means that the liver can take up any surplus glucose before it reaches the rest of the body.

In an active person, all glucose and its breakdown products are eventually used to produce ATP, most of it inside the mitochondria. Excess glucose that cannot be used immediately or stored as glycogen is converted into **fat**, which is stored in the liver, around the gut, and under the skin. People who consistently eat more food than they need will become obese.

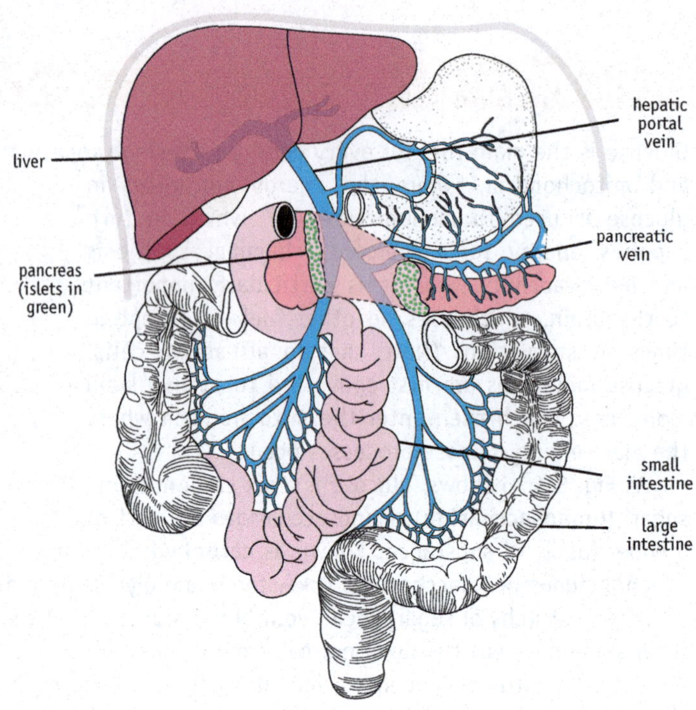

Fig. 3.4.38 Body organs involved in the uptake and transport and storage of glucose are shown here in colour. Notice that the liver is 'downstream' of both the pancreas and the small intestine.

4

Control of blood glucose

Except in emergencies, the concentration of glucose in the blood is controlled by two hormones: **insulin** and **glucagon**, both of them polypeptides (small protein molecules). Although the concentration of blood glucose goes up after meals, in healthy individuals it is regulated within limits. See Fig. XX.

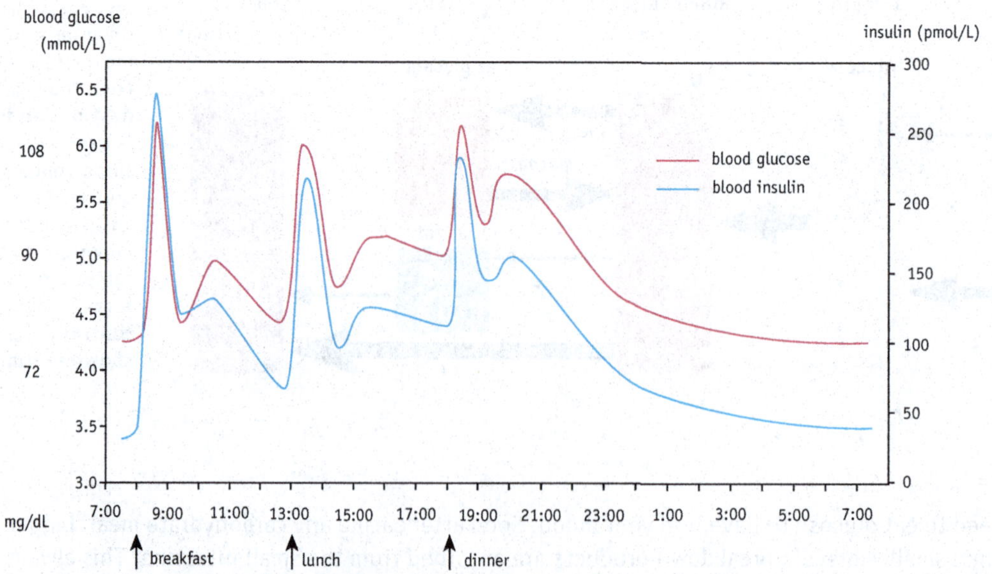

Fig. 3.4.39 Changes of blood glucose and insulin in a healthy individual over a 24-hour period. Insulin prevents after-meal blood glucose peaks from going even higher.

ISBN: 9780170355582

After a high-sugar snack it's usual to feel full soon afterwards, as a result of suddenly increased blood glucose, but then feel even more hungry an hour or so later. The hungry feeling is caused by overshoot, with a sugar rush triggering a sudden peak of insulin, which causes blood glucose levels to fall below normal. Fig. 3.4.39 illustrates some of this effect after three ordinary (non-sugary) meals.

Main sensor and controller

Insulin and glucagon are two hormones, both secreted by tiny patches of tissue located in the **pancreas** and known as the **islets of Langerhans**. There are about a million of these, each with alpha and beta cells. **Alpha cells** (α) secrete glucagon, and **beta cells** (β) secrete insulin (Fig. 3.4.40).

The islets are completely independent of nerve control. They detect (sense) changes in blood glucose concentration, and release the appropriate hormone in correct amounts. So the islets are both sensors and controllers. Their control mechanisms allow glucose levels to deviate by about 20 per cent around the 'set point'.

Insulin and glucagon have **antagonistic** (opposing) effects, as Fig. 3.4.41 shows.

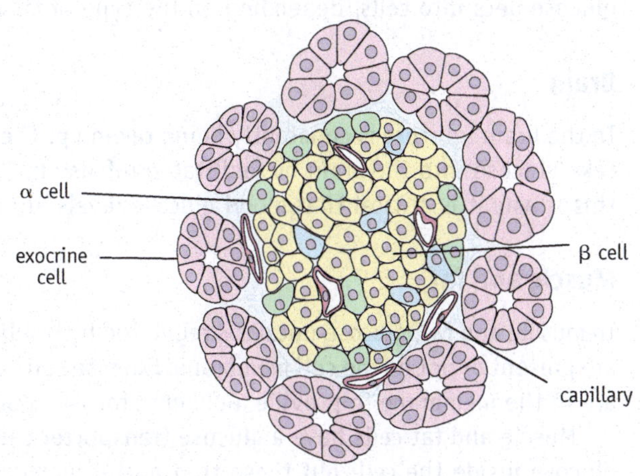

Fig. 3.4.40 Diagram showing one islet of Langerhans with alpha and beta endocrine cells. (Exocrine refers here to cells that secrete enzymes into a duct, not hormones.)

- Insulin responds to high blood glucose, and reduces blood glucose concentration.
- Glucagon responds to low blood glucose, and increases blood glucose concentration.

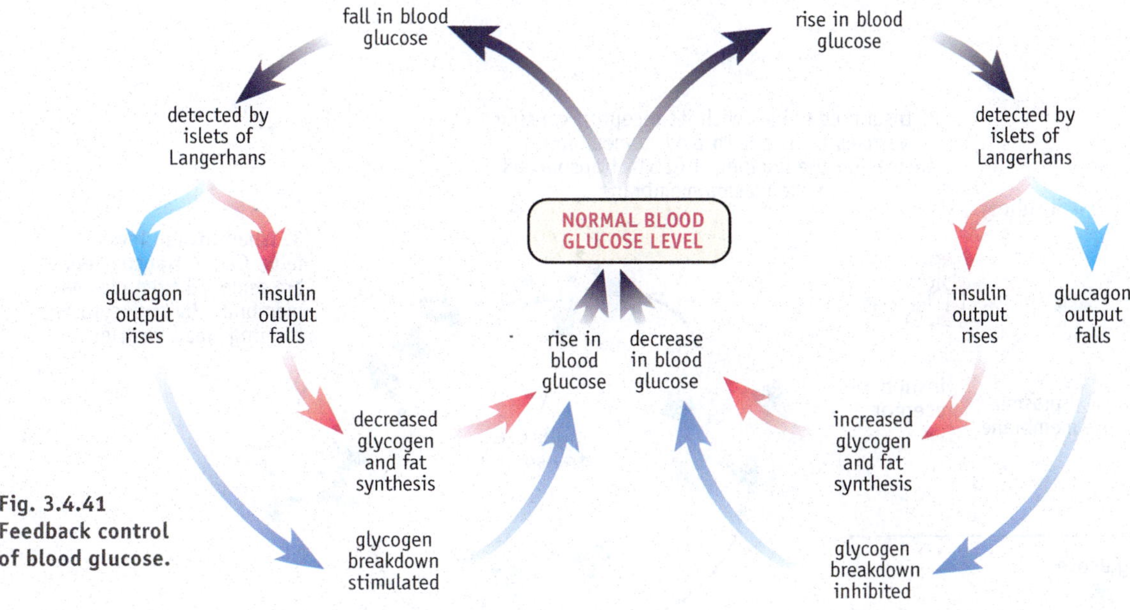

Fig. 3.4.41 Feedback control of blood glucose.

Main effector

The liver, skeletal muscles and fat cells are the main targets of insulin, while glucagon targets the liver only.

- When liver cells receive insulin they convert glucose to glycogen, and store it.
- When liver cells receive glucagon they convert glycogen to glucose, and release it.

These two responses are linked to maintain blood glucose within the limits shown in Fig. 3.4.39 and Table 3.4.1. We could describe liver cells as being 'sensors' of insulin and glucagon, but only the pancreas senses blood glucose.

E

How glucose gets into cells

Glucose molecules are too big to pass through cell membranes by simple diffusion. There are two ways that glucose gets into cells, depending on the type of tissue.

Brain

In the brain, glucose is constantly being taken up. There are glucose transporters in the cell membrane that take glucose into the brain by facilitated diffusion. The brain must have a constant supply of glucose and this is why it is critical that blood glucose levels are maintained.

Muscle and fat

In muscle and fat, glucose uptake is regulated by insulin receptors that control whether glucose transporters are present or not on the cell membrane. Glucose can't get across cell membranes unless specific transporters are in the membrane to provide a channel for the glucose to move through.

Muscle and fat cells have a glucose transporter called GLUT4 on the plasma membrane. It can transport glucose inside the cell, but these transporter molecules are present on the surface of the cell only when insulin is present. When insulin is absent the GLUT4 is inside the cell so cannot transport glucose.

When insulin is present it binds to an insulin receptor on the cell surface, causing the intracellular part of the molecule to change shape. This activates enzymatic activity in the intracellular portion of the receptor. In this way a signal is transmitted from the extracellular environment to the intracellular one without the hormone having to enter the cell.

The insulin receptor can now trigger a chain reaction of enzymes that ultimately makes the vesicles containing the GLUT4 move to the plasma membrane. These vesicles fuse with the plasma membrane so the GLUT4 is now inside the plasma membrane, where it can transport glucose into the muscle or fat cells.

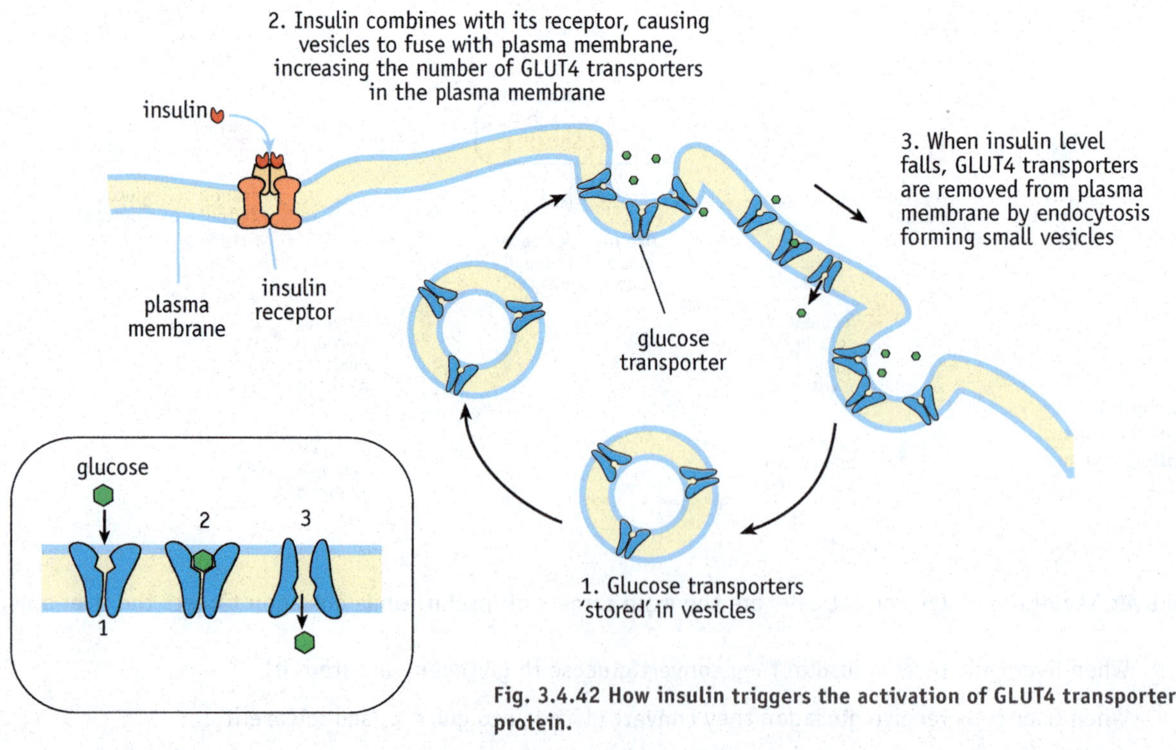

Fig. 3.4.42 How insulin triggers the activation of GLUT4 transporter protein.

 ISBN: 9780170355582

Glucose in emergencies

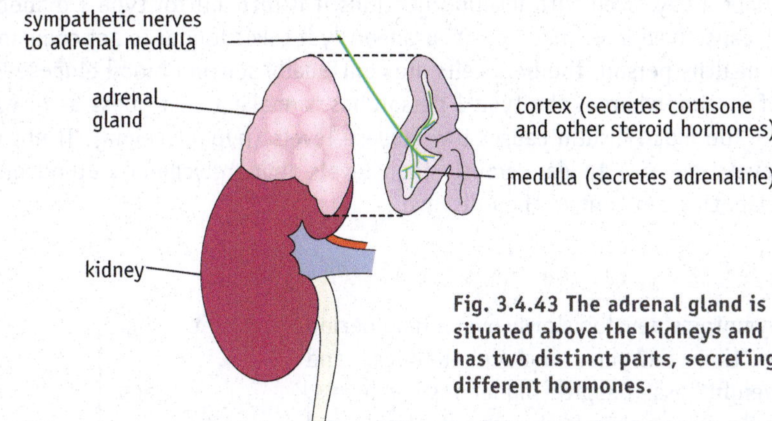

Fig. 3.4.43 The adrenal gland is situated above the kidneys and has two distinct parts, secreting different hormones.

Insulin and glucagon are involved in regulating blood glucose under normal conditions such as after meals. However, other hormones become involved in times of emergency. **Adrenaline** is secreted by the adrenal medulla in times of sudden fear and danger. Adrenaline has a number of effects, such as increasing heart rate and blood pressure, and also causes rapid breakdown of glycogen in the liver and release of glucose into the blood.

Stress of a different kind occurs in starvation, when the body begins to use its own protein as a source of energy. **Cortisol**, one of many hormones secreted by the adrenal cortex, stimulates the production of glucose from non-carbohydrate sources such as amino acids in proteins.

When things go wrong: diabetes

Diabetes has been known for more than 2000 years, but only in the 1920s was its link with insulin discovered. It is sometimes known as diabetes mellitus because urine can become sugary. Previously a condition mainly affecting older people, type 2 diabetes has now become very common worldwide and is increasing rapidly, even among teenagers.

Two types

Diabetes is actually two different diseases with quite different causes, but similar results.

Type 1 diabetes affects fewer than one person in 100, and is caused by the auto-immune destruction of beta cells, so no insulin is produced. Type 1 diabetes can appear at any age, but most often around age 12.

Type 2 diabetes is caused by food and lifestyle factors as well as genetic influence, and has now reached epidemic proportions. Previously in less than 3 per cent of the population, type 2 now affects from 10 per cent to 30 per cent of some groups, with people of Polynesian and Indian ancestry especially prone to it. In type 2, insulin continues to be produced by the pancreas, but the cells in the body become resistant to it, and as a result inhibit the entry of glucose. Obesity is a major contributor to type 2 diabetes.

Diabetes develops gradually and at its earlier pre-diabetic stages is reversible — if lifestyle changes are made. By the time full diabetes develops it is almost impossible to reverse. When blood glucose falls below 3 mmol/L (hypoglycaemia), the sufferer becomes confused and may become unconscious from lack of glucose supply to the brain. When blood glucose stays above 11 mmol/L (hyperglycaemia), other problems develop.

Some long-term consequences

1. **Kidneys.** When blood glucose levels increase above 11 mmol/L, glucose starts to appear in the urine. This creates an osmotic imbalance and so more water starts to move out of the blood, causing excessive volumes of urine — which in turn creates excessive thirst. More seriously, high blood glucose levels also cause permanent damage to the glomeruli (Unit 4). Diabetes is the biggest cause of kidney damage and of people needing dialysis.
2. **Ketosis.** Diabetes results in by-products known as ketone bodies, which tend to reduce blood pH and become physiologically dangerous. Ketones can cause the breath of badly controlled diabetics to smell of nail polish remover.
3. **Eyes.** Diabetes eventually causes peripheral vascular disease (PVD) — damage to small blood vessels. This can result in damage to the retina (retinopathy), which leads to blindness.
4. **Circulation.** PVD also causes problems to blood supply to feet and hands. Persistent infections and gangrene set in, and a high proportion of advanced diabetics need amputations.
5. **Heart.** Diabetes is linked to increased chances of coronary artery disease (atherosclerosis).

Treatments for type 1 diabetes

Type 1 diabetics have to monitor their food intake very carefully, and also inject insulin subcutaneously, several times a day. Even with insulin injections it is difficult for type 1 diabetics to properly control their glucose levels. Because insulin is injected subcutaneously it takes longer to act compared with insulin secreted by the pancreas. In a healthy person, the beta cells are continually sensing blood glucose levels and so release just the right amounts of insulin, whereas the type 1 person has to make a best guess as to when to inject.

Too much insulin causes low glucose levels (hypoglycemia). If not enough insulin is used, then blood glucose levels can rise to dangerously high levels (hyperglycemia). Blood glucose meters have revolutionised the way diabetics can control their disease.

Type 2 diabetes: diagnosis and causes

Symptoms develop slowly over a long period of time and may include tiredness and weight loss. Despite higher insulin levels, cells do not absorb glucose effectively and glucose levels rise. The situation is known as insulin resistance and if untreated can lead to full-blown diabetes. The incidence of type 2 is rising dramatically worldwide and is linked with 'modern' foods and a lack of exercise.

Diagnosis of type 2 is now based on a blood test for glycosylated haemoglobin. Previous tests involved taking an oral glucose tolerance test (OGTT) before eating in the morning. This starts with a drink containing 75 g glucose, followed by monitoring blood glucose for several hours. Sample results are shown in Fig. 3.4.47.

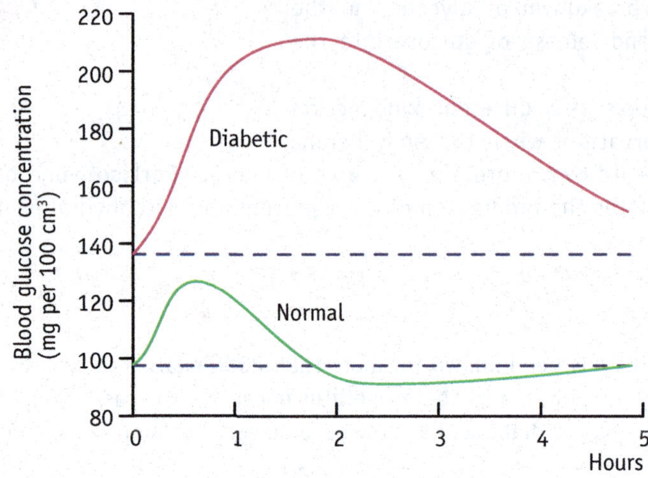

Fig. 3.4.44 Changes in blood glucose after OGTT, in a normal person and in a diabetic person.

4

Type 2 prevention

Once type 2 diabetes has developed to a certain point, it inevitably deteriorates because cells have already become resistant to insulin. However, diabetes is not accidental and not inevitable. Type 2 is mainly caused by lifestyle choices, which means that prevention is possible. The main recommendations, starting in childhood, are:

- an active lifestyle with regular exercise, avoiding couch potato habits
- eat less food in total, as obesity is a major risk factor
- eat less high-sugar food, especially fewer drinks that contain over 5 per cent sugar
- when faced with a choice of starchy foods, choose ones with a low glycaemic index (GI), as they are digested and absorbed more slowly and reduce the 'sugar rush' effect. Example: wholemeal bread instead of soft white bread.

 ISBN: 9780170355582

Check your understanding

1 Write matching words in the blank column. Choose from this list: *polysaccharide, sucrose, hyperglycaemia, glucagon, glycogen, insulin, monosaccharide, hypoglycaemia, mitochondria, liver.*

a	A word for single six-carbon sugars such as glucose	
b	Carbohydrates starch and glycogen are in this category	
c	The destination of blood in the hepatic portal vein	
d	Describes high blood glucose levels	
e	Secreted by beta cells and reduces blood glucose	
f	Secreted by alpha cells and raises blood glucose	
g	Describes low blood glucose levels	
h	Example of a double sugar with 12 carbon atoms	
i	Where glucose metabolites are eventually used	
j	Chemical form in which surplus glucose is stored	

2 Predict the effect in each of the following situations by writing *increases* or *decreases* or *no effect.*

a The effect of increased blood glucose on insulin production. ____________

b The effect of increased insulin production on blood glucose levels. ____________

c The effect of liver glycogen on insulin production. ____________

d The effect of increased adrenaline production on blood glucose levels. ____________

e The effect of increased blood glucagon on liver glycogen. ____________

f The effect of increased blood glucagon on blood glucose levels. ____________

g The effect of exercise on glucagon production. ____________

h The immediate effect of sugary meal on insulin production. ____________

i The immediate effect of a purely protein meal on insulin production. ____________

3 Complete the following sentences.

a Surgical removal of the pancreas has serious health consequences because

____

____

b Insulin and glucagon have antagonistic effects, which means that

____

____

c Type 2 diabetics often cannot be helped by insulin injections because

____

____

d The liver is anatomically well placed to regulate the amount of blood glucose after a meal because

____

____

9780170355582

4 Calculate (in grams) the total amount of blood glucose circulating in a person who has 5 L blood and normal mid-range glucose levels.

____

5 Describe exactly where insulin is produced, and also describe what kind of substance it is chemically.

____

____

6 Explain the survival value of adrenaline's effect on glycogen in the liver.

____

____

____

7 Explain why diabetes sometimes leads to limb amputation.

____

____

____

8 Explain what is meant by 'low-GI' foods, and suggest how they can help prevent diabetes from developing.

____

____

____

____

9 Use the graph showing blood glucose and insulin levels over 24 hours (Fig. 3.4.39) to provide figures on (state the units in each case): **a** the lowest glucose level ____________ **b** the highest glucose level ____________ **c** the approximate time delay between a meal and a rise in blood glucose ____________ **d** the approximate time delay between an insulin peak and a blood glucose decline ____________.

10 Complete this diagram by writing a few words in each box. The 'external' box has been done for you to indicate what is needed in the others.

external change: sugary meal eaten

sensor	**controller**	**effectors**	**output:**

____________ reverses the original changes

ISBN: 9780170355582

Unit 6 | O_2 and CO_2 control

What happens to your body when you get aerobically fit? How is it that two people the same weight can walk up the same hill at the same speed with one struggling for breath and the other not? A background to these and other questions is covered in the next few pages.

Cell respiration

Almost all living things — including humans — depend on energy released from complex reactions involving glucose and oxygen. These reactions occur in two stages: first **glycolysis**, and then **respiration**. Also known as **aerobic respiration**, the second stage happens inside **mitochondria**. Together these reactions release 17 kJ energy from each gram of glucose, and can be simplified as follows:

glucose + oxygen → water + carbon dioxide + lots of energy

A similar chemical process releases energy without the help of 'free' oxygen. It is known as **anaerobic metabolism** (sometimes incorrectly called anaerobic respiration) and can be simplified as follows:

glucose → lactic acid + a small amount of energy

Humans 'switch on' these anaerobic processes only when oxygen supply is insufficient to meet the demand for energy, such as when running fast.

The CO_2 produced by respiration is removed from the cells and eventually from the body. The rest of this unit deals with the supply of O_2 and the removal of CO_2.

Gas exchange

Gas exchange is the diffusion of O_2 and CO_2 in opposite directions across a surface. Most animals have specialised surfaces for this role: gills in fish, **lungs** in mammals. In mammal lungs, trachea and bronchi are surrounded by rings of cartilage to keep them from being squashed. **Bronchi** lead to a system of **bronchioles**: air tubes less than 1 mm across, and with no cartilage rings. (See later information on asthma.)

Bronchioles lead to **alveoli**, tiny air-filled endings where the actual gas exchange happens. There are about 300 million in each lung, each surrounded by a dense capillary network (Fig. 3.4.45). Capillaries and alveoli have extremely thin walls so that air and blood are separated by only 0.5 µm — a distance less than one tenth the diameter of a red blood cell. Each capillary lies between adjacent alveoli, so capillaries are actually surrounded by air.

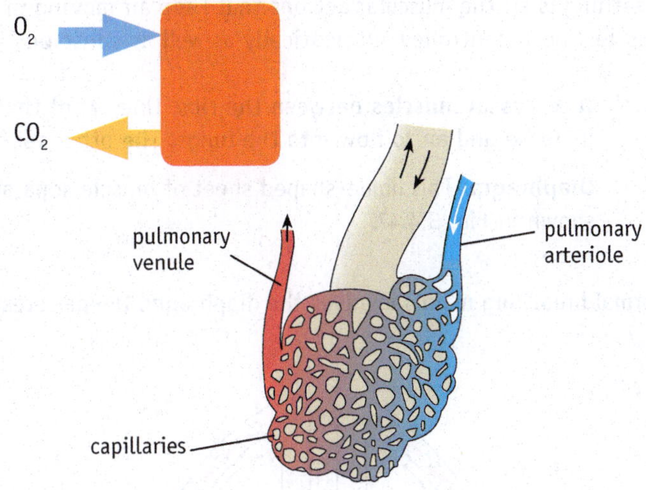

Fig. 3.4.45 A capillary network surrounding a cluster of alveoli (singular: alveolus).

Blood cells passes through each capillary in less than a second, and in this brief time O_2 is loaded into the blood and CO_2 is unloaded. Oxygen diffuses from the air to blood plasma and then into red blood cells, where it combines with haemoglobin to form **oxyhaemoglobin**. At the same time, CO_2 diffuses out of the blood and into the alveoli.

9780170355582

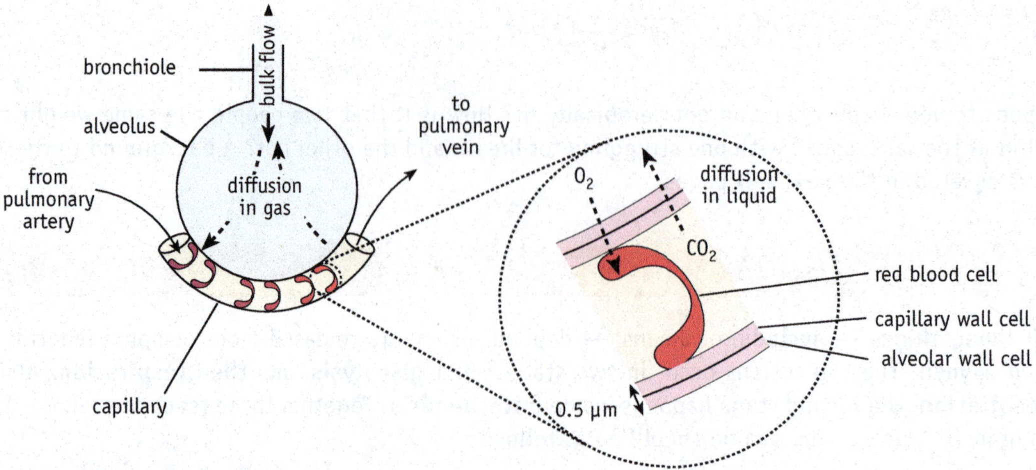

Fig. 3.4.46 One alveolus with one nearby capillary, showing the paths of O_2 and CO_2 diffusion. Red blood cells are briefly bent into U shapes as they squeeze along the capillary.

During quiet breathing only about one tenth of alveolar air is changed at each breath, which explains why it has more CO_2 and less O_2 than inhaled 'outside' air, as the table shows.

Gas	Inhaled air	Exhaled air	Alveolar air
O_2	21%	17.4%	13.8%
CO_2	0.04%	4.5%	5.5%

Breathing

4

Breathing is all the muscular actions that keep air moving in and out of the lungs. There are two sets of breathing muscles, both controlled automatically as well as consciously:

- **Intercostal muscles** between the ribs. One set of these moves the ribs up, causing the chest volume to increase and air to flow into the lungs. The other set of intercostal muscles does the reverse.
- **Diaphragm.** This dome-shaped sheet of muscle separates the abdominal and chest cavities. Its action is shown in Fig. 3.4.47.

Normal breathing mainly involves the diaphragm. Deeper breathing involves all three sets of muscles named above.

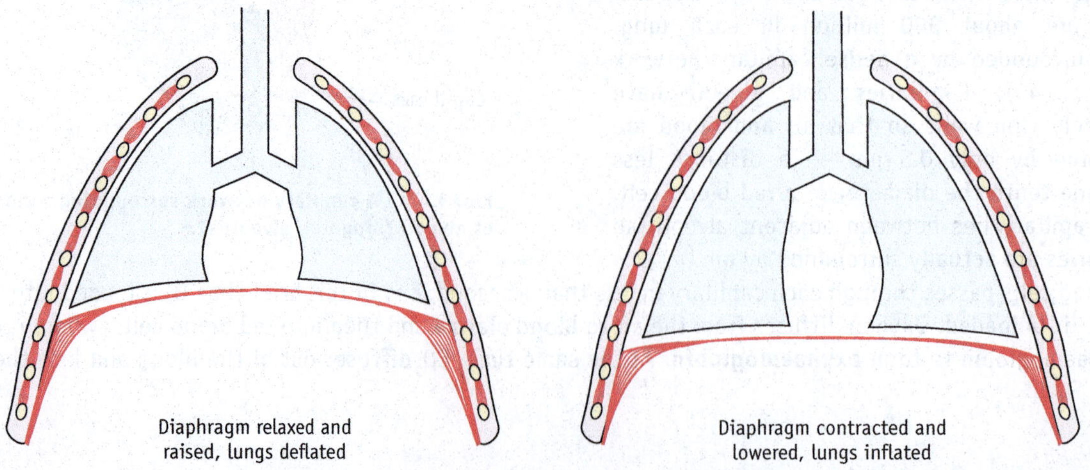

Fig. 3.4.47 When the diaphragm relaxes it moves up, pushing air out of the lungs. When the diaphragm contracts it moves down again, expanding the lungs, causing air to enter.

ISBN: 9780170355582

Homeostatic control

In healthy individuals the O_2 and CO_2 content of tissue fluid remains almost steady, despite frequent changes in the rate of cell respiration. This is achieved by regulating:

- the rate and depth of breathing (control details are given below)
- cardiac output, and also the distribution of blood to different body parts (Unit 3).

Most of the time breathing is automatic. A **breathing centre** in the medulla (base of the brain) has two centres. The **expiratory centre** is normally only active at times of high oxygen demand. The **inspiratory centre** uses different nerves to communicate with the diaphragm and the intercostals muscles.

At rest, you take about 14 breaths a minute, 0.5 L each breath; a ventilation rate of about 7 L a minute. At times of peak activity this can rise to over 150 L a minute. The control system sensors (in the medulla) are very sensitive to changes in blood CO_2, but not very sensitive to changes in O_2. (There are O_2 sensors known as carotid bodies.)

When your muscles are working hard they demand more oxygen, and levels of CO_2 in the blood begin to rise at the same time. Technically speaking, the breathing centre is responding to slight changes in **blood pH**, not to CO_2 itself. Explanation: CO_2 combines with water in the plasma to form carbonic acid, a weak acid. Although it has an important effect, the pH change is very slight; blood pH ranges between 7.35 and 7.45.

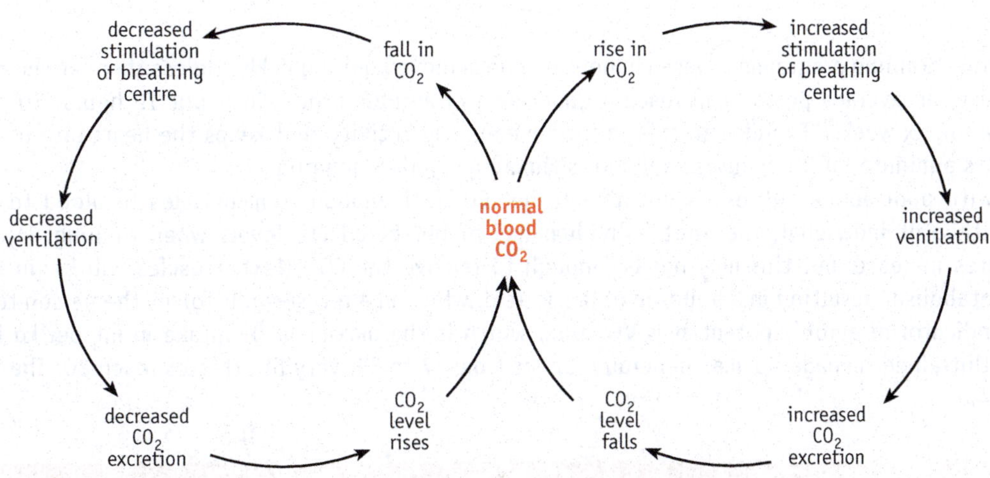

Fig. 3.4.48 Homeostatic control of CO_2 levels in the blood.

What happens during exercise

During high-energy activity such as a training session, several changes affect the rates at which CO_2 is supplied and CO_2 removed:

- **cardiac output** increases up to five times (see Unit 3)
- artery **vasoconstriction** reduces blood flow to less essential regions such as the gut
- artery **vasodilation** (= opening) increases blood flow to hard-working muscles
- autonomic nerves cause generalised vasoconstriction throughout the body, thus raising **blood pressure**
- increased CO_2 and lactic acid production in hard-working muscles causes **haemoglobin** to unload more oxygen than it does in resting muscle.

Aerobic fitness

There are many aspects to physical fitness, including muscular strength and joint flexibility. Aerobic fitness is the only aspect dealt with here. As you become aerobically fitter, the following changes occur, all of them acting to improve the rates of supply of O_2 and removal of CO_2.

- **A** Changes in the **lungs**, which result in faster uploading of O_2 and downloading of CO_2.
- **B** Increased **cardiac output**.
- **C** Increased **VO_2 max** (see below). However, there is little change in the haemoglobin count or in the number of red cells per cubic millimetre. Normal haemoglobin range is 12–18 g/100mL blood.
- **D** Increased capillary density in **body muscles**, which results in faster loading of CO_2 into the blood and downloading of O_2 from the blood.

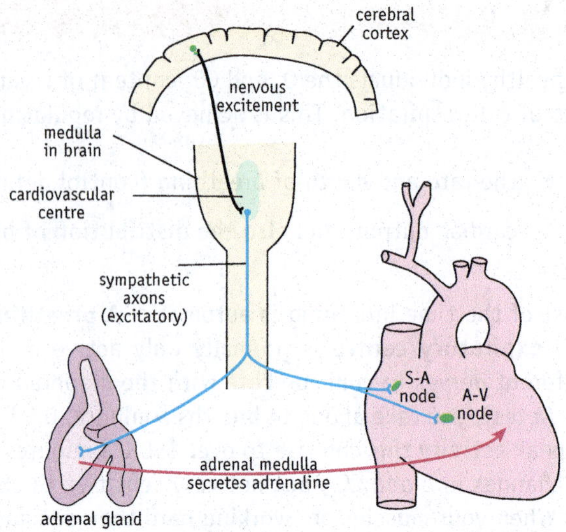

Fig. 3.4.49 Nerve control of the heart during exercise. Under resting conditions, the heart's own pacemaker maintains a steady pulse rate.

With a moderate training programme these changes can be achieved quite quickly. Unless there are medical reasons not to exercise, an average person can reach a good level of aerobic fitness in about 12 hours: 30 minutes four times a week for six weeks. 'Exercise' in this context means any activity that keeps the heart rate in the range of 120–150 beats a minute for 30 minutes: walking, swimming, cycling, jogging.

Anyone with poor aerobic fitness is not able to get CO_2 fast enough from muscles to blood to exhaled air. Compared with a fit individual, the unfit individual has higher blood CO_2 levels when running. Heart rate and breathing rates increase, but this may not be enough to remove the CO_2. Next, muscles will begin to switch to anaerobic metabolism, resulting in a build-up of lactic acid, which in a few seconds forces the person to slow down.

A good indicator of aerobic potential is **VO_2 max**, which is the maximum O_2 uptake in mL per kg body weight per minute. Untrained teenage VO_2 max generally ranges from 37 to 55. Very fit athletes reach 80. The highest ever measured: 94.

When things go wrong

1. **Bronchitis** is inflammation of the bronchi air passages. Result: lots of coughing. Acute bronchitis is caused by viral or bacterial infection, and is often linked to damp cold conditions. Chronic bronchitis is linked to smoking.
2. **Asthma** is brought on by contraction of the muscles in the bronchioles, which causes these airways to become narrower, resulting in wheezing and gasping. Asthma is triggered by a combination of factors, including allergies, but medical science is not certain why it has become so common in recent years.
3. **Emphysema**, also known as chronic obstructive pulmonary disease (COPD), is almost always caused by smoking. Worldwide, it is a major cause of early death.
4. **Pleurisy** is an inflammation of the moist double-layered membrane that surrounds the lungs and lines the rib cage. The condition can make breathing extremely painful, but seldom lasts long.
5. **Pneumonia** involves inflammation of the alveoli and bronchioles, which can start to fill up with fluid, severely limiting oxygen uptake. It is mostly caused by bacterial or viral infections. Although less common than in the past, pneumonia can be fatal if not successfully treated.

ISBN: 9780170355582

E

Into thin air

At all altitudes the proportions of different gases in the air remains the same. At 2000 metres the air pressure is 80 per cent of sea level pressure, which means 20 per cent less O_2 per litre. Air pressure at 4000 m is 63 per cent that of sea level; at Everest summit 33 per cent.

Acute mountain sickness (AMS) can begin as low as 2000 m in some people, 4000 m in others. AMS can happen even in those who are aerobically very fit. It results in headaches, dizziness, fatigue, nausea, confusion. AMS can be a prelude to pulmonary and cerebral oedema, both of which can be fatal. The only effective treatment is rapid descent. The best prevention is slow ascent, no more than 300 m per day, which gives the body time to adjust. For more details, visit altitude.org.

When a person moves from sea level to high altitude, heart and breathing rates increase immediately. Over the following weeks and months a number of other adjustments develop:

- The lowered oxygen level is detected by the **carotid bodies** at the bases of the internal carotid arteries, stimulating breathing and increasing oxygen uptake. It also increases the rate of CO_2 excretion, lowering the CO_2 level of the blood and raising its pH. This would reduce the stimulus for breathing, were it not for the breathing centre becoming less sensitive to a fall in CO_2.
- The haemoglobin content of the blood rises as a result of an increase in the red cell count from 5 million/mm^3 to over 7 million. This is brought about by the hormone **erythropoietin** (EPO), secreted by the kidney.
- The concentration of a substance called **2,3-BPG** in the red cells increases, causing the haemoglobin to release oxygen more readily in the tissues.
- Skeletal muscle fibres become narrower, which decreases the diffusion distance between capillaries and mitochondria.

Some endurance athletes cheat by dosing themselves with EPO, although they might get the same result by training at high altitude. Though EPO enables the blood to carry more oxygen, it carries a risk of heart attack as the blood becomes more viscous.

Fig. 3.4.50 Climbing a 6000 m peak in Nepal. Oxygen enrichment can delay AMS, but some CO_2 is essential. Pure oxygen under pressure is toxic.

Why CO_2?

Why is the breathing centre very sensitive to CO_2 but not to oxygen? Explanation: the proportional changes in CO_2 are much greater. Compared with inhaled air, alveolar air has over 100 times more CO_2 (5.5/0.04), but only a small drop in O_2 (13.8/21). This is probably why land mammals have evolved CO_2 sensitivity, but not O_2 sensitivity. Diving animals like whales and seals are much less sensitive to CO_2 in the blood, which enables them to hold their breath far longer than land mammals can.

4

Check your understanding

1 Write the matching words in the blank column. Choose from this list: *emphysema, oxyhaemoglobin, intercostals, anaerobic, medulla, bronchi, erythropoietin, bronchioles, diaphragm, vasoconstriction.*

a	Two sets of muscles between ribs	
b	Muscle sheet between abdomen and thorax	
c	Form in which O_2 is transported in blood	
d	Responsible for making more red cells	
e	Location of the breathing control centre	
f	Can reduce blood supply to an organ	
g	Chronic obstructive pulmonary disorder	
h	Larger air passages with cartilage rings	
i	Smaller air passages with no cartilage	
j	Metabolic processes producing lactic acid	

2 Complete the following sentences.

a Capillaries and alveoli have extremely thin cell linings because

b When the diaphragm relaxes and moves upwards, it has the effect of

c When the diaphragm contracts and moves downwards, it has the effect of

d Blood carbon dioxide levels tend to rise when

e The breathing centre's response to a slight rise in carbon dioxide is to

3 List four main changes that happen to the body when a person becomes fit (write fewer than eight words on each change).

ISBN: 9780170355582

4 The following are stages in the movement of oxygen from air to mitochondria. (CO_2 travels in the opposite direction, but is not shown. Stage * takes a few seconds, the other stages fractions of a second.) Arrange the following six stages in sequence by writing them in the blank spaces provided. *Diffuses into mitochondria, Combines to form oxyhaemoglobin, Unloaded from blood, Oxygen diffuses into the plasma, Diffuses into muscle cells, Transported in the blood*.*

Oxygen in the air in the alveoli, then:
1
2
3
4
5
6

5 Write a word equation that simplifies the process of aerobic respiration.

6 State the main difference between the requirements of aerobic and anaerobic metabolism.

7 Calculate the ventilation rate of a runner taking 25 breaths a minute, 2 L per breath.

8 Explain why blood pH falls slightly when the body's oxygen consumption increases.

9 A trained athlete of 70 kg has a VO_2 max of 80. Calculate total oxygen consumption (in litres) at this rate, over 15 minutes of maximum effort.

10 Complete this feedback diagram by writing in the responses in each white box to represent how your body responds to increased CO_2 levels in the blood.

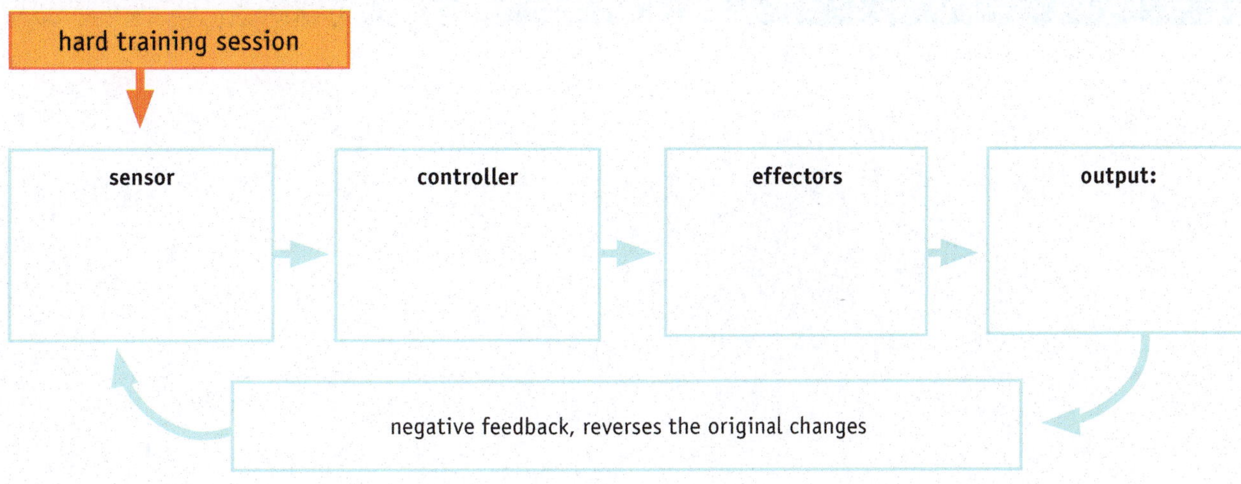

Biology 3.4 Internal environment control

NCEA Achievement Standard 91604: Demonstrate understanding of how an animal maintains a stable internal environment

Internally assessed, 3 credits

Achievement	Achievement with Merit	Achievement with Excellence
Demonstrate understanding of how an animal maintains a stable internal environment.	Demonstrate in-depth understanding of how an animal maintains a stable internal environment.	Demonstrate comprehensive understanding of how an animal maintains a stable internal environment.

Achievement
'Demonstrate understanding ...' involves using biological ideas to describe a control system by which an animal maintains a stable internal environment. Annotated diagrams or models may be used to support the description.

Achievement with Merit
'Demonstrate in-depth understanding ...' involves using biological ideas and/or scientific evidence to explain how or why an animal maintains a stable internal environment. This includes explaining how a specific disruption results in responses within a control system to re-establish a stable internal environment.

Achievement with Excellence
'Demonstrate comprehensive understanding ...' involves linking biological ideas about maintaining a stable internal environment in an animal. This includes at least one of:

- a discussion of the significance of the control system in terms of its adaptive advantage
- an explanation of the biochemical and/or biophysical processes underpinning the mechanism (such as equilibrium reactions, changes in membrane permeability, metabolic pathways)
- an analysis of a specific example of how external and/or internal environmental influences result in a breakdown of the control system.

4

A control system that maintains a stable internal environment (homeostatic system) refers to those that regulate:

- body temperature
- blood pressure
- osmotic balance
- level of blood glucose
- levels and balance of respiratory gases in tissues.

The biological ideas related to the control system includes the:

- purpose of the system
- components of the system
- mechanism of the system (how it responds to the normal range of environmental fluctuations, interaction and feedback mechanisms between parts of the system)
- potential effect of disruption to the system by internal or external influences.

Environmental influences that result in a breakdown of the control system may be external influences such as extreme environment conditions, disease or infection, drugs or toxins, or internal influences such as genetic conditions or metabolic disorders.

ISBN: 9780170355582

Evolutionary processes

Unit 1 | Evolution basics

In biology the word 'evolution' refers to long-term genetic changes in populations. Although we will never know every detail of Earth's history, evidence points towards two absolute certainties:

- The Earth is very old; about 4.6 billion years.
- Living things change over time. We know that whole groups of animals and plants have become extinct, new species have appeared, and that the genetic make-up of a species can, in some cases, change within a few generations.

Evolution underlies all modern biology. Without an understanding of evolution, biology can become a mass of unconnected information. Evolutionary theory is as important to biology as atomic theory is to chemistry. (The word 'theory' is used here in the scientific sense of 'a central idea that explains many facts'.) Our study of evolution is developed in three stages:

- **Evidence** that evolution has occurred (Unit 1)
- **Selection** — the main 'driving mechanism' of evolution (Units 1 and 2)
- **Speciation** — how genetically different populations and new species arise (Units 3 and 4).

Evidence for evolution

The idea of evolution goes back more than 2000 years. In 1859 Charles Darwin assembled many facts supporting the idea, and much more evidence for evolution has been discovered since then. Four kinds of evidence are given here, with more details available in *Excellence in Biology NCEA Level 3*.

Evidence from comparative anatomy

In many kinds of animal we can find structures that have the same basic pattern, but completely different functions. The best examples are the **pentadactyl** (meaning 'five-finger') limbs of mammals, birds and reptiles — including fossil ones. It is particularly obvious in mammals that have totally different ways of living, yet the same '1-2-5' internal bone structure in their front and back legs. Similarity between groups as different as whales and bats is unlikely to have arisen by coincidence or by design. It can best be explained by all mammals having evolved from one kind of ancestor that had the 1-2-5 arrangement. Evolution tends to modify what already exists. Even horses, which are specialised one-toed runners, have modifications of the same pentadactyl arrangement.

Homologous structures: have the same underlying features but may be specialised for different functions, which indicates shared origins. Example: bat wing and human arm.
Analogous structures: have very similar functions but completely different anatomy, which probably indicates different origins. Example: bat wing and butterfly wing.

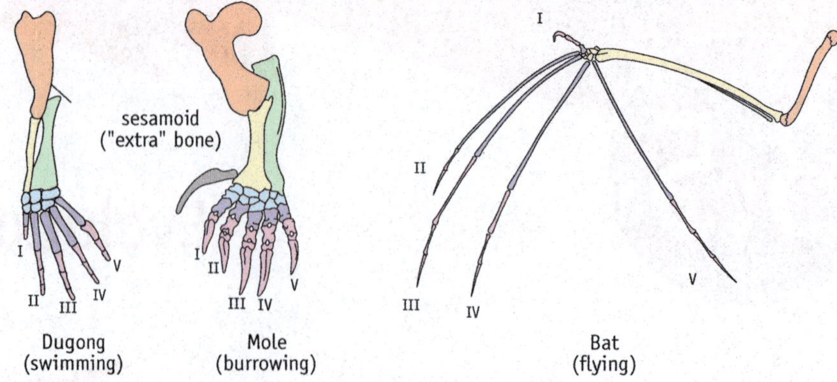

Fig. 3.5.1 The fore-limbs of three very different mammals: adapted for swimming, burrowing, and flying. In all three animals the same underlying component bones are present, but their proportions are very different.

Evidence from fossils

In 1861 a new fossil was discovered in a German quarry. Given the name *Archaeopteryx*, it showed clear reptile features such as a long bony tail and jaws with teeth. But it also had feathers, an obvious bird feature. *Archaeopteryx* is one of many examples of fossils that represent partway links between different groups.

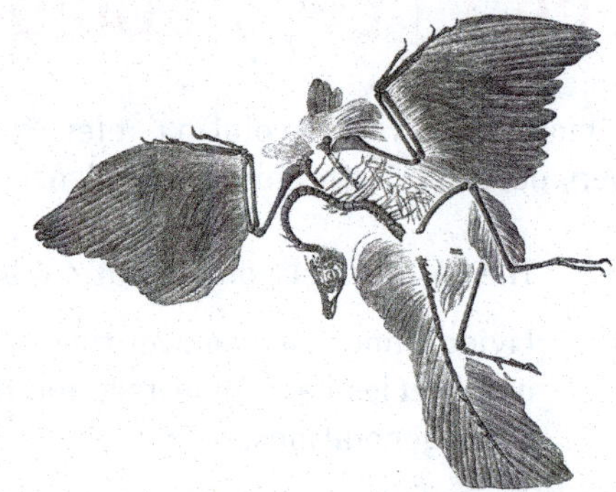

E

Whales have a number of highly specialised features, some of which can be seen in the skeleton of Hector's dolphin (Fig. 3.5.2).

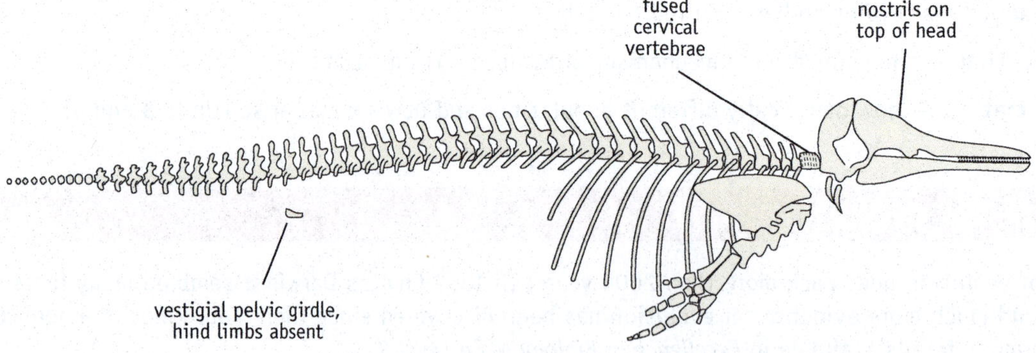

Fig. 3.5.2 Skeleton of Hector's dolphin.

The skeletons of present-day whales include features suited to life in water. For example:

- Hind limbs are absent and the pelvis is vestigial — though the buds of hind limbs are present in the embryo stage, and dolphins are occasionally born with hind limbs.
- Nostrils are at the top of the skull and form the 'blowhole'.
- Inner ear highly modified for detection and direction-finding of sound underwater.
- The seven cervical (neck) vertebrae are fused into a single solid mass.

ISBN: 9780170355582

Whales are descended from land mammals. In recent years a series of fossils has been found intermediate between whales and terrestrial mammals. The drawing shows one extinct type of intermediate stage.

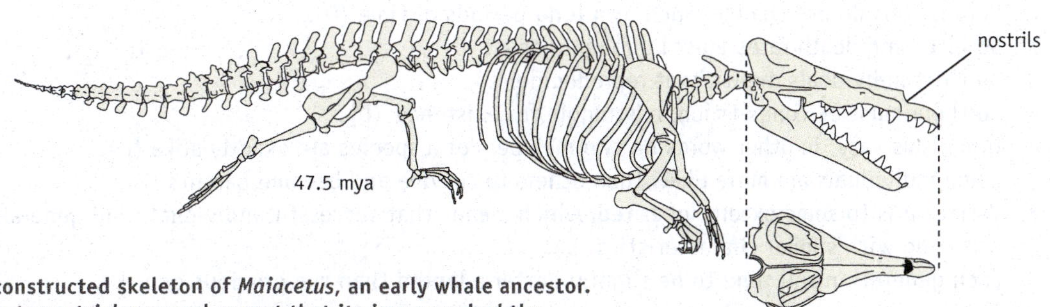

Fig. 3.5.3 Reconstructed skeleton of *Maiacetus*, an early whale ancestor. It resembled a terrestrial mammal except that its inner ear had the characteristic whale specialisations, and its nostrils were partly towards the top of the skull.

Evidence from molecular biology

Recent research has produced huge amounts of information from analysing giant molecules, specifically DNA and proteins. It is now possible to compare the amino acid sequences of proteins, and also the base sequences of DNA in genes that code for these proteins. This kind of evidence enable differences to be expressed as numbers. This takes away difficulties associated with human judgement — it makes comparisons *objective*, not *subjective*. Data can show how much particular sequence differs from other sequences, revealing how closely or distantly any two species are related, as Table 3.5.1 shows.

Species	Number of differences in haemoglobin sequence compared with humans
human	0
gorilla	1
monkey	8
dog	15
kangaroo	38
chicken	45
frog	69

Table 3.5.1 The number of amino acid differences in the beta chain sequence of haemoglobin: seven animals compared.

Evidence from biogeography

Example: the ratites are a southern hemisphere group of birds including ostrich, kiwi, emu, rhea, cassowary and kiwi — all similar in many ways. Being flightless they could not possibly have crossed the vast ocean distances separating them. Best explanation: the ratite group originated in one landmass (Gondwana), which then broke up and drifted apart, with different kinds of ratite then evolving into different types in isolation from each other.

Fig. 3.5.4 Cassowary, a flightless close relative of kiwi.

Darwin and natural selection

In 1859 Charles Darwin published *The Origin of Species*, a book in which he came up with a radically new idea on *how* evolution works. Darwin had never heard of DNA and had little understanding of genetics, so his original ideas have been modified in recent years. However, the central idea has been confirmed by recent evidence.

Darwin's breakthrough was to propose a mechanism for evolution, which he called **natural selection.** His idea was based on a series of observations (O) and deductions (D). These can be summarised as:

1. All organisms can produce far more offspring than are needed to replace the parents (O).
2. Populations do not change much over long periods of time (O).
3. So birth and death rates must be roughly equal (D).
4. So most individuals die without reproducing (D).
5. So there must be competition, a 'struggle for existence' (D).
6. Organisms vary; in other words no two members of a species are exactly alike (O).
7. Some individuals are more likely than others to survive and become parents (D).
8. Variation is to some extent inherited, which means that successful individuals will generally produce offspring with similar characteristics (D).
9. Each generation will tend to be slightly better-adapted than the previous one (D).

Darwin put forward his idea of natural selection as a hypothesis. Scientists now regard his main hypothesis as confirmed, and no one has come up with a better scientific explanation. However, understanding of natural selection has changed since Darwin's time. Important new understandings include:

- DNA and how genes work.
- Darwin saw natural selection in terms of survival. The present-day view is that natural selection depends on reproductive success, not on survival alone.

Natural selection is also known as 'survival of the fittest', though Darwin did not like the expression. 'Biological fitness' is the ability of an animal (or plant) to become a successful parent, which in most situations has nothing to do with 'strength and speed' fitness.

Natural selection is very good at explaining how species evolve and adapt, and how new species appear. Natural selection is not about the origins of life, and biology has very little evidence on this.

Evolutionary change is mostly too slow to be directly observed. However, human effects on the environment have recently been so massive and fast that there are now many examples of rapid evolution in existing life-forms:

- Evolution of resistance to DDT in insects.
- Evolution of resistance to heavy metals in plants in and near polluted sites.
- Evolution of antibiotic resistance in bacteria such as MRSA.
- Evolution of new strains of virus, such as influenza, HIV, Ebola.
- Evolution of a nylon-digesting strain of the bacterium *Flavobacterium* living in wastewater from a nylon factory in Japan. Nylon does not occur in nature, so this is an entirely new feature.

History note 1

Jean-Baptiste Lamarck was one of the first to accept the idea of evolution. In 1809 he proposed a 'use and disuse' theory, attempting to explain how evolutionary change works. He believed that bodily features change in response to need and to use, and that these changes are genetically passed on. Lamarck's ideas have been generally abandoned, because there is no evidence that DNA is changed by need or by lack of need. Kakapo didn't become flightless because they had no need for wings; they became flightless because small-winged individuals that put less energy into flying achieved greater reproductive success.

History note 2

Darwin knew little about how inheritance works, because he had never heard of discoveries made by **Gregor Mendel,** a monk whose life overlapped with Darwin's. Mendel found that genetic material behaves like particles that can be reshuffled into a vast number of different combinations. (We now use the word genes, not particles.) Unfortunately, his discoveries were ignored until 20 years after his death.

ISBN: 9780170355582

Natural selection depends on genetic variety: if all individuals are genetically the same, then selection has nothing to 'work on'. Living things have two ways of creating genetic variety: mutations and sex.

- **Mutations** are uncommon and apparently random events.
- **Sex.** Three features of sexual reproduction cause new gene combinations to appear. (1) The random allocation of chromosomes to gametes that occurs during meiosis; (2) chromosome crossing-over, which also occurs during meiosis; (3) the random encounter of eggs and sperm at fertilisation. Together these features create an almost infinite amount of variation, which explains why children never look exactly like their parents.

These aspects — genetic variation, inheritance, different kinds of mutation — were dealt with in Level 2 Biology, so are not covered again here. However, it may be helpful to revise these topics.

Check your understanding

1 Write matching words in the blank column. Choose from this list: *Lamarckism, speciation, ratites, Archaeopteryx, Mendel, mutations, biogeography, Darwin, sex, pentadactyl.*

a	Discovered the rules of inheritance in the 1800s	
b	Inheritance of body features that are developed by constant use	
c	Suggested that natural selection is the mechanism of evolution	
d	Cause infrequent and sudden changes in genetic variety	
e	Causes genetic differences between offspring	
f	A classification group of birds that includes ostriches, kiwis, emus	
g	A vertebrate limb with a five-digit arrangement	
h	The process by which new species evolve	
i	An extinct animal intermediate between reptiles and birds	
j	Study of the distribution of animals and plants	

2 For each of the pairs listed below, decide whether the two features are **analogous**, or **homologous**, or **both**, or **neither**. Write your one-word answers in the spaces provided.

a monkey hand and bat wing ____________________

b monkey hand and octopus tentacle ____________________

c bat wing and butterfly wing ____________________

d bat wing and whale flipper ____________________

e whale flipper and cat whiskers ____________________

f cat whiskers and insect antenna ____________________

g bat wing and seagull wing ____________________

h seagull wing and penguin flipper ____________________

i bellbird wing and falcon wing ____________________

j mosquito proboscis and human eye ____________________

5

3 This question is based on Table 3.5.1 (see page 137) giving the number of amino acid differences in the beta chain sequence of haemoglobin. Using the figures provided and backing up your answer with figures, evaluate how comparatively close or distant the evolutionary relationship is between:

a monkey and gorilla

b monkey and kangaroo

c dog and kangaroo

d chicken and frog

e gorilla and human

4 Describe what is meant by a 'pentadactyl' limb.

5 Explain why pentadactyl limbs in animals as different as monkeys and bats are considered to be evidence for evolution.

5

6 Describe the part that each of these plays in evolution: **a** mutations, and **b** sexual reproduction.

7 Multiple resistant MRSA bacteria are resistant to almost all antibiotics, a situation that has appeared only in the past 20 years. Explain how this antibiotic resistance may have evolved.

ISBN: 9780170355582

8 'Falcons evolved excellent eyesight because they need it to catch their prey.' Evaluate this statement in terms of how biological evolution works.

9 'Survival of the fittest' is an expression sometimes used. Evaluate 'fittest' and 'survival' in terms of how biological evolution works.

Unit 2 | Genes in populations

Allele frequency

Every individual eventually dies — but genes continue for as long as a species survives. The proportion of different alleles in a population can change for many reasons: migration, early death of some individuals, more successful breeding by others.

This unit explains what can cause changes in the proportions of different alleles in gene pools. The proportion of an allele is also known as its frequency, and we can calculate allele frequencies either as a percentage or else on a 0 to 1 scale. Example: if a small population of kakapo happens to have only one kind of allele for a particular gene, we say the allele's frequency is 1.0 (100%). If all members of a population have the genotype *Aa*, then the frequency of each allele is 0.5.

gene: a unit of inheritance. Chemically, a gene consists of a length of DNA that codes for a polypeptide.
alleles: alternative forms of a gene. Alleles occur in pairs.
genotype: an individual's genetic make-up for a particular pair of alleles.
phenotype: the outward 'expression' of a gene, in some cases visible in a feature such as colour.
genome: all the genes in one individual.
gene pool: all the genes in a population.
population: a group of organisms of the same species living in one area.

Example

The two-spot ladybird beetle exists as two colour forms: red and melanic (black). This colour difference is controlled by a single gene, with the melanic allele (*A*) dominant to red (*a*). Melanic beetles can be homozygous (*AA*) or heterozygous (*Aa*). Red beetles are *aa*.

Fig. 3.5.5 shows an imaginary small population of 8 beetles: 4 red and 4 melanic. Of the 4 melanic beetles, 2 are heterozygous. From this, we can work out the frequency of the *A* allele. There are 8 beetles, each with 2 alleles, making 16 alleles altogether. Of these, 6 are *A* and 10 are *a*, so the proportion of *A* alleles is 6/16 = 0.375 (37.5%). By subtraction, the frequency of *a* must be 0.625, since the two frequencies add up to 1. In this example the frequencies of the two alleles are different, even though the two phenotypes are equal in number.

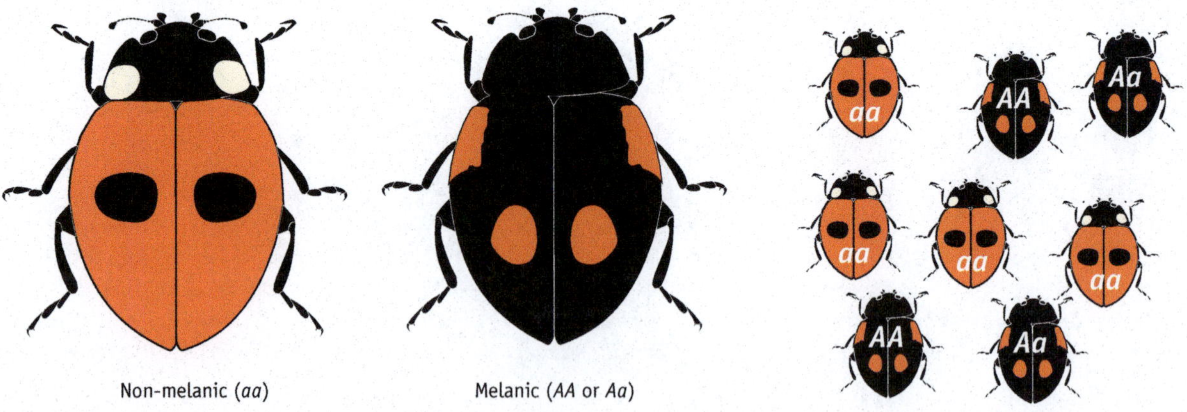

Fig. 3.5.5 Left: Red and melanic (black) forms of the two-spot ladybird. Right: A population of two-spot ladybirds. Red forms are homozygous recessive; melanic is dominant.

ISBN: 9780170355582

Factors affecting allele frequency

Gene pools change over time. Alleles can be removed from a gene pool by death or emigration, and added to the pool by birth or immigration. Overall, changes in gene pools are shaped by two kinds of influence:

- **Selection**. This includes **natural selection**, and also human-guided **selective breeding** (see 3.7, Unit 1).
- **Chance**. Random chance is a feature of genetic drift and the founder effect.

Selection

The end result of natural selection is that certain alleles become more common over time. Other alleles are more likely to be removed, due to early death or failure to breed. Individuals that are consistently more successful in leaving descendants than others are said to be 'fitter'. (The word 'consistently' eliminates chance effects due to small numbers.)

Selection is not efficient, and does not immediately 'weed out' all the less well-adapted individuals. The survival or reproductive advantage of better-adapted phenotypes may be very small, but in the long run some alleles become more common.

Darwin distinguished between two forms of selection in nature:

- **Natural selection**, which causes different survival rates in individual and their offspring.
- **Sexual selection**, which depends on success in finding a mate.

In either case the result is the same: some individuals pass on their genes, others do not.

Whether it relates to survival or to mate-finding, selection can have different results, such as **directional** selection, **stabilising** selection, and **disruptive** selection.

Directional selection

This happens when selection 'pushes' a particular allele frequency to become either more or less common. Directional selection can result in an increase (or decrease) in average size, weight, speed, wing size, ability to resist drought, ability to exploit new kinds of food, etc. The case study on page 144 gives one example in detail. In general this kind of selection can be shown by the graph below.

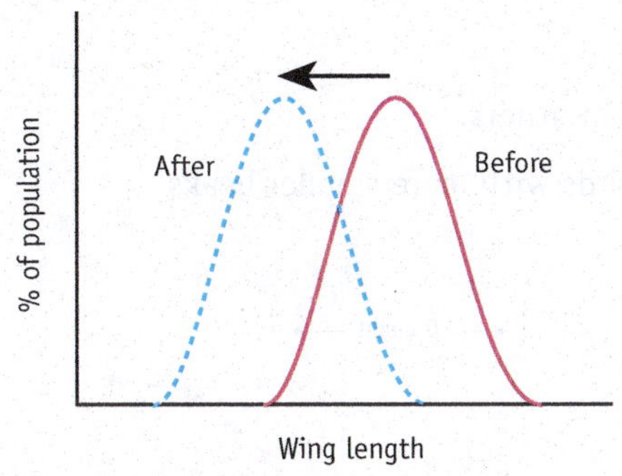

Fig. 3.5.6 Directional selection must have affected kakapo in the past. The graph shows a situation where selection has favoured short-wing phenotypes, with the end result a reduced frequency of alleles for long wings.

Kakapo.

Stabilising selection

Stabilising selection exists where selection favours average individuals. It happens when reproductive success is greatest for average individuals, with extremes being selected against. Stabilising selection is represented by the graph below, which is based on the same research on finches described in the case study. In non-drought conditions, finches with larger beaks tended to die younger, which meant that selection favoured a decrease in beak size. Once beak size had reached a stable optimum, selection favoured birds with average-sized beaks.

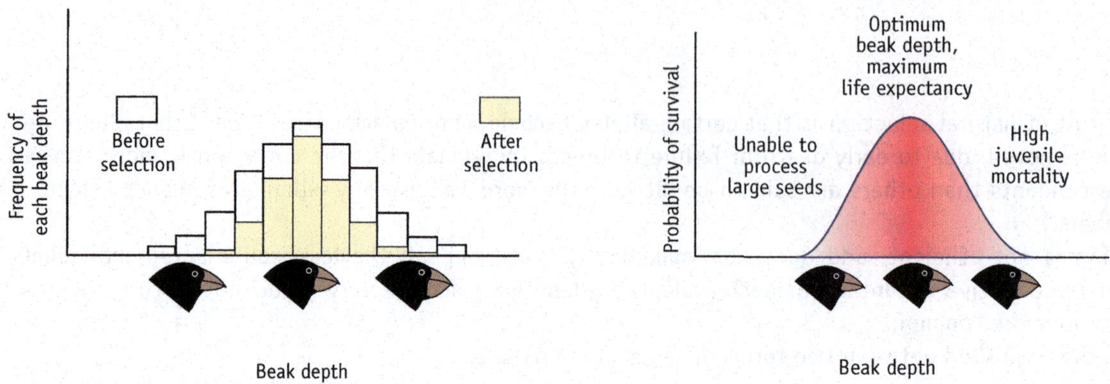

Fig. 3.5.7 Stabilising selection in finches on a Galapagos Island. Beak size differences are exaggerated in these diagrams.

Disruptive selection

This can occur where average individuals are selected against, with higher chances of survival and reproductive success for individuals at the extremes, such as the smallest and biggest individuals.

E

Selection case study

Valuable research has been done on ground finches (*Geospiza fortis*), seed-eating birds that live in the remote Galapagos Islands. For over 20 years, Peter and Rosemary Grant studied these birds on a tiny 34-hectare island, Daphne Major. They caught, measured and banded almost every one of the ground finches on the island. Among their many observations:

- Beak depth varies, some birds having deeper (thicker) beaks than others.
- Birds with deeper beaks tend to feed on larger, harder seeds; birds with more slender beaks preferring smaller seeds that were more easily crushed.

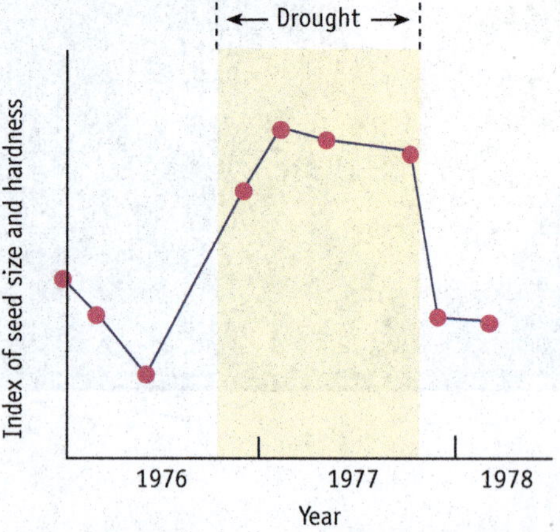

Fig. 3.5.8 Increase in seed size and hardness during a drought.

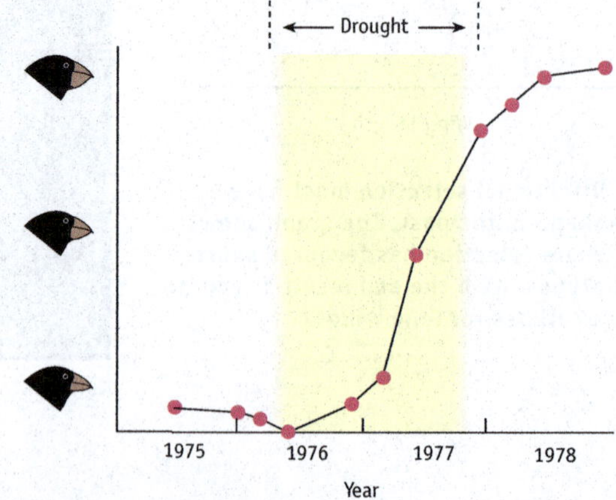

Fig. 3.5.9 Directional selection increased the mean beak depth during a drought.

5

ISBN: 9780170355582

In 1976 a two-year drought began and plants produced fewer seeds. As a result of increased competition for food, smaller seeds were depleted and the proportion of larger seeds rose (Fig. 3.5.8). At the same time the bird population crashed from about 1200 to about 180. Mortality was not random. Because they were able to process the large seeds, birds with deeper beaks had lower death rates compared with birds with more slender beaks. By the time the drought was over, mean beak depth was more than it was at the beginning (Fig. 3.5.9). The Grants found that parents with deeper than average beaks had offspring that resembled them. As a result, average beak depth increased markedly during the drought.

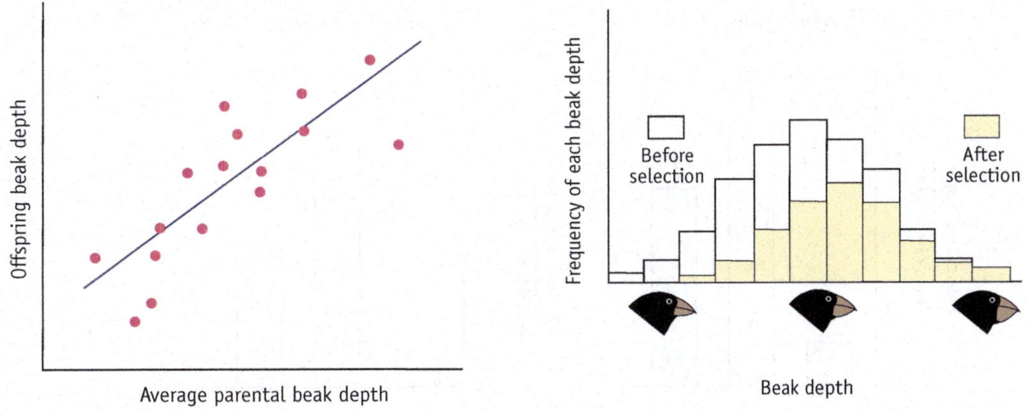

Fig. 3.5.10 The effect of the drought on beak depth in ground finches.

Sexual selection

Sexual selection takes place when some individuals are more successful in attracting mates, and as a result produce more offspring. Sexual selection can take different forms such as:

- **Contest**, where males compete with one another to be chosen by as many females as possible, or else for ownership of a territory in which females choose to rear their young. In most cases these contests take the form of display rituals. Full-on combat is unusual, even in animals with lethal weaponry, probably because even winners can die of wounds.
- **Advertising**, where the most colourful or best-singing males are most attractive to females. This happens in many birds, although in a few types the females are more brightly coloured.

Fig. 3.5.11 A male peafowl's spectacular colours are the result of sexual selection. The situation is presumably a compromise, with the biggest and brightest 'advertisements' often causing early death because these males are less able to escape predators. Not many species have evolved such extreme adaptations as these.

9780170355582

E Sexual dimorphism

In both contests and in advertising, the different mating strategies of males and females may lead to **sexual dimorphism**, a situation in which males and females have evolved different sizes and appearance. The degree of sexual dimorphism is greatest in animals that are polygamous, with each male mating with many females, for example gorillas. In primates that live in pairs, male and female are similar in size and appearance and generally mate for life, for example gibbons.

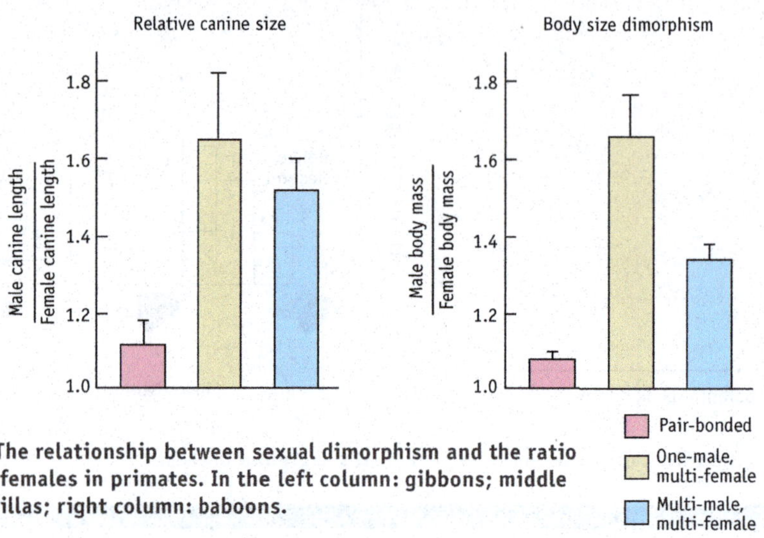

Fig. 3.5.12 The relationship between sexual dimorphism and the ratio of males to females in primates. In the left column: gibbons; middle column: gorillas; right column: baboons.

Chance

Gene pools can be affected by random chance. Example: when a planktonic crustacean is eaten by a whale it is simply a case of being in the wrong place at the wrong time.

Genetic drift

Genetic drift is loss of alleles due to chance events, which in small populations can cause sudden changes in allele frequency. Imagine a population of 20 goats on a remote island, some of them black, some brown. In this small gene pool the alleles for black and brown are equally common, each with a frequency of 0.5. In a landslide, seven goats are killed. As chance has it, five of the seven are brown. This accident will reduce the frequency of the allele for brown colour.

Once a particular allele has low frequency, there is a greater risk of further events wiping it out altogether. New Zealand has many endangered species in considerable danger of allele loss through genetic drift. The Chatham Islands black robin is one such example, at one stage reduced to a single female and four males.

Founder effect

The founder effect occurs in any situation where a few individuals become founders of a large population, which will then have the genes carried by those original few. For example all the wild hares in New Zealand are descendants of six individuals that were introduced and released in the 1800s. Result: very little genetic diversity in their descendants, compared with the 'source' population in Europe.

Genetic bottlenecks

A bottleneck occurs in any situation where a large population crashes to near extinction, then recovers. The new population will have only the genes of the surviving few, so little genetic variability. New Zealand provides many examples. Little spotted kiwi were heading for extinction, so five individuals were put on predator-free Kapiti Island in 1912. This saved the species, but caused a genetic bottleneck in the 2000-plus that survive today.

Micro- and macro-evolution

Everything described in this unit — different types of selection, genetic drift, etc. — can explain small-scale changes in gene frequency. This is known as micro-evolution. Larger scale changes — the evolution of new species and even entire groups of species — is macro-evolution, and is dealt with in Units 3 and 4.

 ISBN: 9780170355582

Check your understanding

1 Matching pairs. Using the blank table below, write the letter of the term that matches the corresponding description.

1	A process in which certain genotypes are more likely to reproduce than others	A	allele frequency
2	All the genes in a population	B	directional selection
3	Change in allele frequency due to chance when a small group splits from parent population	C	founder effect
4	Changes in allele frequency in a small population due to chance	D	gene pool
5	Loss in genetic diversity resulting from an extreme reduction in population numbers	E	genetic bottleneck
6	Selection acting against change in allele frequency	F	genetic drift
7	Selection for ability to obtain a mate	G	selection
8	Selection resulting in a progressive change in allele frequency	H	sexual selection
9	The proportion of an allele in a gene pool	I	stabilising selection
10	All the organisms of one species living and breeding in one area	J	population

1	2	3	4	5	6	7	8	9	10

2 a Identify two factors that can introduce new alleles into a population.

b Identify four factors that can alter the frequency of existing alleles in a gene pool.

3 In a population of 100 sparrows, a gene has two alleles, *B* and *b*. Twenty sparrows have the genotype *BB*, 30 are *bb*, and 50 are heterozygous *Bb*. Calculate the frequency of *B* and *b*.

4 a Describe the similarity between genetic bottlenecks and the founder effect.

9780170355582

b Explain the difference between genetic bottlenecks and the founder effect. Name at least one New Zealand example of each.

5 'Both the founder effect and the bottleneck effect can lead to genetic drift.' Discuss this statement.

6 Tieke (saddlebacks) have been rescued from near extinction.

a Explain what has caused their present low amount of genetic variety.

b Explain why their lack of genetic variety could pose a conservation problem in their future.

5

7 Explain how a peacock's bright colours could be a result of sexual selection. Also explain how its colours could be selected against natural selection.

8 Explain why competition between male lions for breeding opportunities seldom involves full-on combat.

ISBN: 9780170355582

9 Define what is meant by 'stabilising selection'. In fewer than 20 words, describe one actual example.

10 Define what is meant by 'directional selection'. In fewer than 20 words, describe one actual example.

11 Explain how mutations and sex provide the raw material for evolution.

12 Copper is an essential micronutrient for plants and animals, but is toxic in even moderate concentrations. The waste soil around copper mines is heavily contaminated, but *Agrostis tenuis* and other species of grass have evolved tolerance to copper. *Agrostis tenuis* has very small seeds and is wind-pollinated.

Tolerance can be measured in terms of the rate of root growth in solutions containing a standard concentration of copper. The histograms (page 150) show the variation in copper tolerance in adult plants and in plants grown from seeds collected from adult plants, at two sites. One site is copper-mine waste soil; the other is uncontaminated soil 5 metres beyond the edge of the mine waste.

a Describe how the variation in copper tolerance in *Agrostis* differs at the two sites.

b Explain why plants growing in uncontaminated soil show some tolerance to copper.

c Explain why the variation in copper tolerance in waste soil is greater in plants grown from seed than it is in their 'parent' plants.

9780170355582

d In experiments into the competitive ability of copper-tolerant plants, equal numbers of tolerant and non-tolerant plants were grown both separately and together in soil *not* contaminated with copper. All other conditions were the same. When grown separately, tolerant and non-tolerant plants grew at similar rates. When they were grown together, the non-tolerant plants grew more rapidly. Suggest how this fact may relate to your answer to **b**.

____

____

____

____

e Explain how resistance to copper probably evolved.

____

____

____

____

____

____

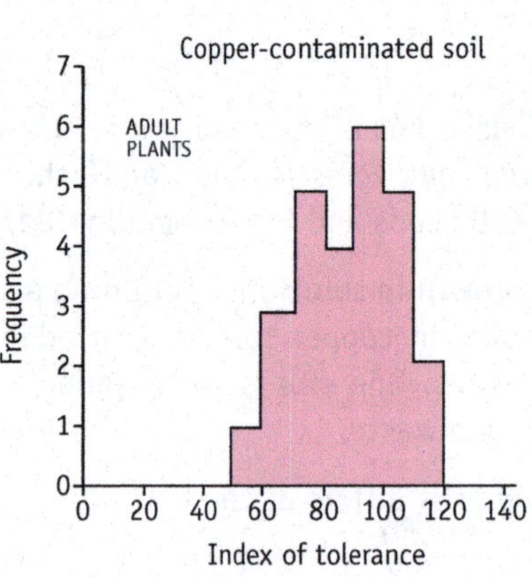

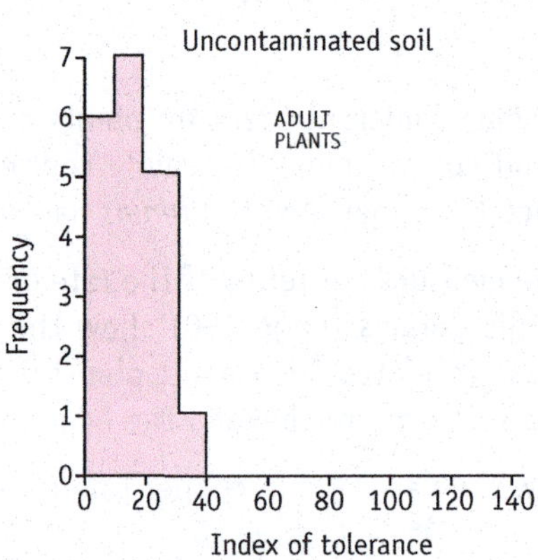

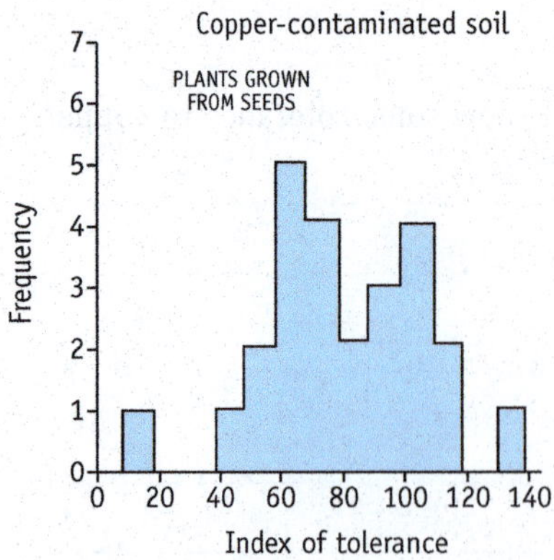

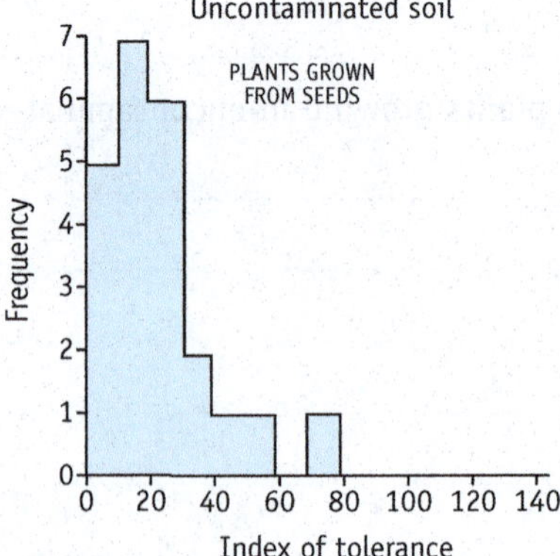

5

ISBN: 9780170355582

Unit 3 | New species

A species is a group of actually or potentially interbreeding natural populations that is reproductively isolated from other such groups. (Definition by evolutionary biologist Ernst Mayr.)

The above definition looks obvious. Everybody knows that goats don't normally breed with sheep; they are different species. But reality can be more complex. Example: zoo lions will interbreed with tigers, yet we don't consider them to be the same species.

Also, species don't always live in areas with clear boundaries. Commonly a species will consist of several localised populations (**demes**), partly isolated from each other by geographical features. Each deme has its own gene pool, and in some cases these demes may remain separate for thousands of years. In other cases individuals move between populations, which keeps gene pools mixed. This mixing is called **gene flow.**

Fig. 3.5.13 Kaka inhabit both North and South Island forests. Being strong fliers, individual birds sometimes move between the islands. This helps maintain gene flow between two slightly different gene pools, and prevents the two populations from evolving into separate species.

Why don't different species interbreed?

Different species don't or can't normally interbreed for at least one of several reasons:

- The species may be **allopatric**, living in geographically different areas with no gene flow.
- The species may be **sympatric** (live in the same area) but are prevented from interbreeding by biological barriers called **isolating mechanisms**. These isolating mechanisms may be **pre-zygotic** (i.e. they prevent fertilisation), or they may be **post-zygotic.**

Most fish and many kinds of marine animals have external fertilisation. Eggs and sperm are poured out into the surrounding water to take their chances, which means a risk that the wrong kind of sperm might fertilise an egg. There are a number of pre-zygotic and post-zygotic ways in which cross-species breeding is prevented.

Fig. 3.5.14 Trout mating. Egg and sperm meet in the surrounding water.

Pre-zygotic isolating mechanisms

These prevent fertilisation happening between related species. Various mechanisms include:

- Different breeding seasons. Example: *Pinus radiata* and *Pinus muricata* release pollen in different seasons.
- Different mating behaviour. They ignore each other's songs and pheromones and other signals.
- Many insect-pollinated flowers can only be pollinated by particular kinds of insect.
- Sperm are unable to fertilise an egg of a different species, either because the sperm cannot survive in their reproductive tract, or because chemical differences prevent the wrong sperm from entering eggs.

Post-zygotic mechanisms

If sperm do fertilise eggs of another species, there are several reasons why the resulting hybrids may fail:

- Hybrid not viable. The zygote may not develop properly, or the hybrid may be weak.
- Hybrid infertility. Hybrids may be perfectly 'fit' in the physical sense, but sterile and therefore biologically unfit. Example: horses (with 64 chromosomes) and donkeys (62 chromosomes) can mate and produce healthy hybrid offspring, known as mules. However, mules are sterile, as they have 63 chromosomes.
- Hybrid breakdown. Example: in certain varieties of rice and in cotton, the F_1 hybrids are fully fertile but the F_2 and later generations have low fertility.

Mule, an example of a sterile hybrid.

Word meanings
zygote = a fertilised egg
sym = together
allo = other, or foreign
patria = fatherland

How do new species arise?

Speciation — the process of new species evolving — can happen in different ways. Note: many biologists consider gradualism to be a different process to speciation.

1 One species slowly changes over time into another, a process known as **gradualism** (aka anagenesis). In these cases an entire population changes without any branching-out. Example: tuatara.

2 **Divergence** (aka cladogenesis), shown here in blue (Fig 3.5.15). One species gives rise to two or more new ones, resulting in more branches of the evolutionary tree. A 'branch' and its several 'twigs' are known as a **clade.** Fossil evidence shows that quite often there are long periods with little change (stasis), and short periods of comparatively sudden change. This kind of situation is known as **punctuated equilibrium.** The ancestral species may become extinct, or it may continue. Bursts of speciation seem to happen when a crucial aspect of the environment suddenly changes. Example: kea and kaka.

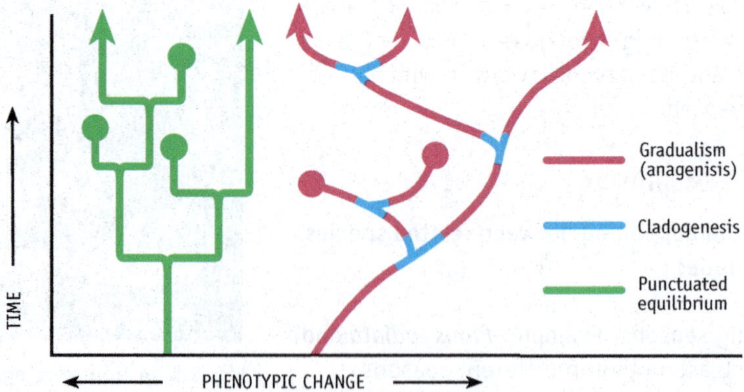

Fig. 3.5.15

Speciation as a result of geographic isolation

Speciation commonly happens where two populations become separated from each other for a long time, isolated by a geographic barrier between them. These barriers can be oceans, mountains, deserts, any unsuitable habitat.

The word for this kind of speciation is **allopatric** ('foreign-land'). If gene flow ceases for long enough and there is a slow accumulation of genetic change, then the two populations will eventually become different species. In some cases speciation can happen in sympatric ('together-land') populations. This is described on page 155.

ISBN: 9780170355582

What could cause two allopatric populations to become genetically different?

- Mutations, which are very unlikely to be the same in two separate populations.
- Natural selection, especially if conditions are different in the two separated areas.
- Genetic drift and the founder effect, especially if one of the populations is very small.

The longer the period of allopatry and the greater the environmental differences, the more different the two populations will become. At earlier stages they can be labelled as 'races' and 'subspecies', but eventually they may become genetically distinct different species.

1. A single population

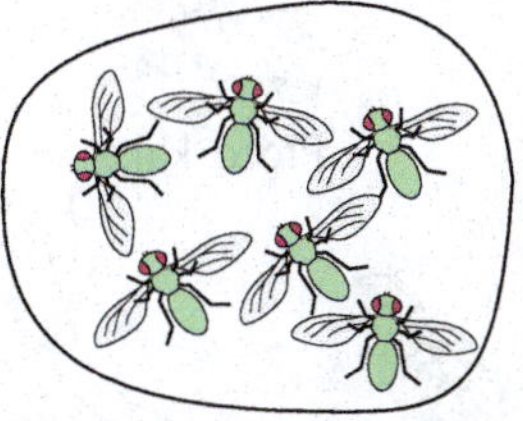

2. Formation of two allopatric populations by some form of geographical barrier

3. Selection pressures in the two populations differ, and since there is no gene flow between them, the gene pools begin to diverge

4. Barrier to gene flow may disappear, allowing the two populations to overlap. They are now two sympatric species.

Fig. 3.5.16 Four stages of allopatric speciation.

Allopatric speciation in parrots

New Zealand wildlife is unique in many ways, such as the absence of land mammals (except for bats), the existence of 'living fossils' like tuatara, plus flightless birds such as kiwi and moa.

The explanation lies in the geological history of New Zealand. About 200 million years ago (mya) there was a southern super-continent, Gondwana. About 70 mya this began to break up into Africa, India, Australia, South America and Antarctica. New Zealand began to split away about 80 mya, before the evolution of mammals, and carrying with it many primitive plants and animals, a sort of 'moa's ark'. After the arrival of humans and with the introduction of mammals, many birds declined or became extinct.

As well as several kinds of small green parakeet (kakariki), New Zealand has three large parrot species:

- kakapo (*Strigops habroptilus*). Flightless, nocturnal, formerly widespread, now highly endangered.
- kea (*Nestor notabilis*). Adapted for mountain habitats, South Island only.
- kaka (*Nestor meridionalis*). Forest parrots, with slightly different North and South Island subspecies.

The ancestors of these parrots diverged into two groups about 60–80 mya, soon after the Tasman Sea was formed (Fig. 3.5.17). One of these two groups gave rise to kakapo. About 3 mya the other group (*Nestor*) split and became two populations: the ancestors of kea and kaka. About 400,000 years ago the kaka group diverged again, giving rise to the North and South Island subspecies. These approximate dates have been inferred from DNA studies.

Kea and kaka are closely related and similar in appearance. We don't know for certain what geographic barriers caused their common ancestor to separate into two groups. It's likely that ice-age climate conditions restricted one population to the South Island, and these evolved into kea. We know that forests were reduced to small patches in the North Island, and it is perhaps here that kaka evolved. When forests slowly spread southwards again, kaka populations moved closer to kea, but were by now too different to interbreed with them.

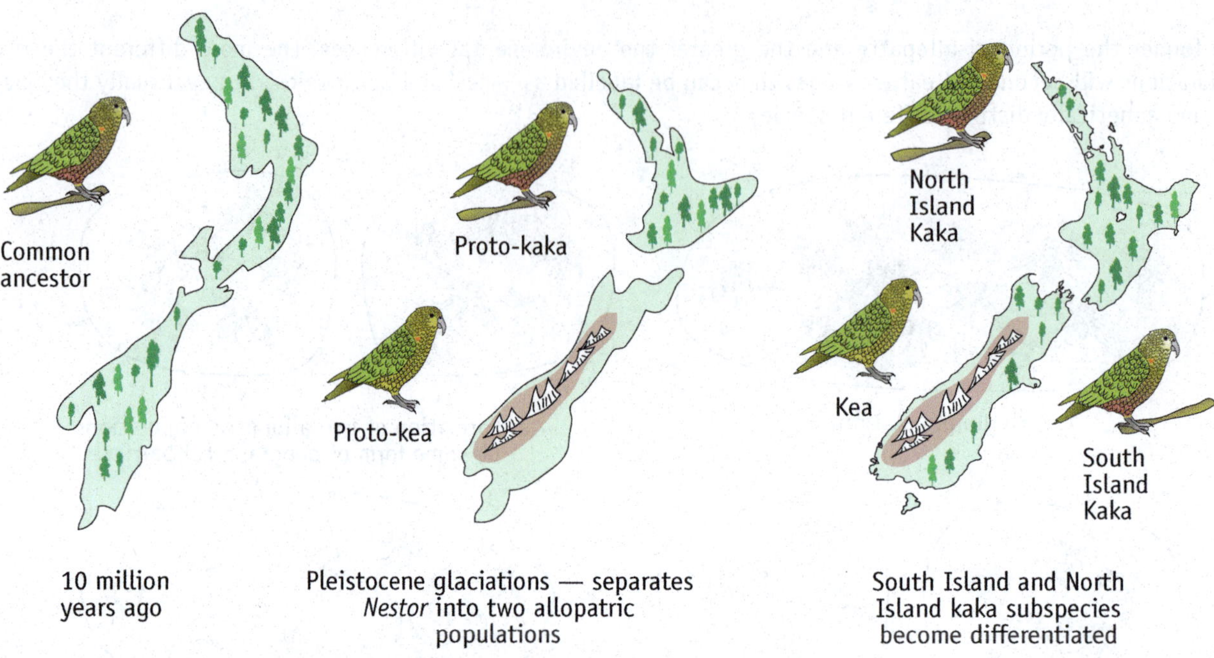

Fig. 3.5.17 Speciation in New Zealand parrots in the genus *Nestor*.

Geographical barriers

Geographical isolation is often not 100 per cent complete. Seeds and insects get blown across oceans, birds fly across deserts. Even barriers like these can be crossed, which means to some extent gene pools are continuously exchanging genes. Over time, geographic barriers like deserts can grow then disappear again. In New Zealand, two factors have been responsible for creating barriers between populations.

Mountain building

The movement of tectonic plates during the last few million years created the Southern Alps. As a result, the South Island became divided into two very different climatic zones, with high rainfall and mild temperatures in the west, and drier with greater temperature extremes in the east.

Associated with mountains are vegetational zones, resulting in ecological 'islands'. Example: in Marlborough and Nelson, the land snail (*Powelliphanta hochstetteri*) occurs as a number of subspecies, each occupying an 'island' of high ground above 650 metres.

Climate change

Climate change can also isolate populations by changes in sea level. During the Pleistocene ice ages, sea level fell worldwide to about 100 metres below what it is today, and New Zealand became a single island. When that ice age ended, terrestrial ice sheets melted and sea level rose, separating a single landmass into islands.

Changes in sea level can isolate freshwater organisms. During the most recent ice age, the Patea, Whanganui, Rangitikei and Manawatu rivers were tributaries of one big river that emptied into the sea at one single mouth. This meant that freshwater fish could move from one river to the other. But when sea levels rose, these tributaries became separated by seawater, which prevented gene flow and caused new species to evolve.

ISBN: 9780170355582

Sympatric speciation

Speciation can happen within one population living in one area, with no geographical isolation. We call this sympatric speciation (*sym* = together, *patria* = fatherland). This is quite common in plants, and is sometimes the result of mutation processes known as polyploidy.

diploid: having two copies of each chromosome in each somatic cell (2*n*); the normal situation
triploid: having three copies of each chromosome (3*n*)
tetraploid: having four copies of each chromosome (4*n*)
polyploid: having multiple copies of each chromosome (3*n*, 4*n*, 6*n*, etc.)
auto-polyploid: if the process happens within one species
allo-polyploid: if the process involves chromosomes from more than one species

Speciation by polyploidy

Polyploidy is any mutation that involves the whole genome, and increases the number of chromosomes to 3*n* or 4*n*. Polyploidy is the result of **non-disjunction**: chromosomes failing to separate properly during cell division. All the chromosomes finish up in the same nucleus, which then has more chromosomes than it should.

Polyploidy is rare in animals but common in plants. Many important food plants are polyploid, including wheat, oats, potatoes. Another example: the New Zealand genus *Melicytus*, which has 11 separate species, one of them the well-known mahoe. Seven *Melicytus* species have 32 chromosomes as their normal diploid number. Two have 64 chromosomes, one has 96, one has 48. All of these are multiples of $n = 16$. Polyploidy can occur suddenly during meiosis or at fertilisation, potentially creating an 'instant species' in all descendants. New polyploid organisms can breed amongst themselves, but not with their parent population.

E

Aneuploidy

Aneuploidy is a situation where cells have extra copies or missing copies of individual chromosomes. (Not copies of the entire genome, as is the case in polyploidy.) Aneuploid mutations can happen during cell division and in most cases the resulting offspring are sterile — as with Down syndrome in humans (47 chromosomes instead of 46, an example of trisomy). Aneuploidy is common in plants, for example in some species of *Hebe* (Unit 4). If tetrasomy happens, the offspring may be fertile, so can potentially give rise to a new species.

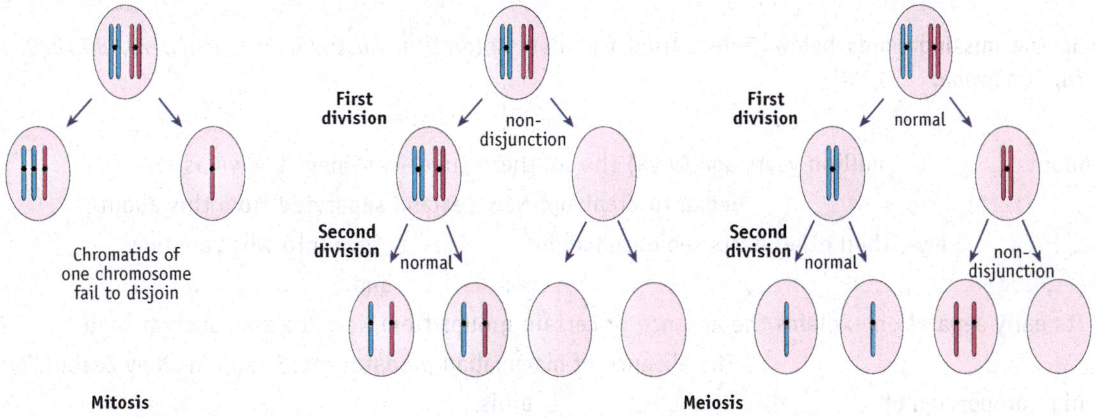

Fig. 3.5.18 Non-disjunction in mitosis and meiosis. Only one chromosome pair is shown.

When non-disjunction occurs in mitosis in a shoot tip, all the descendant cells have the same chromosomal abnormality. If the shoot develops flowers, the gametes will inherit the abnormality. If non-disjunction occurs in meiosis in the stamens or ovules, the gametes may carry the abnormality. Various results are possible:

- If a gamete with an extra chromosome joins with a normal gamete, the zygote will have three copies of the chromosome involved, and will be **trisomic**.
- If a gamete lacks a particular chromosome and joins with a normal gamete, the zygote will have one copy of the chromosome and will be **monosomic**.
- If two gametes both carry an extra copy of a chromosome, the zygote will have two extra copies of the chromosome and will be **tetrasomic**.

5

Check your understanding

1 Matching pairs. Using the blank table below, write the letter of the term that matches the corresponding description.

1	An evolutionary 'branch' and its 'twigs'	A	allopatric
2	Multiple sets of chromosomes	B	clade
3	Group of organisms whose members are sufficiently alike to be able to reproduce and produce fertile offspring	C	polyploidy
4	Inherited feature that tends to prevent species from interbreeding with other species	D	deme
5	Population partly isolated from other populations of the same species	E	isolating mechanism
6	Process by which one species gives rise to two or more species	F	speciation
7	Sharing the same geographical area	G	species
8	Inhabiting geographically separate areas	H	sympatric
9	Before fertilisation	I	gene flow
10	Transfer of individuals and their genes between two populations	J	pre-zygotic

1	2	3	4	5	6	7	8	9	10

2 Fill in the missing words below. Select from this list: *Antarctica, Australia, mammals, 70, 80, 220, flightless, Africa, Gondwana.*

About __________ million years ago (mya) the southern super-continent known as __________________ began to break up. New Zealand separated from this about __________ mya, then other parts separated about __________ mya into what are now __________________, __________________ and __________________. Its early separation explains the absence of certain groups from New Zealand, such as land __________________. The absence of mammalian predators also explains New Zealand's high proportion of __________________ birds.

3 Identify one point of functional similarity between pre-zygotic and post-zygotic isolating mechanisms.

____

____

____

4 List three kinds of pre-zygotic isolating mechanisms.

____

____

____

ISBN: 9780170355582

5 List three kinds of post-zygotic isolating mechanisms.

6 Discuss whether lions and tigers should be placed in the same species. Give at least one reason why this should be the case, and at least two reasons why they should be considered different species.

7 List three examples of geographical barriers that are likely to reduce gene flow.

8 Explain how polyploidy can bring about 'instant' species.

9 a Name one genus in which some species have arisen by polyploidy. __________

b Summarise the evidence that some of these species are in fact polyploid.

10 In Australia the frog species *Litoria ewingii* and *L. verreauxii* are sympatric over part of their ranges, as the map shows. Their mating calls are represented in the four sonogam diagrams underneath the map. It is possible that the mating calls are a reproductive isolating mechanism.

L. ewingi

L. verreauxi

L. ewingi + L. verreauxi

(a) *L. ewingi* (allopatry)

(b) *L. verreauxi* (allopatry)

(c) *L. ewingi* (sympatry)

(d) *L. verreauxi* (sympatry)

a Explain what is meant by 'sympatric'.

b Explain what is meant by 'reproductive isolating mechanism'.

c Using the sonograms, compare the two species calls where they are allopatric.

d Using the sonograms, compare the two species calls in areas where they are sympatric.

e Suggest how selection could have produced the mating call change in the region where the two species are sympatric.

11 This activity relates to pukeko and takahe, two bird species native to New Zealand.

- The species look similar, but do not interbreed even when they live in the same area.
- Pukeko are common birds in Australia, where they are known as swamp hens.
- Swamp hens/pukeko are capable of flying across the Tasman Sea.
- Some pukeko arrived in New Zealand about 400 years ago. Evidence: no pukeko bones before then.
- Takahe have been in New Zealand more than 10,000 years. Evidence: takahe bones found in swamps.

Using the above information, suggest and hypothesise how these two related but genetically distinct species evolved in New Zealand.

5

ISBN: 9780170355582

Unit 4 | Patterns in evolution

Evolutionary rates

Some plants and animals have changed little over time, with dragonflies and tuatara among the living animals that are closely similar to ancestors of 100 million years ago. Brachiopods (lamp shells) have hardly changed at all in 500 million years. In most cases evolution moves faster. Example: fishes in Africa's Lake Victoria, where geological and DNA evidence suggest that approximately 500 new species have evolved in the last 100,000 years — a very rapid rate of speciation.

Fig. 3.5.19 Tuatara have continued in New Zealand with little change, even though similar reptiles became extinct millions of years ago in other parts of the world.

Adaptive radiation

Adaptive radiation is the evolution of many different forms from a common ancestor. Adaptive radiation is one result of speciation — it's not just another name for speciation. Adaptive radiation leads to a number of related species exploiting a diverse range of niches. This 'niche diversity' can come about in different ways, with two categories mentioned here.

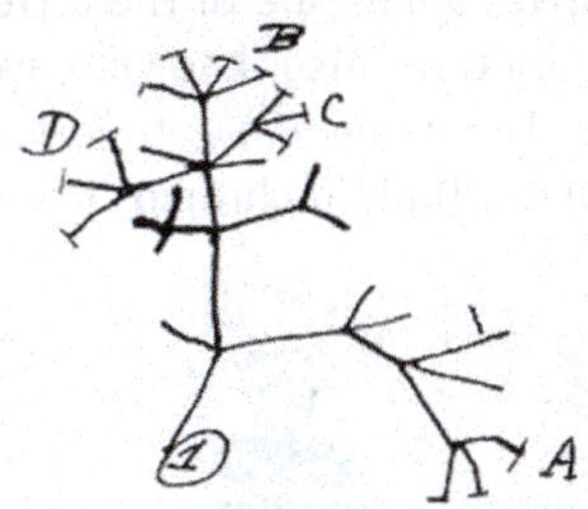

Fig. 3.5.20 The Galapagos Islands of the Eastern Pacific have several finch species, each with a different beak type adapted for a different food. This represents their adaptive radiation. The sketch was done by Darwin in the 1830s when he first began to form ideas about evolution of new species.

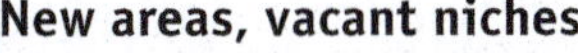

New areas, vacant niches

Vacant niches tend to happen in new areas, and also in areas devoid of competitors. Both situations can favour adaptive radiation. Example: finches in the recently formed Galapagos Islands.

Evolution of new features

This often occurs where newly evolved features equip a species to out-compete others. A 'package' of successful adaptations can be thought of as an evolutionary success story, enabling an ancestral type to produce (over time) many similar but different species, with the whole group having variations on the same ancestral features. Examples: owls (130 species), parrots (350 species).

Fig. 3.5.21 Owls range in height from 12 cm to 50 cm, with all 133 different species sharing the same features: big forward-facing eyes, powerful hooked beak, near-silent flight. They have undergone adaptive radiation into a wide variety of niches worldwide, with different species specialising in different prey, from fish to insects to possums.

5

E

Adaptive radiation in *Hebe*

Hebe is a genus of shrubs with about 90 species, including koromiko. All but one are native to New Zealand, and most are endemic. *Hebe* is one of several closely related genera in Australia, New Guinea and South America. New Zealand species have adapted to a wide range of habitats, ranging from alpine zones to forests to coastal cliffs. Alpine species have to survive strong winds and cold, so tend to be low-growing with small leaves. The evolutionary history of *Hebe* species leads to questions like:

- What are the evolutionary relationships between the species?
- What was the timing of the speciation events?
- What selection shaped the evolution of the 90 species?

Evidence from preserved pollen suggests that *Hebe*-like plants appeared more than five million years ago, corresponding to the rise of the Southern Alps. DNA evidence suggests that most *Hebe* species arose more recently, during the Pleistocene ice ages. The changes in sea level and formation of ecological 'islands' probably played important roles in the geographical isolation that is an essential part of allopatric speciation.

DNA analysis has clarified the evolutionary relationships of various *Hebe* species. The number of base pair differences between two species gives a measure of the difference between them, making it possible to construct the most probable evolutionary tree. Also, knowing average rates of mutation, scientists can put an approximate time scale to the tree. The genus *Hebe*, together with the Australian genus *Derwentia*, are derived from a common ancestor, *Veronica*. Diploid chromosome numbers are shown in brackets.

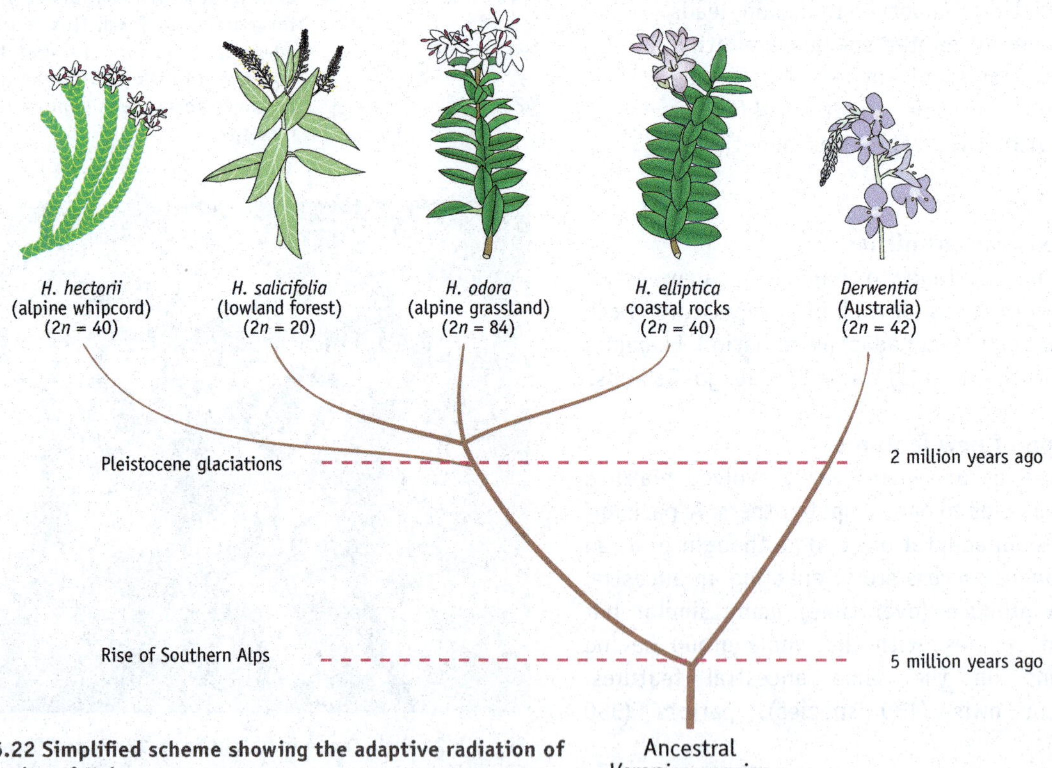

Fig. 3.5.22 Simplified scheme showing the adaptive radiation of four species of *Hebe*.

The original 'founder' of New Zealand *Hebe* probably arrived from Australia, perhaps as seeds carried by birds. Later, the founder population would have become fragmented by changing sea levels, mountain-building, volcanism and glaciation.

Two *Hebe* species are also found in South America: *H. elliptica* and *H. salicifolia*. They have DNA base sequences almost identical to those of New Zealand populations, so must have arrived relatively recently from New Zealand, probably as seeds carried by oceanic birds.

5

ISBN: 9780170355582

Polyploidy

In addition to the allopatric speciation described above, some *Hebe* species very likely originated sympatrically by changes in chromosome number. The common ancestor of the *Hebe* species probably had a diploid chromosome number of 42, as in *H. cupressoides*. If so, those with a diploid number of 84, e.g. *H. armstrongii*, are tetraploid. *H. salicifolia* and *H. elliptica* ($2n = 40$) are nullisomics ($2n - 2$). *H. leiophylla* ($2n = 80$) could have arisen as a tetraploid derivative of such a nullisomic. There are even hexaploids ($2n = 120$, and $2n = 126$), which probably arose through hybridisation followed by chromosome doubling. Hybridisation possibly also played a part in speciation without chromosome number changes, since many *Hebe* species hybridise freely — evidence of their close evolutionary relationships.

Fig. 3.5.23 One of New Zealand's 80 species of *Hebe*.

Note: The genus name was recently changed from *Hebe* to *Veronica*.

Convergent evolution

When species occupy similar niches in different regions, they are called **ecological equivalents.** Example: antelope in Africa, kangaroos in Australia. **Convergent evolution** is any situation where animals (or plants) from different groups have evolved similar features. They have become outwardly similar in response to having similar niche requirements. Though similarities can be striking, there are usually differences that reveal independent origins. Structures that are similar in function but have evolved independently from different origins are known as **analogous structures.** Some examples:

- Dolphins (mammals) and sharks (cartilaginous fish) are unrelated. Both are streamlined and outwardly similar, because both are fast-swimming predators.
- Dugongs and dolphins are different groups of aquatic mammals. Dugongs have evolved a horizontal tail fin very like those of other aquatic mammals, the dolphins.
- Australian marsupials show many convergences with the placental mammals. Example: the marsupial 'wolf' (Fig. 3.5.24).
- The eyes of cephalopods (octopus, squid) and vertebrates look similar, but there are major differences. The vertebrate retina has light-receptors at the back (Fig. 3.5.25). The cephalopod retina has the light-sensitive layer in front of the nerves.

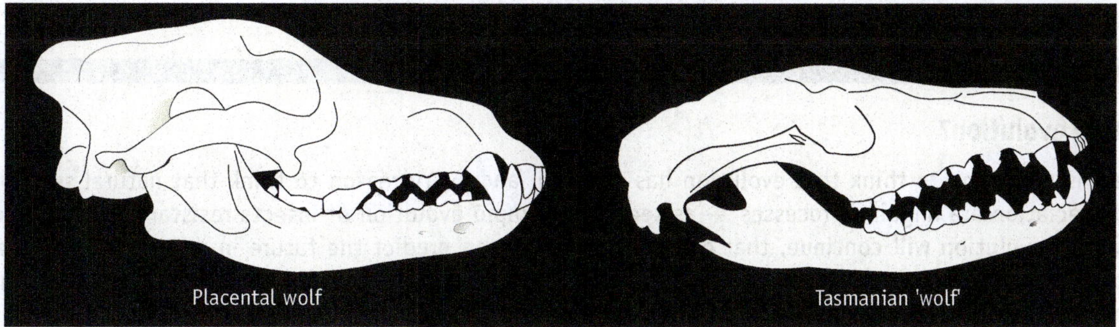

Fig. 3.5.24 Convergent evolution in placental wolf and the extinct marsupial 'wolf', aka 'Tasmanian tiger'.

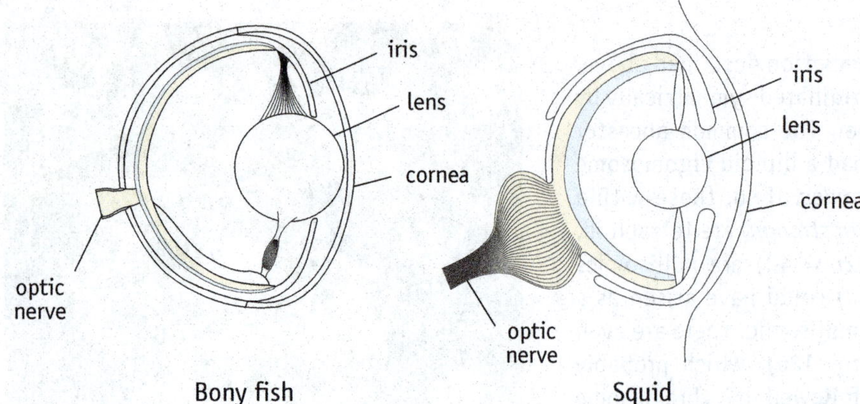

Fig. 3.5.25 Convergent evolution in vertebrate eye and cephalopod eye. Differences in their light-sensitive layers strongly suggest that these similar-looking eyes had independent origins.

Co-evolution

Co-evolution is a process in which one species affects the evolution of another. Some types:

- Parasites and host species; tapeworms could not have evolved without their host animals.
- Predators and prey. Lions have influenced the evolution of zebras; which have influenced lion evolution.
- Mutualistic relationships. In many cases flower have evolved shapes suited to pollination by particular insects, and insect structures have evolved in response. See *Excellence in Biology NCEA Level 3*.

Fig. 3.5.26 In many cases hummingbird beak shapes have co-evolved with particular flowering plants.

Gradualism (aka anagenesis)

One species slowly changes over time into another. In these cases an entire population changes without any branching-out. Example: tuatara.

Punctuated Equilibrium

Fossil evidence shows that quite often there are long periods with little change (stasis), and short periods of comparatively sudden change. The ancestral species may become extinct, or it may continue. Bursts of speciation seem to happen when a crucial aspect of the environment suddenly changes. Example: kea and kaka.

E

Future evolution?

There is no reason to think that evolution has stopped, and every reason to think that natural selection and speciation are ongoing processes — as seen in the rapid evolution of insects resistant to pesticides. Although evolution will continue, that does not mean we can predict the future in detail. Mutations are unpredictable, and the responses of living things to future environmental changes are also unpredictable. Some major present-day groups may vanish — as the dinosaurs did — and other groups that are presently unimportant may speciate to occupy vacant niches. Humans may currently be a part-exception to the principles of evolution, as cultural evolution has become much faster than biological evolution — as explained in 3.6, Unit 6.

 ISBN: 9780170355582

Check your understanding

1 Write matching word(s) in the blank column. Choose from this list: *convergent, co-evolution, adaptive radiation, analogous, endemic, placental, marsupial, ecological equivalent, niche, polyploidy, punctuated equilibrium.*

a	Structures similar in function, evolved independently from different origins	
b	The evolution of many different forms from a common ancestor	
c	The way of life for which an animal or plant is specialised	
d	An animal or plant that occurs only in one particular region	
e	A situation with long periods of little change, then periods of rapid evolution	
f	A situation where different species occupy similar niches in different regions	
g	Having multiple sets of chromosomes	
h	Evolution in which different groups evolve similar features	
i	A process in which one species affects the evolution of another	
j	Mammals that develop in a uterus, supplied by a placenta	
k	Mammals that develop in a pouch	

2 Identify two kinds of situations that make adaptive radiation likely to occur.

3 Convergent evolution is a common feature in evolution. Among the marsupial mammals there are types very similar in appearance equivalent to placental mammals (shown here in brackets). Examples: quoll (cat), Tasmanian tiger (wolf). Using either of these pairs, explain how the similarities probably evolved.

4 Look at the drawings on page 162 of vertebrate and squid (cephalopod) eyes.

a Describe three points of similarity between their structures.

5

b Describe one point of difference between their structures.

5 New Zealand has about 37 species of gecko. It is likely that geological changes led to their speciation.

a Give a name for this kind of speciation.

b Describe and explain the factors that may have led to this kind of speciation.

6 **a** Describe the evidence that the genus *Hebe* evolved in New Zealand, and not elsewhere.

b Below are some New Zealand *Hebe* species with their diploid (2*n*) chromosome numbers. Species also occurring in South America are marked by an asterisk. Refer to Fig. 3.5.23.

*H. elliptica**	40
H. odora	84
*H. salicifolia**	40
H. brachysiphon	120
H. evenosa	118

5

The haploid (*n*) chromosome number in *Hebe* ancestors was almost certainly 21. If this is so, describe the changes in 'ploidy' that could account for each of the following species:

i *H. odora*

ii *H. salicifolia*

iii *H. brachysiphon*

ISBN: 9780170355582

Biology 3.5 Evolutionary processes

NCEA Achievement Standard 91605: Demonstrate understanding of evolutionary processes leading to speciation

Externally assessed, 4 credits

Achievement	Achievement with Merit	Achievement with Excellence
Demonstrate understanding of evolutionary processes leading to speciation	Demonstrate in-depth understanding of evolutionary processes leading to speciation	Demonstrate comprehensive understanding of evolutionary processes leading to speciation

Achievement
'Demonstrate understanding ...' involves using biological ideas and/or scientific evidence to describe evolutionary processes leading to speciation.

Achievement with Merit
'Demonstrate in-depth understanding ...' involves using biological ideas and/or scientific evidence to explain how or why evolutionary processes lead to speciation.

Achievement with Excellence
'Demonstrate comprehensive understanding ...' involves linking biological ideas and/or scientific evidence about evolutionary processes leading to speciation. The linking of ideas may involve justifying, relating, evaluating, comparing and contrasting, or analysing the evolutionary processes that lead to speciation.

Evolutionary processes involve the following biological ideas:

- role of mutation
- gene flow
- role of natural selection and genetic drift
- modes of speciation (sympatric, allopatric)
- reproductive isolating mechanisms that contribute to speciation (geographical, temporal, ecological, behavioural, structural barriers, polyploidy)
- pattern such as divergence, convergence, adaptive radiation, co-evolution, punctuated equilibrium, and gradualism.

Scientific evidence for evolution, which may include example from New Zealand's fauna and flora, will be selected from:

- fossil evidence
- comparative anatomy (homologous and analogous structures)
- molecular biology (proteins and DNA analysis)
- biogeography.

5

Exam-type questions

QUESTION ONE

Hector's dolphin.

New Zealand is home to Hector's dolphin, the world's rarest and smallest dolphin. They live in shallow coastal waters and are highly endangered, often because they get caught in set nets placed close to the shore. There are two isolated populations which appear to have no gene flow between them, are genetically distinct, and are considered to be different subspecies. One small population (often known as Maui's dolphin), occurs only along the western North Island coast, from Taranaki northwards. The larger Hector's dolphin population occurs along the east and southern coasts of the South Island. It is suspected that in time these two populations could evolve into two different species.

Discuss the probable evolution of Hector's dolphin.

- Name the type of speciation that may be occurring.
- Explain how New Zealand's geological past could have caused the two populations to become isolated in the first place.
- Outline the probable sequence of events that must have occurred to lead to the formation of the two subspecies.
- Predict what needs to occur if the two subspecies are to evolve into different species.

– Type of speciation defined ...

– Explain how barriers could form in the sea (consider ice ages, sea depth, land bridges and NZ being one island) ...

– Explain what can cause sea levels to change ...

– Describe how geographic barriers can cause populations to become separated ...

– Suggest how different regions can cause different selection pressures; give examples ...

– Explain what makes some individuals 'fitter'; and explain 'fitness' ...

– Explain how some alleles become more common ...

– Explain why genetic drift is more likely in small populations ...

– Explain what events can lead to new species with barriers to gene flow ...

Use this page to create key points plan that could form the basis for a longer answer to be done on your own paper.

5

ISBN: 9780170355582

QUESTION TWO

The genus *Hebe* has undergone rapid evolutionary diversification in form, together with chromosomal changes including polyploidy. The table below lists eight of the many species that occur in New Zealand, together with their haploid chromosome numbers. Further information is supplied on page 160.

Species	Habitat conditions	Morphology	Chromosome number (*n*)
H. cupressoides	Subalpine east of the main mountains of the South Island.	Whipcord plant with scale-like leaves, growing up to 2 m tall.	21
H. cheesemanii	Rocks on drier mountains of the South Island.	Semi-whipcord plant; shrub up to 0.3 m tall.	21
H. ochracea	Mountains of the northwest South Island.	Semi-whipcord plant; shrub up to 0.3 m tall.	62
H. hectorii	Wet subalpine scrub and tussock of the South Island.	Whipcord plant; erect, rigid plant that grows up to 0.75 m tall.	20
H. imbricata	Drier mountains of the South Island.	Whipcord plant; erect, much-branched rounded shrub up to 0.6 m tall	20
H. elliptica	Coastal.	Leaves 1.5–4 cm long; bushy shrub up to 2 m tall.	20
H. venustula	Subalpine mostly North Island.	Leaves 1–2 cm long; erect bushy shrub up to 1.5 m tall.	60
H. stricta	Common in lowland and subalpine areas, mostly on banks in the North Island.	Leaves 4–5 cm long; woody shrub up to 4 m tall.	20

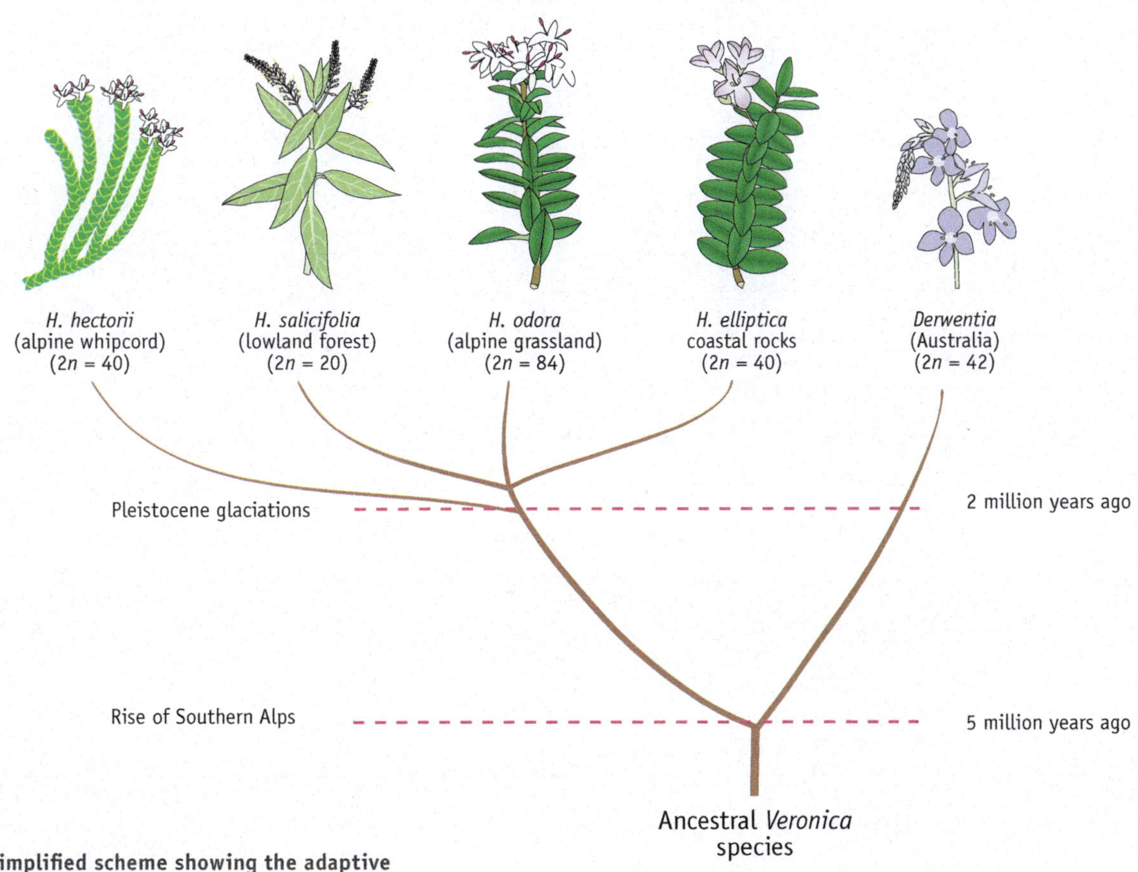

Highly simplified scheme showing the adaptive radiation of a few species of *Hebe*

Discuss the evidence for the role of each of the following processes in the evolution and diversification of hebe in New Zealand.

- Explain how different selection pressures can be generated by environmental changes resulting from mountain building and glaciation.
- Explain how mutations, particularly polyploidy, can result in speciation. Refer to specific examples named in the table.
- Name the type of speciation that can result from polyploidy.

Use this page to create a key points plan or a mind map that could form the basis for a longer answer to be done on your own paper.

ISBN: 9780170355582

QUESTION THREE

New Zealand wrens are an ancient group of endemic birds that evolved in isolation over the past 45 million years. All are small, all are insectivorous. Some were flightless, others are able to fly. As the diagram shows, only four species survive to the present day, with seven others becoming extinct in recent times. The two rifleman species fly, live in the forests, and pick insects off the bark of trees. The two rock wren species inhabit high-altitude areas in the South Island and forage in tussock grass.

Of the extinct species, the curved-beak wren *Dendroscansor* had long strong legs and used its beak to probe crevices in tree trunks to extract grubs. The two *Pachyplichas* ('thick-thigh') species were also flightless, with strong legs and non-perching toes similar to a kiwi. Stephens Island wrens scurried around the island's boulders like mice — but the whole species was unfortunately brought to extinction by the lighthouse keeper's cat.

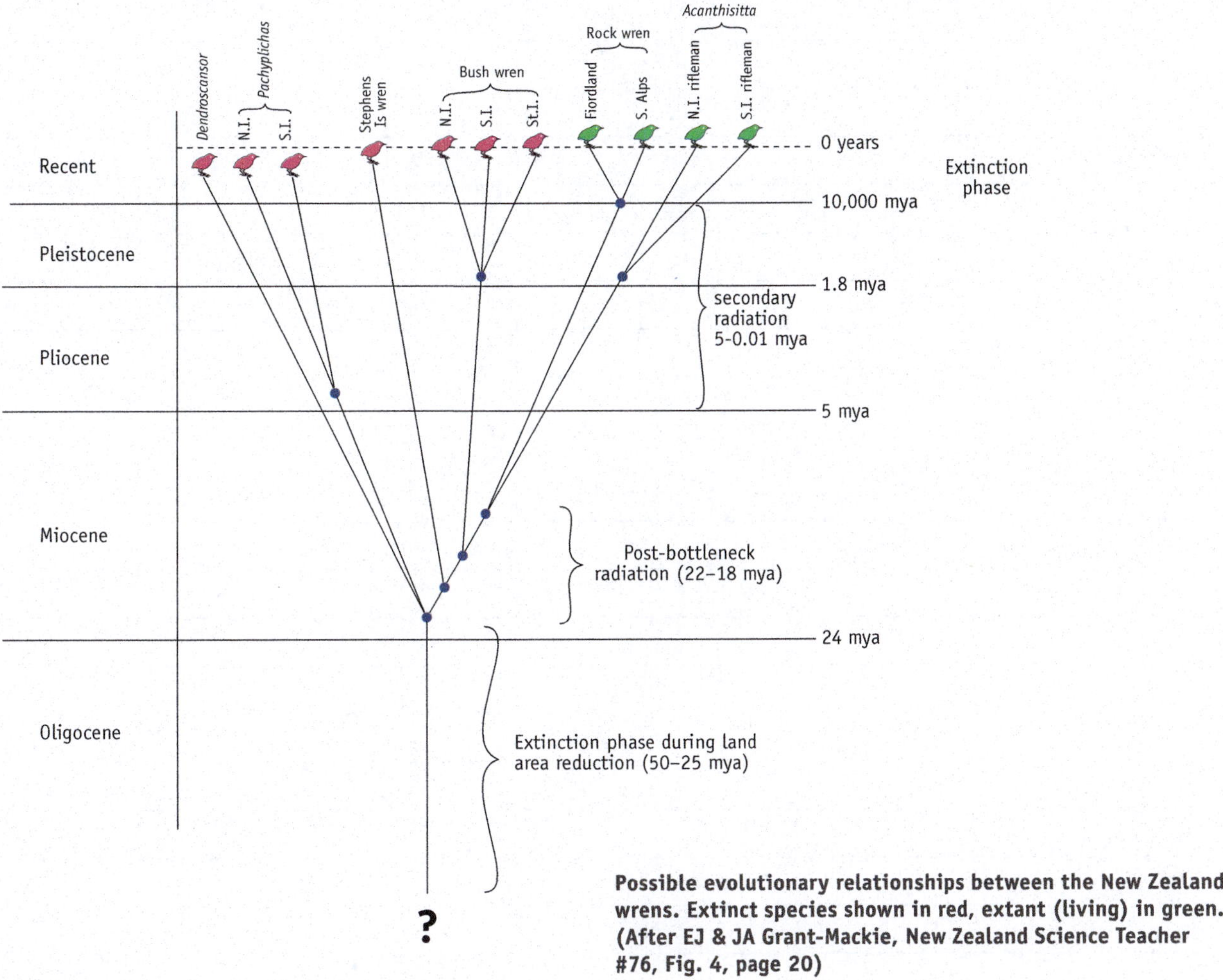

Possible evolutionary relationships between the New Zealand wrens. Extinct species shown in red, extant (living) in green. (After EJ & JA Grant-Mackie, New Zealand Science Teacher #76, Fig. 4, page 20)

Study the information above, and answer the following question.

New Zealand wrens exhibit many evolutionary patterns. Using direct examples from both the description and the diagram, outline the geological events and ecological factors that may have played a part in the wren group. Give special attention to evolutionary patterns such as such as convergent evolution, divergent evolution, and adaptive radiation.

Use this page to create a key points plan or a mind map that could form the basis for a longer answer to be done on your own paper.

ISBN: 9780170355582

QUESTION FOUR

New Zealand short-tailed bat

Ancestors of the New Zealand short-tailed bat (*Mystacina tuberculata*) arrived from Australia about 35 mya. There were no mammals in New Zealand at this time and the bats probably had a varied food source. Over time these bats have evolved ground-living behaviour. Although they can still fly, they crawl on the ground using their folded wings as front legs. They make use of fallen fruit and seeds on the forest floor, and collect nectar and pollen from low plants. In some ways they are the ecological equivalent of mice. These bats are crepuscular, being most active at dawn and dusk throughout the year. (They are quite different to the long-tailed bat which arrived only one million years ago and lives like a typical bat, catching insects in flight.)

The wood rose (*Dactylanthus taylorii*) is a low-growing totally parasitic flowering plant. It has no leaves, and feeds off the roots of pate trees (*Schlefflera*). The wood rose flower exudes a musky smell like sweat. The bat and the wood rose have evolved a mutualistic relationship where the bat gets pollen and high-energy nectar, and the wood rose is cross-pollinated in return. The wood rose is endangered, because rats and mice, although pollinating it, also destroy the plant and its fruit.

Discuss the evolution of the short-tailed bat and the wood rose. Include the following.

- Give a definition of 'ecological equivalent'.
- State the specific name for the type of evolution that the wood rose and short-tailed bat demonstrate, and explain how it is likely to have arisen.
- Explain the evolutionary mechanisms probably involved in the short-tailed bat of today having evolved from the original ancestor.

You may include aspects such as mutation, gene flow and the role of natural selection and genetic drift in your answer.

Use this page to create a key points plan or a mind map that could form the basis for a longer answer to be done on your own paper.

QUESTION FIVE

Various groups of unrelated species often end up with very similar adaptations. Examples are organisms that live in the sea and have evolved a streamlined body shape with fins to assist with manoeuvering. Sharks, dolphins, penguins and an extinct reptile ichthyosaur all look very similar, yet have unrelated vertebrate origins.

Discuss the type of evolution that results from different organisms occupying a similar niche. You should address the following.

- Name the particular type of evolution described.
- Explain how natural selection has resulted in the organisms looking so similar yet with different vertebrate ancestors. Include reference to the pentadactyl limb in your answer.

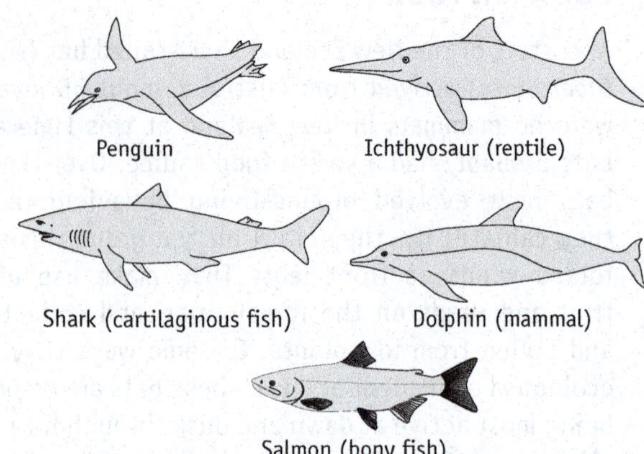

Similarity in body shape in four vertebrates belonging to different classes.

- Name the type/pattern of evolution.
- Explain/define 'niche'.
- Briefly outline how natural selection works.
- Suggest how natural selection might cause different species to become adapted for a previously vacant or under-occupied niche (specifically refer to water as the medium).
- Explain the adaptive advantage of shape in fast-swimming animals.
- Define/ explain/ illustrate 'pentadactyl limb'.
- Use this as examples of homologous structures (not the same as analogous), perhaps using bat/ monkey limbs as examples to compare their different uses and relate to structure.

Use this page to create a key points plan that could form the basis for a longer answer to be done on your own paper.

ISBN: 9780170355582

5

QUESTION SIX

The hammer orchid is one of six related species from Western Australia. It has a flower that resembles the body colour and shape of a female wasp, and also has pheromones similar to those of female wasps. Female thynnid wasps cannot fly, and crawl up the stems of plants to wait for a male to carry them off and mate, usually in midair. Because of the orchid flower's appearance and smell, male wasps are lured to land on the orchids.

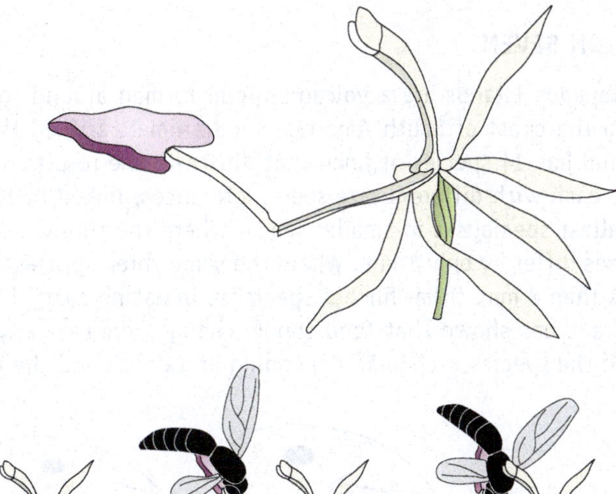

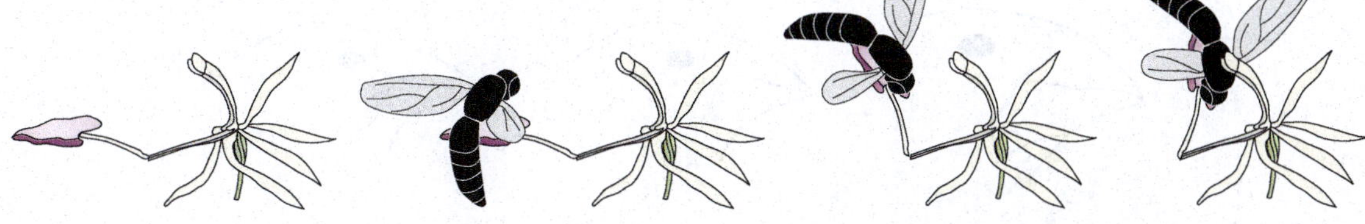

As the male wasp struggles with the flower, the landing pad moves vigorously forward and back. This resembles a hammer action, striking the wasp's thorax into the stamen or stigma, depending on the developmental stage of the orchid. The wasp is covered in pollen and might then fly to the next hammer orchid to repeat the process. The relationship is not mutualistic, since the wasp gets nothing from the flower. If a female wasp is placed beside a hammer orchid, a male can spot the difference, so to be successful the hammer orchid times flowering to the few days each year before the female thynnid wasps emerge.

Discuss the evolution of the hammer orchid and its relationship with thynnid wasps, including the following.

- The specific name given to the process whereby different species evolve to closely copy and resemble another.
- Describe the possible events that led to natural selection favouring orchids that flower at a particular time.
- Explain why the hammer orchid has put energy into copying the sexual partner of an insect. Also suggest the advantages and disadvantages such a strategy has to both the orchid and the wasp.

Use this page to create a key points plan or a mind map that could form the basis for a longer answer to be done on your own paper.

QUESTION SEVEN

The Galapagos Islands are a volcanic group formed around four million years ago, and are situated about 1000 km from the coast of South America. Land animals arrived there by either being windblown or rafting on logs. The island has 14 species of finch that illustrate the results of adaptive radiation. Three species are seed-eating finches, each with different-size seed preferences, linked to beak depth. The largest generally takes large seeds, the smallest specialises in smaller seeds. Where the three species of seed-eater species are allopatric, the mean beak sizes differ by only 1 mm. Where the same three species are sympatric on Santa Cruz island, the beaks differ by more than 2 mm. Other finches specialise in eating cacti, flowers, buds and insects. Research by Rosemary and Peter Grant has shown that food supply changes dramatically with climate, and that finch mortality rates vary between the species each year, depending on rainfall and the type of seeds available.

Large ground finch
(Geospiza magnirostris)

Medium ground finch
(Geospiza fortis)

Small ground finch
(Geospiza fuliginosa)

Discuss the main factors contributing to the evolution of these three Galapagos finches. Make sure you address the following points in your answer.

- Define what is meant by allopatric and sympatric species. Explain why these finches have evolved greater differences in beak size where they are sympatric, compared with allopatric situations.
- Explain how the different beak sizes could have evolved from a common ancestral type. Name this particular type of selection pressure. You may draw a diagram to assist your answer.
- Explain the part that island geography and climate probably played in the adaptive radiation of these finches. Suggest what reproductive isolating mechanisms are likely to reinforce the species separation.

Use this page to create a key points plan or a mind map that could form the basis for a longer answer to be done on your own paper.

5

ISBN: 9780170355582

QUESTION EIGHT

The New Zealand *Polystichum* ferns have undergone considerable adaptive radiation since arriving here from Australia. They occupy habitats from coastal to alpine regions, and from well-lit forest margins to the understorey of dark forest. This radiation must have occurred within the last 13 million years, as a combination of chloroplast DNA sequences and fossil data both suggest a split from Australian species about 13 million years ago (not, as was first thought, during the break-up from Gondwana). The radiation has been attributed to the significant ecological changes accompanying the Pleistocene glaciations. Ferns reproduce by spores and prefer damp habitats, as the gametophyte stage and fertilisation are dependent on external water.

Discuss how **geological** and **biological** processes may have led to the adaptive radiation of New Zealand *Polystichum* ferns. Include how the fern may have arrived into New Zealand 13 million years ago, and how speciation may have occurred, resulting in the different species seen today.

Use this page to create a key points plan or a mind map that could form the basis for a longer answer to be done on your own paper.

QUESTION NINE

Ten species of moa once lived in New Zealand and all are now extinct. They are classified into at least four genera. Kiwi, the only remaining ratite in New Zealand, has only one genus with five species. The diets of moa and kiwi were thought to be a major influence on each group's capacity to diverge into separate species and genera. Moa were herbivorous and varied greatly in size, whereas kiwi are nocturnal, feed on invertebrates in the leaf litter, and are relatively small.

Discuss the possible reproductive isolating mechanisms that would have allowed the moa to remain as ten separate species. Include in your answer:

- At least three pre-zygotic and three post-zygotic mating mechanisms.
- An explanation of the adaptive advantage of reproductive isolating mechanisms.

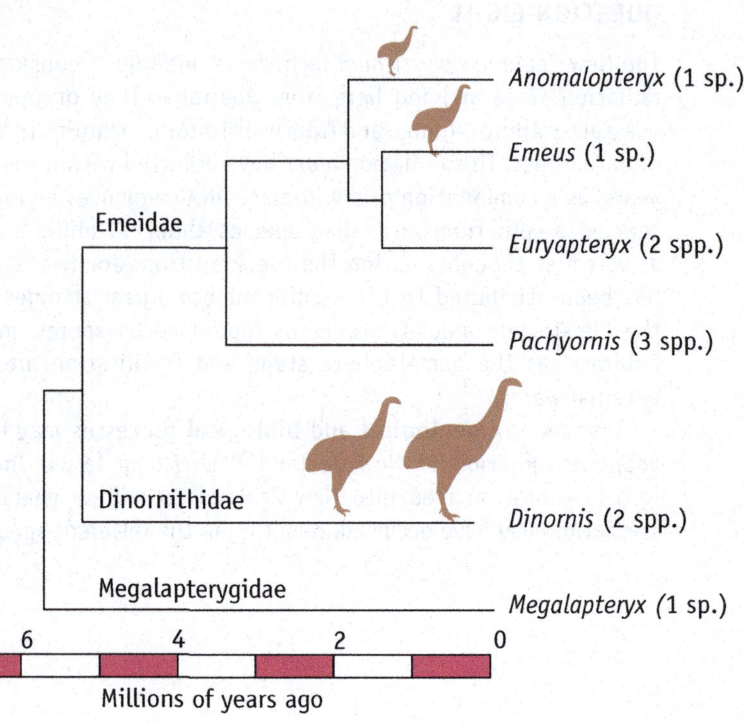

– Define 'species'.

– Define 'reproductive isolating mechanisms'.

– Outline three pre-zygotic isolating mechanisms.

– Outline three pre-zygotic isolating mechanisms.

– In your answer refer to the stimulus material above. Refer to when and where the different species existed.

– Explain the adaptive advantage to the ratites of remaining different species. How does this species-separation save energy? What could energy be used for instead?

Use this page to create a key points plan that could form the basis for a longer answer to be done on your own paper.

5

ISBN: 9780170355582

QUESTION TEN

Tuatara

The tuatara (*Sphenodon punctatus*) is often described as a living fossil. The last remaining example of its genus, the tuatara has remained relatively unchanged over 180 million years, whereas other related species became extinct. Tuatara once lived throughout the mainland of New Zealand but now survive in the wild on only 32 offshore islands. These are characteristically free of rodents and other introduced mammalian predators, which are known to prey on eggs and young as well as compete for invertebrate food. The islands are usually occupied by colonies of breeding sea birds that contribute to the fertility and hence the richness of invertebrate and lizard fauna needed by tuatara.

Discuss possible reasons for the tuatara remaining little changed, surviving glaciations and other environmental changes over the past 60 million years, whereas other reptile species have undergone adaptive radiation. Name the type of evolution that tuatara have shown, and describe how this type of evolution differs from punctuated equilibrium.

Use this page to create a key points plan or a mind map that could form the basis for a longer answer to be done on your own paper.

3.6 Human evolution

Unit 1 | Primates, rocks, dates

Humans are primates

In our mental abilities and creativity, humans are unique — but when it comes to anatomy, humans are little different from other mammals. Animal classification is nowadays based on anatomy and proteins and DNA, and for many reasons humans are placed in the Primate order. At this stage we need to know about the following three groups, the main features of each, plus some examples.

Primates. This is a mammal group of about 200 species, including humans, apes, monkeys, lemurs. Primates are adapted to arboreal living (tree life), which helps explain their main features:

- All primates have **grasping (prehensile) hands** they can use for climbing, or to pick things up.
- All have **forward-facing eyes** (stereoscopic vision), essential for judging distances and a common feature of animals that jump or climb.
- Most are **omnivorous**, with teeth specialised neither for plant food nor meat.
- Most have **colour vision** and a poor sense of smell. Odours are less important at treetop level.

Hominids. This is a Primate subgroup that includes humans, their immediate ancestors, plus the four 'great apes': gorilla, chimpanzee, bonobo, orang-utan. Apes differ from monkeys in having no external tail. The gibbons, 15 'lesser ape' species from South-East Asia, are placed in a separate group.

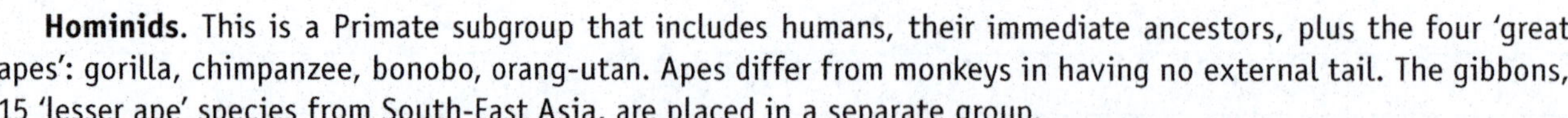

Hominins. This is a Hominid subgroup made up of humans and their human-like ancestors. There is only one surviving human species: *Homo sapiens*. Several other hominin forms are now extinct, including *Homo habilis* and *Australopithecus*. Bipedalism (upright walking) is the distinctive feature that sets hominins apart from all other primates.

All present-day ape species — and also humans — differ from monkeys in several ways, most visibly:

- Apes have especially **mobile shoulder joints**, with long hands used as 'hooks', with thumbs reduced and not fully opposable. These features are adaptations for **brachiating**, a specialised ape method of moving through forests by swinging from branch to branch. (Gorillas and chimpanzees walk on their knuckles because their hands are curved inwards, adapted for brachiating.)
- The **tail** is reduced to a tiny stump of fused vertebrae and is not visible externally.

ISBN: 9780170355582

E

One classification of the primates is shown in Fig. 3.6.1.

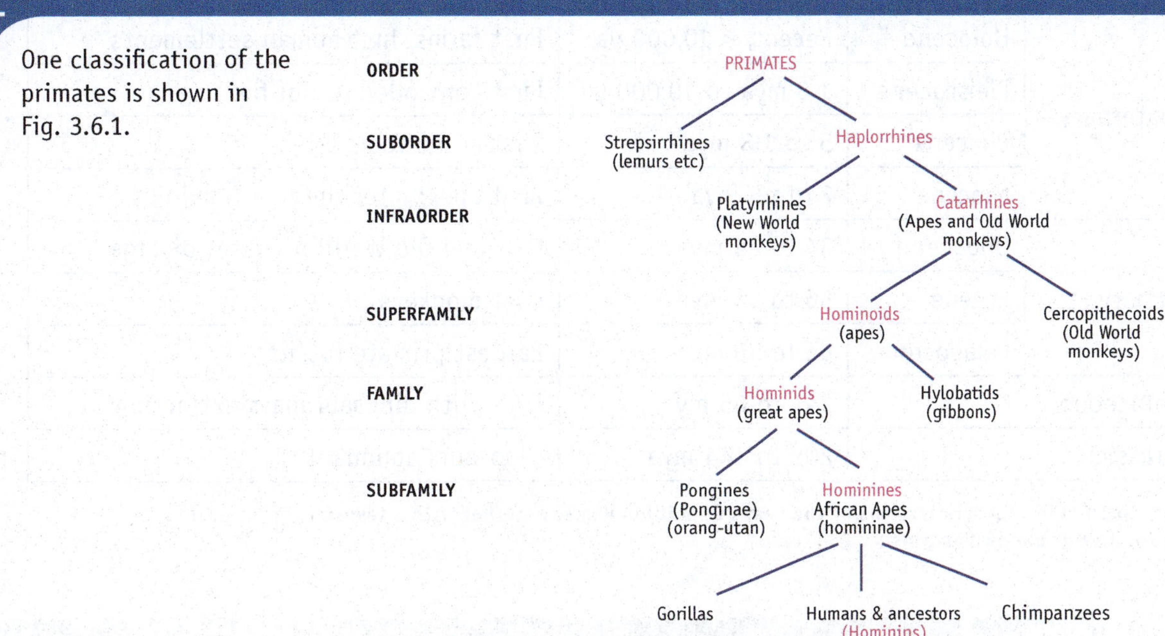

Fig. 3.6.1 A modern classification of primates.

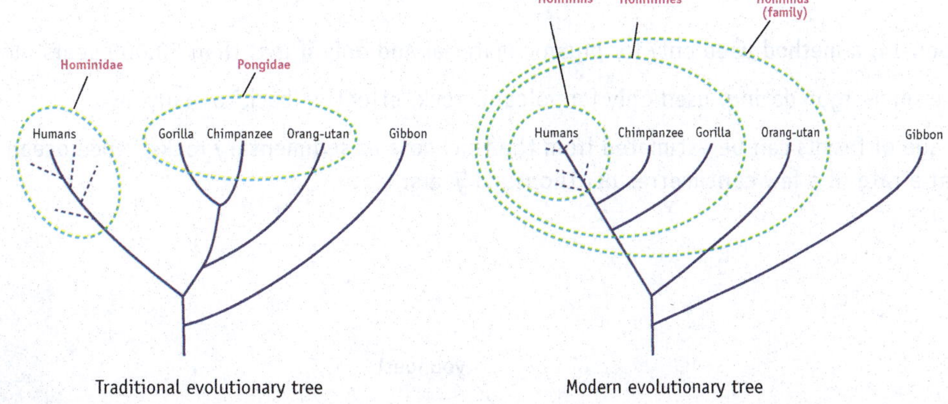

Fig. 3.6.2 Relationships between humans and other apes is shown here in one older classification; also one more modern classification based on molecular similarities and differences. Although classification systems are based on evidence, more evidence keeps arriving, and to some extent any classification arrangement is a matter of opinion.

Geological time

The most direct evidence of trends in hominin evolution comes from **palaeontology**, the study of the fossils. In most cases a dead body rots away, but under some conditions minerals slowly replace hard parts such as skeleton and teeth. Surrounding sediments gradually harden into **sedimentary rock**, which usually consist of distinct layers, or **strata**.

All hominin evolution has taken place in the last five to six million years. The age of fossils and sediments can be given in years, but sometimes names are used for each time period and epoch (Table 3.6.1).

Period	Epoch	Dates	Significant events
Quaternary	Holocene	Recent, < 10,000 ya	First farms, first human settlements
	Pleistocene	1.8 mya to 10,000 ya	First controlled use of fire
	Pliocene	5 to 1.8 mya	First stone tools
	Miocene	24 to 5 mya	First apes; later the first hominins
Tertiary	Oligocene	34 to 24 mya	New and Old World primates diverge
	Eocene	56 to 34 mya	First monkeys
	Palaeocene	65 to 56 mya	Earliest primate fossils
Cretaceous		144 to 65 mya	Ends with dinosaur mass extinction
Jurassic		205 to 144 mya	Dinosaurs abundant

Table 3.6.1 Geological subdivisions of the past 205 million years, together with a few significant events that are part of our own origins.

Dating fossils

If fossil A is found in a deeper stratum than fossil B, then A is older than B — unless the sediments have been disturbed. Actual age in years can be estimated by several methods, a few described here:

- carbon-14, a method used only for organic material and only if less than 50,000 years old
- potassium-argon dating, used only for volcanic rock, effective back to many mya
- the age of fossils can be estimated from the thickness of sedimentary rocks, since ocean sediments build up at a rate of a few centimetres per thousand years.

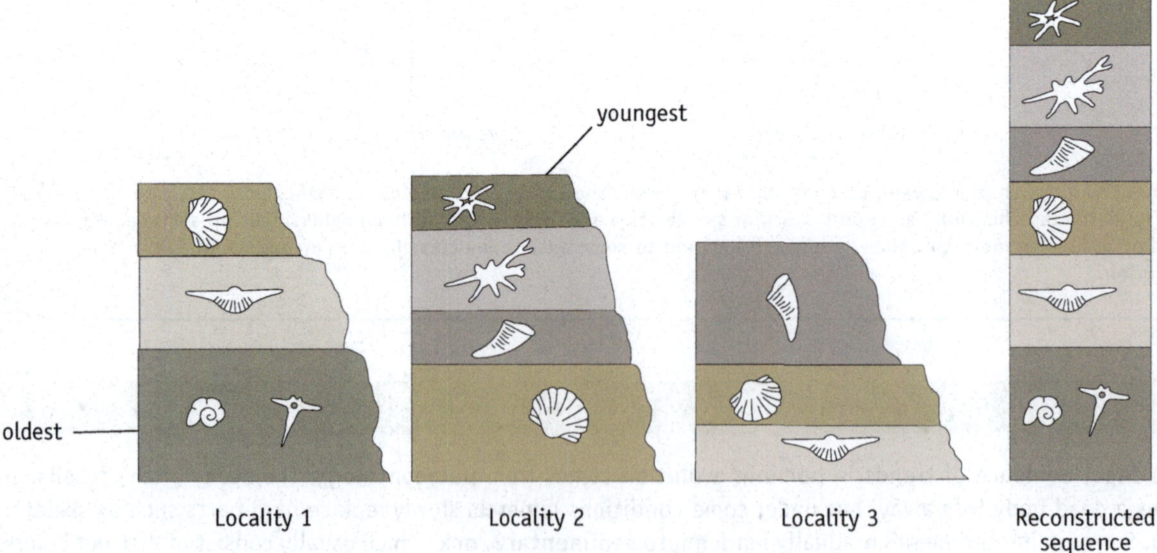

Fig. 3.6.3 Overlapping fossil sequences in different places enable extended sequences to be worked out.

ISBN: 9780170355582

E

Radioisotopic dating in general

Every element exists as several **isotopes**, forms that are chemically identical but differ in their atomic mass. Some isotopes are radioactive; each atom eventually 'decays' to an atom of a different kind, giving off particles and radiation in the process.

For any radioactive isotope, the rate of decay happens at a constant rate. This rate is expressed as a **half-life**, which is the time for half the isotope to break down to another isotope.

Imagine 32 grams of an isotope with a half-life of one year. After a year there would be 16 grams remaining, after two years there would be 8 grams, after five years there would be 1 gram, and so on. The other 31 grams have not been lost; they have become a different isotope (Fig. 3.6.4).

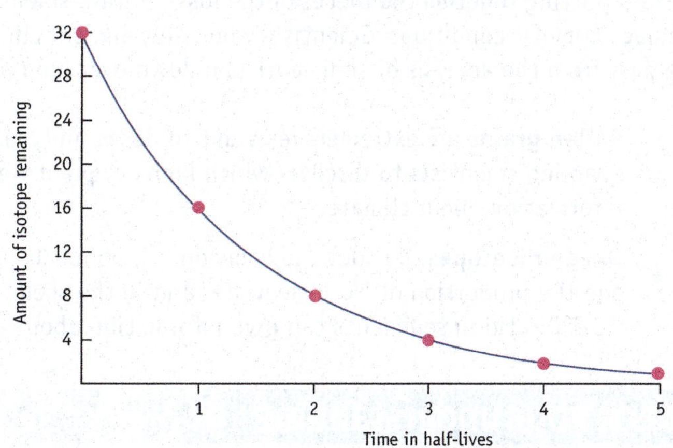

Fig. 3.6.4 Change in amount of a parent isotope as it decays.

The calculated dates are seldom exact values. Some commonly used dating methods are described below.

Carbon-14

Carbon-14 isotope is continuously produced in the upper atmosphere by the action of cosmic rays on 'ordinary' nitrogen-14 (^{14}N). Eventually, each ^{14}C atom decays back to ^{14}N.

Initially the ^{14}C atoms are oxidised to CO_2, some of which is taken up by plants in photosynthesis. The ^{14}C passes along the food chain together with the normal ^{12}C. The moment an organism dies it ceases to take in carbon, so its ^{14}C begins to decrease.

Compared with the other radioisotopes used in dating, the half-life of ^{14}C is short; about 5730 years. After 57,300 years (10 half-lives), the amount remaining is $(\frac{1}{2})^{10}$ or 1/1024 of the original. The practical limit for the carbon-14 method is about 50,000 years. Carbon-14 is used to date organic specimens such as wood, bone or animal shells of calcium carbonate.

Potassium-argon

K-Ar dating is used to date volcanic rock or ash. Dating volcanic rock immediately above a fossil gives a minimum age for the fossil. One famous set of footprints at Laetoli in East Africa shows two sets of unmistakably human footprints walking across freshly fallen volcanic ash. Other footprints nearby include elephants. The ash has been dated at 3.6 mya.

The K-Ar method depends on the fact that about 0.01 per cent of natural potassium is the isotope ^{40}K, and that this decays to argon-40, which remains trapped in the rock. If the rock is heated, the argon escapes and can be collected and measured. Argon begins to accumulate as soon as the rock cools after being ejected from a volcano, so its 'age' is the time since the last eruption.

Fission track

When uranium-238 decays to lead, the uranium atoms emit particles of such high energy that they make tracks about 25 micrometres long in the surrounding rock. In glass-like minerals these can be seen under the microscope and counted. The number of tracks shows the number of ^{238}U atoms that have decayed since the rock was last molten.

Thermo-luminescence

This method is used to date artefacts (manufactured objects) such as pottery and charred flint tools. It depends on the fact that clays and other minerals contain traces of radioactive elements, which emit electrons as they decay. The electrons are trapped within the crystalline structure of the clay. When it is heated the clay emits the energy of the stored electrons in the form of light. The longer the time since the pottery was last heated (i.e. in manufacture), the more electrons are trapped and the greater the luminescence when it is subsequently heated in a laboratory.

Ancient climates

Besides putting together the pieces of the fossil jigsaw, scientists need to know how these creatures lived, and this includes climatic conditions. Scientists who study ancient climates (palaeo-climatologists) can deduce much about the past from the analysis of sediments laid down over long periods. Two methods have provided useful evidence:

- **Pollen grains** are extremely resistant to decay and many end up in marshes. Species can be identified enabling scientists to discover which kinds of plant were common in a past time. This can also give information about climate.
- **Oxygen isotopes.** Besides the common ^{16}O, about 0.2% of natural oxygen is isotope ^{18}O. During an ice age the proportion of ^{18}O in seawater and in the skeletons of marine microorganisms rises. Analysis of the $^{18}O/^{16}O$ ratio in sediments can give information about ancient climates.

Check your understanding

1 Name two features that are distinctive of all primates.

2 Explain the difference between hominid and hominin.

3 List the names of four kinds of great ape.

4 Suggest why gibbons are called 'lesser apes'.

5 Describe what is meant by 'brachiating'. List three adaptations for this method of movement.

6

6 Explain why apes such as chimpanzees have long hands and thumbs that are not fully opposable.

7 Explain how each of the following may be an adaptation for arboreal (tree) life:

a Forward-facing eyes with stereoscopic vision.

ISBN: 9780170355582

b Poor sense of smell.

____

____

c Hands with separate fingers and opposable thumbs.

____

____

d Colour vision and the ability to distinguish red from green.

____

____

____

____

8 Summarise three methods of dating fossils, plus main uses of each.

____

____

____

____

____

9 Complete the following by filling in the missing words.

Fossils are found only in ____________ rocks. The deeper the ____________ in which a fossil is found, the earlier it was buried and the ____________ it is.

10 Give the approximate dates for each of the following:

a The first monkeys ______________________________

b The first apes ______________________________

c The first hominins ______________________________

d The Pleistocene epoch ______________________________

11 State what kind of dating method would be used to determine the age of each of the following:

a a 15,000-year-old wooden spear ______________________________

b a one-million-year-old skull buried in volcanic ash ______________________________

c a 4000-year-old piece of pottery ______________________________

12 If a newly formed piece of charcoal contains 1 picogram of carbon-14, how much will it contain after three half-lives of this isotope? ______________________________

6

Unit 2 | Hominin beginnings

Main evolutionary trends

Hominin evolution began more than five million years ago. Over this vast time span several human-like forms have appeared and disappeared, with only one surviving to our present time: *Homo sapiens*. All *H. sapiens* are human, and all other hominins can be considered 'pre-human', although the dividing line is a matter of opinion.

Much of what we know about the distant past is based on fossils, which tell us much about **biological evolution**. 'Biological' refers to any structure, physiology or behaviour controlled by DNA. (Cultural evolution is different: see Unit 6.) Fossils provide evidence about the structure of extinct pre-humans, plus what they ate, and even how they behaved. We can also learn much by comparing humans to other still-living hominids such as chimpanzees. When all this evidence is put together, we see seven main evolutionary trends over the past five million years:

- an early change from walking on four legs to walking on two legs (quadrupedal to **bipedal**); this involved major alterations to skull, back, pelvis, knees, feet, leg length
- an increase in **cranial capacity** (which indicates brain volume) from about 400 cc to 1500 cc
- increased size of brain areas associated with **speech**
- **canine teeth** became smaller, jaw reduced in size, but the same number of 32 teeth
- **hands** became more flexible, and thumbs larger
- **less hairy**, and more sweat glands
- changes in **reproductive behaviour.**

When studying these trends, it's important to try and explain how and why they occurred. In particular, these trends can be explained by the process of natural selection, just as in other animals. In dealing with natural selection we need to understand the environment in which early hominins lived.

African origins

According to all the evidence, humans began in Africa, home to our ancestors for millions of years. Only in comparatively recent times did our direct ancestors venture much beyond Africa. Five features stand out about the African setting in which most of our biological evolution took place.

- **Predators.** Lions and leopards are powerful hunters, and were abundant. Pre-humans could not possibly have outrun them, so must have survived on cooperative behaviour and on ability to plan ahead.
- **Climate**. Much of Africa is hot and dry; parts are high and cold.
- **Savanna**. Starting about five million years ago the climate changed and forests began to shrink, leaving widening areas of savanna; open grassland with scattered trees. Long-distance travel became important, and pre-humans evolved efficient walking and running abilities.
- **Food**. African savannas have abundant grazing animals; potentially rich sources of food.
- **Competition**. Successful primates (baboons) were already living in African savannas.

Fig. 3.6.5 Conditions in Africa one to five million years ago were similar to conditions we find there today. Changing climate conditions caused forest areas to shrink, grasslands to expand, with more habitat in open country.

 ISBN: 9780170355582

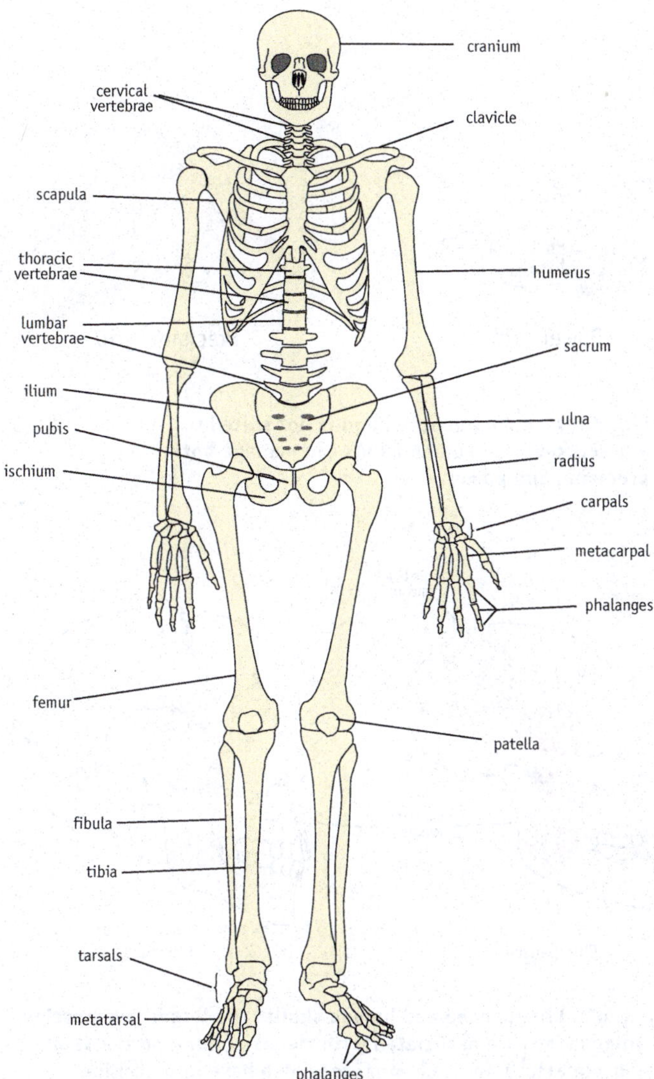

Fig. 3.6.6 All bones in the human skeleton correspond exactly to bones in apes, but the proportions have changed in response to the requirements of walking on two legs. A fossil knee (or pelvis, or skull) is enough to tell us whether an extinct primate walked upright or not.

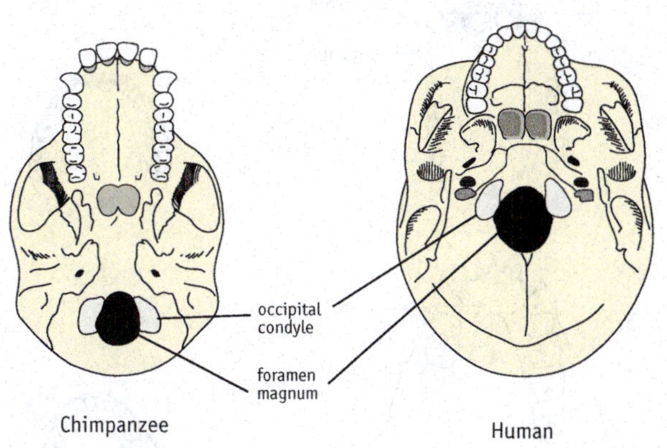

Fig. 3.6.7 Underneath views of chimpanzee and human skulls. The hominin foramen magnum (big opening for the spinal cord) shifted underneath the skull, in order for the eyes to face forwards when standing upright.

Bipedalism

In a number of ways the human skeleton has become specialised for life on two legs. Modern humans are well-adapted for walking and jogging long distances, probably very important for pre-human survival in savanna conditions. (More examples are given in *Excellence in Biology NCEA Level 3*.) Figs 3.6.6 to 3.6.10 illustrate five skeleton features linked to bipedalism.

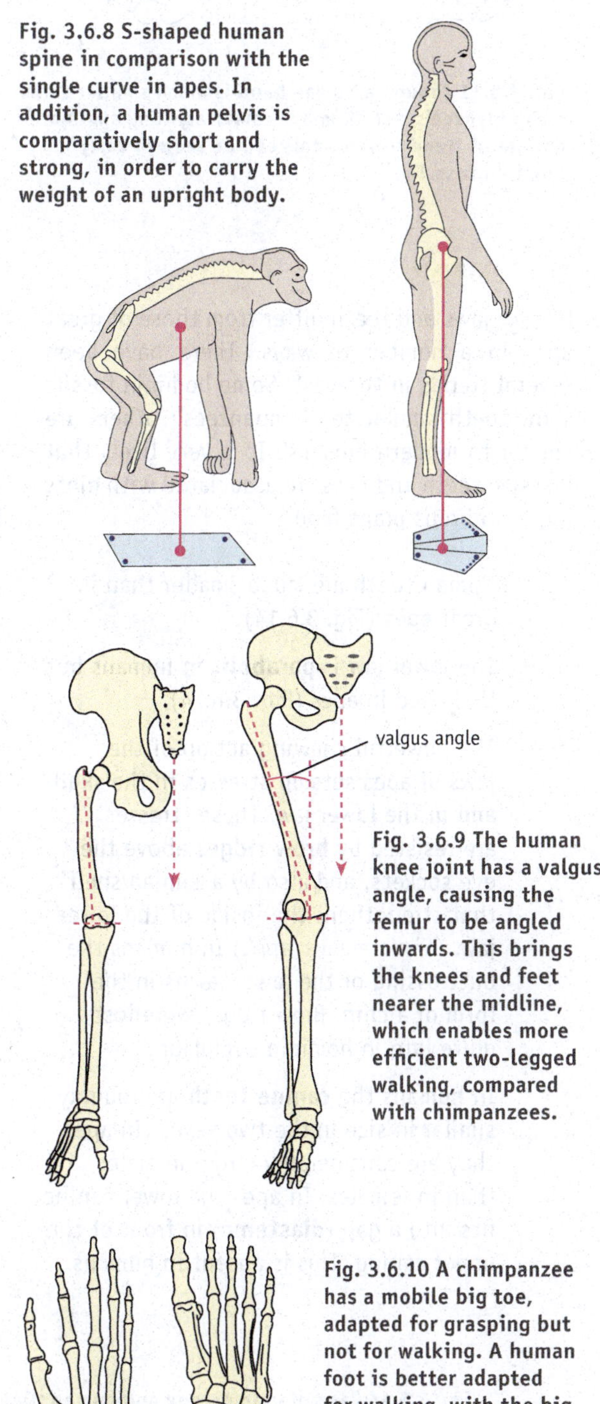

Fig. 3.6.8 S-shaped human spine in comparison with the single curve in apes. In addition, a human pelvis is comparatively short and strong, in order to carry the weight of an upright body.

Fig. 3.6.9 The human knee joint has a valgus angle, causing the femur to be angled inwards. This brings the knees and feet nearer the midline, which enables more efficient two-legged walking, compared with chimpanzees.

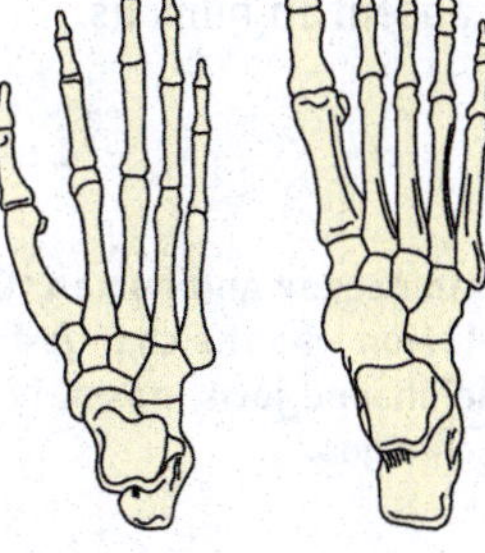

Fig. 3.6.10 A chimpanzee has a mobile big toe, adapted for grasping but not for walking. A human foot is better adapted for walking, with the big toe pointing forwards.

Hands

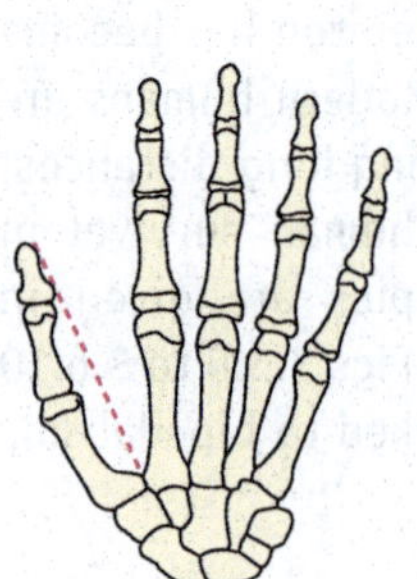

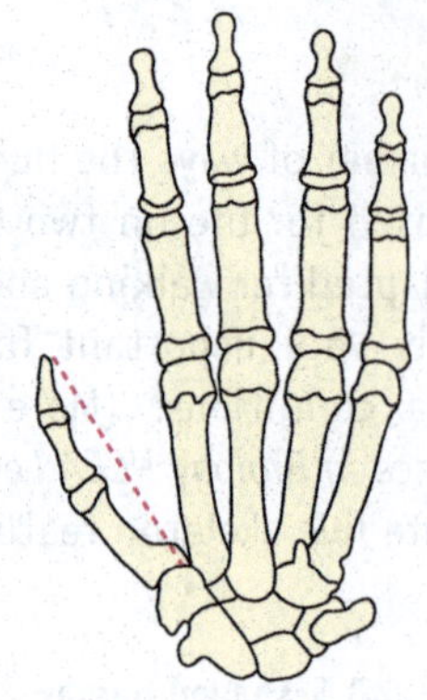

Fig. 3.6.11 Though a human hand is much smaller than a chimpanzee's, the thumb is relatively long and more mobile. A trend towards this can be seen in early hominin fosssils.

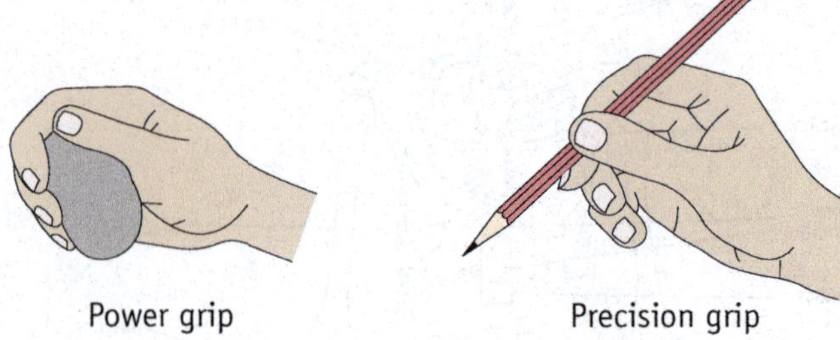

Fig. 3.6.12 A chimpanzee hand is not suited to a precision grip; human hands can manage both precision and power.

Teeth and jaws

Human jaws and teeth differ from those of great apes in a number of ways. There have been several trends in the past. Some hominin fossils show teeth similar to chimpanzees'; others are similar to modern humans'. It is very likely that massive teeth and jaws are associated with diets high in fibrous plant food.

- Human **teeth** are much smaller than in great apes (Fig. 3.6.14).
- The lower jaw is **parabolic** in humans but U-shaped in apes (Fig. 3.6.14).
- The powerful chewing action of the jaws of apes sets up stresses in the skull and in the lower jaw. These stresses are resisted by **brow ridges** above the eye sockets, and also by a 'simian shelf' that strengthens the inside of the lower jaw. (*Simia* means 'ape'.) In humans the buttressing of the lower jaw is in the form of a chin. Brow ridges were lost quite late in hominin evolution.
- In humans the **canine teeth** are roughly similar in size in the two sexes. In apes they are considerably larger in males than in females. In apes the lower canine fits into a gap (**diastema**) in front of the upper canine. This is absent in humans.

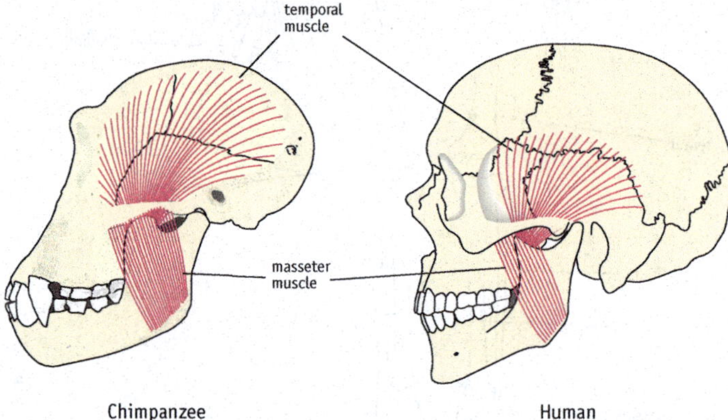

Fig. 3.6.13 Chimpanzee and human skulls. The larger jaw muscles of chimpanzees are associated with ridges of bone on the skull for muscle attachment. Chimpanzees also have large canine teeth, a feature of hominids that was lost during hominin evolution.

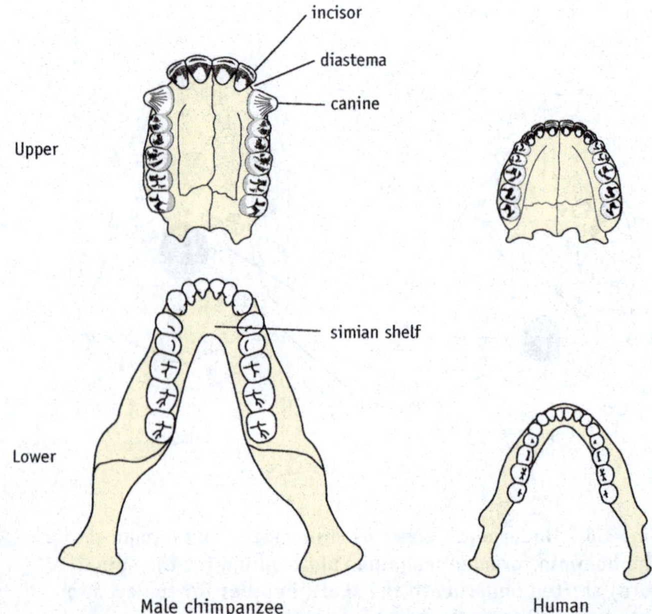

Fig. 3.6.14 Jaws of chimpanzee and human. One trend in hominin evolution was the change from U-shaped to parabolic-shaped jaws, possibly associated with diet changes.

6

ISBN: 9780170355582

Keeping cool

Compared with all other primates, humans are sweaty and non-hairy. Human skin has a higher density of sweat glands, and over most of the body hairs are short and fine — although the density of hairs is similar to that of other primates'.

We do not know whether pre-humans were hairy of not, but it is certain that hair became thinner at some stage, and sweat glands more abundant. Why? Humans evolved in tropical Africa. Our ancestors lived mainly in the open and (like most other primates) were active in the daytime. Under these conditions it is difficult to keep body temperature below 37 °C. Evaporation of sweat is the main way of achieving this, and hair loss probably helped. Going against this reasoning is the fact that tropical Africa has many kinds of hairy mammals, including baboons.

Brains and spoken language

Complex spoken language was probably the greatest advance in human evolution. We do not know for certain when an ability to speak began to evolve, but can get clues from fossil skulls. The capacity for speech lies partly in the organisation of the brain, and partly in the structure of the larynx (voice box), pharynx, tongue and lips.

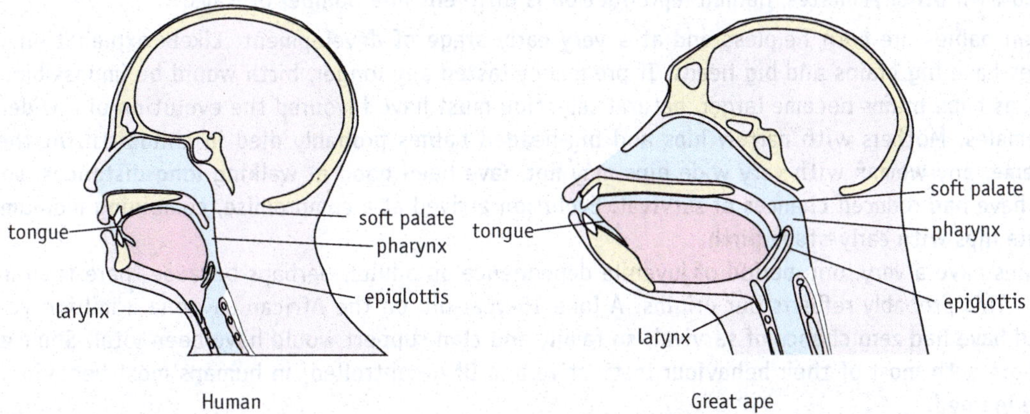

Fig. 3.6.15 The human vocal tract compared with an ape's. The shorter pharynx region in apes is one reason they cannot have spoken language.

When adjustments are made for body size, human brains are the largest in the animal kingdom. Most of the size increase is in the cerebrum. The cerebral cortex is the site of the most complex mental processes, including language. Two small regions of the cerebrum, both usually on the left side, are closely involved with language. **Wernicke's area** is a sensory region concerned with the interpretation of sound. **Broca's area** is a motor region, responsible for the organisation of sounds into meaningful sequences.

Brain size does not necessarily equate with intelligence — we know that Neanderthals had larger brains than ours — but size probably does give a rough indication. Also, in some fossils the inside of the braincase shows convolutions that match folding of the cerebral cortex, including Broca's area.

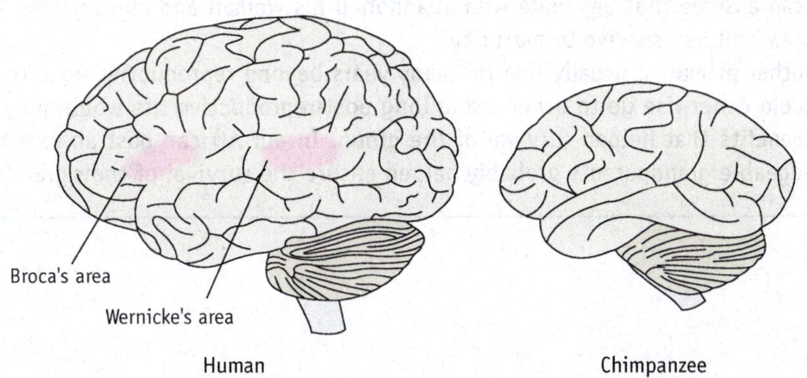

Fig. 3.6.16 Brain of human compared with chimpanzee. Average human cranial capacity is 1350 cm^3, average in chimpanzees is 400 cm^3. When humans are compared with chimpanzees, most of the size difference is in the frontal lobe of the cerebrum.

Reproduction and development

Reproductively, humans differ from other primates in a number of ways:

- Human babies are born at a very early stage of development.
- There is a prolonged period of juvenile dependence, followed by an adolescent growth spurt.
- Compared with chimpanzees and gorillas, humans have less size difference between male and female.
- The timing of ovulation in females is hidden; there is no obvious outward sign.
- Women cease ovulating in middle age.

Why is human reproduction so different?

Compared with other primates, human reproduction is different in a number of ways:

1. Human babies are born helpless and at a very early stage of development. Likely explanation: human babies have big brains and big heads. If pregnancy lasted any longer, birth would be impossible. In the past, as baby brains became larger, natural selection must have favoured the evolution of a wider pelvis in females. Mothers with narrow hips and big-headed babies probably died in childbirth. At the other extreme, any woman with very wide hips may not have been good at walking long distances, so would also have had reduced chances of survival. Evolution arrived at a compromise, combining medium-width female hips with early-stage birth.
2. Humans have a very long period of juvenile dependence on adults, perhaps because there is so much to learn. This probably reflects our origins. A lone 15-year-old on the African savanna a million years ago would have had zero chance of survival, so family and clan support would have been vital. Some animals are born with most of their behaviour instinctive and DNA-controlled; in humans most behaviour needs to be learned.
3. There is a big male-female size difference (sexual dimorphism) in chimpanzees, gorillas and orang-utans. This sort of difference is usually associated with polygamy, with the biggest males getting the most females. In *H. sapiens* there is much less size difference between male and female. This may be associated with natural selection favouring monogamous males. Rearing children on the African savanna a million years ago must have been extremely risky, and beyond the capacity of any single mother. Males who stayed loyal to mother and children probably had more offspring survive. Males who abandoned mothers and moved on may have had fewer offspring survive.
4. In all other primates, females have highly visible changes to their genital area around the time they ovulate, and this is the only time that males take a close interest. Natural selection must have favoured this sex-attraction signal to maximise the chances of successful fertilisation. In humans, ovulation is concealed — and happens at a time roughly halfway between menstrual periods. This very likely evolved as a way of keeping males interested in females throughout the year, for many years. Ongoing sex attraction probably became a means of increasing loyalty, which was essential for the successful rearing of children. We can assume that any male who abandoned his woman and child on the African savanna would have had few children survive to maturity.
5. Humans, unlike other primates, usually live for many years beyond reproductive age. They use food and resources that could otherwise go to others, so a long post-reproductive life would only have evolved if it also brought benefits that helped survival of the group. In our African past an extended family that included knowledgeable grandparents probably helped ensure the survival of their grandchildren.

 ISBN: 9780170355582

Check your understanding

1 Complete the following table to sum up structural differences between humans and apes. In each space, write a short description to clarify that difference.

Structure	*H. sapiens*	Great apes, e.g. chimpanzee
Brow ridge		
Foramen magnum		
Canine teeth		
Spine shape		
Pelvis shape		
Leg length		
Knee joint		
Hands		

2 Describe the function of the foramen magnum.

3 Explain how the changed position of the foramen magnum was an adaptation for upright walking in early hominins.

4 Explain the advantage of an opposable thumb, and explain why in apes the thumb is not fully opposable.

5 Early hominins had much longer 'hind' legs than is the case for apes such as chimpanzees. Suggest a link between these long legs and environmental conditions in Africa four or five million years ago.

6 According to one idea, humans have thin hair as an adaptation to help cooling. Give one item of evidence that supports this hypothesis. Also give one item of evidence against it.

7 Suggest one advantage to pre-human hominins of a precision-grip ability.

8 Explain how walking was (and is) made more efficient by the valgus angle.

9 Describe three ways in which human reproduction and growth differs from that of chimpanzees.

10 Explain why the female pelvis is wider in *H sapiens*, in comparison with female chimpanzees.

6

11 Suggest how these two following facts might have affected in what kind of places early hominins lived in Africa.

- Much of Africa is dry and without permanent rivers.
- It is known that pottery and water-carrying technologies were only developed in recent times.

ISBN: 9780170355582

Unit 3 | Australopithecines

Australopithecus africanus

Until the 1920s most scientists assumed that humans first evolved in Europe or Asia, but this changed in 1924 when anatomy professor Raymond Dart in South Africa was given a skull and lower jaw found in a quarry near Taung. It was a young primate with a brain no larger a chimpanzee's, but also had three features typical of modern humans: a short face, small canines, and a foramen magnum that gave proof of upright walking.

Dart realised the importance of this fossil and named it *Australopithecus africanus* (meaning 'Southern ape from Africa'). It was the first of a series of fossils known as the australopithecines, and backed up Charles Darwin's idea that human ancestors became two-legged before they became brainy.

In the 1930s many more hominin fossils were found in South Africa. These were of two general types: a slender type (gracile) named *Au. africanus*, and a more solidly built (robust) type later named *Paranthropus robustus*. All clearly had a mixture of human and ape-like features:

- Cranial capacity was small: 430 to 520 cm^3 for *Au. africanus*; about 450 cm^3 for *P. robustus*.
- Both species walked upright (were fully bipedal). Evidence:
  (a) the foramen magnum was situated under the skull;
  (b) a valgus angle in the knee joint;
  (c) a forward-facing big toe.
- Canines were relatively small, as in modern humans.

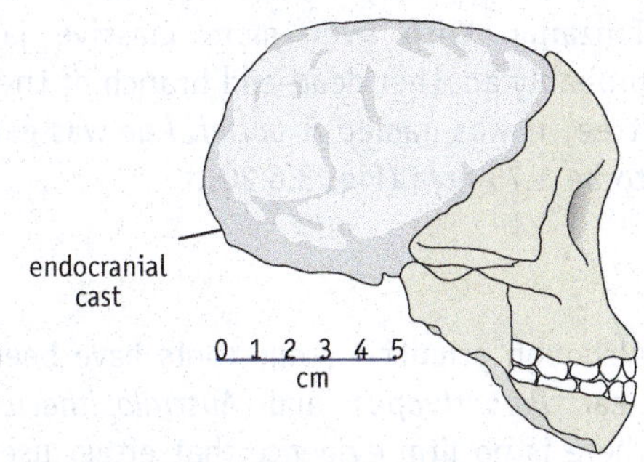

Fig. 3.6.17 Face and jaws of the Taung child, *Australopithecus africanus*. The short face is typical of modern humans.

Of the two species, the skull of *P. robustus* was less human-like. The molars were massive, proof that it was mainly a plant eater. A crest of bone (sagittal crest) along the top of the skull was evidence of powerful jaw muscles (Fig. 3.6.19).

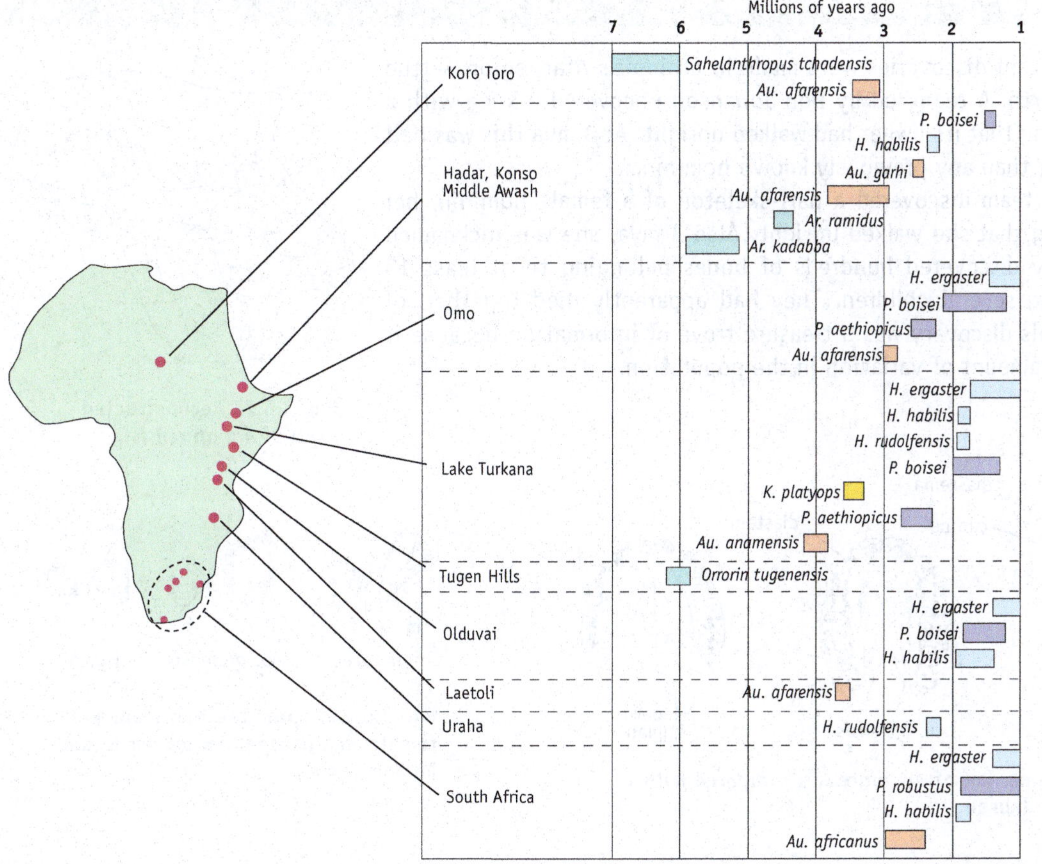

Fig. 3.6.18 Map showing some of the most important human fossil sites in Africa older than 1 mya. All known pre-human fossils more than 1.8 million years old are African, providing strong evidence of where we began.

The South African fossils were found in what had originally been limestone caves, in which there were no datable deposits. However there were abundant fossils of other animals, whose age was known with reasonably accuracy because they were also known from other sites that could be dated. Using this method of 'faunal correlation', it was estimated that *Au. africanus* lived about 3 to 1.5 mya. *P. robustus* lived about 2 to 1.5 mya. It was probably a side-branch in the human evolutionary tree, with no living descendants.

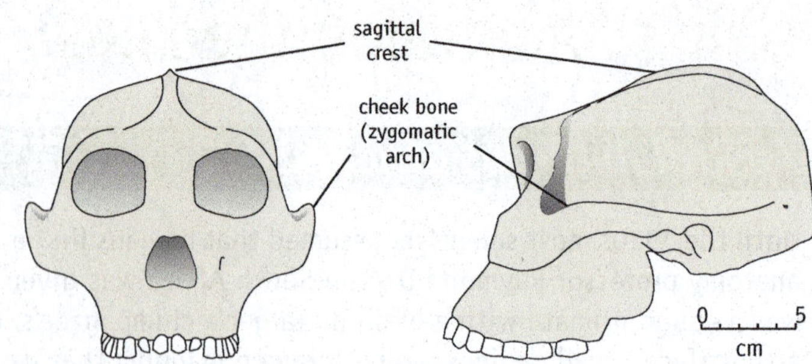

Fig. 3.6.19 *P. robustus*, its big saggital crest showing it had massive muscles for chewing tough food.

Another side branch: *Paranthropus boisei*

Another fossil, similar to *P. robustus*, was found in 1959 by Mary Leakey at Olduvai Gorge in Tanzania. With even more massive jaws and probably another dead-end branch of the human 'tree', it was named *P. boisei*. Age was estimated to be 1.75 mya (Fig. 3.6.20).

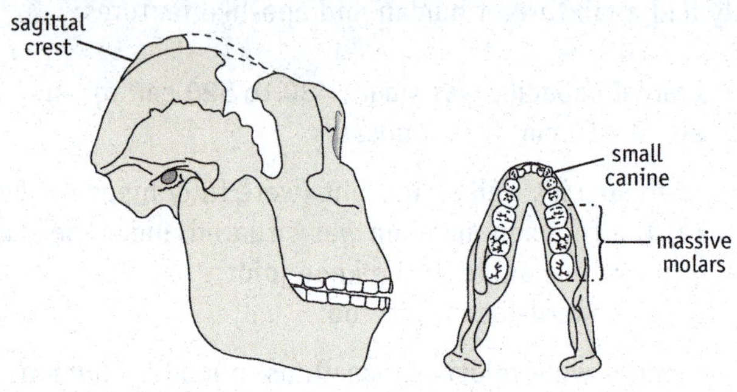

Fig. 3.6.20 Skull and lower jaw of *P. boisei*.

Did Australopithecines use tools?

Although primitive stone tools have been found near *Paranthropus* and *Australopithecus* sites, there is no firm evidence that either used stone tools. The difficulty is that hominin species which did use stone tools also lived in the same areas, but much later. Since chimpanzees are known to use sticks and stones, it's possible that the australopithecines did the same.

Australopithecus afarensis: Lucy

In 1973 some important discoveries were made in Ethiopia's Afar region — the hottest place on earth. A team led by Don Johanson uncovered a knee with a valgus angle, showing that its owner had walked upright. At 3 mya this was half a million years older than any previously known hominin.

A year later the team discovered a part-skeleton of a female hominin, her pelvis shape proving that she walked upright. Also 3 mya, she was nicknamed 'Lucy'. In 1975 they discovered hundreds of bones belonging to at least 13 individuals including several children. They had apparently died together, of unknown causes. This discovery was a treasure trove of information because it gave an idea of the amount of variation in the population.

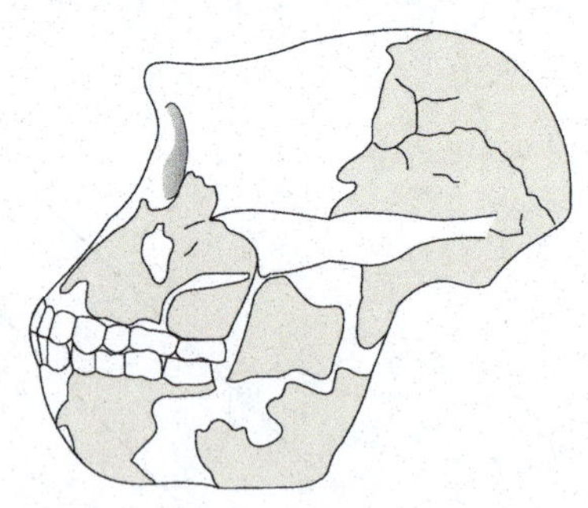

Fig. 3.6.21 Reconstructed skull of *Au. afarensis*.

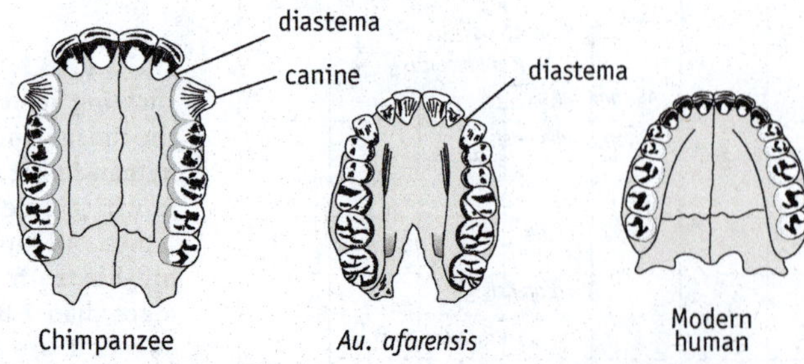

Fig. 3.6.22 The upper jaw of *Au. afarensis*, compared with a chimpanzee and a human.

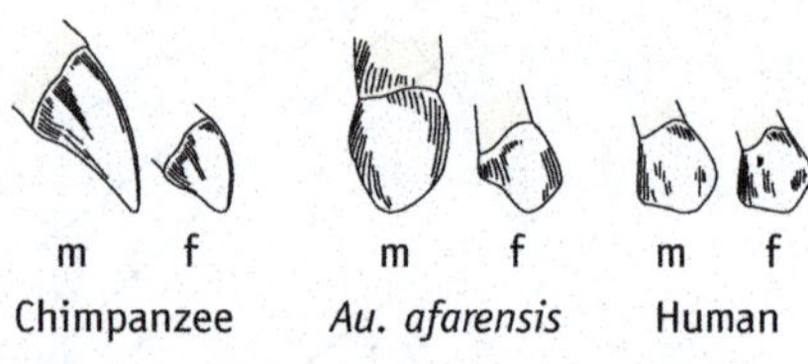

Fig. 3.6.23 Canine teeth of male and female chimpanzee, *Au. afarensis*, and human.

6

ISBN: 9780170355582

Named *Australopithecus afarensis*, their most important characteristics were:

- Fully bipedal; proved by the short, broad hip girdle, the valgus angle, the arched feet, forwardly directed big toe, and position of the foramen magnum.
- Brain between 380 and 450 cm^3, roughly the same as a chimpanzee's (Fig. 3.6.21).
- Arms were relatively long. Ridges on the limb bones showed that they were well-muscled.
- Finger and toe bones (phalanges) were somewhat curved as in the great apes. This could mean that they were partly arboreal, or it could simply have been an evolutionary 'leftover'.
- A small diastema in front of the upper canine teeth, and the canines were longer than in humans.
- Clear sexual dimorphism. Males had longer canines, were about 1.7 m tall, and weighed about 68 kg. Females were just over 1 m tall and weighed about 33 kg.

E

The oldest hominins

Between 1992 and 1994, an expedition to Aramis in Ethiopia discovered an almost complete female skeleton, dated 4.4 mya. She was about 1.2 m tall, with body mass of about 50 kg. The skeleton was so fragile that it took three years to extract and several more to reconstruct. Altogether, it was 15 years after its discovery before the analysis was published and given the name Ardipithecus ramidus. The most important features are:

- Skull fragments showed the foramen magnum was forward-placed, proving a bipedal posture.
- Her big toe was directed semi-sideways, suggesting that her foot was prehensile. This suggests (but does not prove) that she could climb trees and also walk upright.
- Her jaw was shorter than a chimpanzee's.
- The tooth enamel was thin, a characteristic of present-day chimpanzees and gorillas.
- The canines were intermediate in form between those of chimpanzees and *Au. afarensis*.
- From the abundant fossil plant and animal material recovered from the site, it is likely that *Ar. ramidus* lived in woodland rather than grassland.

In 1997 and in 2002, an expedition to the Awash region of Ethiopia found teeth and skull remains that were even more primitive than *Ar. ramidus*. Named *Ar. kadabba*, these were dated at between 5.8 and 5.2 mya — close to the date of divergence of hominins and the great apes that had been calculated from molecular data. Numerous other fossils have been found, some of which are described in *Excellence in Biology NCEA Level 3*.

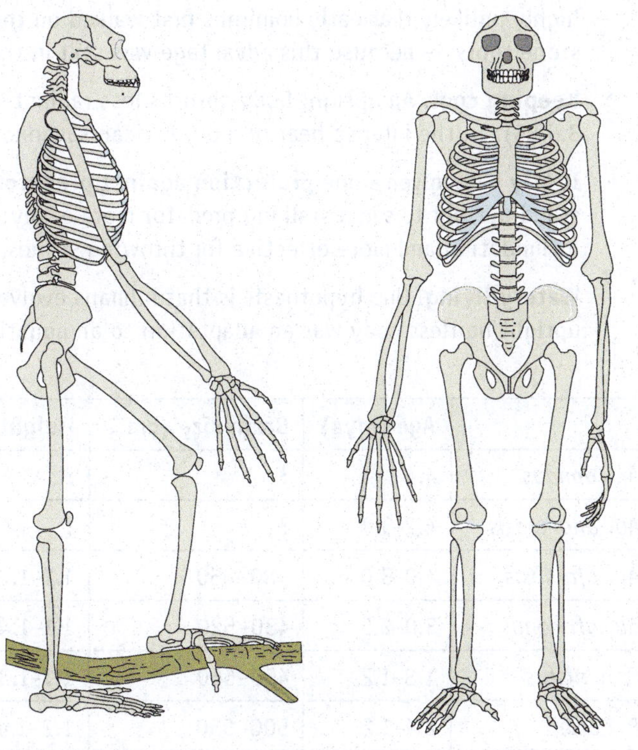

Fig. 3.6.24 ***Ardipithecus ramidus.***

Costs and benefits of ground-living

About 5 mya the African climate gradually became drier. Forests shrank and grasslands spread. These changing conditions probably forced some hominins to spend more time in the open, and some would have adapted to this — while others died out. Was life in the open any better? Both tree-living and ground-living have advantages and disadvantages:

- Arboreal (tree) life provides safety from ground predators.
- On the ground there is potentially a wider and richer diet.

The amount of time spent on the ground must have been a compromise between these two conflicting needs.

A dramatic discovery was made at Laetoli in Tanzania, in fossilised volcanic ash dated 3.6 mya. The ash shows two sets of clearly human footprints, giving absolute proof that some human-like creatures were walking upright at that time. Molecular evidence suggests that hominins diverged from other apes about 5.8 mya, so bipedalism must have evolved in less than 2.2 million years (5.8 – 3.6). Considering the major changes in skeleton and leg muscles, this was rapid evolution.

What could have been the possible advantages of bipedalism? We cannot be sure which of these advantages were important 3 or 4 or 5 mya, but there are several possibilities:

- **Carrying infants.** Baby apes hang on to their mother's long hair. If *Australopithecus* were not hairy, then mothers must have carried babies in their arms.
- **Carrying food.** Apes eat food where it is found. Modern human hunter-gatherers usually collect food some distance away from where it is eaten.
- **Tools and weapons.** Being bipedal would have greatly increased the ability to use sticks as digging tools and weapons. Chimpanzees and baboons are known to deter leopards by brandishing sticks. Hominins began to walk on two legs perhaps around 5 mya, but stone tools were first made perhaps 2.6 mya. It is highly unlikely that early hominins first walked on their hind legs in order to free their hands for making stone tools — because this advantage was still in their distant future.
- **Keeping cool.** An upright body absorbs less radiant heat from the sun than a four-footed one (Fig. 3.6.25). In the intense heat of a dry African savanna, keeping cool is important for survival.
- It may have given some **protection against predators.** In regions with long grass, some prey animals stand upright to see a stalking predator more easily. Even meerkats do this. Also, being upright is more intimidating and more effective for throwing stones.
- **Watery living.** One hypothesis is that humans evolved in swamp habitats or along seashores, and that an upright hairless body was an adaptation to an aquatic stage. There is no fossil evidence for this.

	Age (mya)	Brain size (cm^3)	Height (m)
Ar. ramidus	4.4	?	?
Au. anamensis	4.2–3.9	?	?
Au. afarensis	4.0–3.0	380–450	1.1–1.7
Au. africanus	3.0–2.5	430–520	1.1–1.4
P. robustus	1.8–1.2	450–550	1.1–1.3
P. boisei	2.4–1.2	500–530	1.2–1.4

Table 3.6.2 Key features of six australopithecine types.

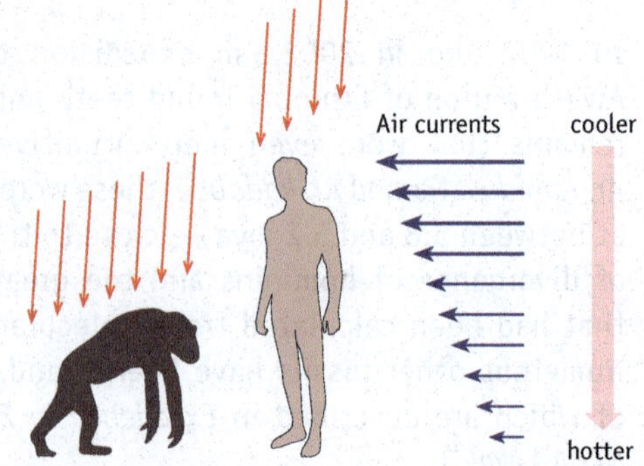

Fig. 3.6.25 In the midday sun, a quadrupedal ape absorbs more radiant heat from the sun than a bipedal ape.

6

ISBN: 9780170355582

Check your understanding

1 Complete this table to summarise some of the main African hominin fossil discoveries.

Place	In which country is it located?	Fossil hominin discovered here (genus and species name, if known)	When they lived (mya)
Taung			
Olduvai (Unit 4)			
Afar			
Awash			
Aramis			
Laetoli			
Turkana (Unit 4)			

2 For *Ar. ramidus*, describe briefly:

a The evidence for tree climbing.

b Evidence of bipedalism.

c Two points of similarity to chimpanzee-like apes.

d Two points of difference to chimpanzee-like apes.

3 Write matching word(s) in the blank column. Choose from this list: *A. africanus*, *Paranthropus*, hominins, sagittal crest, *A. afarensis*, *Australopithecus*, *Ardipithecus*.

a	Genus of australopithecine with massive jaws and molars	
b	Genus of australopithecine with smaller jaws, probably omnivorous	
c	Fossil nicknamed 'Lucy'	
d	One of the earliest fossil genera of australopithecine	
e	The first australopithecine fossil to be found	
f	Primate group consisting of the bipedal humans and their ancestors	
g	Ridge along mid-line of skull to which jaw muscles are anchored	

6

4 For each of the four possible advantages in bipedalism, complete the sentence by explaining the possible advantage of bipedalism, or its possible connection to the environment that early hominins lived in.

a Bipedalism may have given protection against predators because

and increased survival rates because

b Bipedalism may have been linked to use of tools and weapons because

and increased survival rates because

c Bipedalism may have been linked to hot African conditions because

d Bipedalism may have been linked to carrying infants because

5 State the meaning of 'gracile' and name one early hominin that fits this description.

6 State the meaning of 'robust' and name one early hominin that fits this description.

7 Describe one feature of *Australopithecus* that is apelike, and three features that are humanlike.

8 Compared with all other primates, humans are very sweaty and not hairy. Explain how these two features might be related to bipedalism.

6

9 Discuss this statement: 'Early hominins became bipedal to free their hands for making stone tools.'

ISBN: 9780170355582

Unit 4 | First stone tools, first fire

One of the early hominins — possibly *Australopithecus afarensis* — gave rise to bigger-brained types that have been given the scientific name *Homo*, meaning 'man'. The earliest two species of the genus were *H. habilis* and *H. rudolfensis*, the main evolutionary trends during their million-years-plus being:

- Increase in brain size. The average cranial capacity of australopithecines was around 400 cm^3; the earliest *Homo habilis* had brains around 650 cm^3.
- The first stone tools — although it is possible these were developed earlier.

Homo habilis

The first fossils were found by Louis and Mary Leakey at Olduvai, Tanzania, and were dated at 1.75 mya. Cranial capacity was estimated to be about 650 cm^3. Abundant stone tools lay nearby. The teeth were smaller than in australopithecines, suggesting perhaps that some food cutting was being done with stone tools. The Leakeys named these fossils *Homo habilis*, 'habilis' meaning 'handy'.

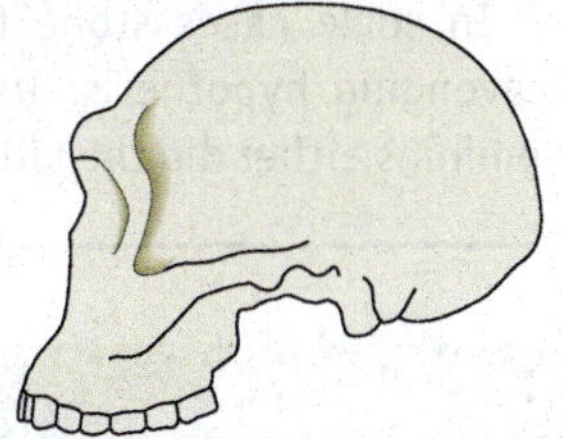

Fig. 3.6.26 Skull of *Homo habilis*.

Homo rudolfensis

A year before the discovery of *H. habilis*, a skull was found in Kenya near Lake Turkana, aka Lake Rudolf (Fig. 3.6.27). Dated at about 1.9 mya and later named *H. rudolfensis*, it had a cranial capacity of about 750 cm^3, only 250 cm^3 less than that of the smallest modern humans.

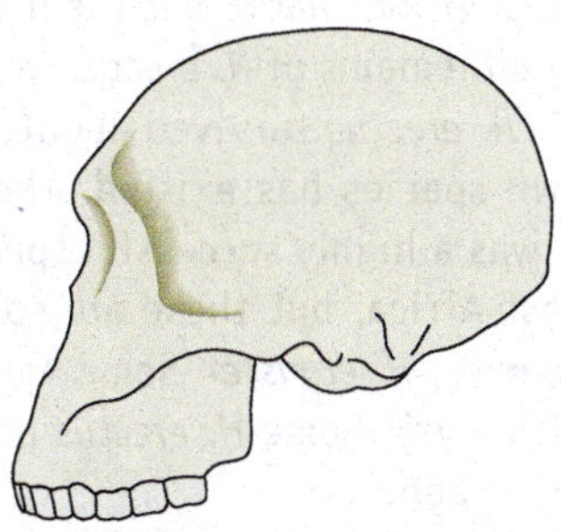

Fig. 3.6.27 Skull of *H. rudolfensis*.

The first stone tools

Stone tools associated with *H. habilis* and *H. rudolfensis* are called 'pebble tools' or **Oldowan** — because they were first found at Olduvai. Similar ones have been found in South Africa, Ethiopia, Kenya and Europe (Fig. 3.6.28). They must have been made and not 'natural' because the flat faces are concentrated at one end. Trials show they were made by striking one pebble with another.

The oldest stone tools so far discovered were near Hadar in Ethiopia, dated about 2.6 mya. It is probable that the flakes struck from the pebble were themselves used as cutting tools. These tools are extremely common, with thousands lying around in some places. Presumably unsuccessful attempts were thrown away, and new pebble tools were made when old ones became blunt.

Studies of the wear patterns have shown that some flakes were used to cut meat, others to cut wood. The ability to cut meat into pieces would have enabled large animals to be butchered. These simple tools may have been used for such purposes as cracking bones to extract marrow, and crushing tough plant food.

Making effective stone tools is not easy. (Try it sometime.) These early makers of stone tools had to start by selecting appropriate materials, then know how to produce sharp edges, then how to use it. All of this probably involved natural selection, with cleverer large-brained individuals being more successful at obtaining food. More food would have meant more babies surviving to adulthood, which is how natural selection works. These babies may have been cleverer, like their parents, and more likely to get high-protein food which would have helped brain development.

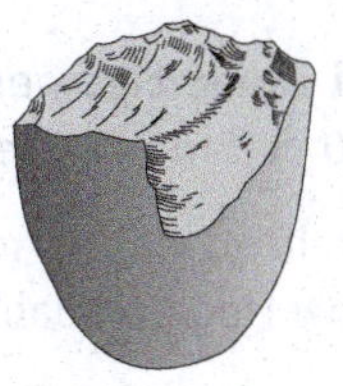

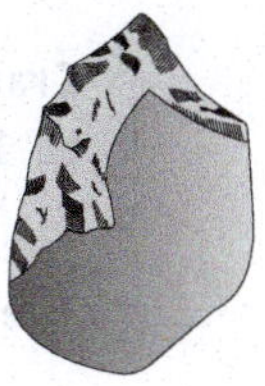

Fig. 3.6.28 Oldowan tools, typically rounded river-pebbles sharpened at one end, often used some distance from where they were shaped. On average each pebble was hit five times to sharpen one end.

6

E

Scavengers or hunters?

Scientists once thought that early hominins lived only by hunting big game. It was assumed that hunting, with its demands of skill and teamwork, provided the selection pressure for the evolution of high intelligence. Another hypothesis: they were not hunters but instead lived by scavenging food left by lions and leopards. Evidence suggests that both hypotheses are correct and that perhaps these hominins were opportunists, not specialists.

Anthropologists have experimented by scavenging in the African bush, without using any modern technology. They found it is not difficult to locate a kill by watching for signs such as circling vultures. They also found that once lions and hyenas have abandoned a kill, it becomes easy to chase away the vultures, then crack open some leg bones to get at the marrow inside.

Clues on the behaviour of extinct hominins also come from scanning electron microscope examination of scratch marks on fossil prey bones. It has been found that the marks made by stone tools and lion teeth are quite different. Stone flakes leave fine parallel scratches when used on bone.

In some cases stone tool marks have been made over existing carnivore marks, which supports the scavenging hypothesis. In other cases carnivore marks have been made over tool marks, suggesting that hominins either did the killing themselves, or else got to dead animals before other scavengers such as hyenas.

Homo erectus

In the 1890s, the fossil remains of a hominin were discovered on the island of Java (Indonesia) — the earliest outside Africa. Originally known as 'Java Man', it was later given the species name *Homo erectus* on the mistaken assumption that it was the first upright-walking human species. Later, more fossil remains of *H. erectus* were found in China, Africa and Georgia.

H. erectus survived about 1.7 million years — 10 times longer than our own species has existed. They spread across two continents, suggesting it was a highly successful species. The oldest forms lived about 1.9 mya in East Africa, but these are sometimes considered to belong to a separate species, *H. ergaster*. Some Asian specimens found in Java are almost as old (1.8 mya). Some *H. erectus* populations survived to as recently as 143,000 years ago.

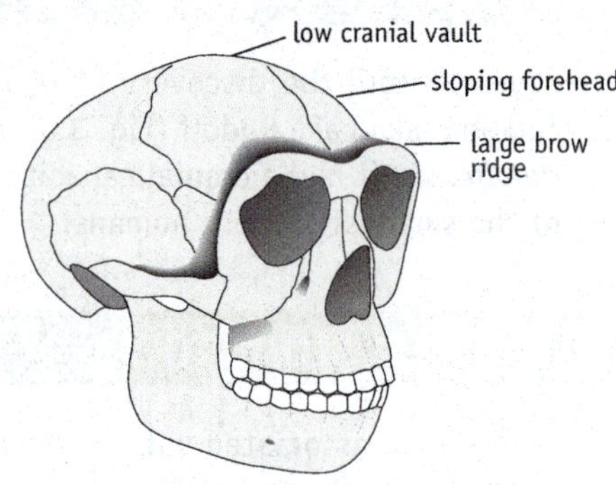

Fig. 3.6.29 Reconstruction of skull of *H. erectus* from Zhoukoudian in China.

Characteristics

H. erectus varied greatly and achieved wide distribution, but all shared the following features:

- **Cranial capacities** were larger than in *H. habilis*, ranging from just over 800 cm^3 in the oldest specimens to 1250 cm^3 in more recent ones.
- The forehead was narrow and had a prominent **brow ridge** even in smaller, probably female, individuals. The brow ridge probably resisted the forces set up in chewing.
- Strong **neck muscles**. Evidence: the skull had a transverse ridge above the neck, with a large area for muscle attachment.
- The **lower jaw** was strongly built, with no chin.
- **Teeth** were smaller than in *H. habilis*, but larger than in modern humans.
- All *H. erectus* sites are associated with **Acheulean stone tools**.
- There is good evidence they used **fire** deliberately. Details below.

6

 ISBN: 9780170355582

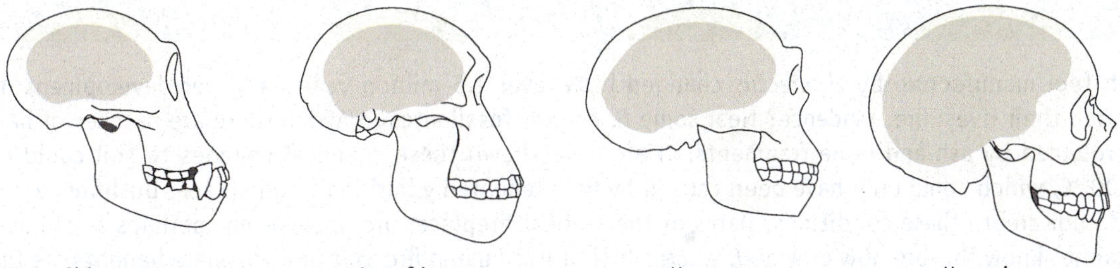

Chimpanzee *Au. africanus* *H. erectus* *H. sapiens*

Fig. 3.6.30 Changes in the relative sizes of the brain and face in human evolution.

E

Tools and culture

The earliest *H. erectus* fossils are associated with pebble tools, but their most characteristic tools were 'hand axes' in which the entire stone was shaped into two main faces (Fig. 3.6.32). Tools of this type are known as **Acheulean** (also spelled Acheulian). Together, the Oldowan and Acheulean cultures are known as the Lower Palaeolithic. (Palaeolithic means 'Old Stone Age'.)

Experiments have shown that the pattern of wear in stone tools (when seen under the microscope) is characteristic of the kind of use to which the stone is put. Some Acheulean 'hand axes' had been used to cut meat, others had been used to bore holes in wood.

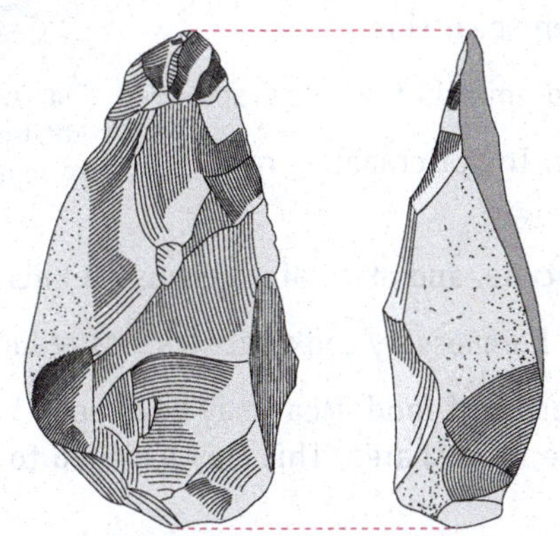

Fig. 3.6.32 Acheulean tools were sharpened along two edges using up to 50 'shaping strikes'; and were much heavier and more sophisticated than Oldowan tools.

Acheulean tools first appeared about 1.7 mya in East Africa. By 1 mya they had appeared in Israel, and by 500,000 years ago their use had spread to Europe and India. Stone tools cannot be made from any kind of rock, and only certain kinds of rock such as flint and obsidian are suitable. Stone tool making required the ability to recognise suitable kinds of rock and to pass on stone-shaping skills to others. Although it is impossible to be sure about timing, spoken language may also have begun to evolve by this stage.

Optional hands-on practical activity. Make stone tools of the type described in this and later units. Once you have made some sharp stone flakes, they could be used as knives. Use these to skin a freshly killed animal such as a rabbit. You will find that it is almost impossible to do the task without some sort of implement. Rule: no modern or metal technology is allowed. Suggestions: start with a hard rock such as basalt, and do this outside. Safety requirement: use eye protection to prevent stone fragments hitting your eyes.

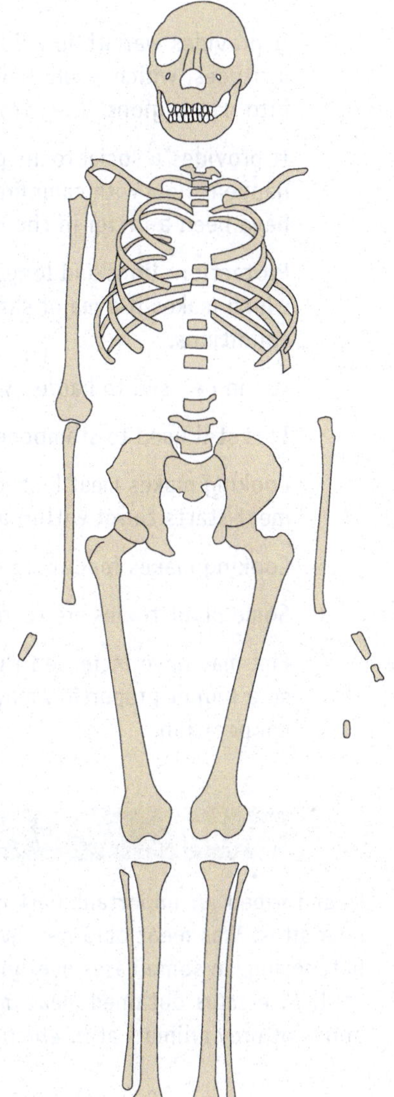

Fig. 3.6.31 An almost complete skeleton of a male juvenile *H. erectus* was discovered on the shores of Lake Turkana (Lake Rudolf) in Kenya. Based on the incomplete development of his bones, this 'Turkana boy' was estimated to be nine years old and already 1.6 metres tall, suggesting that adults would have been at least as tall as modern humans.

9780170355582

Fire

Although tool manufacture by *H. erectus* changed little over 1.5 million years, another development must have transformed their lives: fire. Evidence? Near some *H. erectus* fossil sites in Africa there are patches of heat-altered soil, surrounded by ash and bone fragments. Trials have shown these chemical changes to soil could only occur above 400 °C, which could only have been caused by fires repeatedly burning in one place. Bushfires and lightning strikes do not create these conditions. Dates of the earliest fireplaces are unclear, but perhaps as old as 1.5 mya.

We cannot know for sure how or why *H. erectus* first started using fire, but nine possible benefits are listed here. These benefits are not pure guesswork; we have a good idea from observations of present-day hunter-gatherers such as Khoisan people of the Kalahari Desert.

Fig. 3.6.33 Lions were major predators of humans until recent times. Fire was probably our main form of defence.

- It provides warmth in cold climates and at high altitudes, which would have enabled *H. erectus* to spread into new regions, away from tropical conditions.
- It provides a social focus point after dark, just as happens now with campfires. Nightly gatherings could have been a factor in the development of language.
- Protection: lions and leopards will not go near fire, which makes it a major safety factor under African conditions.
- It can be used to harden wooden spear tips.
- It is still used to stampede herd animals towards traps.
- Cooking makes meat last longer. In hot climates, raw meat starts to rot within a day.
- Cooking makes food more digestible, and also safer because it kills parasites such as tapeworms.
- Some plant toxins are rendered harmless by cooking. Sickness reduced by cooking.
- Fire may have increased the sharing of food. Meat may have been brought back to base to be cooked, so a higher proportion may have been shared. This may have led to more sophisticated social rules for cooperation.

Meat eating

Meat formed an important part of the diet of *H. erectus*, as shown by the large numbers of fossil animal bones near sites. Was meat obtained by hunting or by scavenging? Examination of bones show the cut marks typical of butchering, in some cases overlying lion tooth marks.

If *H. erectus* obtained meat mainly by scavenging, they must have been very good at it. The sheer number of bones of prey animals at *H. erectus* sites suggests that meat was a major food of earlier hominins.

Check your understanding

6

1 Compare the brain capacities of *H. erectus*, *H. habilis*, *H. rudolfensis*, *Au. africanus*.

ISBN: 9780170355582

2 List features that make stone tools recognisable as part of the Oldowan culture.

3 Explain why fossils found at Olduvai were given the species name '*habilis*'.

4 Describe fossil evidence that hominins sometimes scavenged off the kill of predators such as lions.

5 Explain the likely adaptive advantage of tool-using capabilities, by using specific examples to suggest how stone tools might have increased reproductive success in *H. habilis*.

6 Chimpanzees sometimes use stones to crack open nuts or sticks to get ants out of logs. Discuss whether there is a clear line between this 'tool-using' behaviour and the use in early hominins.

7 The list below gives the first part of sentences that relate to the likely uses of fire by *H. erectus*. Complete each of the five sentences by explaining how that particular 'use' may have extended the life span of individuals and possibly been of benefit to their whole group. Your answers should relate to short-term survival advantages, not to genetics or long-term evolutionary benefits.

a Fires provide warmth at night, which meant that

b Cooking kills bacteria in the meat, which meant that

c Fires repel lions and other predators, which meant that

d Fire can be used to harden wood, which meant that

e Fires provide a social focus point at night, which meant that

8 Summarise evidence that *H. erectus* probably used fire.

9 Describe the main differences between Oldowan and Acheulean tools.

10 Identify which hominins were responsible for making these types of tool:

a Oldowan

b Acheulean.

11 Explain the possible significance of the 'Turkana boy' discovery.

6

 ISBN: 9780170355582

Unit 5 | Neanderthals, Denisovans and more

When did we first become human? There may never be a final answer because there was a gradual transition from *H. erectus* to *H. sapiens*. For simplicity, in this book we will consider any *Homo sapiens* to be human. Between *H. erectus* and *H. sapiens* is a collection of fossils generally grouped into two species: *H. heidelbergensis* and *H. neanderthalensis*. Fossil and molecular evidence shows that of these, only *heidelbergensis* could have been ancestral to modern *H. sapiens*.

Even *H. sapiens* from the distant past are described as 'modern' humans. This does not mean 'modern' as regards technology or culture; it means modern in the sense that their physical features were no different from those of people living today.

Homo heidelbergensis

H. heidelbergensis first appeared in the fossil record about 850,000 years ago and lasted until about 100,000 years ago. Evidence suggests they probably originated in Africa and quickly spread throughout Europe, Asia and Africa. They differed in a number of ways from *H. erectus* (Fig. 3.6.34):

- An increase in cranial capacity to an average of 1200 cm^3, only slightly smaller than the modern *H. sapiens* average of 1350 cm^3.
- A higher cranial vault (roof of skull).
- A decrease in size of the teeth and jaws.
- Though still very prominent, the brow ridges were partly separated, instead of a single ridge spanning the whole forehead as in *H. erectus*.

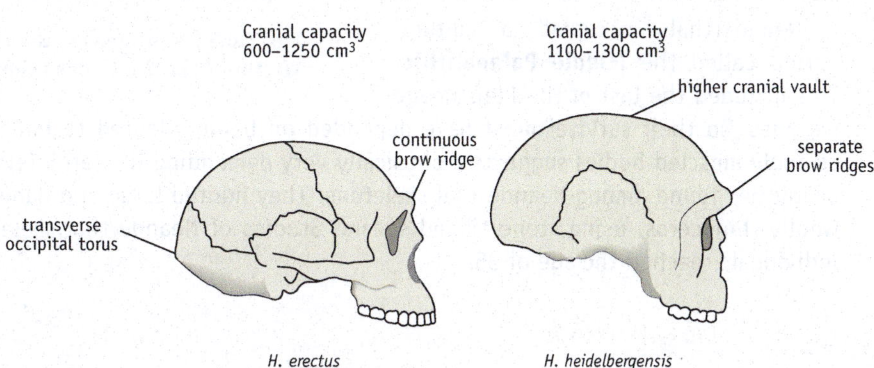

Fig. 3.6.34 Comparison between skulls of *H. erectus* and *H. heidelbergensis*.

Hunting and tool-making

Many *H. heidelbergensis* sites are known, but only a few provide solid evidence for large-scale hunting. At one cave site in Spain, dated 800,000 years ago, many animal bones were found with marks of stone tools. In some cases stone tool marks were overlaid by later animal tooth marks, suggesting that those animals scavenged off *H. heidelbergensis* kills.

One of the most significant innovations in tool-making was the invention of the **Levallois** technique between 250,000 and 300,000 years ago. It originated in Africa, but its name comes from a Paris suburb where such tools were first found. Each tool was made from a large flake struck off a prepared core. The flake was then further shaped by striking small pieces from its edges. Several large flakes could be produced from a single core.

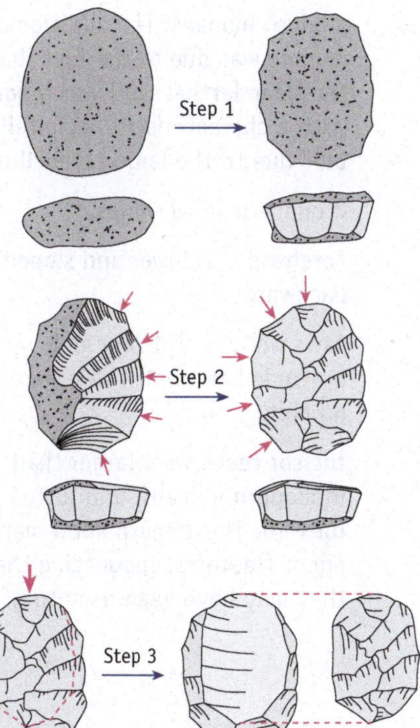

Fig. 3.6.35 The Levallois technique. It took many actions to strike stone flakes off the edges of the core, producing a number of sharp flakes and a main stone tool with many sharp edges.

6

The Neanderthals

Neanderthal remains have been found throughout Europe and in parts of Western Asia, and are by far the best-known non-modern humans (Fig. 3.6.36). The name comes from the first discovery of their bones, in Germany's Neander valley.

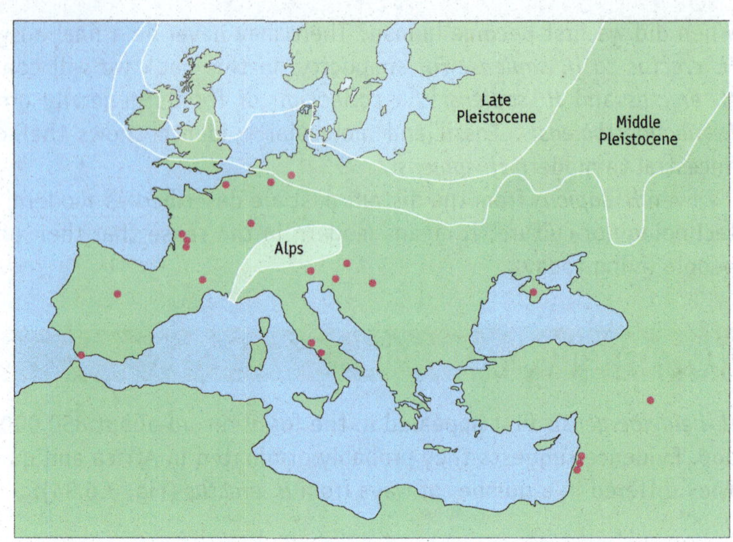

Fig. 3.6.36 Map showing the main Neanderthal sites in Europe and Western Asia. White lines show the extent of ice sheets and glaciation.

Time span

The oldest Neanderthal remains have been found in a cave at Atapuerca, Spain, and consist of at least 28 people who lived between 350,000 and 400,000 years ago. The youngest remains found are from Croatia, dated at 28,000 years ago.

Neanderthals occupied a cultural period called the **Middle Palaeolithic.** This included the last of the Pleistocene ice ages, so their survival must have depended on being adapted to harsh conditions and extreme cold. Their strongly muscled bodies suggests a physically very demanding life, an inference backed up by the high frequency of injuries found among Neanderthal skeletons. They hunted large and dangerous animals such as cave bears and woolly rhinoceros, using stone-tipped spears. Studies of Neanderthal skeletons show that fewer than one in 10 individuals reached the age of 35.

Physical characteristics

Some physical features of Neanderthals compared with modern humans:

- Average cranial capacity was 1500 cm^3, compared with 1350 cm^3 in modern humans. The additional volume was due to the fact that the Neanderthal skull was longer, with a characteristic 'occipital bun' due to the large cerebellum.
- Prominent brow ridges.
- Forehead was lower and sloped backward.
- Jaws were very strong and protruded forward. There was no chin.
- Incisor teeth were larger than in modern humans, and jutted forward. These teeth show many micro-fractures, suggesting that they may have been used to grip.

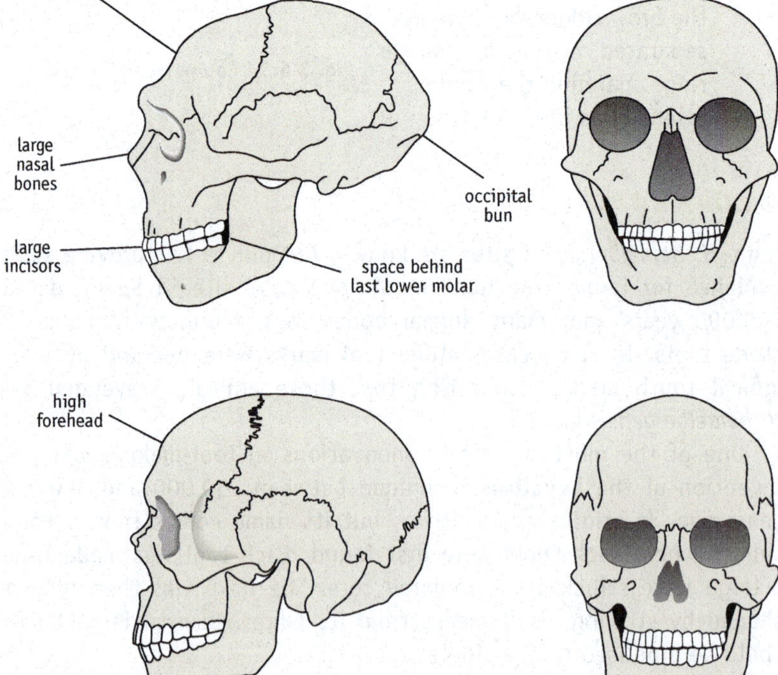

Fig. 3.6.37 Neanderthal (top) and modern human (bottom) skulls compared.

6

ISBN: 9780170355582

- The nasal (nose) bones jutted out more than in modern humans, and the nasal cavity was longer. This may have been an adaptation to cold conditions, for warming inhaled air.
- The forearm and lower leg were relatively shorter than in modern humans. The limb bones were very strongly built, with prominent ridges for muscle attachment.

Neanderthal tools and clothing

Most Neanderthal stone tools were skilfully made using the Levallois technique. The Neanderthal tool culture itself was known as **Mousterian**. Implements included blades, points, burins (a kind of chisel) and scrapers. Microwear studies have shown that most were used to work wood and scrape animal hides.

There is indirect evidence that they clothed themselves in animal skins. Their incisors showed extreme wear, suggesting these teeth may have been used like pliers to hold skins while they were being scraped. It is unlikely that they could have survived the Pleistocene ice ages without clothing.

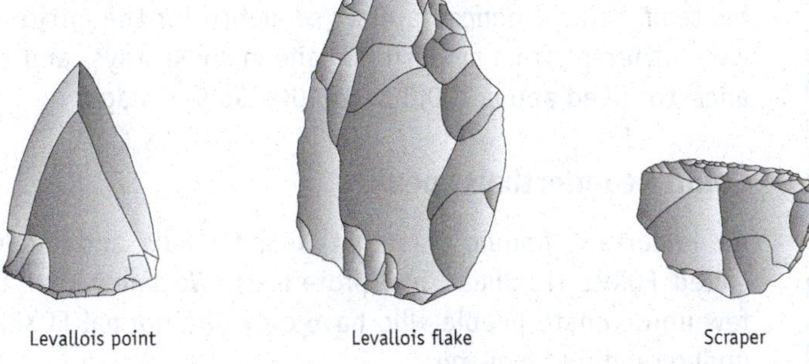

Fig. 3.6.38 Some Neanderthal implements. Their tools were more finely made than Acheulean hand axes and far more varied.

Burial of the dead, care for the disabled

Neanderthal people probably buried their dead. Evidence:

- A high proportion of intact skeletons. If bodies were simply abandoned, most would have been ripped apart by scavengers.
- At Shanidar Cave in northern Iraq, the skeleton of a middle-aged Neanderthal man was found to be circled by pollen grains from colourful flowers. Likely explanation: his family placed flowers around the body before it was covered with soil, a custom that continues to this day, and something that non-humans never do.
- Bones of prey animals have been found alongside skeletons, in some cases accompanied by stone tools, suggesting that Neanderthals believed they were helping the person in the afterlife.

One skeleton in France was of an older man who had lost most of his teeth and clearly suffered from severe arthritis. The Shanidar Cave skeleton had a withered right arm. Neither of these individuals could have made much practical contribution to the survival of his group, yet they survived with the help and support of others.

Were Neanderthals artistic?

Until recent years it was believed that art was a unique achievement of modern humans and that earlier pre-humans were concerned only with physical survival. Recently, evidence has been found of personal adornment. A 50,000-year-old Neanderthal site in Spain revealed a number of mollusc shells that had been pierced as if strung together in a necklace.

At one Neanderthal cave in Slovenia, investigators discovered a bear femur with holes bored into it so that it resembled a flute. It was dated at 43,000 years old, and may be evidence that Neanderthals made music.

E

Links to modern humans

In recent years it has been possible to extract DNA from well-preserved Neanderthal skeletons. Mitochondrial DNA (mtDNA) was studied first. This has the advantage of being inherited solely from the mother, so change cannot occur by recombination. Also, most cells have 500 to 1000 mitochondria, so many copies are available.

By 1997 the Swedish geneticist Svante Pääbo had extracted DNA from a Neanderthal arm bone. By 2010 his team had announced a draft sequence for the entire genome. Their analysis showed that Neanderthals were different from modern humans in some ways, and that the most recent human-Neanderthal common ancestor lived about 300,000 to 400,000 years ago.

Could Neanderthals speak?

An important finding was that Neanderthals and modern humans share a peculiar variant of a gene called FOXP2 (forkhead box protein 2). We know that this gene is important in language, because the few unfortunate people who have only one normal FOXP2 allele have great difficulty in making sounds or understanding language.

Though the FOXP2 gene is present in all mammals and in birds, humans and Neanderthals appear unique in sharing two mutations in this gene that are absent in all other mammals. This suggests that Neanderthals could speak, and also that the FOXP2 mutations occurred before Neanderthals split from modern humans.

What happened to the Neanderthals?

Studies of Neanderthal DNA show that they could not have evolved into modern humans. It is very likely that Neanderthals were out-competed by modern people moving into Europe from the Middle East, around 40,000 years ago. Recent research shows that there must been some interbreeding of Neanderthals and the new arrivals. Evidence: modern humans from Europe and Asia share an average of 2.5 per cent of their DNA with Neanderthals. Africans do not have any Neanderthal DNA, proving that Neanderthal evolution occurred after modern humans left Africa.

Why caves?

Most Neanderthal (and other) remains have been found in caves. It is quite likely that only some groups used caves as homes, but that most groups lived and hunted in open country far from any caves. If these groups built temporary shelters of wood, their shelters would not have survived long. Any bones and burial sites in or near caves had a much better chance of lasting thousands of years, and eventually being discovered.

The Denisovans

6

At the Denisova Cave in Siberia, archaeologists found a small human-like finger bone, a molar tooth and a toe bone. A bracelet and other artefacts found with the bones were carbon-dated at about 41,000 years. When DNA in the bone and tooth was analysed, the results suggested that Denisovans were related to Neanderthals:

- Denisovan mtDNA differs from modern mtDNA by nearly twice as many base pairs as Neanderthals differ from modern humans. This suggets that Denisovans last shared a common ancestor with modern humans about one million years ago.
- Between four and six per cent of the nuclear DNA of Melanesians is identical to Denisovan DNA. (Melanesians are people of New Guinea, New Caledonia, Vanuatu, Fiji.) This suggests that Denisovans interbred with modern humans in South-East Asia. Further studies showed that Australian aborigines and some inhabitants of the Philippines and Polynesia also have some Denisovan ancestry.

ISBN: 9780170355582

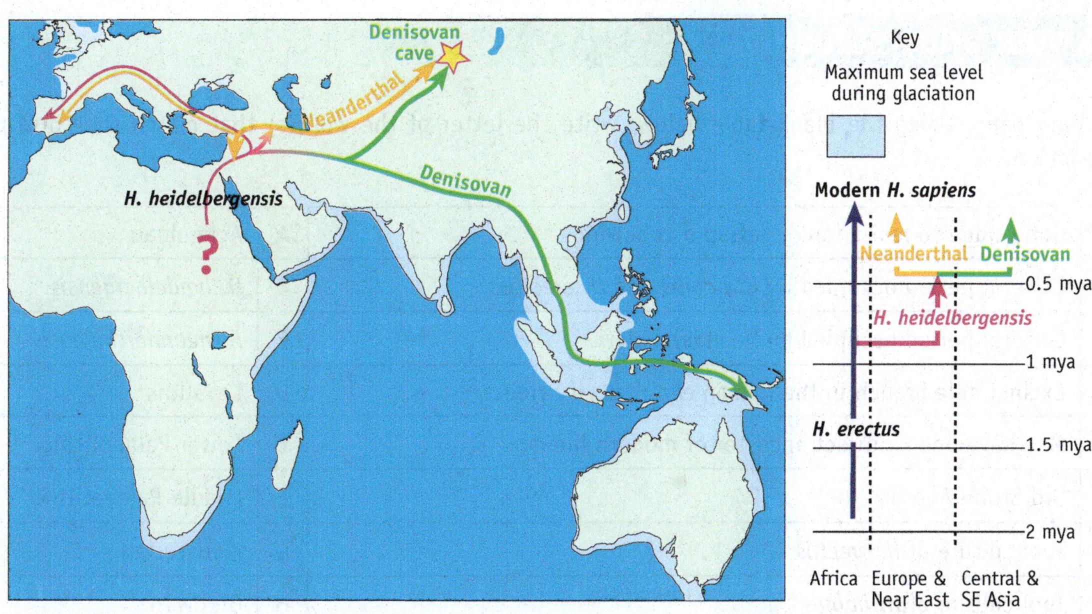

Fig. 3.6.39 Three Homo species and their possible connections. Neanderthals occupied Europe for over 300 000 years. *H. denisova* is known only from one cave in Siberia, but genes of their type also appear in New Guinea and Australia.

Homo floresiensis

A cave on Flores Island (Indonesia), produced a remarkable discovery in 2003: the remains of a female human-like creature about 1 metre high. The remains consisted of a skull, mandible, parts of the backbone, pelvis, legs and feet. It was nicknamed 'the hobbit' (Fig. 3.6.40).

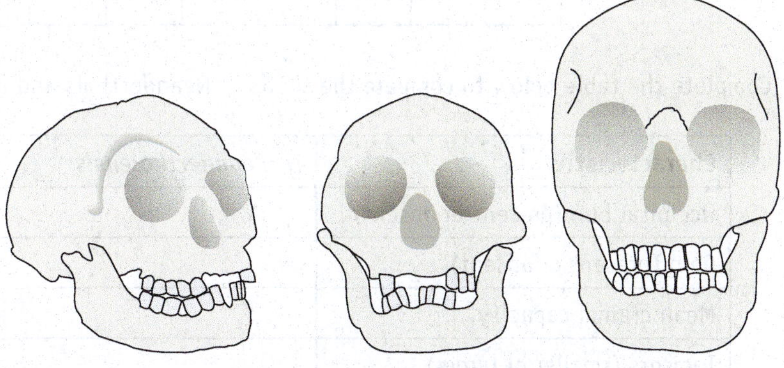

Fig. 3.6.40 Skull of *H. floresiensis* (left and centre) compared with that of *H. sapiens*. The cranial capacity is tiny, but other features are like those of modern humans.

The brain was 380 cm^3, about the size of a chimpanzee's — very small even when body size is taken into account. In 2004 the partial remains of another eight, similar individuals were found. The butchered remains of Komodo dragons and pygmy elephants, together with charred bones and fire-cracked rocks, indicates that these creatures were hunters who used fire.

The age of the specimens ranged from 94,000 years to a very recent 12,000 years old. Also remarkable: Flores is surrounded by deep water, so that even during ice ages it could only have been reached by boat.

Despite the fact that its brain was smaller than any other species of *Homo*, the researchers decided to place it in the genus, and to call it *Homo floresiensis*. It may have evolved from a local *H. erectus* population, then survived in isolation until very recently. Should this 'hobbit' be considered human or not? Questions like this are unanswerable until more pieces of the jigsaw are discovered.

Check your understanding

1 Matching pairs. Using the blank table below, write the letter of the word(s) that match the corresponding description.

1	Bony ridge to resist forces set up by chewing	A	Acheulean
2	Cultural period occupied by *H. habilis* and *H. erectus*	B	*H. heidelbergensis*
3	Cultural period occupied by Neanderthals	C	*H. neanderthalensis*
4	Extinct side branch in the human evolutionary tree	D	Levallois
5	May have been a direct ancestor of modern humans	E	Lower Palaeolithic
6	Old Stone Age	F	Middle Palaeolithic
7	Tool culture of *H. erectus*	G	Mousterian
8	Tool culture of *H. habilis*	H	Oldowan
9	Tool culture of Neanderthals	I	Palaeolithic
10	Tool-making technique used by *H. heidelbergensis* and also Neanderthals	J	Brow ridge

1	2	3	4	5	6	7	8	9	10

2 Complete the table below to compare the skulls of Neanderthals and modern humans.

Characteristic	*H. neanderthalensis*	*H. sapiens*
Occipital bun (present or absent)		
Chin (present or absent)		
Mean cranial capacity		
Incisors (smaller or larger)		
Nasal cavity (smaller or larger)		
Brow ridges (present or absent)		
Forehead (low or high)		

3 Describe three kinds of indirect evidence that Neanderthals had clothing.

4 Describe evidence that Neanderthals cared for older and disabled people.

ISBN: 9780170355582

5 Describe evidence that Neanderthals cared for their dead.

6 Explain how we can be sure that Neanderthals originated in Europe or Asia, and not in Africa.

7 Describe two human-like features of *H. floresiensis*.

8 Describe two ways in which *H. floresiensis* were completely unlike modern humans.

9 Hypothesise on the possible origins of *H. floresiensis*, including which hominins they evolved from, and how they may have got to the island of Flores.

10 Describe from where the Denisovans probably originated. State which modern human groups may be most closely related to them, and identify the evidence for this.

11 List four or more ways in which Neanderthal stone tools were an advance on those of earlier stone cultures.

9780170355582

Unit 6 | The first modern humans

Discovery, distribution, time span

In archaeology, 'modern' describes any *H. sapiens* humans who were anatomically (physically) the same as us, even if their cultures were totally different. In 1868 the pre-historic remains of anatomically modern *H. sapiens* humans were found at Cro-Magnon in France. Since then, all Europeans similar to these have been known as Cro-Magnon people, with the earliest remains in Europe carbon-dated at 40 kya (thousand years ago).

The very earliest skeletons of modern humans discovered anywhere are in Ethiopia, dated 195 kya. Remains found in Israel prove that by 120 kya, some humans had already begun to move out of Africa, but evidence suggests these early 'Asian' groups eventually died out — possibly because of the Neanderthals already living there. A much later movement of human groups out of Africa began around 60 kya. These people, probably fewer than 3000 in number, became the ancestors of all present-day humans now living beyond Africa.

Physical characteristics of modern humans

Modern humans differ from the *H. neanderthalensis* and *H. heidelbergensis* in a number of ways:

- Cranial capacity is slightly smaller in *H. sapiens*, averaging about 1350 cm^3.
- Brow ridges are smaller; the large forehead is steeper.
- A prominent chin.
- Jaws and teeth are smaller, especially the incisors.
- Limbs are more slender, possibly because technological skills replaced muscle power.

Cultural evolution

Enormous changes have occurred since the first modern *H. sapiens* evolved perhaps 200 kya. Almost all these changes have been **cultural**, not biological. Genetically, we have changed little in the last 200,000 years. By 'culture' we mean language, customs, art, technology, skills, beliefs — anything that is acquired by learning. Culture does not depend on DNA.

Other animals (for example chimpanzees, elephants) also have cultures that vary between different groups. One feature that distinguishes our species from others is that cultural change has accelerated, with the past 300 years of cultural evolution having changed the world more than three million years of biological evolution.

Cultural evolution and biological (genetic) evolution differ in the following ways:

- **Storage:** Genetic information is stored in DNA. Cultural information is stored in the mind. (Since the invention of writing, on paper and now digitally.)
- **Origins:** Genetic change begins with mutation and recombination. Cultural change begins with imagination and inventiveness.
- **Speed:** Genetic evolution is slow. Cultural evolution can be very fast by comparison.
- **Purposeful:** Genetic evolution works by trial and error (natural selection). Cultural evolution can anticipate future needs and be purposeful.
- **Transmission:** Genetic information can only be transmitted from parents to offspring. Cultural information can be transmitted from anyone to anyone, even from dead to living. Ideas travel freely.
- **Change:** Genetic information remains fixed during the lifetime of each individual. Cultural information is acquired, modified and transmitted throughout life.

 ISBN: 9780170355582

E

Biological and cultural evolution are fundamentally different, but have probably interacted in complex ways. According to the manner of this interaction, we can distinguish four phases:

1 Brain size increased to the point where significant cultural change became possible.

2 Cultural change began to provide a stimulus for further increase in brain size — in other words, biological and cultural evolution became linked in a **positive feedback** cycle (Fig. 3.6.41).

3 Brain size stopped increasing, probably because the advantages of big brains came into balance with childbirth-related disadvantages, resulting in stabilising selection.

4 The past 200,000 years of human evolution has been almost entirely cultural, and change has been at an ever-increasing rate.

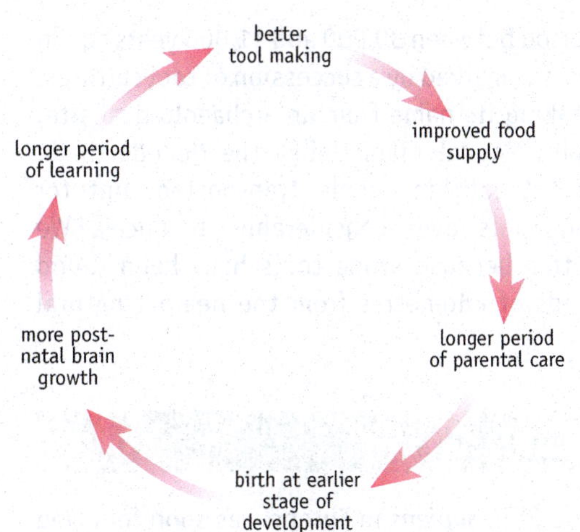

Fig. 3.6.41 Possible feedback between genetic and cultural change.

Stages in cultural evolution

There are many stages with many different names, but only a few of the main ones are listed here.

Broad category	Name of 'age'	Who?
Industrial Revolution		Worldwide *H. sapiens*
Agricultural Revolution		Worldwide *H. sapiens*
'Metal ages'; first bronze, then iron, then steel		Worldwide *H. sapiens*
'Stone ages'	Neolithic	*H. sapiens*
	Upper Palaeolithic	*H. sapiens*
	Mousterian	*H. neanderthalensis*
	Acheulean	*H. erectus*
	Oldowan	*H. habilis*
	(none)	*Australopithecus*

Tool technology

From about 50 kya onwards — marking the start of the Upper Palaeolithic period — technology of hunting suddenly became more sophisticated, with more intricate stone and bone tools. The most important features of these *H. sapiens* tools were as follows:

- They were more finely made (Fig. 3.6.42).
- They made much use of bone, antler and ivory as well as stone (Fig. 3.6.42).
- They combined one kind of material with another to make composite tools. (Fig. 3.6.43).

- Tools were used to make other tools, an achievement that enabled later rapid strides in technology. Particularly important: the *burin*, a stone chisel used to work wood, antler or bone.

The period between 30,000 and 11,000 years ago in Europe was marked by a succession of tool cultures, each taking its name from an archaeological site. Example: Magdalenian. Unlike the Neanderthals, Upper Palaeolithic people transported flint for making tools over considerable distances. We know this because stone tools have been found hundreds of kilometres from the nearest natural source.

Hunting

The rise of *H. sapiens* in Europe was soon followed by the extinction of a number of large mammals, including mammoths and woolly rhinoceros. Similar mass extinctions of prey animals occurred soon after the arrival of humans in Australia (where about 50 large mammal species vanished quite suddenly), North America, and also New Zealand (moa extinction). The most likely explanation: modern humans indulged in overkill. This is backed up by the huge numbers of prey animal bones in places such as Buffalo Jump in Canada.

Bows and arrows were independently invented in several parts of the world by 20 kya. They offered a significant advantage over spears, as any hunter could now kill from greater distances. By 17 kya the spear thrower (atlatl) had been invented. This hooked on to the end of a spear, enabling it to be thrown faster and further.

Harpoons were invented before 17 kya. Together with fishhooks, harpoons were a key technology in parts of the world where cloudy conditions caused people to be chronically short of vitamin D — which in sunny climates is naturally made in the skin. Sea fish are rich in vitamin D, so harpoons helped humans spread into cooler, more cloudy areas.

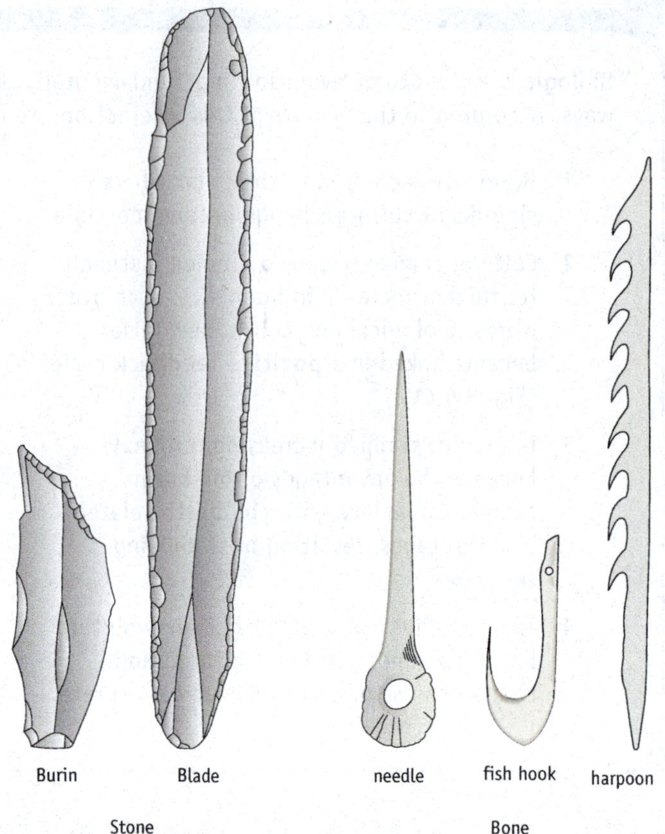

Fig. 3.6.42 Some Upper Palaeolithic stone and bone tools. Perforation techniques made needles possible, hides to be sewn, enabling humans to move into colder areas. Flint was a favoured material for stone blades.

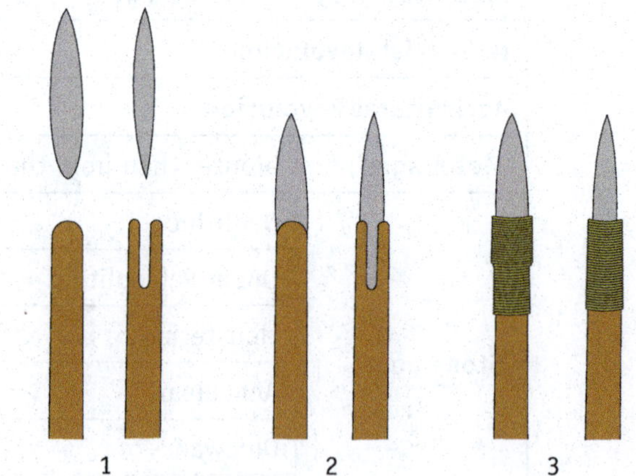

Fig. 3.6.43 A Neanderthal spear at three stages of its production. Composite materials made sharp spearheads possible.

6

Improvements in the use of fire

A million years ago *H. erectus* probably used fires that had been naturally started (e.g. by lightning), but it was only in relatively recent times that *H. sapiens* learned how to make fire. One way was to use the natural mineral iron pyrite to strikes sparks hot enough to ignite tinder. The earliest example of such a 'firestone' has been found in Belgium, alongside remains dated at 15 kya.

A development of great significance: making fires hotter by directing air through channels in the earth. The long-term significance of ducted air was that it created temperatures high enough to make pottery and (later) metal from ores. Pottery was not developed until 13 kya — and rapidly became important because it enabled people to carry water and so live further from rivers, and also to cook in containers.

ISBN: 9780170355582

Palaeolithic art

The earliest symbolic art — mostly necklaces and engravings — is from Southern Africa, dated at 71 kya. From around 30 kya bone carvings and cave paintings became increasingly common in Europe and elsewhere. Why did people spend so much time on this? One hypothesis is that art resulted from increased food supply. With lives less dominated by hunger, hunter-gatherers had more time on their hands. However, this does not explain what drives artistic creativity.

Another hypothesis: greatly increased brain size resulted in creative and imaginative capacities far beyond what was needed for simple survival. People painted, carved and decorated because art results in emotional satisfaction and personal self-expression. Beauty became an end in itself. One eventual result: thousands of years later the development of writing enabled people to use words and symbols to represent objects and ideas.

Life expectancy

From skeletons of early modern people it has been possible to calculate life span. On average women died earlier than men, presumably because of the hazards of childbirth. Most men died before they reached 50. One interesting difference between the skeletons of early *H. sapiens* and those of the Neanderthals is that *H. sapiens* showed much less evidence of injury or disease, probably because superior technology was providing safety against physical hazards.

Brain size

One clear trend in hominin evolution is the increase in brain size, especially from *H. erectus* onwards (Fig. 3.6.44). The advantages of big brains are not obvious, because many animal species are highly successful despite having small brains.

Humans brains are three times bigger than any other primate brain and come at a great cost. Our brains take up to 25 years to develop fully, use up much of the body's nutrition, and big-headed babies make birth hazardous. There must have been strong adaptive advantages to justify these costs.

We cannot know what *H. erectus* were using their brains for, but are certain these hominins were too slow and weak and defenceless to have survived dangerous African settings on their physical capabilities alone. It is likely that increased brain size evolved through natural selection for abilities such as teamwork, communication, memory, language, cooperation, adaptability, evaluating the motives of others, plus an ability to devise strategies based on past experience.

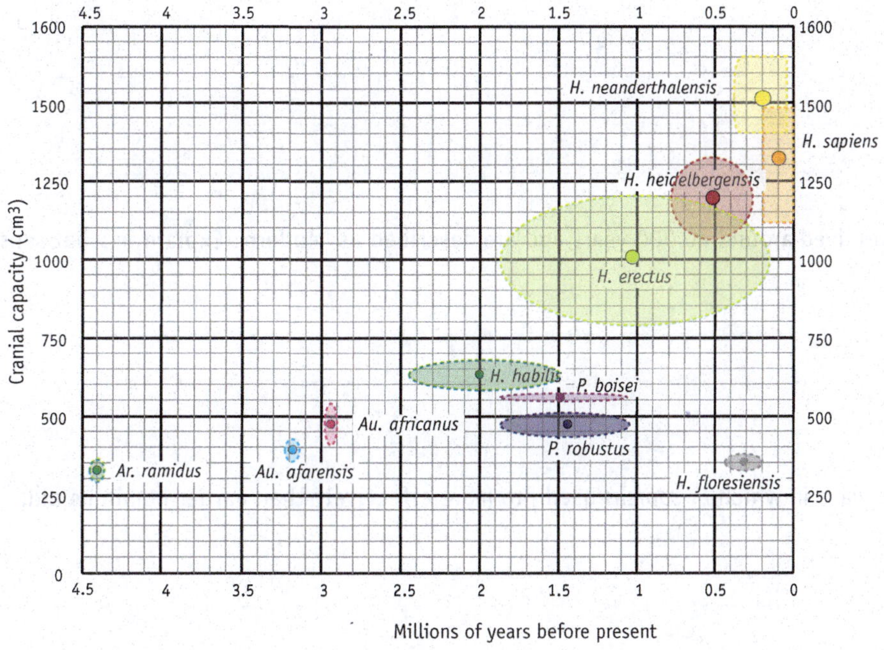

Fig 3.6.44 Brain size of 11 different hominins.

Check your understanding

1 Compare biological and cultural evolution by completing this table.

	Biological evolution	Cultural evolution
Comparative speed of change		
The underlying causes of change		
How information is stored		
How information is transmitted from one generation to the next		
Two actual examples of this kind of change in humans		

2 Describe the evidence for large-scale organised hunting overkill by Palaeolithic and Neolithic *H. sapiens*.

3 *H. sapiens* who lived around 40,000 years ago are described as 'modern'. Explain in what sense 'modern' is used here.

4 Describe two ways in which *H. sapiens* used fire more effectively than earlier hominins did.

 ISBN: 9780170355582

5 Match each of the skulls A–D in the diagram with one of these species: *H. sapiens; H. neanderthalensis; H. erectus; P. boisei*. In each case, give a reason for your choice.

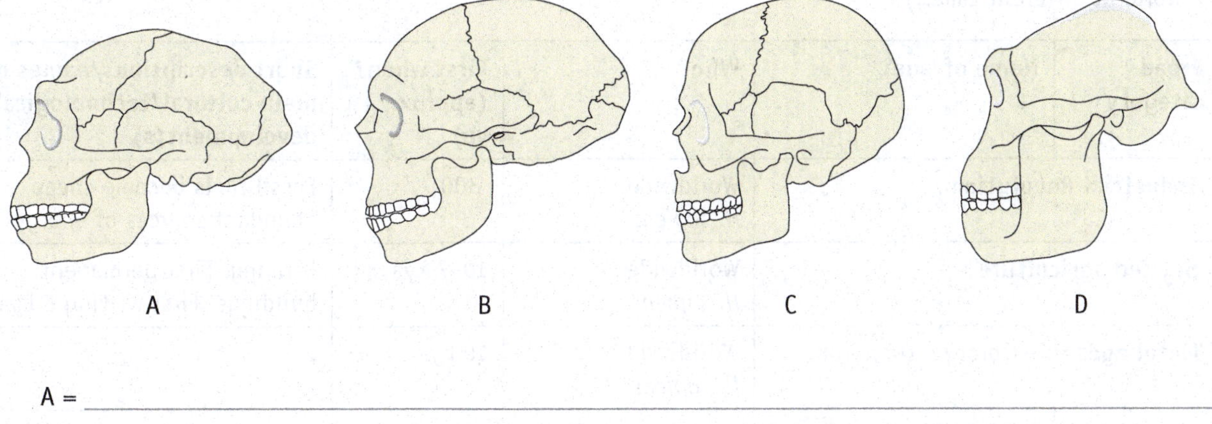

A = ______________________________

B = ______________________________

C = ______________________________

D = ______________________________

6 Identify the culture associated with each of the tools Q–T in the diagram below.

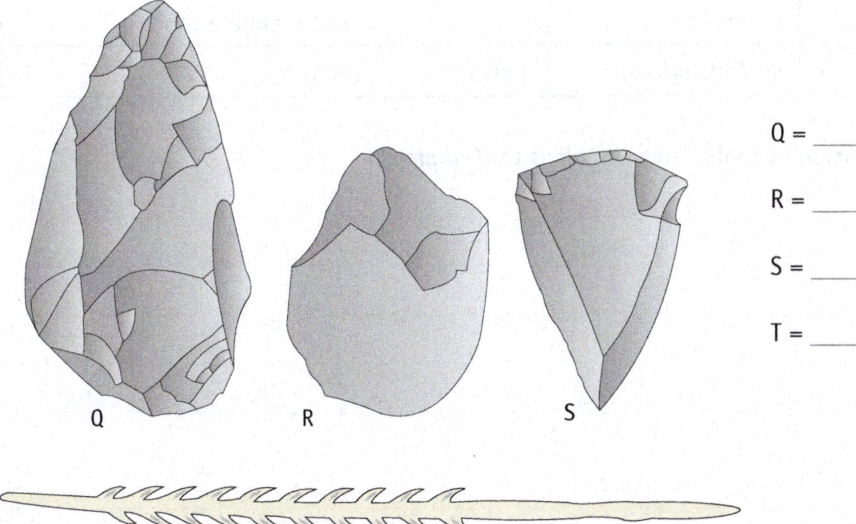

Q = ______________________________

R = ______________________________

S = ______________________________

T = ______________________________

7 Complete this table by writing facts in each of the empty boxes, using information contained in this and previous units. (Dates are approximate, as in many cases the same transition happened in different parts of the world at different times.)

Broad category	Name of 'age'	Who?	First when? (approx. ya)	Short descriptions/names of main cultural/technological development(s)
Industrial Revolution		Worldwide *H. sapiens*	300	Fossil fuels become cheap, abundant sources of energy
Settled agriculture		Worldwide *H. sapiens*	10–7 kya	Farming. First permanent buildings. First writing 6 kya
'Metal ages'; first bronze, then iron		Worldwide *H. sapiens*	10 kya	
'Stone ages'	Neolithic	*H. sapiens*		
	Upper Palaeolithic	*H. sapiens*		
	Mesolithic	*H. neanderthalensis*		
	Lower Palaeolithic	*H. erectus*		
		H. habilis		Simple pebble tools
	(none)	*Australopithecus*	4 mya	(none?)

8 Discuss trends evident in the evolution of tools, from *H. habilis* to *H. sapiens*.

ISBN: 9780170355582

Unit 7 | The spread of *Homo sapiens*

There are two different ideas as to where modern humans originated: the *Multiregional Hypothesis* and the *Out of Africa Hypothesis*. Both agree that human ancestors originated in Africa, and that the original split between the hominin line and the great ape line took place in Africa. The two ideas differ as to what happened after hominins left Africa.

This is more than a science debate; it is also political. According to the 'Multiregional' idea, human populations are different 'races' because they had different origins long ago, but according to the 'Out of Africa' idea, all humans are closely related.

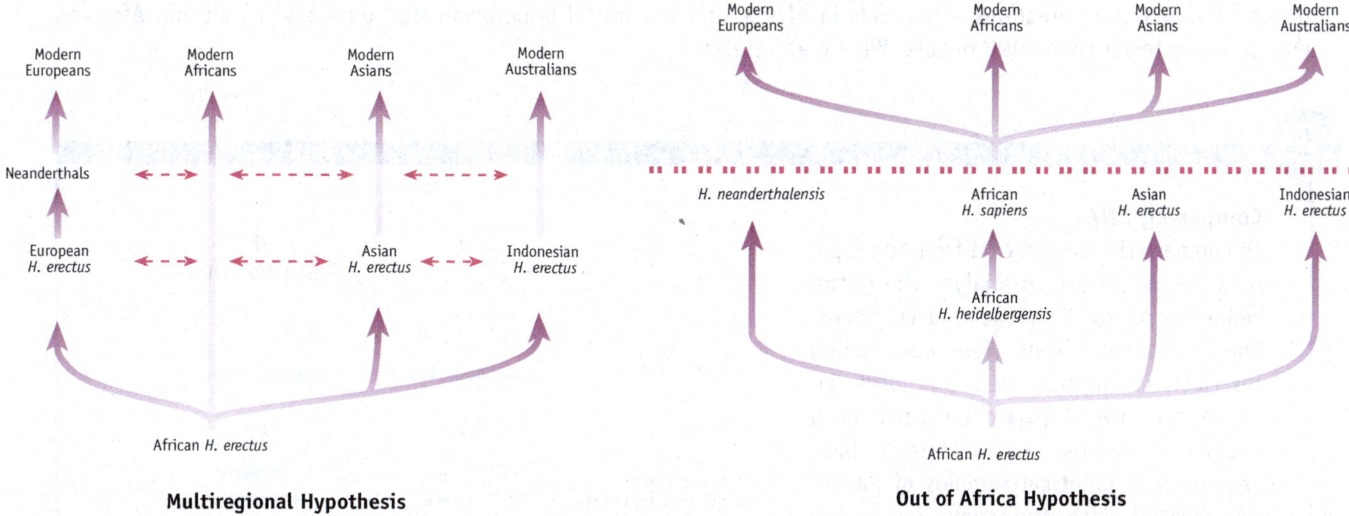

Fig. 3.6.45 Two hypotheses for the origin of modern humans.

Multiregional Hypothesis

In this view, modern Africans, Asians, Europeans and Australian aborigines all evolved independently from different local populations of *H. erectus*. The most recent common ancestor of different modern human groups may have been African *H. erectus* about 1.8 mya, or perhaps more recently from *H. heidelbergensis*. Some of the resulting different modern human groups later became blended by interbreeding.

Supporting evidence:

- In a number of places there are fossils intermediate between *H. erectus* and *H. sapiens*.
- Modern Europeans have on average about 2.5 per cent Neanderthal DNA, showing that interbreeding took place in the past.

Out of Africa Hypothesis

In this view there was a single origin for all present-day *H. sapiens*. Between 100 kya and 200 kya, a group of anatomically modern humans evolved in Africa from one local *H. erectus* group. Much later, perhaps 60 kya, some groups spread to Europe, Asia and Australia, replacing any existing *H. erectus* populations they came across.

Supporting evidence:

- The earliest *H. sapiens* fossils are found in Africa (in Ethiopia), 195,000 years old. The earliest *H. sapiens* fossils outside Africa are 120,000 years old, and found in the part of Asia nearest Africa. Elsewhere across the world, the earliest fossil *H. sapiens* fossils are less than 60,000 years old.
- When DNA of present-day people from five continents was compared, it was found that African populations showed the greatest variation, more than the rest of the world put together.
- The strongest evidence comes from studies of mtDNA (see below).

Evidence from mtDNA: 'Mitochondrial Eve'

Mitochondria contain a very small amount of DNA (mtDNA), only 37 genes. mtDNA is useful because it is inherited only from mothers. Unless there has been a mutation, your mtDNA is identical to your mother's mother's mother. Since the mutation rate of mtDNA is known, it is possible work out when two populations separated.

Many people from different parts of the world have had their mtDNA tested. As expected, people from the same ethnic group showed fewer differences than people from different ethnic groups. If the degree of difference between samples of DNA from different populations is taken as a measure of their relatedness, then it is possible to construct an evolutionary tree. According to calculations based on mtDNA, the most recent female shared ancestor of modern humans lived in Africa between 150 kya and 230 kya. Present-day people are all descended from this one woman — a 'Mitochondrial Eve'. According to another calculation, everyone alive today descends from a population of fewer than 14,000 breeding individuals in Africa, and the initial population that gave rise to all non-Africans was probably fewer than 3000 people. We are all related.

E

Comparing DNA

To compare the mtDNA of different people it is not necessary to analyse the entire sequence of all 37 mitochondrial genes. The first comparisons were done using restriction enzymes (see 3.7, Unit 3). These cut DNA at particular sites; each enzyme recognises a different base sequence. If identical samples of mtDNA are treated with the same restriction enzyme, they yield the same pattern of fragments (Fig. 3.6.46). These can be separated and their sizes determined by gel electrophoresis. The early research on mtDNA involved only a small region of the mitochondrial genome, but later studies compared the entire sequence of 16,569 base pairs.

By treating mtDNA from a given individual with different restriction enzymes and then determining the sizes of the fragments produced, the relative positions of the restriction sites can be worked out and represented as a restriction map.

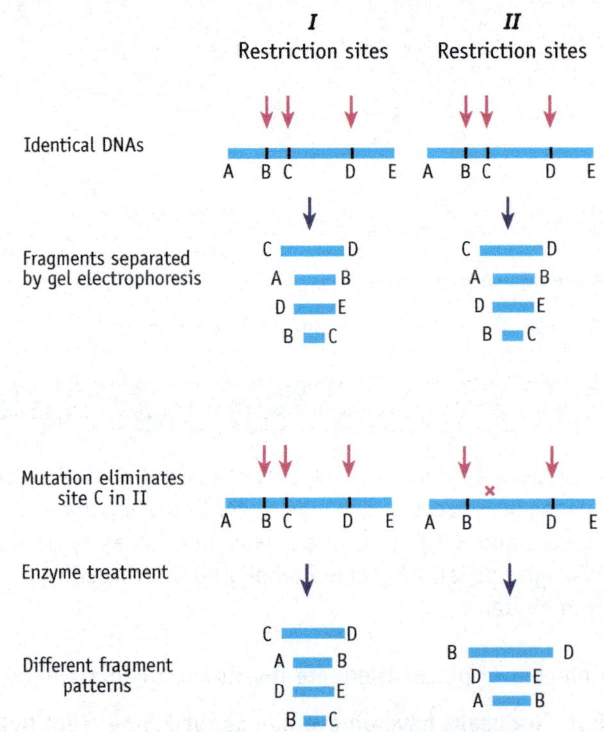

Fig. 3.6.46 How mutation changes the pattern of mtDNA fragments produced by a restriction enzyme.

Recently, nuclear DNA has been extracted from Neanderthal bones. Results: except for Africans, modern humans have between 1 and 4 per cent Neanderthal DNA. This showed that after having left Africa, modern *H. sapiens* replaced Neanderthals, but with some interbreeding. Neanderthal DNA was found in present-day populations from France, China and New Guinea, which shows that interbreeding with Neanderthals must have occurred early, before Eurasian populations split into separate groups. A similar picture has emerged from analysing nuclear DNA from the recently discovered Denisovans (Unit 5), who interbred with modern humans in East Asia.

Overall, evidence supports the 'Out of Africa' hypothesis, but there are also multiregional differences as a result of some past interbreeding with Neanderthals and Denisovans.

6

ISBN: 9780170355582

Beyond Africa

Around 120 kya small numbers of *H. sapiens* began to move out of Africa. The main movements out of Africa occurred around 60 kya.

Modern humans reached Australia around 45 kya, Europe 40 kya, North America less than 20 kya. Spread would have been helped by the Pleistocene ice age, when sea levels were about 70 metres lower than they are today. Most recent of all: human expansion into the Pacific within the last 5000 years. This began in Asia and took place over several thousand years in a series of voyages by sailing canoes.

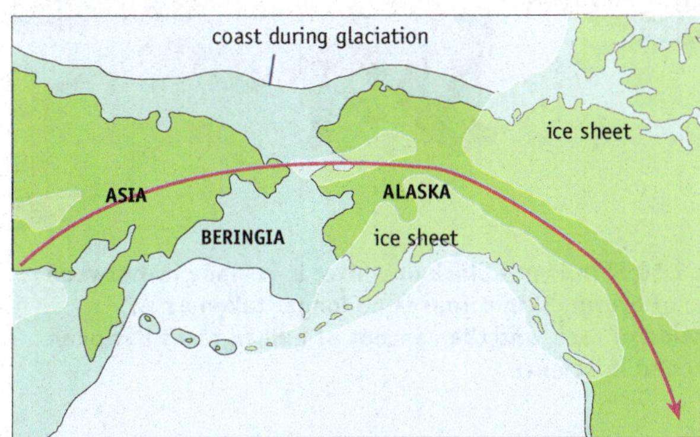

Fig. 3.6.47 Probable route by which humans reached North America where the oldest stone tools have been dated at 15,500 ya. DNA from ancient and modern native Americans has shown that native Americans share a common ancestry with people native to southern Siberia.

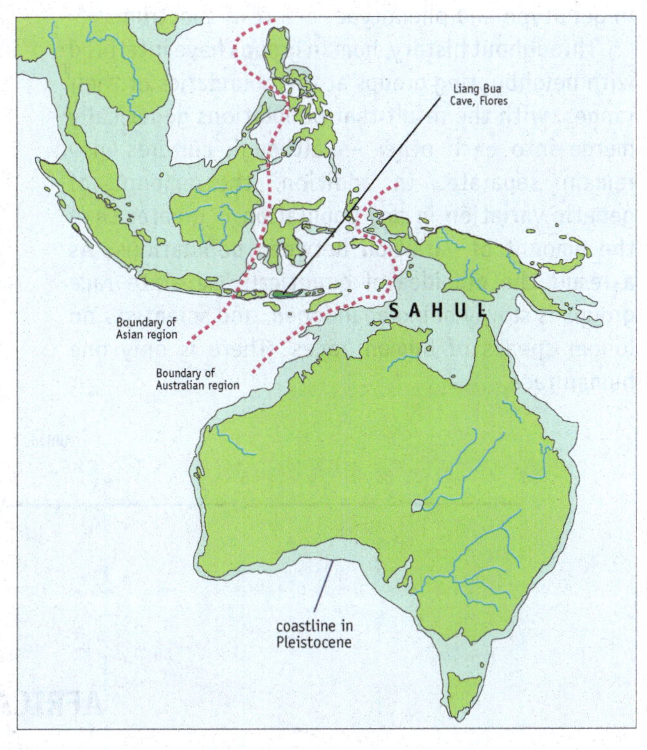

Fig. 3.6.48 Lower sea levels during a Pleistocene ice age caused Australasia and New Guinea to be linked. Humans first reached here about 45 kya. Despite lower sea levels, there was still a stretch of deep water that could only have been crossed by some kind of boat or perhaps by raft.

Skin colour

Fossils tell us nothing about skin colour, but we are certain that until very recently all humans were dark-skinned. Reasons: (1) our ape relatives are all dark-skinned; (2) melanin, the skin pigment, is known to protect against sunburn and skin cancer; (3) human populations in very sunny climates are darkest-skinned of all — although none are literally black.

Pale skin colour evolved in some groups in northern Europe and Asia, probably when humans first moved into areas previously covered by ice when Pleistocene glaciation was ending. This skin colour change probably happened less than 10 kya, as an adaptation to a new environment of cloudy climates with little sunshine. Under these conditions pale skin became an advantage because it enabled people having this genetic feature to make more vitamin D, a process that happens naturally in the skin in the presence of light.

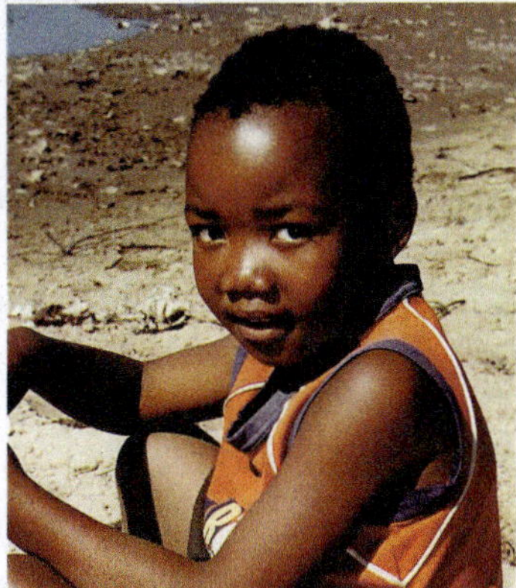

Fig. 3.6.49 In regions where sunshine is more intense, natural selection favours darker skin colour, because this gives protection against sun damage. In more cloudy regions, natural selection favoured pale skin as a way of preventing vitamin D deficiency.

6

The human race

Until as recently as the 1970s, it was believed that humankind consisted of separate race groups: African (black), Caucasian (white), Asian, Polynesian, and so on. However, recent DNA evidence tells us that humankind does not consist of clearly separate race groups, but is a **cline**. 'Cline' is the technical word for an extended population with continuous variation in genotype and phenotype; a sort of spectrum.

Throughout history, human groups have interbred with neighbouring groups at the boundaries of their ranges, with the result that populations genetically merge into each other — although cultures may remain separate. In addition, the amount of genetic variation in any population is greater than the amount of variation between populations. As a result the old idea of genetically separate race groups is slowly being abandoned, and scientists no longer speaks of human 'races'. There is only one human race.

Fig. 3.6.50 Skin is not black or white; it is many in-between shades of brown. Skin colour is no longer taken as an indication of race, and the concept of human races has been abandoned in science.

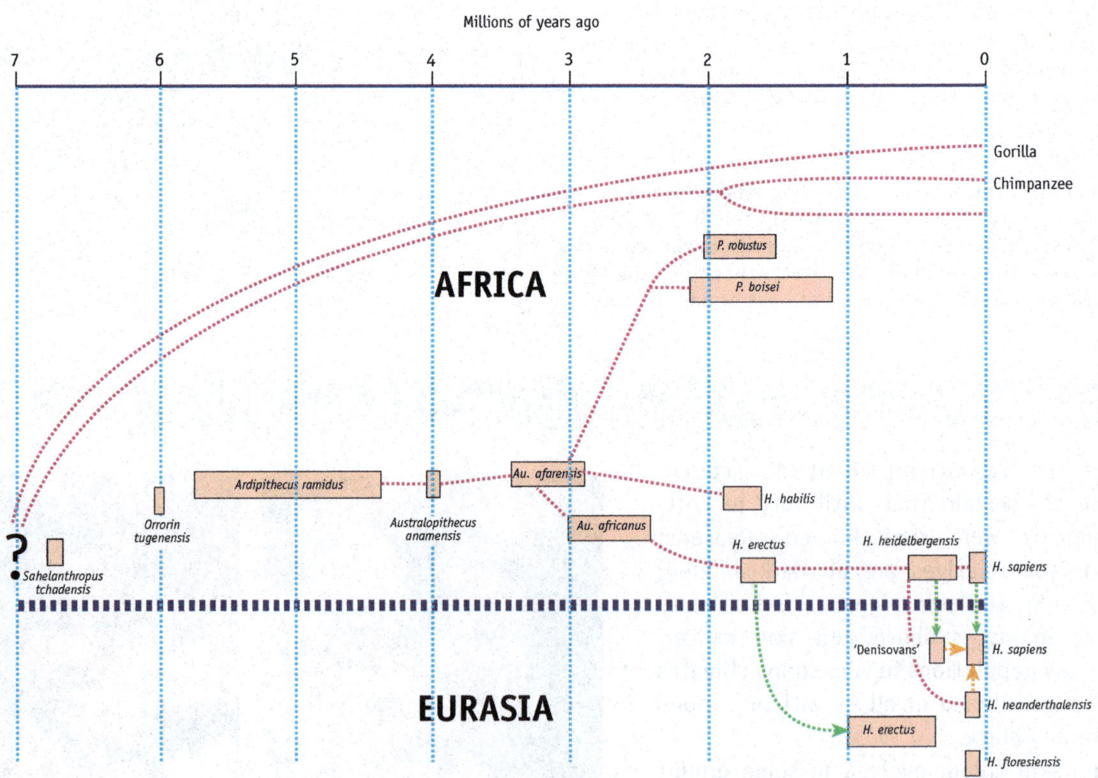

Fig. 3.6.51 One of several possible human evolutionary trees. The 'tree' has not been finalised, as new discoveries are being made almost every year, and adjustments are made to include new evidence.

 ISBN: 9780170355582

Check your understanding

1 There are two competing hypotheses to explain the origin of *Homo sapiens*.

a Name and summarise each hypothesis.

b Describe evidence that supports the 'Out of Africa' hypothesis.

2 State how modern humans reached:

a North America.

b Australia.

3 Explain how pale skin colour was (until modern times) an advantage to humans who lived in Northern Europe.

6

4 Explain, in terms of natural selection, how dark skin colour is an advantage to humans who live in tropical sunny climates.

5 The present world human population of over 7 billion shows much less variation in mtDNA than the few thousand chimpanzees in Africa. Suggest two possible reasons for this.

6 It is suggested that all humans alive today are descended from one single female who lived about 200 kya. Summarise the evidence for this conclusion.

7 Explain what is meant by a 'cline'. Also explain why the idea of separate human 'races' has been abandoned in science.

 ISBN: 9780170355582

Unit 8 | Neolithic revolutions

Hunter-gatherers

By the end of the Pleistocene ice age around 12 kya, humans had spread over almost all major land areas. The main exceptions: icy regions and Pacific islands. Neanderthals and *H. erectus* were extinct. World population of *H. sapiens* was tiny, less than 1 per cent of present-day numbers.

People were genetically the same as they are now, but culturally very different. Whether in forests or semi-desert, all lived in small groups and obtained their food by hunting and gathering. All were nomads, with groups moving from one place to another as food supplies dictated. Different cultures developed sophisticated technologies using stone, wood and bone.

Metals were not used. These were late Stone Age people, aka 'Neolithic'. Writing had not yet developed so we have no direct written history, but we know for certain that farming did not exist and neither did towns. If people built shelters, these were made of wood and animal hides, so nothing remains. Only 400 generations ago, everybody everywhere was a hunter-gatherer.

Fig. 3.6.52 The !Kung peoples of Southern Africa are one of the few groups that continue their hunter-gatherer way of life into the 21st century. Although they are fully modern humans, their culture is similar to ones that existed across much of the world tens of thousands of years ago. (The !Kung people, aka Khoisan, have a unique language with many click sounds represented by ! and x.)

Agricultural revolutions

Gradually and in stages, some nomad groups began to settle in preferred places for years at a time, deliberately planting seeds for their group's future food supply. We do not know exactly why these changes started to happen, but do know 'farming revolution' towards a settled lifestyle slowly began at different times and different places, mostly in fertile river valleys in regions that include Turkey, Iraq, Egypt, India, China, Peru and New Guinea. Agricultural revolution in these areas began between 10 kya and 6 kya. Since growing crops need to be protected from wild animals, this meant that people were now obliged to live in one place, sometimes for years. Staying in one place led to people building semi-permanent homes, digging wells and organising irrigation.

These agricultural revolutions — aka Neolithic revolutions — brought immense changes:

- more food means that fewer children die each winter, so populations increase
- settlements develop into towns with populations of thousands
- permanent buildings made of stone
- division of labour: stonemasons, farmers, metal workers, musicians, etc.
- centralised control: rulers who decide what was to be built and where and by whom.

Fig. 3.6.53 A farmer in Nepal with a wooden scratch-plough, almost exactly the same technology as early farmers used thousands of years ago.

Domestication of plants and animals

Modern hunter-gatherers such as the !Kung use a wide range of plant foods. Farming, the new way of living in Neolithic times, soon depended on a much smaller range of plants. In different regions the main food supplies became the wild versions of wheat, barley, rice, corn and potatoes. The wild ancestors of these plants produced little food, but careful selection of seeds from more productive plants eventually resulted in more productive crops and many different varieties of each. New technologies developed, such as sickles (for cutting grain) and querns (grindstones for crushing seeds). Even today, more than 80 per cent of all human food worldwide depends on these five plant species.

From guinea pigs to camels, humans have domesticated about 20 mammal species. Dogs were first, in pre-farming times. During the agricultural revolution, wild sheep and goats and cattle were domesticated in western Asia, pigs in Europe, llamas in Peru. Centuries of selective breeding produced animals that became better food producers and less wild in their behaviour. Animal products included leather, milk, meat and wool. Wild horses were tamed mainly for their carrying ability. Domestic cats are descended from African wildcats, probably first used to protect grain stores from rats and mice.

Fig. 3.6.54 Descended from the Asiatic wolf (shown here), dogs were domesticated more than 15,000 years ago, probably beginning with adopted wolf cub pets that probably became useful hunting companions for nomadic groups. Over time, selective breeding produced tamer wolf-dogs and eventually many different dog varieties.

Metals

At roughly the same time as agricultural revolutions were occurring, Neolithic farmers in Europe, Africa and Asia discovered how to get useful metals from rocks. In Europe the sequence of discovery was first copper, then bronze, then iron. People discovered — perhaps accidentally — that certain kinds of rock heated to high temperatures with carbon (a process of chemical reduction) would produce hard metals. They soon found that metals were superior to stone when used for sickles and axes — and later as weapons of war. Steel was a much later invention. Long before bronze and iron were developed, both gold and silver had been used for jewellery, but both are too soft for practical use. Gold and silver both exist as pure metals in nature, so do not need reduction.

Fig. 3.6.55 Iron was first used to make spearheads around 10,000 years ago in Africa.

E

Lessons from history

The shift from a hunter-gatherer way of life to settled farming eventually led to towns and cities and growing populations, together with more opportunities for knowledge and new thinking and creativity. The result could be described as 'civilisation'. History provides many examples of civilisations that suddenly declined. The commonest cause: collapse brought about by a combination of deforestation, local climate change, soil loss, followed by decline in food production. Example 1: Southern Iraq 4000 years ago had forests and grasslands. Centuries of bad farming turned it into salty desert where little now grows. Example 2: Rapanui (Easter Island), where Polynesian settlers cut down almost all the trees, which led to soil loss, starvation and population collapse. It remains to be seen whether humankind will be wise enough to avoid large-scale environmental decline in the future.

One consequence of settled living: a great increase in conflict. Neighbouring tribes of hunter-gatherers seldom fight each other, since they have no more possessions than they can carry and do not see anyone as owning land. Once people settled and began to 'own' land and other possessions, conflict and warfare became facts of life.

ISBN: 9780170355582

Industrial revolution

The Industrial Revolution involved a shift away from basic agriculture towards new technologies in which abundant fossil fuels (first coal, later oil) replaced muscle power (both human and animal) as the main sources of energy. This transformation began in England and Scotland in the 1700s then rapidly spread across the world. Rates of industrial and technological change continue to accelerate. Agriculture has become closely linked to industry, with fertilisers and farm output depending on cheap fossil fuels. At sea, large-scale industrial fishing has caused fish numbers to plummet. It is debatable whether natural ecosystems can sustain 7 billion humans at high standards of living. Decisions made over the next 50 years may decide whether or not humankind will halt the over-exploitation of resources.

Check your understanding

1 Define what is meant by 'nomads'.

2 Name one group of nomads whose original culture is still in existence today. Their way of life is sometimes described as 'hunter-gathering'. Suggest what they are 'gathering'.

3 Name five species of food plants that have been domesticated from wild ancestors.

4 Name 10 species of mammal that have been domesticated from wild ancestors. For each of these species, state one of its likely uses in Neolithic times.

6

5 Name seven regions of the world where agricultural revolutions took place in Neolithic times.

6 *H. sapiens* and its closely related ancestors have been in existence about one million years. Calculate what proportion of one million years these ancestors lived as hunter-gatherer nomads, before farming first began.

7 Explain, by using a flow diagram, or words only, the likely cause-and-effect series of events that linked the Neolithic agricultural revolution with increased population, and also with division of labour into specialist skills.

8 Suggest what became eventually the most important consequences of the agricultural revolution.

9 Describe how iron is obtained from some kinds of rock. Suggest one major benefit and one major problem that arose from increased use of iron during the 'Iron Age'.

6

 ISBN: 9780170355582

Biology 3.6 Human evolution

NCEA Achievement Standard 91606: Demonstrate understanding of trends in human evolution.

Externally assessed, 4 credits

Achievement	Achievement with Merit	Achievement with Excellence
Demonstrate understanding of trends in human evolution	Demonstrate in-depth understanding of trends in human evolution	Demonstrate comprehensive understanding of trends in human evolution

Achievement
'Demonstrate understanding ...' involves using biological ideas to describe trends in human evolution.

Achievement with Merit
'Demonstrate in-depth understanding ...' involves using biological ideas to explain how or why trends in human evolution occur.

Achievement with Excellence
'Demonstrate comprehensive understanding ...' involves linking biological ideas about trends in human evolution. The linking of ideas may involve justifying, relating, evaluating, comparing and contrasting, and analysing using scientific evidence.

Trends in human evolution refers to change over a period of time in relation to:
- human biological evolution
- human cultural evolution
- patterns of dispersal of hominins. Hominins refers to living and fossil species belonging in the human lineage. This is a subgroup of hominids, a group which includes both humans and the great apes.

Trends in human biological evolution begin with early bipedal hominins and may require comparison with living hominids. These trends involve:
- skeletal changes linked to bipedalism
- changes in skull and endocranial features, including teeth, brain volume, jaw, foramen magnum
- changes in the manipulative ability of the hand.

Trends in human cultural evolution involve:
- use of tools (stone, wood, bone)
- use of fire
- clothing
- abstract thought (communication, language, art)
- food-gathering (hunter-gatherer, domestication of plants and animals)
- shelter (caves, temporary settlement, permanent settlement).

Interpretations of the trends in human evolution are based on current scientific evidence, which is widely accepted and presented in peer-reviewed scientific publications.

Exam-type questions

QUESTION ONE

'The single most significant change during human evolution was the evolution of two legged walking'.

Discuss the statement above, outlining the selection pressures that affected the adoption of bipedalism in early hominins. Also outline the advantages and disadvantages of this method of locomotion.

- Explain how climate change led to environmental differences, in Africa . . .

- Explain how this could have affected competition with other tree dwelling primates . . .

Chimpanzee

Human

- Now state advantage(s) of standing upright . . .

- Link this to energy conservation, and also to increased survival for an individual or group . . .

- State a second advantage of how bipedalism links to increased survival of individual or group . . .

- Also state a disadvantage of bipedalism....

- Explain why this would increase chance of injury or death . . .

Use this page to create a key points plan that could form the basis for a longer answer to be done on your own paper.

ISBN: 9780170355582

QUESTION TWO

Although we share a common ancestor with African apes, a number of features set us apart.

Referring only to the skull, spine, pelvis and knee joint, discuss the functional reasons for the differences between the gorilla and human skeletons.

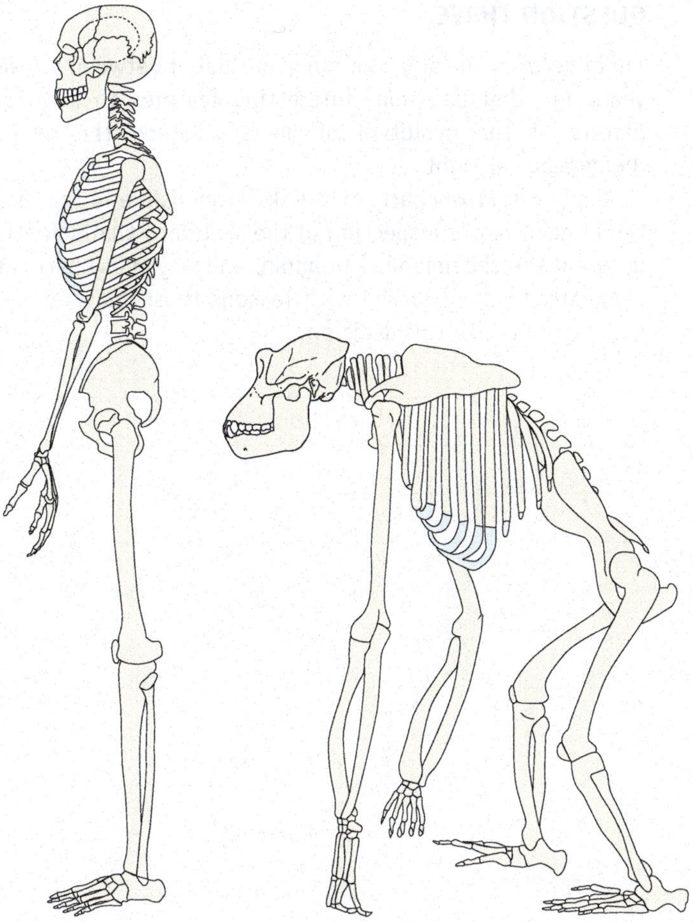

Use this page to create a key points plan or a mind map that could form the basis for a longer answer to be done on your own paper.

QUESTION THREE

Ardipithecus is an early hominin genus dated between 4.4 and 5.8 million years ago that has some interesting features to add to our growing picture of the evolution of humans. Study the reconstruction of *Ardipithecus* at right.

Explain four key parts of the skeleton visible in the diagram (or that would need closer inspection of the skeleton) that scientists look at to decide if the specimen is a hominin, and why these parts are considered peculiarly human. Outline with reasons those features of the skeleton that conflict with this decision.

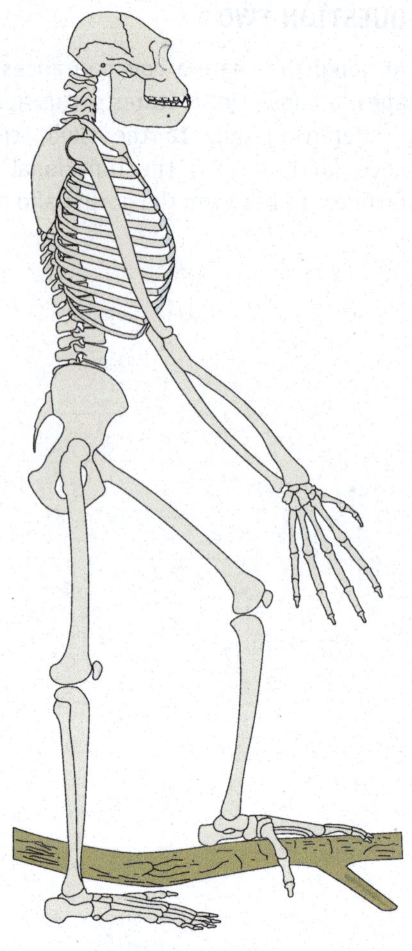

A reconstruction of the skeleton of *Ardipithecus ramidus*.

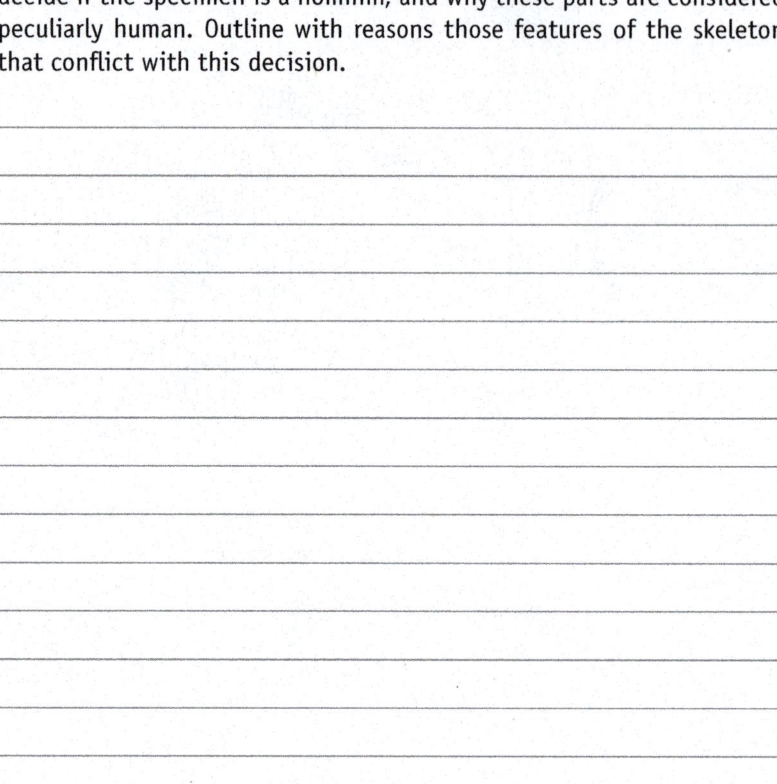

Use this page to create a key points plan or a mind map that could form the basis for a longer answer to be done on your own paper.

ISBN: 9780170355582

QUESTION FOUR

The earliest stone tools date back 2.6 million years and are attributed to *H. habilis*. Successive hominin groups refined and developed the tools until the appearance of *H. sapiens,* where the greatest range of materials and applications of those tools is shown.

Discuss the relationship between cranial capacity, manual dexterity and the development of tool cultures. Use named tool cultures together with the related hominin species to illustrate your answer.

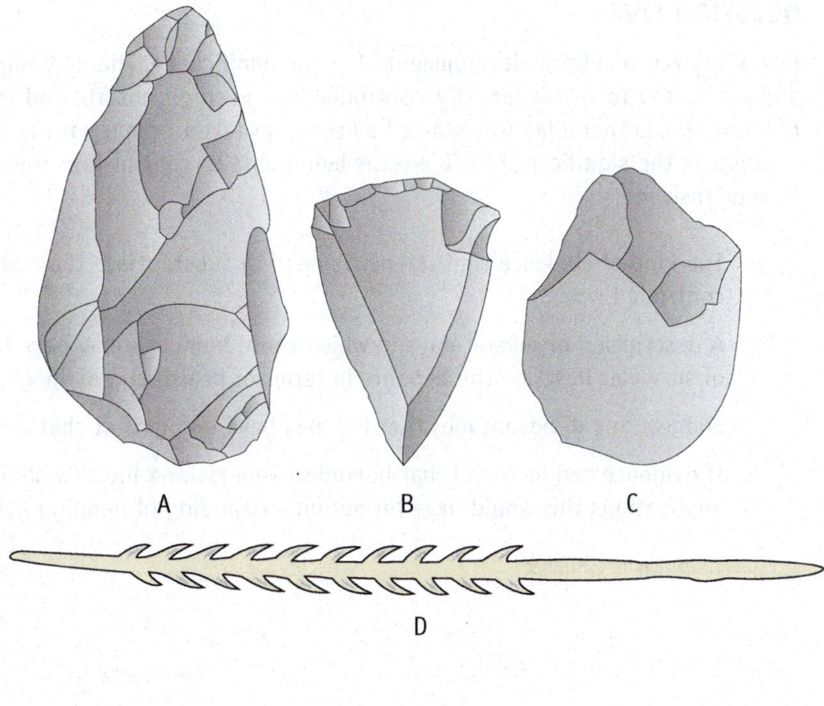

Use this page to create a key points plan or a mind map that could form the basis for a longer answer to be done on your own paper.

QUESTION FIVE

Use of fire was a cultural development of major significance. The first controlled use of fire is dated about 1.6 mya, and attributed to *H. erectus*. (By 'controlled' we mean purposeful and managed, not accidental. We have no way of knowing whether a fire was started by them, or taken from a natural wildfire then maintained for a purpose.)

Discuss the significance of *H. erectus* being able to control fire. You will need to address the following points in your answer.

- The kind of evidence that scientists need to substantiate the claim that groups were using fire in a controlled way.
- A description of several ways in which these hominins may have been using fire to increase their chances of survival. Describe the benefits in terms of health and of specific threats to the survival of individuals.
- Suggest any disadvantages that fire may have brought, at that time.
- If evidence can be found that hominins were making fire as well as controlling it, suggest what implications this would have for our understanding of hominin evolution.

- Explain meaning of 'controlled'.

- Explain what type of archaeological evidence could lead to us concluding that the fires were unlikely to be natural/ accidental.

- Describe at least three probable uses of fire. For each point follow through: explain how it aided survival by removing a named threat to the life of the individual or group. Give some named advantages.

- List possible disadvantages/hazards at that time and the consequences to the survival of the individual or future production of offspring.

- Explain what the ability to make fire (eg by using friction) would imply about this hominin's intelligence.

Use this page to create a key points plan that could form the basis for a longer answer to be done on your own paper.

ISBN: 9780170355582

QUESTION SIX

In 2004 a remarkable archaeological discovery was made in a cave on the island of Flores, Indonesia. Several tiny human-like skeletons were discovered, and later given the name *H. floresiensis*. Due to their small size they were nicknamed 'hobbits'. Skull shape was similar to *H. erectus*, but the brain capacity was less than half as much as *H. erectus* brains, and similar to a chimpanzee brain in size. Internal casts showed that the Wernicke's area was well-developed, suggesting that these hobbits in some ways most closely resembled *H. sapiens*. The tools found in association resemble Mousterian and Upper Palaeolithic tool cultures. The cave also contained the bones of large animals, including elephants.

Compare and contrast the skull features of *H. floresiensis* with that of *H. sapiens*.

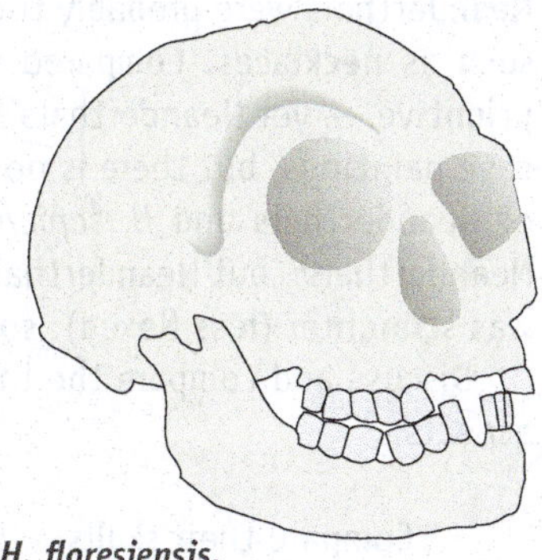

H. floresiensis.

- Suggest why scientists chose to classify the hobbit as belonging to the genus *Homo*.
- Describe the function of the Wernicke's area of the brain, and explain how this area could have been an advantage when *H. floresiensis* hunted large dangerous animals.

- Directly compare and contrast'
  eg
  - list specific structural similarities
    to *Homo sapiens*
  - *H. floresiensis* and *H. sapiens*
    shared structural features include:
    (list at least 4)

- Behavioural similarities include:
  (list at least 2)

- Structural differences between
  H. floresiensis and *H. sapiens*
  include ......

- After reading the stimulus
  material above, state your on-balance
  opinion as to whether these two
  hominins are considered similar
  enough to be classified as the
  same species.

- Describe function of Wernicke's area of the
  brain, and how it may have aided
  the survival of small hominins
  when hunting big dangerous animals.

Use this page to create a key points plan that could form the basis for a longer answer to be done on your own paper.

6

QUESTION SEVEN

Neanderthals were probably the first hominins who buried their dead with care, sometimes together with artefacts such as necklaces. Compared with *H. sapiens* who lived at the same time, Neanderthal stone tools were more primitive — yet Neanderthals had a bigger brain capacity. We know that *H. sapiens* at that time made carvings and cave paintings, but there is no evidence that this was the case with Neanderthals. Comparisons of skull endocasts of Neanderthals and *H. sapiens* show differences of detail. In *H. sapiens* the cerebrum is larger than it was in Neanderthals; but Neanderthals had a comparatively larger cerebellum. The upper part of the Neanderthal pharynx was straighter (less flexed), so it is assumed they could not make a full range of speech sounds.

Discuss and compare the life and survival of Neanderthals and contemporary *H. sapiens*. Include the following aspects.

- Compare their skulls.
- Suggest reasons why Neanderthals did not have a culture as elaborate as that of *H. sapiens*, even though the Neanderthal brain was larger.
- Discuss the significance of burial customs and symbolic art in the life and survival of both Neanderthals and *H. sapiens*.
- Explain the significance of the discovery of Neanderthal skeletons with broken bones that had healed.

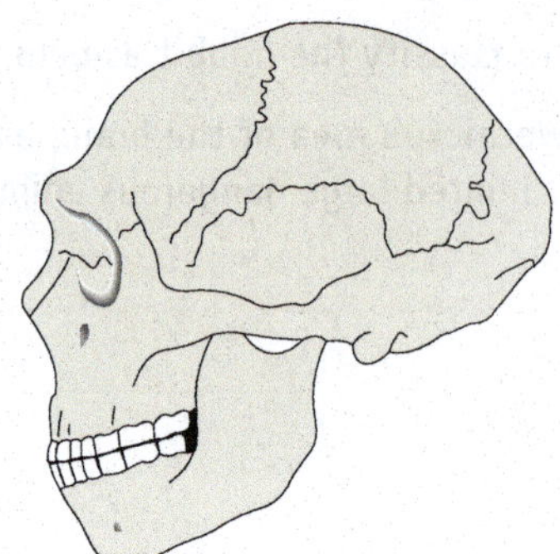

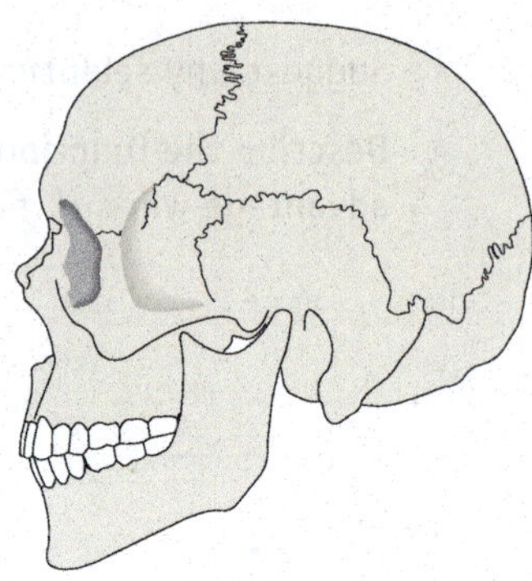

Use this page to create a key points plan or a mind map that could form the basis for a longer answer to be done on your own paper.

ISBN: 9780170355582

QUESTION EIGHT

Two main hypotheses (or theoretical models) have been put forward to explain the origin of modern humans. (1) The 'Out of Africa' or 'Replacement' hypothesis suggests that *H. erectus* emerged from Africa about a million years ago. About 200,000 years ago modern *H. sapiens* evolved in Africa. Much later, about 70,000 years ago, groups of *H. sapiens* extended their range from Africa and replaced any remaining hominins they came across in other parts of the world. (2) The 'Multiregional' hypothesis. This agrees with the one million years ago timescale, but proposes that different *H. erectus* populations around the world evolved independently into different *H. sapiens* groups (races) in Asia, Africa, Europe, and Australia.

Discuss these two models, making sure that you cover the following aspects.

- Explain why mitochondrial DNA and not nuclear DNA is used to estimate the relatedness of various hominin groups.
- Explain how mitochondrial DNA evidence has led to the 200,000 year date referred to above.
- State what specific kind of evidence (fossils and/or DNA) could support or refute one hypothesis or the other.

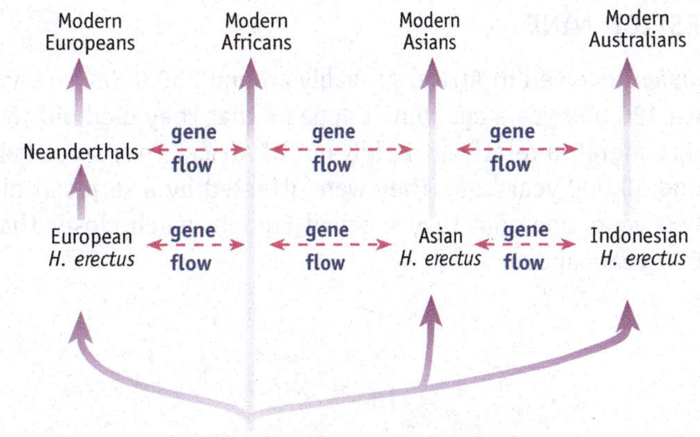

Multiregional hypothesis

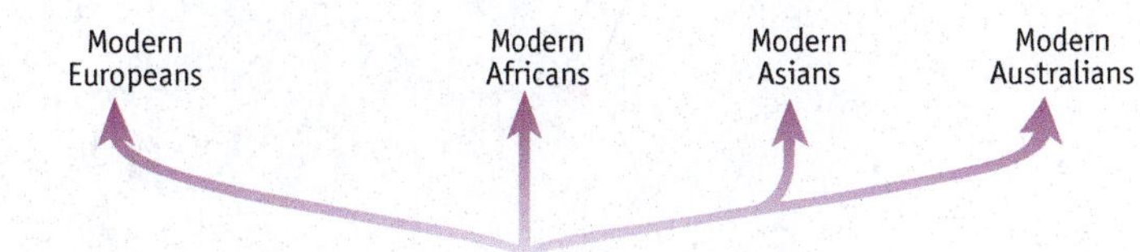

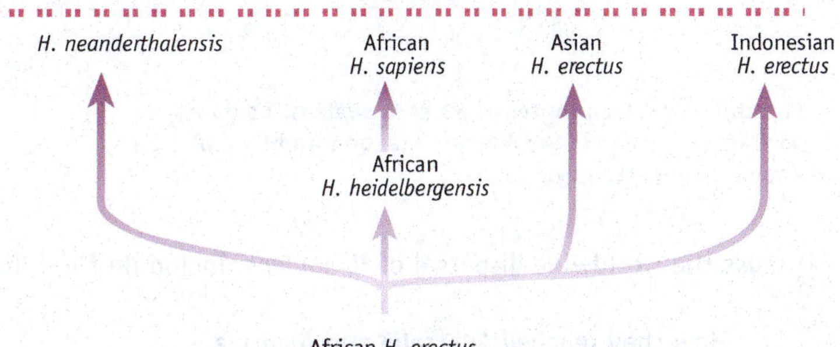

'Out of Africa' Hypothesis

Two hypotheses for the origin of modern humans.

Use this page to create a key points plan or a mind map that could form the basis for a longer answer to be done on your own paper.

QUESTION NINE

H. sapiens evolved in Africa, probably around 200,000 years ago. Fossils show that some groups were living beyond Africa 120,000 years ago, but it appears that they died out. Much later, starting about 60,000 years ago, different groups migrated relatively rapidly out of Africa. They spread along the coast (or inland) to reach Asia and Australia around 50,000 years ago. They were affected by a series of glaciations during these times. It was not until about 40,000 years ago that they reached Europe, much closer than Australia. The Americas were reached only about 18,000 years ago.

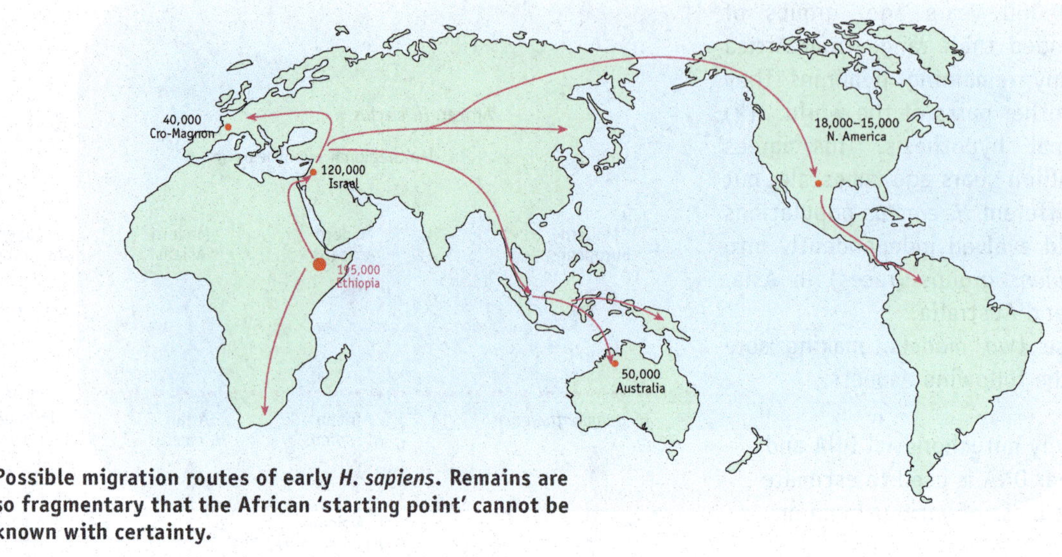

Possible migration routes of early *H. sapiens*. Remains are so fragmentary that the African 'starting point' cannot be known with certainty.

Discuss the worldwide dispersal of *H. sapiens*, including the following aspects.

- How they reached Australia and America.
- Likely rates of travel, in approximate kilometres per century.
- Possible reasons for the late occupation of Europe and America.
- Any specific cultural evolutionary changes required for the move into Europe and America.
- A definition of what is meant by cultural evolution.

Use this page to create a key points plan or a mind map that could form the basis for a longer answer to be done on your own paper.

ISBN: 9780170355582

QUESTION TEN

It is known that as early as 18,000 years ago, wild cereals such as wheat were being harvested in Egypt. Evidence: harvesting sickles and grindstones found from that time. In the millennia following, many other plants and animals were domesticated. This occurred independently in at least three parts of the world. In the Middle East, wheat, barley, sheep and goats were domesticated from about 10,000 years ago. In China, rice, yams and pigs were domesticated from about 7000 years ago. In Central and South America, maize, beans, llamas and guinea pigs were domesticated from about 8000 years ago.

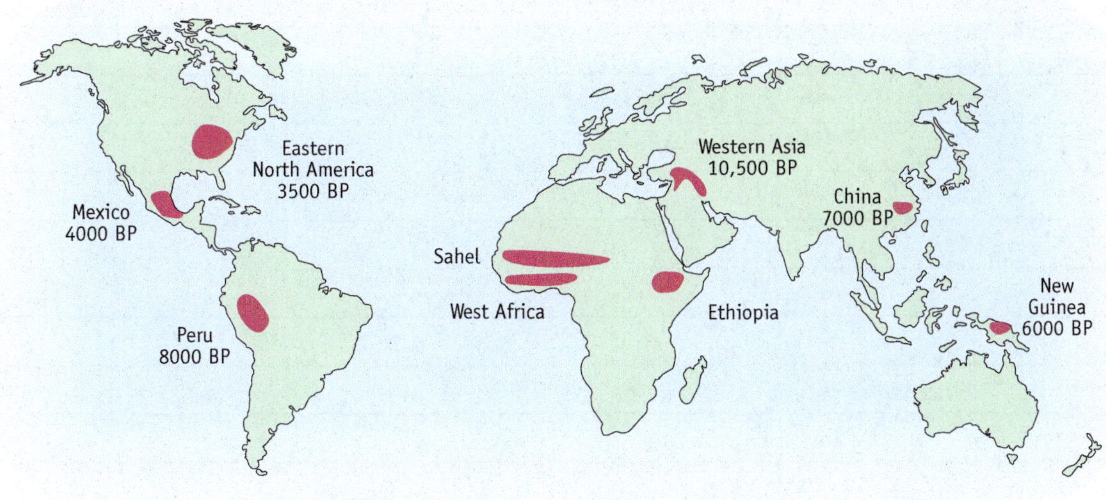

Discuss the impact the domestication of plants and animals must have had on the survival and success of human populations in those areas at those times.

- Include evidence that allows us to be sure which plants and which animals were domesticated, where and when.
- Explain and discuss the advantages and disadvantages of this early farming of domesticated plants and animals, compared with hunting and gathering.

Use this page to create a key points plan or a mind map that could form the basis for a longer answer to be done on your own paper.

 ISBN: 9780170355582

Gene manipulation

Unit 1 | Selective breeding

What is 'gene manipulation'?

DNA discoveries have triggered a rush of new technologies. Molecular biologists are now able to extract DNA, identify DNA, cut DNA at specific points, make billions of copies, transfer genes to other organisms. Gene-transfer technology is known by many different names: gene splicing, gene editing, genetic engineering (GE), genetic modification (GM), transgenesis. Whatever the name, the end results of gene transfers and removals are **GMOs**, short for Genetically Modified Organisms.

For centuries humans have relied on the process of **selective breeding**, with the aim of producing useful plant and animal varieties. Selective breeding and GM share similar goals, but in other ways are very different. Compared with GM, selective breeding is low-tech, simpler, cheaper.

Cloning is any process that makes genetically identical individuals. Example: producing 1000 apple trees all exactly the same. Strictly speaking, whole-organism cloning should not be classed as gene manipulation because it results in uniformity, not change.

GENE MANIPULATION

Selective breeding	(Cloning)	GMO production
Low-tech, used in farming for hundreds of years, creates new varieties, comparatively slow	Makes multiple copies of individuals (or cells) with identical genes	New, high-tech, directly involves DNA, aims to create new gene combinations by moving genes into new or alien situations

Assessment

Each school has its own ways of assessing Biology standard 91607, with some using tests and others using research assignments. This book provides material for both. For individual research assignments your teacher will advise:

- how many weeks are allocated for learning the basics and doing further research
- how and when the final report will be done; e.g. three periods of class time
- how much prepared material you are allowed to bring to report-writing times.

Details of assessment criteria are given on page 260.

Possible topics
Standard 91607 provides choices, enabling students to study one or more of the following kinds of gene manipulation:

- selective breeding (this could include embryo selection, animal breeding, plant breeding, development of new crops)
- whole organism cloning
- transgenesis (i.e. GMOs)
- investigation and modification of the expression of existing genes.

This unit deals with **selective breeding**, mainly in plants. Unit 2 deals with **cloning**, Units 3 and 4 with **genetic modification.**

Whichever of the above four 'manipulations' you select, it's important that you:

- describe its purpose
- describe clearly the techniques and processes involved.

Don't deal excessively with details such as enzyme names, but do focus on the big picture and make it clear what each technique and process is used for.

Implications of genetic manipulation
For each 'manipulation' you deal with (e.g. selective breeding and genetic modification), you need to independently research its biological implications. These implications may include both positive and negative impacts on:

- ecosystems
- genetic diversity
- health and survival of individuals (whether human or 'other')
- survival of populations
- evolution of populations.

You don't have to deal with all of these implications; two or three may be ample.

Selective breeding in plants

For thousands of years, humans have altered their pets, crops and livestock to increase the numbers of those with desired features. This is known as artificial selection, or selective breeding. Dogs and cattle, apples and oranges; all have been greatly changed compared with their original wild ancestors.

Definition: selective breeding is a process of using individuals with desired phenotypes for breeding purposes, and not using those with less desired phenotypes.

In many ways similar to natural selection, selective breeding differs in being goal-directed and comparatively quick. Within a few years it is often possible to produce 'improved' genetic varieties. Among domestic and farm animals these varieties are known as different **breeds**. In the case of plants they are usually called **cultivars**.

Fig. 3.7.1 Teosinte (on the left) is a grass with small tough seeds — and is the ancestor of maize (corn). It still grows in the wild in Mexico. More than a thousand years ago farmers guessed its potential and selectively bred teosinte to develop plants that produce more food. The process is ongoing.

How selective breeding is done in plant crops

Whether it's apple trees or maize plants, humans can decide which individuals are allowed to reproduce. This is done by selecting seeds or cuttings from 'better' individual plants and using these to grow the next generation.

 ISBN: 9780170355582

Favourable traits are passed down and within a few generations they become common. Plant breeders are always aiming to produce crops that will possess desirable characteristics such as:

- higher yields or a different taste
- resistance to disease, frost, drought, higher temperatures.

Natural genetic variation means that individual plants grown from seeds are never the same as each other. Individual plants — whether apple trees or timber trees — that look 'better than most' get noticed. Their seeds are saved, then planted in the expectation that desirable traits will become more common in the next few generations. Selection needs no expensive equipment, and has been going on for centuries.

What causes genetic variation?

Genetic variation is the 'raw material' for selection. Plenty of genetic variability in a species means a wide range of phenotypes to select from. Less genetic variation means less scope for improvement. Genetic variation occurs naturally as a result of:

- **Mutations**. These are unpredictable and rare.
- **Meiosis**. Gamete production includes crossing-over and also random chromosome assortment, both of these creating more variety.
- **Fertilisation**. Under natural conditions it's pure chance which sperm meets which egg, although outcomes can be influenced by transferring pollen between two cultivars with desired characteristics.

E

Mutations occur spontaneously, but breeders can increase the mutation rate of an organism by using radiation or chemicals. Many mutations are harmful, but with luck there will be a few mutants (individuals with mutations) with useful characteristics that have not been found before. Some chemicals (e.g. colchicine) are known to affect meiosis, and can increase the chances of producing polyploid individuals. Polyploidy can quickly produce new varieties and even species. Some important crop plants have been produced in this way.

Crop plant	Probable ancestral haploid number	Present chromosome number	'ploidy' level
oats	7	42	$6n$
peanut	10	40	$4n$
sugar cane	10	80	$8n$
banana	11	22, 33	$2n$, $3n$
cotton	13	52	$4n$

Fig. 3.7.2 Different varieties of maize. The wide range of phenotypes reflects wide genetic diversity.

Fig. 3.7.3 There are now over 3000 cultivars of apples, all derived from ancestral species *Malus sieversii*; which still grows wild in Kyrgyzstan.

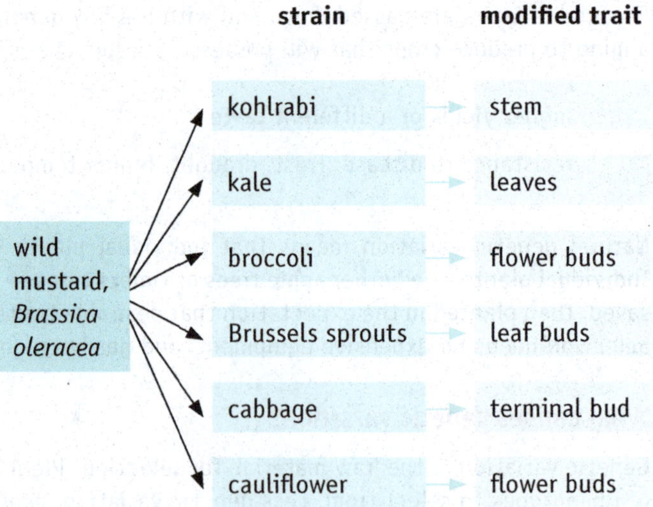

Fig. 3.7.4 Six kinds of 'Brassica' vegetables have been developed from one wild ancestor species. Within each of these kinds there are dozens of cultivars, all of them produced through selective breeding.

The importance of genetic diversity

Selective breeding is effective in producing new cultivars suited to local conditions. However when selecting for particular phenotypes, it is possible that some genes may be unintentionally selected against. In the case of apples, more than 70 percent of world production comes from only 10 of the 3000 known cultivars. There is always the risk that 'unfashionable' rare cultivars may become extinct and that valuable genes may be lost forever — such as genes for resisting a particular virus disease. This risk applies equally to GM crops. Because of these risks, there is a strong need to conserve the original wild ancestors, which are likely to contain genes that have been lost in domestic cultivars. Having diverse genes is a form of insurance.

Many farmed crops are now **monocultures**, which means large areas with just one plant species, and little genetic diversity. Monocultures are economically efficient, but ecologically high-risk. Under these conditions pest numbers can easily explode to disastrous levels.

One example: the Irish famine. Potatoes were a staple food in Ireland, with one cultivar dominating. In the 1840s an outbreak of fungus disease wiped out almost the entire potato crop year after year. A million people died of starvation, and many more were forced to migrate.

One disadvantage of selective breeding is that plants (or animals) can become highly inbred after many years. Under these conditions 'inbreeding depression' can develop, with undesirable recessive traits more likely to appear. Sometimes the situation can be reversed by crossing different cultivars, resulting in **hybrid vigour**.

Fig. 3.7.5 Crop monocultures like this are highly prone to pest problems, so often need large amounts of chemical protection.

ISBN: 9780170355582

Selective breeding in animals

Selective breeding is used for animals as well as plants. Humans have domesticated about 20 species of mammal, with dogs by far the most diverse in appearance, probably because they have been under human control for longer than any other species. Depending on what they want, owners select for dogs' looks, size, health, personality, or ability to learn quickly.

For all animals the methods are simple: individuals with desired features are chosen to breed and pass on their genes. Individuals with few desired features are not allowed to breed.

Fig. 3.7.6 Hundreds of dog breeds have been developed, all derived from the original wild ancestor, the Asiatic grey wolf, probably starting less than 15,000 years ago. Looks, size and temperament are some of the qualities selected for.

Fig. 3.7.7 Many breeds with different uses have been developed since horses were first domesticated over 8000 years ago. All are descended from one wild species, now almost extinct in its native Mongolia.

Biotechnology in animal breeding

Modern technologies such as artificial insemination now make animal farming more efficient, although the basic principles of selective breeding remain unchanged.

Artificial insemination (AI) is widely used for dairy cows, one cost-advantage being that sperm from one bull can be used to inseminate about 500 cows. AI is not for selective breeding purposes alone — it's used because cows have to be in calf before they can produce milk.

Genomic selection is now used alongside AI. DNA analysis is used to check breeding animals to identify those carrying genetic markers for desired features. Genomic breeding values (gBVs) give a measure of how likely an individual is to produce offspring with the desired phenotypes. Genes are not altered in the process.

Check your understanding

1 Define 'selective breeding'.

2 Explain the importance of mutations in selective breeding.

3 Describe the effect that each of these has on genetic variety:

a mutations

b chromosome crossing-over during meiosis

c random allocation of chromosomes to gametes

4 Describe what is meant by 'monoculture'. Also explain why monoculture can be a risky situation.

5 Explain how 3000 apple cultivars could have been created from just one wild species of apple.

6 Greyhounds are extremely fast runners, originally used to catch hares. Suggest how this dog breed was developed.

7 Identify one long-term problem with selective breeding.

7

 ISBN: 9780170355582

Unit 2 | Cloning

Plant propagation

Plants can be propagated in one or both of two ways: from seeds, or by cloning.

- **Seeds** are the result of sex processes in flowers, and sex means that no two seeds are genetically exactly the same. **Variety** is created naturally.
- **Cloning** can be achieved by methods such as cuttings, bulbs, tissue culture, etc. All members of a clone are genetically **identical**, except for the occasional mutant.

From a farmer's point of view there are advantages in having thousands of plants genetically all the same.

- If all ripen at the same time, this simplifies harvesting.
- If all are the same variety and colour, this simplifies marketing.
- Desirable features such as frost resistance can be uniform across an entire field of plants.

Many plants have a natural ability to reproduce vegetatively (i.e. by non-flower non-sex methods). This ability is used by growers for cloning purposes. Examples:

- **bulbs** (e.g. tulips; garlic) and **tubers** (e.g. potatoes)
- **cuttings.** Many kinds of plant can grow from a piece of cut stem or twig if placed in the ground and part-covered with soil. (*Klon* is the Greek word for 'twig'.)

cloning: any process that produces multiple individuals that are genetically identical to each other.
clone: a number of individuals produced by cloning methods. (One individual is not a clone.) A clone can be artificial or natural.
propagation: reproduction; increase in numbers.

Fig. 3.7.8 Tulip field in Holland. Each colour is a clone, derived many years ago from one single bulb. The distinctive colours of different cultivars were originally developed after careful selective breeding, often beginning with a mutation.

Plant tissue culture

Cloning plants is easy. Traditionally, this has meant propagation methods such as cuttings and grafts and bulbs. Recent techniques include plant tissue culture, which enables rapid mass-production from a single parent plant.

Tissue culture involves techniques for growing plants from tiny pieces of leaf or stem or root tissue. These are known as **explants**, and can begin as small as one-cell size. Unlike the situation in animals, plants cells are **totipotent**, which means that every cell has the ability to grow into an entire plant if given sterile and chemically correct conditions.

Fig. 3.7.9 Young grapevines, where a selected fruit-producing cultivar has been grafted on the rootstock and stem of another cultivar that has superior ability to cope with disease. Grafting is a process in which a small piece of stem from one cultivar is made to grow on another that is already in the ground.

9780170355582

Plant tissue culture can be used for plants that have been genetically modified, but exactly the same methods can be used for non-GMOs. In Fig 3.7.10, the first Petri dish shows a step in which plant cells are being genetically modified. By the second dish each disc is starting to produce a mass of unspecialised cells, known as a '**callus**'. By the fourth stage entire miniature plants have been produced. In this way, thousands of genetically identical plants can be produced in a laboratory in just a few weeks. The young plants are then planted in soil outdoors.

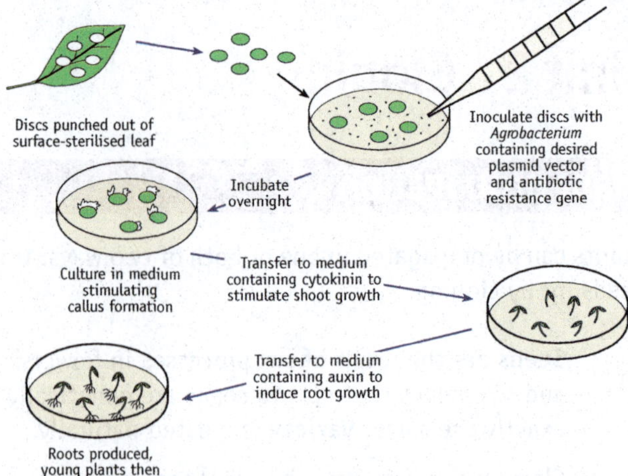

Fig. 3.7.10 Steps in tissue culture, starting with leaf cells. In this case the plant material has been genetically modified at an early stage, but culturing can also be done from non-GM material.

Implications of cloning

Cloning and monoculture technologies can be economically effective in the short-term, but there are long-term implications as well.

- Evolution. Cloning reduces genetic diversity, which in the long run is a major problem as it leaves less scope for improvement by selective breeding.
- Health and survival. If the original tissue or individual plant is found to have a genetic defect, that means the entire clone will have this defect.
- Ecological. As explained in Unit 1, monocultures and especially cloned monocultures are an ecological risk. A cloned population is less likely to survive environmental changes such as the arrival of a new disease. Plants that have been grown from seeds are more variable so will not all be affected in the same way.

Note: All information in this unit relates to whole-organism cloning, but there are also techniques for cloning individual cells and even sections of DNA.

E

Animal cloning

One potential and two actual types of cloning are described here. Whichever method is used, cloning has the long-term evolutionary consequence of lessening genetic variety.

De-extinction and conservation. It is theoretically possible to get a few cells from long-extinct animals, extract DNA, then create a clone. This 'Jurassic Park' scenario is unlikely because DNA molecules are fragile and disintegrate rapidly after death, with only part of the genome remaining after a few years. As a way of dealing with critically endangered animals, it may be better to conserve both them and the habitats on which they depend.

Embryo splitting has been used for many years as part of stock breeding. At the two-cell stage after *in-vitro* fertilisation, the cells are first separated, then each is allowed to develop into a separate embryo, then implanted in surrogate parents. The resulting offspring are genetically identical twins. (The first stage is like the formation of natural identical twins, which form a natural clone.)

Somatic cell nuclear transfer (SCNT). This is how 'Dolly the sheep' was created in 1996. A somatic (body) cell from one breed was injected into an empty egg from another breed, and the resulting embryo implanted in a surrogate-mother sheep. A total of 277 cell fusions failed before Dolly was born healthy. Dolly was not a GMO, but the aim of this procedure was to provide a way of rapidly producing GMO animals with particular genetic modifications. The technology has not been widely adopted.

ISBN: 9780170355582

Check your understanding

1 Define 'clone'.

2 Define 'tissue culture'.

3 Cloning can have evolutionary negative consequences because

4 List three advantages to farmers of cloning plants, as compared with starting from seeds.

5 Explain the main use of grafting, as compared with using one-cultivar cuttings.

6 Suggest the main use of tissue culture, as compared with growing plants from cuttings.

Unit 3 | GMO technologies

Introduction

Since 1983 it has been possible to transfer genes from one organism and to place them into a totally different species. We describe the result as a **transgenic** organism or a Genetically Modified Organism (**GMO**). This unit describes how these transfers are done. The next unit explains why GMOs are made, with different examples and some of their implications.

The genetic code is universal. Example: in all living things, UGG is the RNA codon for tryptophan. Also, any one gene codes for only one kind of polypeptide (or protein). This has led to the assumption that any gene will behave in exactly the same way no matter where it is moved to, whether in a fish or a tomato plant.

As well as creating GMOs, there are many technologies and uses that involve DNA in one way or another:

- Gene profiling for forensic and ID purposes
- Gene profiling to find if a problem gene is present (e.g. for Alzheimer's)
- Embryo selection
- Cloning whole organisms
- Cloning stem cells for medical purposes
- Gene therapy, as used for people suffering from multiple sclerosis or muscular dystrophy. They can be given regular injections of 'improved' genetically modified cells — although this does not change a sufferer's genotype.

Only the last of these uses could be described as some kind of gene 'manipulation', and none of them creates GMOs, so these uses are not described in this unit.

Put simply, five laboratory techniques are used to create GMOs — taking DNA from one kind of living thing and getting it to 'take up residence' in the nuclei of another:

1 **Cutting** DNA, using restriction enzymes.
2 **Joining** DNA strands, using ligase.
3 **Sorting** DNA strands, using gel electrophoresis.
4 **Copying** (amplifying) DNA strands, using PCR or else plastids.
5 **Inserting** copies of the 'new' transgenic DNA into cells.

The rest of this unit assumes basic knowledge of DNA structure, DNA replication, protein synthesis and bacterial reproduction. If you are hazy about these, it may be a good idea to revise some Level 2 information first.

1 Cutting DNA, using restriction enzymes

Restriction enzymes act like chemical 'scissors', cutting DNA wherever they encounter a specific sequence of bases called a **restriction site**. These enzymes are naturally produced by bacteria as a defence against viruses; they 'restrict' viruses by cutting invading DNA. Each restriction enzyme is named according to the bacterium from which it was extracted.

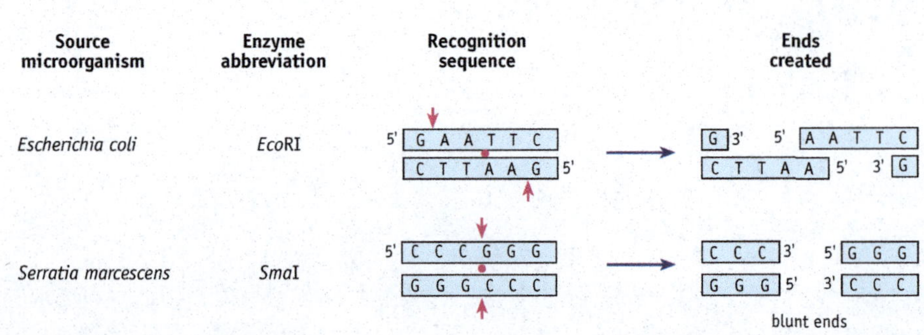

Fig. 3.7.11 Recognition sequences of two commonly used restriction enzymes.

7

ISBN: 9780170355582

Most restriction recognition sequences are palindromic, meaning that they read the same forwards as backwards. Recognition sequences are defined by reading one strand in the 5′ ⟶ 3′ direction. Example: *Eco*RI recognises and cuts the sequence 5′ G A A T T C 3′.

Restriction enzymes are of two kinds:

- Some produce staggered cuts and **sticky ends.** When DNA from two sources has been cut with the same restriction enzyme, the ends can easily join by complementary base pairing.
- Others cut the two strands opposite each other, generating **blunt ends.**

2 Joining DNA strands, using ligase

DNA ligase is an enzyme that acts like a 'stapler', joining DNA fragments together. DNA fragments from different sources can easily be joined if they have sticky ends that were made using the same kind of restriction enzyme. When the two kinds of DNA are mixed, their complementary ends 'anneal', forming weak bonds. The fragments are then joined more strongly using DNA ligase (Fig. 3.7.12).

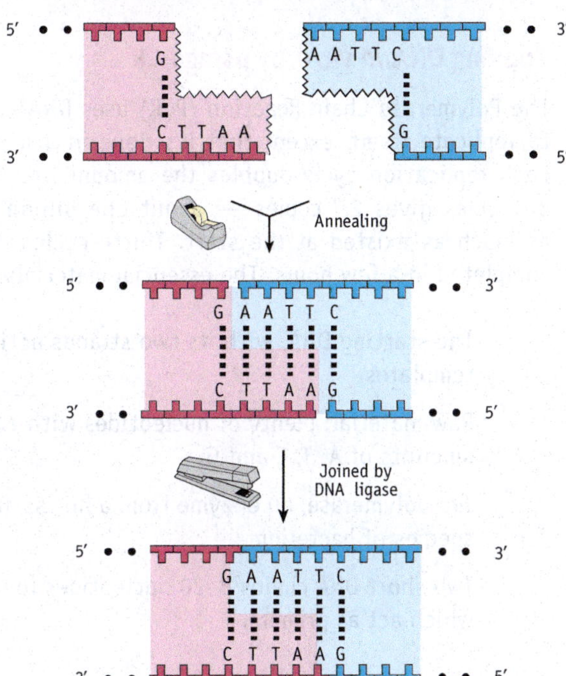

Fig. 3.7.12 DNA ligase joins two sections of DNA that have sticky ends.

3 Sorting DNA strands by size, using gel electrophoresis

When DNA fragments — each anywhere from hundrec thousands of bases long — are placed in a gel in an ele field, the negatively charged phosphate groups drag tl… towards the positive pole (anode). Longer fragments move more slowly through the gel. Result: DNA separates out into a series of bands, each band representing millions of same-length fragments (Fig. 3.7.13).

The bands become visible if the DNA is first labelled with a substance that fluoresces in UV light. Using fragments of known length, their rate of movement can be measured and used as standards to measure fragments of unknown length. In this way, particular sections of DNA can be separated from other sections.

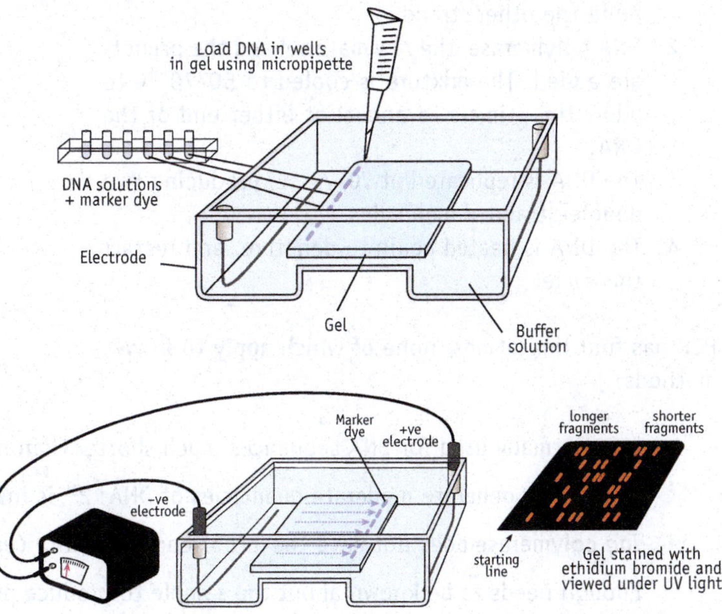

Fig. 3.7.13 Using gel electrophoresis to separate DNA fragments. Short fragments travel further.

4 Copying DNA strands

There are two ways of making multiple copies of DNA, whether it is genetically modified or not:

- ***In vitro*** ('in glass') method; the polymerase chain reaction (PCR).
- ***In vivo*** ('in life') methods; using bacteria or viruses.

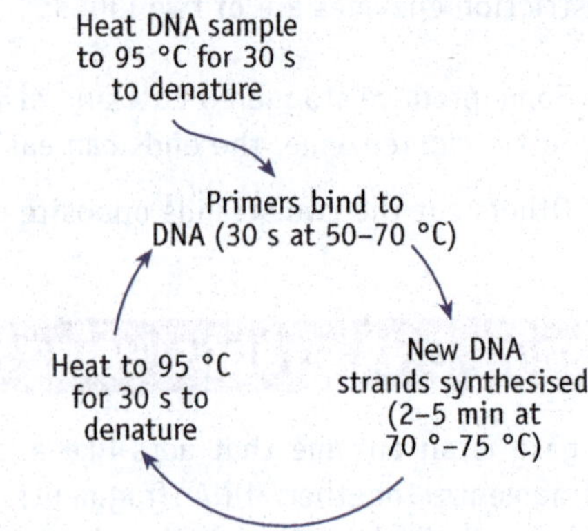

The PCR cycle

Whichever method is used, the result is a **clone**; a large number of identical copies of DNA.

Copying DNA *in vitro*, by using PCR

The Polymerase Chain Reaction (PCR) uses DNA's ability to replicate itself, except that it's done in a machine. Each replication cycle doubles the amount of DNA, so 30 cycles gives 2^{30} copies — about one billion times as much as existed at the start. Thirty cycles can be completed in a few hours. The essential materials are:

- The starting DNA, with its two strands acting as templates.
- Raw material: plenty of nucleotides with equal amounts of A, T, C and G.
- *Taq* polymerase, an enzyme from a hot-spring species of bacterium.
- Two short DNA chains 8–20 nucleotides long, which act as primers.

The steps are as follows (Fig. 3.7.14):

1. The DNA is heated to 95 °C to denature it (separate the strands). Each is then used as a template to build the other strand.
2. DNA polymerase, the raw material and the primers are added. The mixture is cooled to 50–70 °C to allow the primers to anneal at either end of the DNA.
3. The DNA is replicated at 70–75 °C, producing two double-stranded molecules.
4. The DNA is heated again to denature, and restart the cycle.

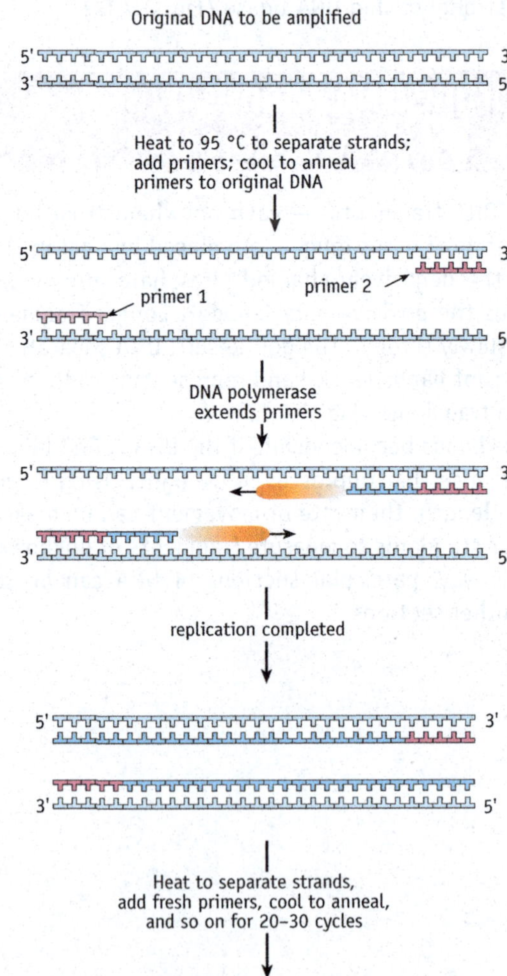

Fig. 3.7.14 Polymerase Chain Reaction

PCR has four limitations, none of which apply to *in vivo* methods:

- It is normally used for DNA sequences much shorter than most genes.
- It can only generate moderate quantities of DNA; 2^{30} is insufficient for some purposes.
- *Taq* polymerase does not have the 'proofreading' ability (unlike *in vivo* methods).
- Enough needs to be known about the sample to produce primers. If the gene in question is completely unknown, PCR cannot be used.

7

ISBN: 9780170355582

Copying DNA *in vivo*, by using plasmids

To clone larger amounts of DNA, *in vivo* methods are used, most commonly by inserting DNA into a bacterium or virus that then acts as a **vector** or carrier. (For use of viruses as cloning vectors, see *Excellence in Biology NCEA Level 3*.) Inside bacteria are **plasmids**, small chromosomes usually present as 20 to 30 copies per cell and replicating at the same time as the main chromosome does. Plasmids have two features that make them useful as transgenesis vectors:

- They can be taken up by other bacteria, even of other species.
- They contain genes for antibiotic resistance, which can be used to identify their presence.

To insert foreign DNA into a bacterium involves the following (Fig. 3.7.15):

1. Plasmids and the DNA are mixed with a restriction enzyme. Both are cut in the same way, producing compatible sticky ends.
2. DNA ligase is then added, producing recombinant plasmids.
3. The recombinant plasmids are added to a culture of the appropriate kind of bacterium. Some take up the plasmids.
4. The bacteria are then allowed to multiply and the transformed bacteria are identified.

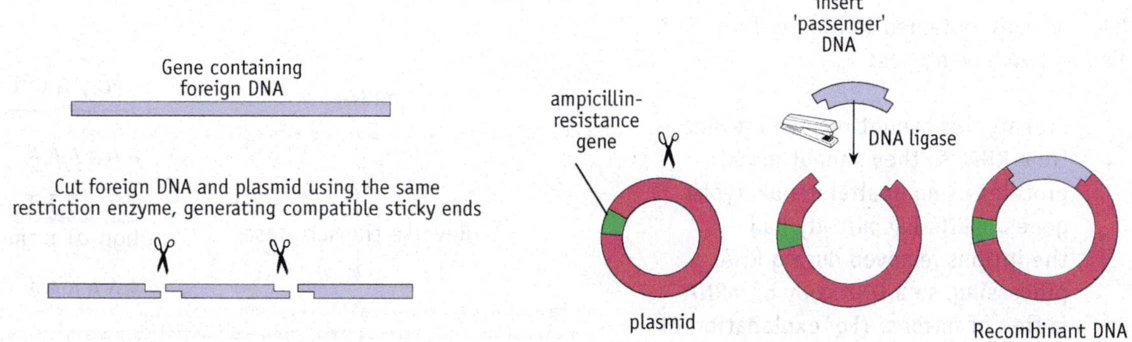

Fig. 3.7.15 Inserting DNA into a plasmid.

5 Inserting recombinant DNA into cells

The final steps in the laboratory stages of this technology are to insert DNA into target cells. Five different techniques are named here. A is used mainly for animal cells, usually egg cells; D specifically for plants. 'Successful' cells then need to be identified and grown into a whole living organism.

A **Microinjection.** DNA is injected directly into the nucleus of a target cell.

B **Biolistics.** Microscopic gold particles are given a thin coating of transgenic DNA, and the particles are then blasted into the target cells. Most cells are destroyed, some survive, and a few take up the DNA. Gold is used because it is non-toxic.

C **Using a virus as a carrier.** Viruses are genetically engineered to make them harmless, given transgenic DNA, then allowed to infect target cells. HIV is used (under strict control) because it will target almost any cell.

D **Electroporation.** Cells are subjected to a brief electric shock, which produces minute holes in the plasma membrane, allowing DNA to be taken up from the surrounding solution.

E ***Agrobacterium*.** These bacteria are used to insert genes into plants — though it only works with dicotyledons. (Details of the process are in the 'Excellence' box below.) After cells have been treated in this way, they are grown into miniature plants using sterile tissue-culture methods as described in Unit 2.

For the five methods described on the previous page, success rates are very low, with only a small proportion of cells incorporating the recombinant DNA into their chromosomes. Also, there is little or no control over where the DNA is incorporated, which makes the processes unreliable, so most plants will fail to produce the desired features. Success rates are generally much less than one in 1000 plants. For this reason, huge numbers of GMO plants (pine trees, for example) need to be produced and trialled for there to be a reasonable chance of finding a few that have (for example) softer wood suitable for papermaking.

E

Plasmid identification, gene libraries

Only a very small proportion of bacteria take up the plasmids. This is solved by using plasmids containing a gene for resistance to an antibiotic such as ampicillin. If the bacteria used are sensitive to ampicillin, only those that have taken up the plasmids will grow, which enables the transgenic bacteria to be identified.

Treatment with a restriction enzyme generates millions of DNA fragments that collectively make up the entire genome. Between them, the transformed bacteria contain different fragments of the entire genome, and constitute a **gene library**. Only a tiny proportion of the bacterial colonies will contain the gene of interest, so these must first be isolated from the others. This is done with a gene probe.

Reverse transcription: making DNA from RNA

DNA is usually obtained indirectly from RNA. This has two advantages:

- Prokaryotes cannot remove introns from RNA, so they cannot make proteins using unaltered eukaryotic genes. mRNA has already had the introns removed during RNA processing, so a DNA copy of mRNA is free of introns. (For explanation of introns, see *Excellence in Biology NCEA Level 3*.)
- In a multicellular organism, each cell only translates some of its genes, so there are far fewer kinds of mRNA.

Because the genetic code is universal, bacteria can be used to mass-produce DNA from any organism — including eukaryotes. The problem of introns is overcome by using mRNA to make DNA using the enzyme **reverse transcriptase**. This can be used *in vitro* to convert mRNA into a DNA copy (Fig. 3.7.16).

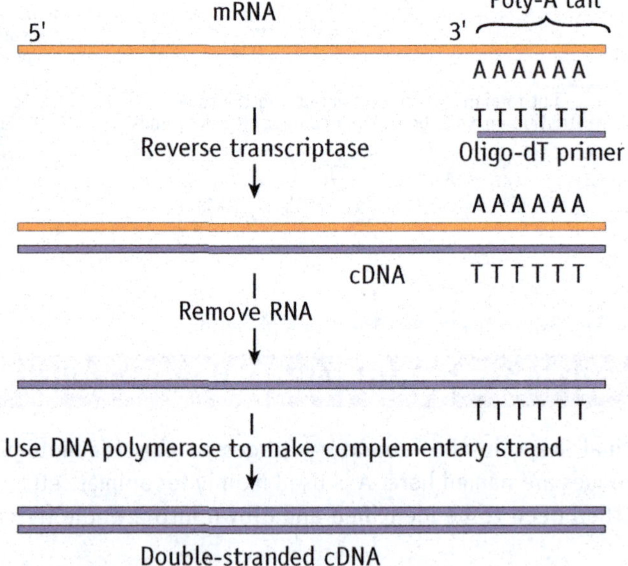

Fig. 3.7.16 Making cDNA from mRNA using reverse transcriptase.

Agrobacterium techniques

The most common method of inserting genes into cells of dicotyledonous plants uses the bacterium *Agrobacterium tumefaciens*. In nature it causes tumour-like growths called galls. On entering a wound, the bacterium inserts a *tumour-inducing* (**Ti**) plasmid into a host cell at the site of the wound. Part of the plasmid, called **T-DNA**, is incorporated into a chromosome of the host. The T-DNA contains genes causing the host cell to divide, producing the gall. Once the T-DNA has been incorporated into the chromosome, it is replicated along with it, so the gall grows independently of the bacteria (Fig. 3.7.17).

7

 ISBN: 9780170355582

The *Agrobacterium* used to insert genes into plant cells have had the gene causing gall formation deleted, and they have genes for resistance to an antibiotic such as *kanamycin*. Fig. 3.7.17 shows how *Agrobacterium* is used as a vector to introduce a gene into a plant cell.

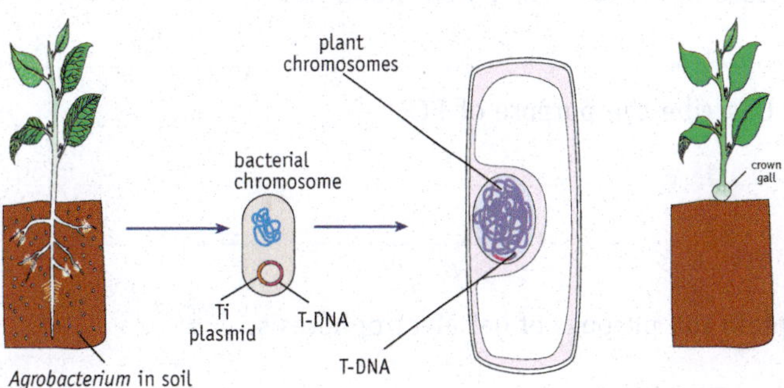

Fig. 3.7.17 *Agrobacterium* causes crown gall disease by inserting part of its Ti plasmid into the host genome.

Using *Agrobacterium* as a vector involves the following operations:

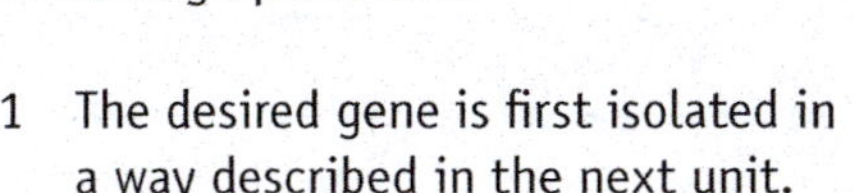

1 The desired gene is first isolated in a way described in the next unit.

2 The gene is spliced into a plasmid of *Agrobacterium* and cloned as described earlier in this unit.

3 Cells of the host plant are grown in tissue culture (see below), and treated with the engineered *Agrobacterium*, together with an antibiotic such as kanamycin. This serves to identify those bacteria into which the engineered plasmid has been inserted, since only these bacteria can grow in the presence of the antibiotic.

4 From the cultured cells, entire plants are then grown.

Agrobacterium does not attack monocotyledons, so for cereals and some other important crop plants, other methods are used. These include electroporation (after the cell walls have been digested away to produce naked cells called *protoplasts*), and the biolistic method, in which minute beads of tungsten or gold are coated with DNA and fired into intact plant cells. Gold is used because it is non-toxic. Biolistics destroys most cells, and its success rate is low.

Check your understanding

1 Describe the purpose of using restriction enzymes when making recombinant DNA.

____

____

2 Explain why it is useful to have different kinds of restriction enzyme when making recombinant DNA.

____

____

3 Explain briefly what is involved in these two stages of joining DNA fragments:

a annealing ____

b using DNA ligase. ____

4 Explain what is meant by the terms *in vivo* and *in vitro*. Name one example of each technique in GMO technology.

____

____

____

5 a State what the letters 'PCR' stand for.

b Describe the purpose of PCR.

6 Explain the purpose of gel electrophoresis.

7 In gel electrophoresis, bigger DNA fragments do not travel as far compared with smaller fragments because

8 The purpose of using plastids in the making of GMOs is

9 List five methods of transferring DNA into cells.

10 Explain one reason why the success rate of DNA transfer is very low.

11 Describe ways in which selective breeding and the production of GMOs are similar.

12 Describe ways in which selective breeding and the production of GMOs are different.

 ISBN: 9780170355582

Unit 4 | GMO crops: examples and implications

Background

This unit aims to help students carry out a research assignment on some aspect of GMO technology and its implications.

The first GMO crop plant — a variety of tobacco — was developed in 1982, and since then many GMO crops have been developed and patented. Arguments have continued over positive and negative implications of GMO foods, with many arguments based on possibilities and not on solid evidence. Production and acceptance of GM foods is high in the USA, lower in Europe. Currently, no commercial genetically modified crops are permitted in New Zealand.

Sources of information

Information on GMOs continues to change rapidly, so that any summary — including this one — can be overtaken by new research. It is important to get recent research information, and not rely mainly on reports from the 1990s. Science is an open book that's still being written.

The other problem is bias. GMO arguments tend to be polarised, which makes it difficult to find online resources that are not biased one way or the other. Websites linked to GMO businesses tend to feature only positive possibilities and outcomes, never negative ones. On the other hand, some websites deal only with negative or failed aspects of GMO crops. When evaluating opinions and evidence, be aware of hidden bias, especially from people who are likely to make money out of a situation.

Fig. 3.7.18 A soybean field being sprayed in order to kill any weeds that might later compete with the growing crop, but not kill the young GMO soybean plants themselves.

Argument or evidence?

Arguments for and against the way GMOs are being used at present usually revolve around implications for:

- Health and safety
- Ecosystems
- Genetic and biodiversity effects
- Gene ownership (most GMOs are patented and owned)
- Food production and farm profitability.

These implications are discussed in this unit. However, opinion alone is not enough — arguments become more convincing if based on evidence. GMO crops have been grown for more than 30 years, giving time for evidence to emerge.

GLYPHOSATE 360 WEEDKILLER
CONTENTS MAKES 50 LITRES OF SPRAY
ACTIVE INGREDIENT: Contains 360g/litre glyphosate as the isopropylamine salt in the form of a soluble concentrate.
PRECAUTIONS: Keep out of reach of children. Store in original container, tightly closed, away from foodstuffs. Avoid contact with skin and inhalation of spray mist. Wash hands and exposed skin after using and before eating meals. Dispose of empty container safely. Avoid contamination of any water supply with chemical or empty container. Do not apply this product on crops that will be consumed as food by humans or animals.
Hazard Classification; Classes 6.3A, 6.4A, 9.1B (HSNO Act 1996)
FIRST AID: If swallowed, DO NOT induce vomiting. Give plenty of water. If in contact with skin wash thoroughly with soap and water.
GENERAL INFORMATION: Glyphosate 360 Weedkiller controls a wide range of grass and broadleaf weeds including couch, kikuyu, paspalum, thistles and most oxalis species. It works by moving through the plant and into the root system killing the entire plant. Brown-off may take 7-14 days after application,

Fig. 3.7.19 Glyphosate is a wide-spectrum herbicide (plant poison). It is used to kill weeds, especially in fields of crop plants genetically modified to resist glyphosate.

Examples of genetically modified crop plants

Use the blank rows to add further examples as you encounter them.

The summaries below are too brief; you will need to do much reading research on your own.

Gene added	To which crops?	Intended purpose and properties *(In brackets: some unintended results, side effects and alternatives.)*
Anti-ripen	FlavrSavr tomato	Slows the ripening process, so potentially increases the storage life of tomatoes and reducing costs to producers. Introduced 1994. *(Not a commercial success. Withdrawn 1997.)*
Bt	corn (maize) soybeans cotton potato	*Bacillus thuringiensis* (Bt) is a soil bacterial species that produces a toxin capable of killing moth and butterfly caterpillars. Synthetic versions of the 'Bt' gene for this toxin were introduced into crop plant genomes to help these plants kill pest moths and butterflies. Additional aim: to reduce farmers' need for other insecticide poisons, some of them very toxic to humans. *(Bt crops also kill non-pest moths and butterflies and possibly other insects, with flow-on effects to other food chains.)*
Glyphosate resistance	corn soybeans canola wheat alfalfa	Glyphosate ('Roundup') is a commercial weedkiller, first developed in 1973. A gene that protects against glyphosate was discovered in bacteria, then introduced into the genome of crop plants in the 1990s. Aim: to enable farmers to spray and kill other (weed) plants but not kill the crop plants, thus reducing the need for ploughing and weed removal. *(A temporary benefit. In the USA over 80 weed species have evolved resistance to glyphosate, so its use has increased to compensate. Reduced biodiversity among wild plant communities on farms. Concerns over chemical safety.)*
Golden rice	rice	Modified to produce beta-carotene in rice grains, to help overcome the problem of vitamin A deficiency, which is common in poorer countries and can cause blindness in children. *(Not proved to work. Golden rice carotene content is low. A simpler and cheaper solution already exists: growing and eating vegetables that are naturally high in vitamin A. In addition, golden rice yields are lower than for other varieties already being gown in nearby areas.)*

Fig. 3.7.20 Maize being harvested. Over 90 per cent of the maize and other main crops grown in the USA are GMOs, with one or more Bt-type genes added. Most of the US maize and soybean harvest is used as stock feed, not for direct human consumption.

7

ISBN: 9780170355582

Examples of GMOs developed for pharmaceutical and other purposes

Use the blank rows to add further examples as you encounter them.

Gene added	**To which organisms?**	**Intended purpose and properties** *(In brackets: some unintended results, side effects, and alternatives.)*
human insulin	bacteria	Purpose: to mass produce cheap insulin for use by diabetics. GMO bacteria are cultured in large vats, and produce human insulin, which is later extracted. Widely used.
human growth hormone (HGH)	cows	Purpose: to induce cows to produce this hormone in their milk. The hope is that potentially HGH could then be extracted and used to help children who have growth problems.
spider-silk	goats	Purpose: to induce goats to produce spider-silk protein in their milk. Spider silk is stronger than steel, and the hope is that spider-silk fibre can potentially be produced in this way.

Health and safety implications with GMO foods

In 30 years there have been few problems with GMO food consumption. Potential issues include: allergic reactions to new proteins, altered nutritional value of foods, toxicity. There has been only one case of widespread poisoning, when GMO bacteria were used to produce tryptophan, an amino acid used as a food supplement. Result: 37 deaths by poisoning in the USA, with 1500 disabled. This involved a bacterial GMO and not a food crop, and no other problem like it has been identified.

A greater health issue has revolved around possible effects of 'Bt' foods on consumers, and on the widespread use of glyphosate. A 2012 study found that in rats fed Bt-containing GM corn, the cancer rate was double that of a control rat group. Glyphosate use may also be linked to a kidney disease epidemic (CKDu) in Sri Lanka and India. At present the weight of evidence indicates that GMO-derived foods are safe to eat. However, little safety testing has been done. Some countries have laws requiring the GMO content of foods to be labelled, most do not.

Farmers who repeatedly spray GMO crops with glyphosate may suffer from accidental poisoning. On the other hand, using GMO soybeans and Bt corn means that farmers can cut down on use of other weed- and pest-control poisons, so possibly on balance they are better off healthwise. We will know for sure only when there is more evidence on long-term health effects.

Ecosystems, implications and survival of populations

According to the World Health Organization among others, some possibilities and realities include:

- **Killing non-target species**, such as non-pest insects including butterflies. This appears to be happening with GMO crops carrying the Bt gene. (Non-target killing also happens with most insecticides, so this is not just a GMO problem.)
- **Other plants at risk**. Biodiversity is diminished by heavy glyphosate use.
- **Soil quality** is at risk of being diminished by heavy glyphosate use, as it appears to have adverse effects on useful mycorrhizal fungi and nitrogen-fixing bacteria.

The impacts of GMO crops and associated chemical use vary according to local conditions, so it may be unwise to see all these implications as applying in every case.

Genetic and biodiversity implications linked to GMO crops

According to the World Health Organization among others, some possibilities and realities include:

- **Resistance in weeds** is evolving as a result of increased glyphosate use. The number of plants registered as herbicide-resistant in the USA rose from two species in 2000, to 85 species in 2012. As farmers attempted to deal with increasing numbers of resistant weeds, glyphosate use per hectare doubled between 2001 and 2007.
- **Resistance by pest insects** to Bt, in the same way that insects evolve resistance to insecticide chemicals. Example: the cotton bollworm had become resistant to Bt by 2009.
- **Gene transfer to other species.** Genes are spread by pollen drift. GM canola is known to freely hybridise with other species of *Brassica*.
- **Uncertain gene behaviour.** Genes inserted into a completely different genome could (and do) behave in unpredictable ways, since genes are influenced by neighbouring genes in ways that we only dimly understand.

Gene ownership: implications

To create a GMO, existing genes are taken from one kind of living thing and placed in another: plant to plant, bacteria to plant, human to bacteria. No completely new genes are made. As described in Unit X, gene transfers need highly specialised skills and equipment, so can be very expensive. By contrast, traditional selective breeding is low-tech and simple. In one respect, both forms of 'gene manipulation' — gene transfer and selective breeding — share similar goals of making improved crop plants, but the methods are totally different.

GMO crops are mostly developed by researchers working for large agri-business corporations. Although in most cases they did not create the genes in the first place, these corporations own the rights and legal patents to their new gene combinations and any resulting seeds. In Europe alone more than 2000 seed varieties have been patented. GMO development is almost entirely driven by the commercial interests of these corporations.

GMO seeds are expensive. For a variety of technical and legal reasons it is not possible for farmers to save some GMO seeds from a harvest and use these for planting the following year. Farmers who have been found with unauthorised GMO crops growing on their farm — even accidentally — have been sued. The traditional custom of farmers saving seeds for future use is being abandoned. A new batch of seeds needs to be bought every year.

Seeds and the patented genes they carry are increasingly owned and controlled by a few corporations. The biggest three — Monsanto, DuPont, Syngenta — between them sell about half of the global seed supply, including most GMO seeds. These corporations also supply chemicals such as glyphosate that many GMO crops depend on.

The implications of restricted gene ownership are serious, and discussions on the matter are only just beginning.

 ISBN: 9780170355582

Food production and farm costs: implications

GMO crops have been grown extensively since the mid-1990s. They were originally developed with various claims and hopes, chiefly:

- improving total farm production (yield in tonnes per hectare)
- reducing the need for chemical pesticides, etc.
- improving the profitability of crop farming.

Results so far have been mixed. For some GMO crops in some areas, outcomes have been positive on some points. In other situations, GMO crops have fulfilled none of the above claims. It is difficult to give global averages, but from USA experience the overall results from GMO crop farming have been:

- farm production: little change on average
- chemical costs: slightly reduced in some cases, higher in others
- seed costs: increased two-fold to four-fold.

GMO crops are sometimes claimed to be the answer to the problems of feeding an expected nine billion humans by 2050. According to the World Bank, an estimated one third of global food output is currently wasted — with the highest proportion of wastage in developed countries. World hunger is caused mainly by inequality, not by insufficient world food production.

Most improvements in crop production over the past 50 years have come about not as a result of GMOs, but through traditional selective breeding methods plus improved irrigation methods. Also, there is now an increasing move to 'biological' farming, which aims to keep industrial chemical inputs as low as possible, and to maximise soil health.

Project suggestions

Biology 3.7 is likely to be assessed on a project basis, so a short list of five possible project ideas is offered below. These range across all of 3.7, not this unit alone. New GMO-related issues and contexts and information will continue to appear, so there are many other project ideas that could be considered.

1. **Selective breeding.** Clarify the similarities and differences between selective breeding and genetic modification. Outline how selective breeding works, its history and uses, in one particular kind of crop plant and/or domesticated animal.
2. **Animal cloning.** Dolly the sheep was the first example of an animal created using SCNT (somatic cell nuclear transfer). Give a detailed account of the technique. Outline the possible future uses and advantages and disadvantages of SCNT. Include practical, economic and ethical aspects.
3. **Future foods?** There are many claims that GM crops will become essential to avoid mass starvation in the future. Discuss this viewpoint critically, taking into account practical aspects of using GMOs compared with the alternatives. Consider mainly practical and economic aspects.
4. **Golden rice.** Investigate how and why this GMO rice was developed. Consider its costs and benefits, its effectiveness, and the alternatives.
5. **Gene ownership.** Who owns genes? Report on why increasing numbers of genes are privately owned, and by whom. Also report on how these gene combinations are produced, and on the future implications of gene ownership.

Biology 3.7 Gene manipulation

NCEA Achievement Standard 91607: Demonstrate understanding of human manipulations of genetic transfer and its biological implications

Internally assessed, 3 credits

Achievement	Achievement with Merit	Achievement with Excellence
Demonstrate understanding of human manipulations of genetic transfer and its biological implications.	Demonstrate in-depth understanding of human manipulations of genetic transfer and its biological implications.	Demonstrate comprehensive understanding of human manipulations of genetic transfer and its biological implications.

Achievement
'Demonstrate understanding ...' involves using biological ideas to describe human manipulations of genetic transfer and its biological implications.

Achievement with Merit
'Demonstrate in-depth understanding ...' involves using biological ideas to explain how humans manipulate genetic transfer and the biological implications of these manipulations.

Achievement with Excellence
'Demonstrate comprehensive understanding ...' involves linking biological ideas about human manipulations of genetic transfer and its biological implications. The linking of ideas may involve justifying, relating, evaluating, comparing and contrasting, and analysing.

Human manipulation of genetic transfer may involve:
- selective breeding (could include embryo selection, animal breeding, plant breeding, development of new crops)
- whole organism cloning
- transgenesis (i.e. GMOs, Genetically Modified Organisms)
- investigation and modification of the expression of existing genes.

Biological implications may involve the impact on:
- ecosystems
- genetic biodiversity
- health or survival of individuals
- survival of populations
- evolution of populations.

7

ISBN: 9780170355582

Glossary

Abiotic factor Physical or non-living factor such as light or temperature
Acheulean Stone tool culture association with *Homo erectus*
Adaptive radiation Relatively rapid proliferation from an ancestral type into new types, which fill a diversity of ecological niches
Adrenaline Hormone produced by the adrenal glands in emergencies, stimulating changes like increase in heart rate and blood pressure
Aerobic Involving oxygen (literally, air)
Agonistic Threat and submission behaviour between members of the same species
Agrobacterium Soil bacterium used to insert recombinant DNA into dicotyledonous plants
Aldosterone Hormone that influences blood pressure
Allele frequency The proportion of an allele in a gene pool compared with all the alleles of that gene
Alleles Alternative forms of a gene. Alleles occur in pairs, with two alleles per gene
Allelopathy Production by plants of chemicals that inhibit growth of potential competitors
Allopatric From or in different geographic regions
Altricial Hatching or being born in a helpless state, totally dependent on parents
Altruism Behaviour where individuals help one another with no reward to themselves
Alveoli Tiny air-filled endings where gas exchange happens in a mammal
Anaerobic metabolism Energy-yielding process by which glucose is broken down in absence of oxygen (sometimes incorrectly called anaerobic respiration)
Analogous Features that are superficially similar but have different modes of development and different evolutionary origins
Annealing Forming a temporary join between DNA fragments by complementary base pairing
Antagonistic Opposing, as in the effects of insulin and glucagon
Anthropomorphism Attributing human feelings and motives to an animal
Ardipithecus One of the earliest fossil genera of Australopithecines
Atlatl Spear thrower, giving greatly improving killing power
Australopithecus Genus of australopithecine with smaller jaws than four-footed apes; probably omnivorous
Autonomic Parts of the peripheral nervous system that are not under conscious control
Auxin Plant growth substance involved in phototropism and gravitropism

Bacteriophage Virus that attacks bacteria; used in cloning DNA
Baroreceptors Blood pressure sensors
Biotic factor Environmental influence due to other organisms, e.g. predators
Bowman's capsule Cup-shaped structure at one end of each nephron
Brachiating Method of moving through trees by swinging from branch to branch using arms
Broca's area Brain centre that organises vocal sounds into meaningful sequences
Brood parasite Animal that uses an animal of another species to rear its own

Carbohydrates Compounds containing the elements C, H and O, with H and O in the ratio 2:1
Carbon-14 Isotope used in dating organic remains less than 50,000 years old
Cerebrum Region of the brain greatly enlarged in apes, most of all in humans
Choice chamber Apparatus used in studying taxes and kineses
Circadian Recurrent behaviour with a period of about a day
Circa-lunar Recurrent behaviour with a period of about a month
Circannual Recurrent behaviour with a period of about a year
Circa-tidal Recurrent behaviour with a period of about 12.4 hours

Clade An evolutionary 'branch' and its daughter 'twigs'
Climax community Final stage of a succession, in which no further change occurs
Cline An extended population with gradients in phenotype
Clone A number of genetically identical individuals produced from one 'parent'. A clone can be artificial or natural
Cloning Any process that produces multiple individuals that are genetically identical to each other
Coding strand DNA strand that has the same base sequence (except for uracil) as mRNA
Co-evolution Evolution in which two or more species affect each other's evolution
Coleoptile Sheath protecting foliage leaves of grass seedling
Commensalism Relationship in which one species derives benefit and the other is neither harmed nor does it benefit
Competition Situation in which demand for a resource exceeds supply
Convergent evolution Evolution of superficial similarity of phenotype as a result of similar selection pressures
Cortisol One of many hormones secreted by the adrenal cortex; stimulates the production of glucose from amino acids
Courtship Prelude to mating in some animal species, with behaviour by both partners acting as mutual stimuli that bring them together
Crepuscular Active around dawn and/or dusk
Cro-magnon Name given to earliest European modern humans
Crypsis Camouflage by resemblance to the background

Day-neutral plant Any plant in which flowering is insensitive to day length
Deme A population partly isolated from other populations of the same species
Dependent variable The variable that is shown in the results in an experiment
Diabetes Disorder(s) in which blood glucose levels cannot be properly regulated
Dialysis Medical procedure that is used to replace some kidney functions
Diapause Seasonally induced pause of growth and development in arthropods, e.g. crickets
Diastema Gap between two permanent teeth; in chimpanzees, between the upper incisor and canine
Directional selection Selection against one end of a range of variation, resulting in a progressive change in allele frequency
Disruptive selection Selection acting against the middle of a range of variation
Diuretic Substance that stimulates urine production
Diurnal Active during the day
DNA ligase Enzyme that joins DNA fragments
Double circulation Blood system in which one side of the heart pumps blood to the lungs and the other side pumps blood to the rest of the body

Ectoparasite Parasite that feeds on the outside of its host
Effector Any structure that produces change, especially in a homeostatic system
Electroporation Inserting DNA into cells using brief electric shock to make tiny holes in plasma membrane
Endemic Found only in that country — e.g. most *Hebe* species are endemic to New Zealand
Endogenous Having an internal origin
Endoparasite Parasite that lives inside its host
Entrainment Resetting an internal clock by some rhythmic environmental cue
Epoch Any sub-part of the Cenozoic Period ('Age of mammals', 65 mya to present)
Exogenous Having an external origin
Exon Section of DNA that codes for amino acids in a polypeptide (cf. intron)
Explant Fragment of plant tissue into which recombinant DNA is introduced, from which new plants can be grown

Facultative Not essential for survival
Firestone Pebble of iron sulfide, used to produce sparks hot enough to make fire
Fission track dating Dating method using the number of tracks left in rock by decaying uranium-238 atoms
Florigen Chemical that transmits flowering signal from leaves to meristems, stimulating them to form flowering buds
Foramen magnum The hole in the skull through which the spinal cord passes
Free-running Being free of external rhythmic influences

Gas exchange The diffusion of O_2 and CO_2 in opposite directions across a surface
Gel electrophoresis Technique for separating DNA fragments of different lengths, using an electric field in a porous gel
Gene A unit of inheritance consisting of a length of DNA that codes for a polypeptide
Gene flow Movement of genes via organisms or gametes, from one population to another
Gene library A culture of transformed bacteria that collectively contain the entire genome of another organism
Gene pool All the genes in a population
Gene probe Short length of single-stranded DNA used to locate a specific DNA sequence

ISBN: 9780170355582

Genome All the genes in an organism
Genotype An individual's genetic makeup for a particular pair of alleles
Germ Cells that can potentially contribute their genes to future generations; the gametes and cells that give rise to them
Glucagon Hormone produced in the pancreas, increasing blood glucose levels
Glycogen A particular kind of polysaccharide, similar to starch
Gravitropism Plant growth response to the direction of gravity
Grazer An organism that feeds off another organism without killing it

Habitat Place where an organism lives
Haemoglobin Protein molecule with the special function of bonding reversibily with oxygen
Half-life The time for half of the amount of an isotope to change to another isotope
Home range Area an animal occupies but does not defend
Homeostasis Regulation of blood and tissue fluid to keep conditions the same (Greek *homeo* = the same)
Homeotherms Animals able to balance heat gain and loss to keep body temperature almost constant, e.g. birds and mammals
Hominid Family containing humans, African apes and orang-utans
Hominin Group consisting of the genus *Homo* and also ancestral genera such as *Australopithecus*
Homo erectus First human ancestor to use fire
Homo habilis Earliest proto-human to make stone tools
Homo heidelbergensis First humans for which there is firm evidence for systematic hunting
Homo neanderthalensis First humans to bury the dead and care for the aged
Homologous Features with the same underlying arrangement indicating the same origins, but may be specialised for different functions
Hormones Chemical messengers that travel in the blood
Hyperglycaemia Blood glucose level higher than normal
Hypoglycaemia Blood glucose level lower than normal
Hypothalamus Small region of the brain with sensor and controller functions in several homeostatic systems

IAA Indolyl-3-acetic acid; the chemical name for auxin
Independent variable The factor that is intentionally changed in an experiment
Insulin Hormone produced in the pancreas; brings about reduction in blood glucose levels
Intron Non-coding segment of a gene
Islets of Langerhans Small groups of hormone-producing cells in the pancreas
Isolating mechanism Inherited feature that tends to prevent species from interbreeding with other species

Ketosis Pathological state in diabetes resulting from production of ketone bodies, reducing blood pH
Kin selection A form of natural selection in which the behaviour of an individual tends to increase the reproductive success of its relatives
Kinesis Orientation resulting from change in *rate* of activity rather than its direction
Klinostat Device for varying the duration of exposure to gravity from one direction
Kya Thousand years ago ('kilo' = thousand)

Lek Mating ritual (and place) in which a territory is established by males and used solely for mating
Levallois A particular tool-making technique associated with Neanderthals
Lipofection Introduction of DNA into cells by surrounding them with lipid droplets, which are taken in by endocytosis
Long-day plant Any plant flowering when photoperiods exceed a critical value, e.g. iris
Lower Palaeolithic The earlier phase of the Old Stone Age
Lunar rhythm Rhythm with a period the same as the time between full moons; 29.5 days

Mesolithic Cultural period between the Palaeolithic and the Neolithic
Metabolism General word covering all chemical activity in living things
Migration Active, regular movement of animals in *anticipation* of future change
Mimicry Deception by close resemblance to another organism
Mitochondria Organelles that produce most of the ATP in cells
Mitochondrial DNA DNA in mitochondria that has provided much information on short-term evolutionary change; inherited only from mothers
Monogamy Relationship between the sexes in which each male mates with only one female in a breeding season
Monosaccharide A 'single sugar' such as glucose; most have six carbon atoms
Mousterian General term for Neanderthal stone tool culture
Multiregional Hypothesis Hypothesis that modern humans evolved independently in Africa, Europe and Asia

Mutualism A relationship between individuals of different species from which both derive benefit
Mya Million years ago
Mycorrhiza Mutualistic relationship between plant roots and a fungus

Nastic movement Plant movement in response to a non-directional stimulus
Navigation Finding the way over unfamiliar regions using knowledge of position and direction
Negative feedback Process in which the output is used to reduce the input, thus bringing about stability
Neolithic The New Stone Age, characterised by the agricultural way of life
Nephrons Kidney tubules; about one million per kidney
Neural spine Extension of vertebra to which neck muscles are attached
Neuron Nerve cell
Niche The sum total of an organism's requirements; its way of life
Nocturnal Active at night
Nucleotide analogue 'False' nucleotide used in DNA sequencing
Null hypothesis A testable assumption that any difference between two sets of figures is due to chance alone

Obligate Essential for survival
Occipital condyle Part of the skull that articulates with the atlas (first vertebra)
Oedema Accumulation of fluid in a body region, resulting in swelling
Oldowan Earliest known stone tool culture associated with *Homo habilis* and *Homo rudolfensis*
Organism A living thing
Osmotic regulation Control of water balance (aka osmoregulation)
Out of Africa Hypothesis that modern humans evolved in Africa and then migrated to Europe and Asia, displacing earlier species

Pair bond Long-lasting relationship between male and female, helping increase the chances of rearing offspring
Palaeontology The study of fossils
Paranthropus Genus of australopithecines with massive jaws and molars
Parasitoid Animal that feeds inside another, eventually killing it or, in some cases, sterilising it
Parasympathetic One component of the autonomic nervous system
Pathogen Organism that produces disease
PCR Polymerase chain reaction; method of cloning short DNA fragments *in vitro*
Phenotype The outward 'expression' of a gene, often showing in a feature such as colour
Photonasty Plant movement in response to change in light intensity
Photoperiod The length of the daytime or, under artificial conditions, exposure to light
Photoperiodism Control of the timing of activities by day length
Phototropin Receptor pigment involved in phototropism
Phototropism Plant growth response to the direction of light
Phytochrome Blue-green pigment involved in many light-mediated processes, such as induction of flowering
Pilotage Finding the way by use of landmarks
Pituitary gland Pea-sized structure at the base of the brain; has a major endocrine function
Plasmid Miniature bacterial chromosome used in cloning DNA by bacteria
Pleistocene The most recent series of ice ages, ending around 12 kya
Plumule The shoot of an embryo plant
Poikilotherm Animal with body temperature that is always close to that of the environment
Polygamy Relationship between the sexes in which each male mates with many females
Polygynandry Situation where the young are reared by several adults
Polysaccharides Long-chain carbohydrate molecules consisting of many sugar units
Population A group of organisms of the same species occupying a given area
Potassium-40 Isotope that decays to argon-40, used in radioisotopic dating
Precocial Hatching or being born at an advanced stage of development
Primates Mammal order containing humans, apes, monkeys and lemurs
Propagation Reproduction; increase in numbers
Punctuated equilibrium Periods of rapid evolution separated by long periods of little change

Quern stone Flat stone used to grind grain

Radicle Root of an embryo plant
Renal Any part or process linked to the kidneys
Restriction enzyme Enzyme that cuts DNA at specific sequences
Reverse transcriptase Enzyme used to make DNA from mRNA
RNA polymerase Enzyme that makes RNA using DNA as a template
RNA processing Process in eukaryotes in which introns are removed from RNA to produce mRNA

ISBN: 9780170355582

SCN Supra-chiasmatic nuclei; the site of the master clock in mammals
Seismonasty Turgor movement in response to vibration
Selection Process resulting in an allele having a different probability of remaining in the gene pool, compared with other allele(s)
Semilunar rhythm Rhythm with a period half that between full and new moon; 14.7 days
Sexual dimorphism Difference in external form of males and females
Sexual selection Selection for ability to obtain a mate
Short-day plant Plant flowering when the photoperiods are shorter than a critical value
Smooth muscle Slow-contracting muscles that are not under voluntary control, e.g. in blood vessel walls
Soma Collective name for those cells that are not ancestral to the gametes and die with the rest of the body
Speciation Process by which one species gives rise to two or more species
Species Group of actually or potentially interbreeding natural populations that is reproductively isolated from other such groups
Stabilising selection Selection acting against the extremes of a range of variation
Stimulus A change in an organism's environment to which it can respond
Stratum Layer of sedimentary rock
Succession Progressive change in the composition of a community over time
Sucrose A disaccharide (double sugar), consisting of a glucose and fructose unit
Sympatric Living in the same geographical region

Taxis Movement of an organism in a direction that depends on that of the stimulus
Teleology Attributing purpose to biological phenomena
Template strand DNA strand used in complementary base pairing to make mRNA
Territory Area that an animal occupies, then defends against others of the same species
Thermoluminescence Dating method using electrons emitted in radioactive decay but trapped in clay
Thigmotropism Plant growth response to contact
Thyroid Gland in neck producing the hormone thyroxine
Tidal rhythm Recurrent behaviour with a period the same as between successive high tides; 12.4 hours
Tissue fluid Fluid between cells; the 'internal environment'
Totipotent Capable of developing into the full range of cell types in an organism
Transcription The making of an RNA copy of a gene
Transformation Introduction of 'foreign' DNA into a bacterium
Translation Using the base sequence in mRNA to make a polypeptide
Tropism Plant growth movement in a direction that relates to that of the stimulus
t-test Statistical test used to compare two sets of continuous data

Upper Palaeolithic Later phase of the Old Stone Age

Valgus angle Angle between shaft of femur and the vertical when femur is in normal standing orientation
Vasodilation Widening of blood vessels
Vernalisation Induction of flowering by a period of cold, e.g. tulips
Virulent Producing severe disease symptoms
Vocal tract Air passage taken by sound from larynx to lips

Wernicke's area Brain centre responsible for interpreting the auditory input of language

Ya Years ago

Zeitgeber Rhythmic environmental cue that resets an internal clock

Answers

3.1 Practical investigation

Unit 1 Practical investigation

1

Investigation	ft/ps?	Y/N?
A Slaters (woodlice/isopods)	ft	Y
B Young tomato plants	ft	N
C Barnacles	ps	Y
D Manuka trees	ps	N
E Mangrove breathing roots	ps	Y
F Commercial disinfectants	ft	Y
G Crickets	ps	Y
H Running shoes	ft	N

2 **a** (one example) If we try planting corn seeds at different depths, then we could find an optimal depth where success rates are highest.
b (one example) Perhaps below a certain amount of citronella oil vapour in the air, mosquitoes will not be repelled.
c (one example) My chosen plant species may have an optimal water pH requirement, and this is likely to be close to pH 7.
d (one example) If we water plants too often or too seldom, then growth rates are likely to be slow.
e (one example) If I increase the yeast surrounding temperature from 10°C to 30°C, then CO_2 production is likely to get faster and faster.

3 **a** (one example) There may be an optimal amount of dissolved fertiliser for *Lemna* growth, and beyond that amount the growth rate won't increase.
b What is the effect of fertiliser concentration on growth rates in *Lemna*?
c Fertiliser concentration
d The growth rate of *Lemna*, perhaps measured by the number of floating leaves per square cm.
e Fertiliser concentration with five values: 1g/L, 2g/L, 3g/L, 5g/L, and plain tap water.
f Same temperature for all, same amount of light, same water conditions in other respects (e.g. pH), same containers, same type of plants, same number of plants at the start.
g The plan does not specify which fertiliser, nor specifies amounts, nor how many amounts. Information is needed on all three points.

Unit 2 Graphs and statistics

1 **a** mean; **b** standard deviation; **c** dependent variable; **d** range; **e** dispersion; **f** skewed distribution; **g** pie chart; **h** histogram; **i** median; **j** normal distribution; **k** scatter graph; **l** line graph; **m** raw data.

2 **a** The 2330 result should be discarded, because it is about 100 times the other values, so is obviously a recording error. Possibly the results should be 23 and 30, but because this is uncertain it's best to dump this result.
b Total for 8 results = 208. Mean = 208/8 = 26.0 mg/minute
c Range = 31 – 22 = 9 mg/minute
d Median = 26 mg/minute

3 **a** independent; **b** dependent; **c** line; **d** scatter; **e** pie.

4 **a** P = 0.2733. The difference between O and E is not significant.
b P = 0.0679. The difference between O and E is not quite significant.
c P = 0.0106. The difference between O and E is significant.
d P = 0.0001. The difference between O and E is highly significant.

3.2 Socio-scientific issue

Answers have not been provided for 3.2 as this standard requires students to work independently.

3.3 Plant and animal responses

Unit 1 Biological clocks

1

1	2	3	4	5	6	7	8	9	10
B	G	H	J	E	C	A	F	D	I

2

1	2	3	4	5	6	7	8	9	10
E	M	G	A	P	O	F	L	D	C
11	12	13	14	15	16	17			
B	J	H	K	I	Q	N			

3 **a** weta, cricket; **b** morepork, kiwi; **c** rabbit, lion; **d** tui, bellbird, starling; **e** barnacle, limpet.

4 Sleep movements in clover leaves, stomatal opening and closing

5 Body temperature, cell division in the skin, urine output

6 The SCN are in the hypothalamus. They receive nerve impulses from the retina; they communicate with the rest of the body via the pineal gland, which secretes the hormone melatonin and which induces sleep and nocturnal decrease in body temperature.

7 **a** The difference between 'entrainment' and 'endogenous' is that 'endogenous' means 'having an internal origin'. Entrainment is the resetting of an endogenous 'clock' by a rhythmic environmental cue.
b We know that the human circadian period is about 25–26 hours, because this is the period of human rhythms under constant conditions such as constant light or darkness.
c The internal bodily cause of jetlag is the lack of synchrony between the endogenous rhythm and external environmental rhythms.
d The function of a *zeitgeber* is to continually 'reset' the internal clock to keep it synchronised with environmental rhythms.

8 **a** actogram; **b** constant darkness; **c** About 25 hours; **d** The animal can begin the appropriate behaviour before the external environmental change 'demands' it.

Unit 2 Seasonal behaviour and photoperiodism

1 **a** photoperiod; **b** florigen; **c** vernalisation; **d** phytochrome; **e** diapause; **f** absorption spectrum; **g** strawberry; **h** hibernation; **i** endotherm; **j** metabolism.

2 **a** 21 December, 14.5 hours; **b** 21 June, 9.5 hours; **c** 21September, 21 March

3 **a** We know that plants perceive day and night length in their leaves and not their flowers, because flowering is only induced if the leaves are exposed to the appropriate photoperiod.
b We know that flowering in short-day plants is actually triggered by long nights, because a brief light interruption to a long night prevents flowering in SDPs and induces flowering in LDPs.
c To switch off flowering in *Chrysanthemum* (a short-day plant, CDL 11 hours), plants being grown indoors should be given nights shorter than 13 hours, or interrupt the night with light.
d Plants (and also animals) use day length as an indicator of time of year, and do not rely on seasonal factors such as temperature, because only photoperiod varies predictably with season.
e The term 'long-day plant' is a misleading, because it is the length of uninterrupted darkness that is important.

4 By interrupting the night the grower was giving the plant a short night, which has the same effect as a long day. To succeed, the grower should not turn on the plants' lights at night.

5 X = SDP; Y = DNP; Z = LDP

6 **a** It must be a short-day plant, since it flowers in I but does not in II, when the days are longer.
b Interrupting the night in the middle as in III prevents flowering, but a night interruption near the beginning (as in IV) does not. Evidently the length of continuous darkness must exceed a certain value to induce flowering.
c A nocturnal interruption with red light has the same effect as white light, but if this is immediately followed by far-red light, the effect of the red light is reversed, and the effect of far-red light can itself be reversed by red light.
d It could be induced to flower by artificially lengthening the night/growing them indoors having lights on for 10 hours or less out of 24.

Unit 3 Animals: finding the way

1 **a** taxis; **b** positive gravitaxis; **c** negative phototaxis; **d** migration; **e** compass; **f** orthokinesis; **g** pilotage;**h** navigation; **i** klinokinesis; **j** kinesis; **k** thigmokinesis.

ISBN: 9780170355582

2 In the polar summer, plankton growth is maximal (zero growth in continuous darkness of winter). Whale calves lose less heat if born in tropical seas.
3 a Migration costs large amounts of energy (which may be partly made up by increased food supplies in the destination). Headwinds can cause them to die before they reach their destination. There may be increased risks of predation.
b Days are much longer the further from the equator, so there is much more time to feed the young.
4 a Three kinds of compass used by migrating birds are solar (sun) compass, stellar (star) compass, magnetic compass (Earth's magnetic field).
b When navigating by sun (or stars), birds need an internal clock, in order to compensate for the apparent movement of sun (and stars).
c Bees are able to navigate using sunlight on a cloudy day, but only if some clear sky is visible.
5 Salmon recognise the stream they were hatched in from its unique chemical 'signature' or odour.
6 Experiments 1 and 2 show that with bar magnets, experienced pigeons can still navigate provided they can see the sun. It seems that they have both a solar and a magnetic compass, and either can substitute for the other. Experiment 3 shows that birds with no previous experience of the sun are able to navigate, but only if their magnetic sense is not interfered with. Use of the sun as a compass appears to be learned, probably using the magnetic compass as a reference. Experiment 4 shows that the birds can only use the solar compass in the afternoon if they have previous experience of the sun's position at that time.
7 A homing pigeon must have a sense of position ('map'), a sense of direction ('compass') and a sense of time.
8 In dry air, the slaters moved more quickly at 20°C than at 5°C, and at both temperatures they moved more quickly in dry air than in humid air. Hydrokinesis. Also thermokinesis.

Unit 4 Plants, orientation, tropisms

1 **a** tropism; **b** thigmotropism; **c** gravitropism; **d** phototropism; **e** radicle; **f** auxin; **g** nasty; **h** thigmonasty; **i** plumule; **j** coleoptile.
2 a 'Positive gravitropism' is one way of saying that the radicle grows downwards.
b Two advantages this positive gravitropism gives the plant are the seedling obtains a more reliable water supply, and better anchorage.
c The main effect that auxin has on cells close to the root tip is to inhibit cell elongation.
d During germination, the plumule shows negative gravitropism, which benefits the young plant by enabling the shoot to reach the light even when it's underground in total darkness.
3 Auxin: indole-3-acetic acid (IAA)
4 a The main effect of auxins on growing stems is to stimulate cell elongation.
b The main effect of auxins on growing root tips is to inhibit elongation.
c Three differences between a tropic and a nastic response are: **i** In tropisms, movement is by growth; in nasties it is by changes in turgor; **ii** A tropism is a response to a directional stimulus; nasties are responses to non-directional stimuli; **iii** Tropisms are not reversible; nasties are reversible; **iv** Tropisms are slower.
d We know that adult Norfolk pines do not have any phototropic response because they grow vertically upward throughout life.
5 E: 3 and 5
6 D, since the greater number of coleoptile tips have been on for the longest time, yielding the greatest amount of auxin to the agar block.
7 C: 1 and 4
8 In both roots and shoots, auxin can stimulate elongation, but this effect occurs at much lower concentrations in roots than in shoots. Concentrations that stimulate elongation in shoots inhibit elongation in roots. In both horizontal shoots and roots, auxin is transported away from the tip along the lower side. This stimulates elongation of the lower side in shoots, causing upward bending, but inhibits elongation of the lower side in roots, causing it to bend downward.

Unit 5 Competition and cooperation

1 **a** interspecific; **b** Gause; **c** ritual; **d** intraspecific; **e** niche; **f** pioneers; **g** allelopathy; **h** antibiosis; **i** agonistic; **j** hierarchy.
2 Competition is behaviour that happens when demand for resources is greater than supply.
3 Gause's Principle: No two species can indefinitely occupy the same niche in the same habitat.
4

Interspecific behaviour	Intraspecific behaviour
Competition: niche differentiation, allelopathy	**Competition:** territory, dominance hierarchy
Cooperation: mutualism	**Cooperation:** parental care, social insects

5 a The main difference between territory and home range is a territory is defended, and a home range area is not.
b Intraspecific competition is generally much more intense than interspecific competition because in most cases there is little or no competition between different species, but lots within a species.
c One big advantage of social animals having ritual threat and submission behaviour, compared with settling disputes by fighting, is that it saves energy, and there is less likelihood of either contestant being injured or killed.
6 A submissive individual on balance benefits from staying with the group because the advantages of group life such as protection from predators probably outweigh the disadvantage of stress and perhaps getting less food.
7 Grooming probably reduces conflict, partly because low-ranked individuals grooming dominant individuals in a monkey group are more likely to confirm their place in the hierarchy.
8 a In the case of cleaner fish, the advantage to each species is that the cleaner fish gets food, and the larger fish gets awkward parasites removed.
b In a mycorrhizal mutualism arrangement, the advantage to each species is the underground fungus gets organic foods from the green plant, which in turn gets a greatly increased road system for absorbing water and nutrients.
c In the case of leafcutter ants, the advantage to each species is ants get food by eating the fungus they cultivate, and the fungus gets food supply brought by the ants.
9 **a** 15; **b** 41; **c** yellow; **d** grey; **e** yellow; **f** grey; **g** yellow, blue, white, orange, violet, red, black, indigo, green, grey; **h** blue and white; **i** The lowest-ranking monkey deferred to the highest-ranking monkey before any full threat; **j** A hierarchy reduces conflict and so reduces the risk of injury to all individuals — even the lowest-ranked.
10 a Both pots A and B are nitrogen-deficient, but in presence of *Rhizobium*, soybean grow far more than *Paspalum*. *Paspalum* is deprived of combined nitrogen but soybean obtains ammonia from *Rhizobium*, which can fix nitrogen.
b *Paspalum* grows far more rapidly when supplied with nitrate (pot C) than when nitrate is deficient (pot B). On the other hand, even when nitrate is supplied (pot C), soybean grows more slowly than it does in pot B. Soybean also grows more slowly than *Paspalum* in pot C, even though nitrate is supplied. This is probably because *Paspalum* that is not deprived of nitrate will compete more strongly with soybean for other essential minerals.
c Soybean grows considerably more in presence of *Rhizobium*, even though nitrate is available. This is probably because in competition for nitrate *Paspalum* is superior, but the ammonia produced by *Rhizobium* in the root nodules is unavailable to *Paspalum*.
d *Rhizobium* gains from the legume supply of energy in the form of carbohydrate produced in photosynthesis.
e The legume gains from *Rhizobium* a supply of usable/available nitrogen in the form of ammonia.
f Clover would probably have an advantage (over grasses) in soils that are deficient in combined/available nitrogen.
11 a By giving away food, there would be a short-term disadvantage: hunger. Hungry individuals are probably less successful in rearing their babies.
b If the bat that receives blood were to 'return the favour' at a later date, there could be a longer-term advantage. This could help the 'receiver' feed its own babies.

Unit 6 Exploitation: predation, parasitism

1 **a** crypsis; **b** alkaloid; **c** predator; **d** aposematic; **e** Batesian mimicry; **f** ectoparasite; **g** exploitation; **h** brood parasite; **i** autotomy; **j** endoparasite.
2 a One important difference between a parasite and a predator is that a parasite doesn't normally kill its host; a predator kills its prey.
b The word 'strategy' as applied to animals in the wild means a combination of adaptive features that promote reproductive success in an organism's niche.
c One important difference between a predator and a grazing animal is that a predator kills whole organisms; a grazing animal kills small parts of many plants without killing any individual plant.
d Compared with free-living animals, most endoparasites put a much larger proportion of their energy into reproduction because less energy has to be devoted to obtaining food and avoiding predators, leaving more energy for reproduction. (Also, very few of their eggs are successful in reaching a new host.)
e Batesian mimicry is the term for any situation in which a tasty species closely resembles a distasteful, dangerous or toxic species.
3 a Mistletoe, feeding on southern beech or other trees
b Shining cuckoo, parasitising grey warblers
4 Behavioural characteristics associated with crypsis: choosing a suitable background; staying still.
5 **a** parasitism; **b** predation; **c** parasitism; **d** grazing; **e** parasitism.
6 a Energy 'cost': the energy needed to build its shell.
b Energy 'saving': it can swim slowly/save energy fleeing predators.
7 Growing a new tail costs energy.
8 Many or most kinds of wild plant have natural chemical defences against attack from slugs and other animals. Very often these chemicals taste unpleasant. Domestic *food* plants have been selectively bred to taste nicer, which in many cases has meant loss of their chemical defences.
9 a Nesting in colonies improves defence against land-based predators, as predators generally can kill only a small proportion of their prey when there is a sudden abundance of prey.
b By dispersing after reproduction, food can be found over a much wider area so competition for food is reduced.
10 Advantage: a group of lions may be better able to pull down and kill large prey animals such as buffalo. Disadvantage of this group strategy: the food has to be shared among many. A solitary hunter such as a leopard has a different disadvantage: it cannot kill big prey and may have lower hunting success rates. Advantage: any prey that it does kill does not need to be shared.

Unit 7 Breeding behaviour

1 **a** precocial; **b** altricial; **c** pheromone; **d** courtship; **e** pukeko; **f** synchronisation; **g** K-strategy; **h** r-strategy; **i** tactile; **j** olfactory.
2 Little or no parental care: e.g. sea urchins, oysters, corals.
3 High level of parental care: e.g. seahorses, mammals, birds, crocodiles.
4 Courtship behaviour: helps to ensure that mating occurs between members of the same species; helps synchronise male and female behaviour.
5 a R-strategy animals do not care for their young, and compensate for this by producing many young.
b In species that have plenty of parental care, the life expectancy of parents can be reduced (compared with non-breeders), because they expend considerable energy in caring for their young.

c A young bird benefits from having a high level of parental care because it starts independent life with a much better chance of survival.
d Rainforest trees generally produce large seeds with a generous food supply because they germinate in shade, so a large energy supply helps the young plants reach a height where they can get sufficient light.

6 a No effect.
b Helpers increase survival; offspring survival increases up to 3 times with increased number of helpers; and survival rates increase with age of the offspring.
c Relatives share some of their genes in common, so by helping a relative, a bird increases the chances of contributing copies of its own genes to the next generation.

7 a This behaviour may reduce the energy cost to the parents
b Since siblings share some of their genes in common, when an individual helps to rear a sibling's offspring it is also helping that same individual's reproductive success, but at an energy cost.

8 Theory 1: male with bright plumage is probably free of parasites, since parasitic infection affects the brightness of the plumage. Theory 2: bright-coloured vigorous male may be more healthy, so may pass on its genes for health and vigour.

3.4 Internal environment control

Unit 1 Homeostasis basics

1 **a** neuron; **b** synapse; **c** tissue fluid; **d** CNS; **e** hypothalamus; **f** endocrine; **g** insulin; **h** plasma; **i** pituitary; **j** peripheral.

2 A 'set point' is one about which a particular variable is regulated. Example: The set point for body temperature is about 37°C.

3 Negative feedback is a mechanism by which changes in the internal environment are automatically corrected. Examples: **i** The higher the blood CO_2 level, the faster it is excreted by breathing; **ii** The higher the blood glucose level, the more insulin is secreted so the glucose is removed faster from the blood.

4 a By 'internal environment' we mean the tissue fluid surrounding the cells.
b By 'negative feedback' we mean a process in which the greater a change from a set point, the stronger the tendency to correct it.
c In temperature control systems, the purpose of a thermostat is to stop the heat-generating process when the temperature exceeds a certain pre-set value.
d The main difference between a static and a dynamic equilibrium is in a static equilibrium there is no change or movement; in a dynamic equilibrium there is constant adjustment around the set point.

5
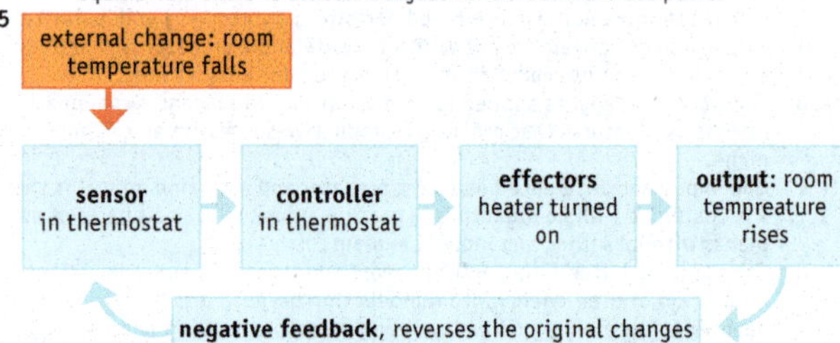

6 In homeostatic systems, effectors are structures that act to correct a departure from the set point. Examples: **i** In response to insulin, the liver removes glucose into the blood, thus opposing a tendency for it to rise; **ii** In response to a drop in skin temperature, smooth muscle in the walls of skin arterioles contracts, reducing blood flow and thus heat loss from the skin.

7 The result would be uncontrolled temperature rise.

8

A General process or stage	B Temperature regulation in humans
External change	Hard game of sport on a warm day
Sensor (detects the change)	Hypothalamus region in brain senses a temperature rise
Controller	Hypothalamus
Effector(s) (the part(s) that brings about action)	Sweat glands become more active
Output (the change brought about by the effector)	Evaporation causes cooling
Result of this change	Body temperature falls slightly

Unit 2 Temperature control

1 **a** hypothalamus; **b** ectotherms; **c** homeotherms; **d** vasodilation; **e** TSH; **f** thyroxine; **g** hypothermia; **h** hyperthermia; **i** poikilotherms; **j** autonomic.

2 **a** increases; **b** increases; **c** decreases; **d** no effect; **e** increases; **f** increases; **g** increases.

3 a Most animals die if their body temperature gets above 42°C because enzymes catalysing metabolic reactions are denatured.
b Animals like lizards move slowly when their body temperature is low because their enzymes work more slowly, slowing their metabolism.
c As regards temperature regulation, the main role of the hypothalamus is to detect changes in core body temperature and to stimulate effectors to make corrective changes.

4 A warm animal can be active even in cooler conditions, making it easier to catch prey and escape from enemies.

5 Blood transports heat away from areas that are too hot (such as active muscle) to sites where heat is lost (skin and lungs).

6 kidneys, heart, brain, active skeletal muscles, liver

7 In response to fall in core body temperature, the hypothalamus stimulates the hair erector muscles to contract. In furry mammals this helps to conserve heat, in humans it just causes 'goosebumps'.

8 An insulating layer of fur prevents movement of air next to the skin and so reduces loss of heat by convection. Air is a poor heat conductor.

9 Penguins live in continuously cold conditions and the heat exchangers are a 'permanent' solution to heat loss. In humans, the need for heat conservation is usually temporary; vasoconstriction can be turned on and off as needed.

10
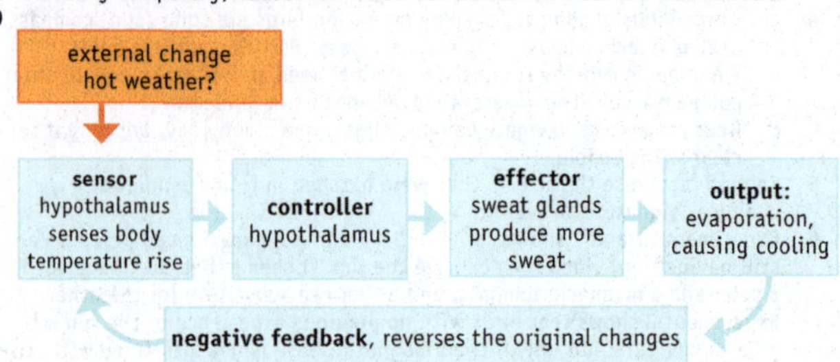

Unit 3 Blood pressure control

1 **a** systole; **b** diastole; **c** arteries; **d** veins; **e** arterioles; **f** capillaries; **g** brachial; **h** carotid; **i** hypertension; **j** hypotension.

2 a Compared with the right ventricle, the left ventricle is more muscular because it has to generate enough pressure to produce tissue fluid in the capillaries, and to force fluid into the kidney glomeruli at a high rate. (Note: pressure is not needed to 'send blood a greater distance', as capillary lengths are the same in lungs and in body.)
b When arteries become less elastic, this can increase blood pressure because they are less able to expand and thus reduce the surge of pressure when the heart contracts.

3 By contracting in one region, they reduce flow to it, and by dilating in another, they increase flow to it.

4 a 60 x 80 = 4800 mL = approx. 5 litres per minute
b 150 x 100 = 15,000 mL = 15 litres per minute
c 60 x 80 x 60 = 288,000 mL = 288 litres per hour

5 Systole is the contraction phase of the ventricles, diastole is the relaxation phase.

6 Pressure of 110/70 refers to systolic pressure 110 mm Hg, diastolic pressure 70 mm Hg

7 Baroceptors are in the walls of the carotid sinus at the base of each internal carotid artery. They respond to stretch, and thus to pressure in the carotid arteries.

8 High blood pressure can be caused by smoking, excessive intake of salt and steroid medication. Pressure can be lowered by reducing salt intake, reducing body weight, not smoking, reducing stress levels, keeping fit, taking necessary medication.

Unit 4 Water control

1 **a** renal artery; **b** renal vein; **c** osmoregulation; **d** glomerulus; **e** ADH; **f** mitochondria; **g** dialysis; **h** hypothalamus; **i** urea; **j** ureter.

2 a Very few protein molecules enter Bowman's capsule because they are too big to get through the sub-microscopic pores in the filter.
b The main direct effect of ADH is to increase the permeability of the collecting duct walls to water, eventually reducing urine output.
c The function of osmoregulation is to maintain a near-constant water concentration in the blood, lymph and tissue fluid.
d The region of the nephrons where most reabsorption takes place is the first convoluted tubules.

3 **a** decrease; **b** increase; **c** increased; **d** increase; **e** decreased.

4 a Most protein molecules are too large to pass through the filter in the glomeruli.
b All the glucose is reabsorbed because it is needed as fuel.
c Glucose is reabsorbed by active transport.

5
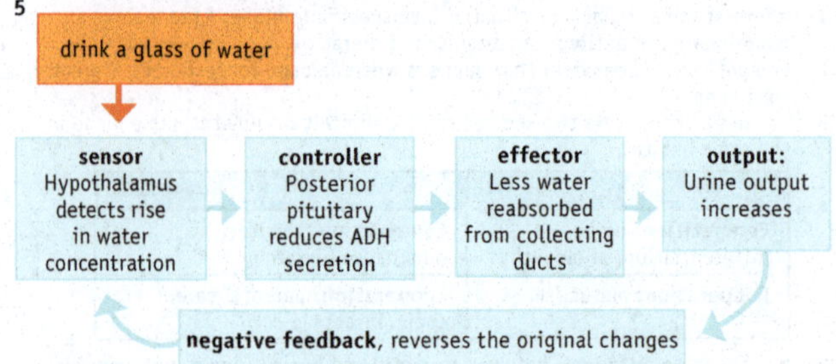

6 Many possible causes of kidney failure, including infection and diabetes. Where possible treat the primary cause first. If kidney function is permanently and severely impaired, the only long-term measure is daily dialysis.

Unit 5 Blood glucose control

1 **a** monosaccharide; **b** polysaccharide; **c** liver; **d** hyperglycaemia; **e** insulin; **f** glucagon; **g** hypoglycaemia; **h** sucrose; **i** liver; **j** glycogen.

2 **a** increases; **b** decreases; **c** no effect; **d** increases; **e** decreases; **f** increases; **g** increases (the *eventual* effect) **h** increases; **i** no effect.

3 a Surgical removal of the pancreas has serious health consequences because insulin secretion stops, leading to severe type 1 diabetes.

ISBN: 9780170355582

- b Insulin and glucagon have antagonistic effects, which means that they have effects that oppose each other: insulin lowers blood glucose level, glucagon raises it.
- c Type 2 diabetics often cannot be helped by insulin injections because type 2 diabetes results from inability to respond to insulin, not the inability to produce it.
- d The liver is anatomically well placed to regulate the amount of blood glucose after a meal because blood flows directly from the small intestine to the liver (via the hepatic portal vein).

4 5 L = 5000 mL = 5000 grams. 5000 grams x 0.09/100 = 4.5 grams

5 Insulin is a small protein molecule, produced in the beta cells of the islets of Langerhans in the pancreas.

6 Adrenaline is secreted in times of emergency when there is likely to be an urgent need for physical exertion and therefore glucose use. It causes the breakdown of liver glycogen into glucose and its release into the blood.

7 Diabetes causes peripheral vascular disease (PVD) in which arterial walls become thickened, reducing blood flow and eventually causing death of tissue 'downstream'.

8 Low-GI foods, after digestion, cause a smaller/more gradual rise in blood glucose level, compared with the effect of high-GI foods.

9 **a** 4.25 mmol/L; **b** 6.2 mmol/L; **c** meal and a peak in blood glucose 40 mins; **d** insulin peak and a subsequent blood glucose minimum 70 mins.

10

external change: sugary meal eaten

sensor Beta cells detect rise in blood glucose → **controller** Beta cells increase insulin secretion → **effector** Liver converts glucose into glycogen → **output:** Blood glucose level falls

negative feedback, reverses the original changes

Unit 6 O_2 and CO_2 control

1

a	intercostal
b	diaphragm
c	oxyhaemoglobin
d	erythropoietin
e	medulla
f	vasoconstriction
g	emphysema
h	bronchi
i	bronchioles
j	anaerobic

2
- a Capillaries and alveoli have extremely thin cell linings because diffusion of gases is much faster over short distances.
- b When the diaphragm relaxes and moves upwards, it has the effect of decreasing the volume of the lungs, so exhaling air.
- c When the diaphragm contracts and moves downwards, it has the effect of increasing the volume of the lungs, so inhaling air.
- d Blood carbon dioxide levels tend to rise when rate of respiration rises or if breathing voluntarily pauses.
- e The breathing centre's response to a slight rise in carbon dioxide is to stimulate the breathing muscles to work harder.

3 Heart output increases; gas exchange capacity increases; capillary density in muscles increases; VO_2 max increases.

4

Oxygen in the air in the alveoli, then:
1 Oxygen diffuses into the plasma
2 Combines to form oxyhaemoglobin
3 Transported in the blood
4 Unloaded from blood
5 Diffuses into muscle cells
6 Diffuses into mitochondria

5 glucose + oxygen → carbon dioxide + water + energy

6 Aerobic respiration uses oxygen (and occurs in mitochondria and produces lots of ATP); anaerobic metabolism does not use oxygen (and occurs in cytoplasm and produces less ATP).

7 25 x 2 = 50 L per minute

8 CO_2 forms carbonic acid when dissolved in water. As respiration increases, carbonic acid levels rise, causing pH to fall slightly.

9 80 mL/kg/min x 70 kg x 15 min = 84,000 mL = 84 L

10

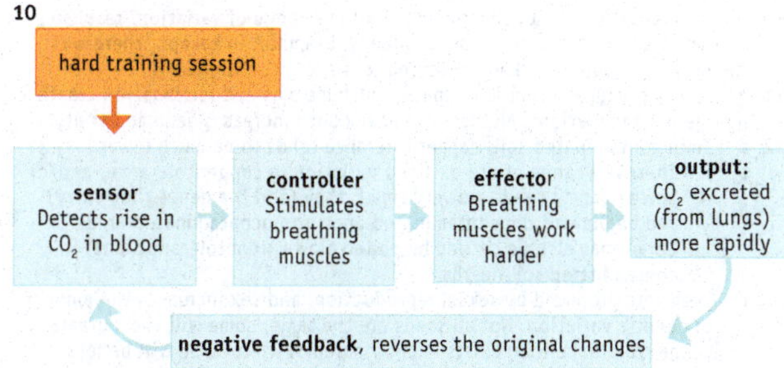

3.5 Evolutionary processes

Unit 1 Evolution basics

1 **a** Mendel; **b** Lamarck; **c** Darwin; **d** mutations; **e** sex; **f** ratites; **g** pentadactyl; **h** speciation; **i** *Archaeopteryx*; **j** biogeography.

2 **a** homologous; **b** analogous; **c** analogous; **d** homologous; **e** neither; **f** analogous; **g** both; **h** homologous; **i** both; **j** neither.

3
- a 7 differences (8 – 1) indicates a fairly close relationship.
- b 30 differences (38 – 8) indicates a very distant relationship.
- c 23 differences (38 – 15) indicates a distant relationship.
- d 24 differences (69 – 45) indicates a distant relationship.
- e 1 difference (1 – 0) indicates a very close relationship.

4 'Pentadactyl' literally means a five-fingered limb. It is characteristic of amphibians, reptiles, mammals and (highly modified) in birds.

5 Among tetrapod (four-limbed) vertebrates, limbs are adapted for functions as diverse as climbing (e.g. monkeys), running (e.g. dogs), swimming (e.g. seals) and flying (e.g. bats). In all these, the limb plan is fundamentally similar, suggesting that an ancestral pattern became modified for different functions.

6
- a Mutations are the ultimate source of new genetic material.
- b Sexual reproduction is the means by which existing genetic material is 'reshuffled' into new combinations.

7 To begin with almost all individual *Staphylococci* were sensitive to (killed by) antibiotics. A tiny minority of mutants were resistant to antibiotics like penicillin when they were first introduced. In this new 'penicillin' environment these few bacteria would have survived and eventually replaced the sensitive bacteria. A tiny minority of these penicillin-resistant bacteria would have had a second mutation making them resistant to (say) streptomycin, and so on, until bacterial populations were resistant to most kinds of antibiotics.

8 'Useful' alleles do not evolve because they are needed. What happens is that some allele variations, originating by chance, increase the probability of reproductive success, and so become more common over time.

9 Individuals that have a better than average chance of surviving and reproducing tend to make a greater contribution to the next generation. The 'fittest' individuals are those leaving the greatest number of descendants. For example, in a cryptic species of insect, the 'fittest' individuals are those that are most successful in avoiding predation by blending with their background.

Unit 2: Genes in populations

1

1	2	3	4	5	6	7	8	9	10
G	D	C	F	E	I	H	B	A	J

2
- a Mutation, immigration
- b Selection, genetic drift, immigration, mutation, (in very small populations) emigration

3 Number of *B* alleles = (20 x 2) + 50 = 90, so frequency of *B* = 90/200 = 0.45. By subtraction, frequency of *b* = 1 – 0.45 = 0.55.

4
- a In both cases, the 'new' population is tiny. Bottleneck: Little Spotted Kiwi. Founder: hares.
- b In the founder effect, the new population are emigrants from a 'parent' population, e.g. hares and hedgehogs are all descendants of a few individuals introduced into New Zealand in the 19th century. In a genetic bottleneck, the new population are survivors from a massive reduction of the parent population resulting from some catastrophic reduction, e.g. the Chatham Islands robin was reduced to a single female and four males. Little spotted kiwi have recovered from perhaps just five individuals.

5 In both founder and bottleneck situations, a population is reduced to small numbers. In either case, reproductive failure due to chance events can have significant effects on allele frequencies in a small surviving population.

6
- a Tieke were almost wiped out by rats and cats, so their descendants — the present-day survivors — only carry a small proportion of the alleles in the original gene pool.
- b This poses two threats. First, many of these 'lost' alleles could have been of potential benefit in surviving future environmental change. Second, as a result of inbreeding, certain disadvantageous recessive alleles would be more likely to be expressed, threatening the survival of the individuals possessing them.

7 Males with the brightest colours are most likely to be chosen by females, so the offspring are more likely to carry alleles causing bright colours. On the other hand, the most conspicuous males would be more likely to be eaten by predators. As a result, there is a balance between the advantage of finding a mate and the disadvantage of being eaten.

8 Since even the winner of combat could get seriously injured, it is to the advantage of both contestants to settle a conflict by threat rather than combat.

9 Stabilising selection acts against the extremes of a range of variation. Example: before modern medicine, babies with smallest and largest birth-weights were more likely to die, selection favouring the average.

10 Directional selection acts against one end of a range of variation, resulting in a progressive change in allele frequency. Example: in kakapo, there was selection in favour of kakapo spending less energy on flight.
11 Mutations produce new alleles. In sex, both meiosis and fertilisation create new gene combinations. Mutations and sex both increases genetic variety.
12 a In uncontaminated soil, copper tolerance tends to be much lower.
b i There is a range of pre-existing variation in copper tolerance, and/or
ii Since *Agrostis* seeds are very small, they (and the genes they carry) can be blown from contaminated areas to uncontaminated areas. Genes may also be carried by pollen blown from tolerant plants in contaminated soil nearby.
c Seeds are produced by sexual reproduction, and sex increases the amount of genetic variation. Not all seeds are the same; some will show greater copper tolerance than exists in their parents, while some will be less copper-tolerant then their parents.
d These results support the view that tolerance is disadvantageous in uncontaminated soil.
e When copper mining began, the population would have consisted mainly of plants that did not tolerate copper. Natural selection probably favoured those that grew the fastest. As a result of mutations, a small minority would have had some resistance to copper. In contaminated areas, natural selection would strongly have favoured those plants that could tolerate copper, with growth rates being a less important feature.

Unit 3 New species

1

1	2	3	4	5	6	7	8	9	10
B	C	G	E	D	F	H	A	J	I

2 About 220 million years ago (mya) the southern super-continent known as Gondwana began to break up. New Zealand separated from this about 80 mya, then other parts separated about 70 mya into what are now Antarctica, Australia and Africa. Its early separation explains the absence of certain groups from New Zealand, such as land mammals. The absence of mammalian predators also explains New Zealand's high proportion of flightless birds.
3 Pre-zygotic and post-zygotic isolating mechanisms both act to prevent gene flow between different species.
4 Pre-zygotic isolating mechanisms: different mating signals; different breeding seasons; sperm cannot penetrate the egg of another species.
5 Post-zygotic isolating mechanisms: hybrids may be sterile; hybrids fertile but physically less robust; hybrids offspring less viable.
6 For: Lions and tigers interbreed in captivity. Against: The offspring are weaker than either parent; clear differences in appearance and behaviour (lions are social and live in open country, tigers solitary, forest dwellers).
7 Mountain ranges, seawater separating rivers, vegetational zones, deserts
8 Polyploidy can bring about 'instant' species because offspring created by polyploidy are unable to interbreed with the population from which they arose, as a result of having different chromosome numbers.
9 a *Melicytus* (e.g. mahoe).
b Evidence of polyploidy: all species of *Melicytus* have chromosome numbers that are multiples of 16, e.g. *M. ramiflorus* 32, *M. alpinus* 48, *M. micranthus* 96.
10 a 'Sympatric' means living in the same geographical area or region.
b A reproductive isolating mechanism is an inherited feature that acts to prevent interbreeding between different species.
c Where the two species are allopatric, their calls are very similar.
d Where sympatric, *L. ewingii* has a call that is similar to allopatric *L. ewingii* populations, but the call of *L. verreauxii* is quite different. Thus it appears that after the two species became sympatric, the mating call of *L. verrauxii* diverged from that of *L. ewingii*.
e In regions where the two species are sympatric, there may be (or may have been) some interbreeding. If the hybrids were not fully viable, natural selection would have acted against them. Those individual *L. verrauxii* who had distinctly different calls would be less likely to hybridise, and so leave more viable offspring. If so, natural selection would have increased the difference between the two species sounds.
11 At some time in the distant past, swamp hens flew to New Zealand from Australia; almost certainly wind-assisted. In the absence of mammalian predators, genetically different individuals that spent least energy developing wing muscles had more energy available for growth and reproduction. Over many generations, these birds became flightless and also increased in size, evolving into takahe. During this period of allopatry, various pre-zygotic isolating mechanisms evolved. By the time recent ancestors of pukeko arrived in New Zealand only a few hundred years ago, pukeko and takahe could not interbreed, even when sympatric.

Unit 4 Patterns in evolution

1 **a** analogous; **b** adaptive radiation; **c** niche; **d** endemic; **e** punctuated equilibrium; **f** ecological equivalent; **g** polyploidy; **h** convergent; **i** co-evolution; **j** placental; **k** marsupial.
2 Sudden absence of competition after a group arrives in relatively uninhabited territory. Evolution of a new feature that enables organisms to compete more successfully with other species.
3 In the absence of placental mammal competitors, the ancestors of the Australian marsupials had a wide range of ecological 'opportunities', similar to those available to the ancestors of placental mammals in other parts of the world. Given these similar ecological conditions, marsupials radiated in parallel fashion to their placental equivalents. Quoll evolved as medium-sized agile predators, occupying the same niche as cats elsewhere in the world.
4 a Both squid and vertebrate eyes have: an internal lens; a cornea; retina.
b In the cephalopod (squid) retina the photoreceptors are 'in front' of the nerve cells, in the vertebrate retina they are 'behind'.
5 a Allopatric speciation.
b Changes in sea level causing the joining and separation of North and South island land masses. Rise of the Southern Alps partly separated the wet, mild west zone from drier, more extreme east zone. Any of these geological factors could have separated different populations.
6 a The overwhelming majority of *Hebe* species are endemic to New Zealand.
b i *H. odora* could have resulted from chromosome doubling of a hybrid between two species with $2n = 42$. Less likely, it could be a tetraploid, resulting from somatic doubling of an ancestor with $2n = 42$.
ii *H. salicifolia* could have resulted from fusion of two chromosomes to form a larger one or, less likely, it could be a nullisomic, resulting from loss of a chromosome.
iii *H. brachysiphon* could have originated as a hybrid between a species with $2n = 40$ and another species with $2n = 80$; gametes with $n = 20$ and $n = 40$, giving a hybrid with $2n = 60$ and probably sterile. Subsequent somatic doubling (polyploidy) would give $2n = 120$, restoring fertility.

3.6 Human evolution

Unit 1 Primates, rocks, dates

1 All primates have forward-facing eyes, grasping hands and feet, plantigrade ('flat' hands and feet), large brain (and most have colour vision).
2 **Hominid:** classification group including humans, *H. erectus* etc, australopithecines, chimpanzees, gorilla, orang-utan. **Hominin:** humans. *H. erectus* etc, australopithecines.
3 Orangutan, gorilla, chimpanzee, bonobo.
4 Gibbons are smaller in size than the other apes.
5 Brachiating means swinging from branches by the arms. Adaptations: long hands used as 'hooks'; reduced thumbs; very mobile shoulder joint; broad chest; arms longer than hind legs.
6 Ape hands are more adapted for brachiating, less for grasping.
7 a Binocular vision enables accurate distance-judgement, which is very important to animals that live high above the ground and jump between branches.
b There are few scent trails high above the ground, so there is little advantage in tree-living animals having a good sense of smell. (This also applies to birds.)
c Increases ability to grasp branches when climbing.
d Many fruits are red or orange when ripe, so an ability to see this is important to fruit-eaters.
8 Potassium/argon (suitable for volcanic sediments older than about one million years); carbon-14 is used for dating organic materials younger than about 50,000 years; fission track is used for dating volcanic rocks.
9 Fossils are found only in sedimentary rocks. The deeper the stratum in which a fossil is found, the earlier it was buried and the older it is.
10 **a** 24 mya; **b** 5–24 mya; **c** 5 mya; **d** from about 1.8 mya to 10 kya.
11 **a** carbon-14; **b** potassium-argon; **c** thermoluminescence.
12 1/8 = 0.125 picogram

Unit 2 Hominin beginnings

1

Structure	*H. sapiens*	Apes, e.g. chimpanzee
Brow ridge	Absent or small	Prominent
Foramen magnum	Centrally placed	Near back of skull
Canine teeth	Small	Prominent
Spine shape	S-shaped, with double curvature	Single curvature
Pelvis shape	Bowl-shaped	Long hip bones
Leg length	Long	Short
Knee joint	With valgus angle	Without valgus angle
Thumbs	Long	Short

2 The foramen magnum is the hole in the skull through which passes the spinal cord.
3 A centrally placed foramen magnum enabled the skull to be balanced on the atlas vertebra, reducing the need for strong muscles to keep the head upright. *Also*: having a central foramen magnum rotates the skull, enabling the eyes to face forward when standing upright, not up at the sky.
4 It enables grasping objects such as branches and, in humans, manipulation of objects. In apes, a long thumb would impede brachiation and their thumb is too small to be fully opposable.
5 Long 'hind' legs are an adaptation for bipedalism. Four or five million years ago the African climate became drier with wide areas of open grasslands. These conditions may have contributed to bipedal walking, since this would have allowed objects to be carried (food, infants) over long distances, and also foraging far from trees.
6 For: Humans have a higher density of sweat glands than any other mammal; reduced hairiness/less fur helps evaporation. Against: Other primates in the same environments are quite hairy; e.g. baboons.
7 Precision grip enables fine manipulative movements, such as needed for delicate operations (such as making stone tools).
8 A valgus angle enables the femur to be angled inwards and feet to be situated close to the midline, which enables efficient walking; without the wide stance and waddling walk that happens when feet are far apart, as in chimps. (Compared with chimp walking, human walking uses half as much energy per kilometre.)
9 Female humans don't advertise their ovulation so males don't know when a female is fertile; adults live for a long time after the age of childbearing; human babies are born in a helpless state, and the brain continues to grow long after birth; there is a long period of juvenile dependency.
10 A wide pelvis enables big-headed, large-brained babies to be born.

ISBN: 9780170355582

11 Without some way of carrying water, hominins were limited to areas less than one day's walk from the nearest surface water. In dry seasons, this fact must have restricted their range to river valleys.

Unit 3 The first hominins

1

Place	Country	Fossil hominin	Lived (mya)
Taung	South Africa	*Australopithecus africanus*	3.0–2.5
Olduvai	Tanzania	*Paranthropus boisei, Homo habilis*	2.0–1.0
Afar	Ethiopia	*Australopithecus afarensis* ('Lucy')	3.2
Awash	Ethiopia	*Ardipithecus kadabba*	5.8–5.2
Aramis	Ethiopia	*Ardipithecus ramidus*	4.4
Laetoli	Tanzania	Earliest human footprints	3.0
Turkana	Kenya	*Homo erectus*	1.8

2 **a** Big toe directed partly *sideways*; **b** Long legs? Valgus angle? Big toe directed *partly* sideways; **c** Long arms, canines longer; **d** Jaw shorter.

3 **a** *Paranthropus*; **b** *Australopithecus*; **c** *A. afarensis*; **d** *Ardipithecus*; **e** *A. africanus*; **f** hominins; **g** sagittal crest.

4 **a** Bipedalism may have given protection against predators because it would have enabled their earlier detection, and increased survival rates because perhaps fewer were killed by predators.

b Bipedalism may have been linked to use of tools and weapons because it freed the hands for manipulating objects, and increased survival rates because more successful tool makers may have obtained more food.

c Bipedalism may have been linked to hot African conditions because it may have reduced absorption of midday solar heat; and greater air currents higher up would have helped evaporation of sweat.

d Bipedalism may have been linked to carrying infants because the hands could be free to carry them, and ... perhaps endable longer journeys in search of food.

5 'Gracile' means slender. Example: *A. africanus*.

6 'Robust' means 'stoutly built'. Example: *Paranthropus boisei*.

7 Apelike: small ape-sized brain. Humanlike: knee with valgus angle; forward-directed big toe; small canine teeth.

8 Air movements are stronger higher above ground level, which helps sweat evaporate, even more so if there is little hair to reduce evaporation. Also: bipedalism was probably associated with life away from trees and shade, creating a greater need for cooling in hot climates.

9 Bipedalism originated 4 mya or earlier. According to evidence, tool-making originated nearer 2 mya. Natural selection would not have produced bipedalism at 4 or 5 mya in anticipation of behaviour that was 2 mya in the future.

Unit 4 First stone tools, first fire

1 *Au. africanus* had a mean capacity of about 400 cm^3, *H. habilis* 650 cm^3, *H. rudolfensis* about 750 cm^3, and *H. erectus* varied from 800 cm^3 (early) to 1250 cm^3 (late).

2 Oldowan culture: Called 'pebble tools' because most of the surface was rounded and pebble-like; only one end chipped to create working surfaces.

3 '*habilis*' means 'handy', referring to (presumed) tool-making abilities of *H. habilis*.

4 Electron micrographs of fossil bones of prey animals show that characteristic marks made by stone tools in some cases sometimes overlay marks clearly made by lion teeth.

5 Stones (not teeth) were used to smash bones to get the energy-rich marrow. Stone tools were possibly used in defence against predators such as leopards and hyenas. Individuals who were skilled users of stone tools would have provided more food for their families.

6 Making tools by early humans was more sophisticated than using 'found' objects such as unmodified stones. Chimps use 'found' stones, but also modify twigs to dig out termites. This implies a humanlike sense of purpose, so there is not a completely clear line between human and chimp behaviour in this. However, chimps do not seem to have the human ability to use tools to make other tools, or sophisticated ones.

7 **a** Fires provide warmth at night, which meant that survival was increased in colder weather and hunting could be extended into high mountainous areas of Africa.

b Cooking kills bacteria in the meat, which meant that dangers of food poisoning were reduced, and food lasted longer after cooking.

c Fires repel lions and other predators, which meant that fewer children were killed, and life expectancy increased.

d Fire can be used to harden wood, which meant that spear tips could be more effective, increasing hunting success and food supplies.

e Fires provide a social focus point at night, which meant that social life could be extended, perhaps facilitating the later development of language, plus the reassurance of group gathering.

8 Heat-altered soils have been found dated earlier than 1 mya. Trials have shown that forest fires could not have caused these high temperatures. Probable 1 mya 'campfire' sites have been found associated with ash and animal bones.

9 Edges of Oldowan tools were only cut from one end of a stone. Ascheulean 'hand axes' were much larger and had two main faces edges, formed using far more blows.

10 **a** Oldowan: *H. habilis*; **b** Acheulean: *H. erectus*.

11 The 'Turkana boy' was 1.6 metres tall, yet skeletal features indicated he was only nine years old. This indicates that *H. erectus* adults were of similar height to modern humans.

Unit 5 Neanderthals, Denisovans and more

1

1	2	3	4	5	6	7	8	9	10
J	E	F	C	B	I	A	H	G	D

2

Characteristic	*H. neanderthalensis*	*H. sapiens*
Occipital bun	Present	Absent
Chin	Absent	Present
Mean cranial capacity	1500 cm^3	1350 cm^3
Incisors	Larger	Smaller
Nasal cavity	Larger	Smaller
Brow ridges	Present	Absent
Forehead	Low	High

3 Neanderthals lived in such cold conditions that they must have used clothing to survive. Microwear study of their tools shows they were used to work animal hides. The wear on their incisors suggested they were used like pliers to hold animal skins.

4 Some Neanderthal skeletons had degenerative features showing they would have been incapable of getting food themselves, so must have been looked after by others.

5 Many Neanderthal skeletons were entire, showing they must have been protected from predators. Some were buried with stone tools and parts of prey animals. Some remains were covered with pollen of colourful flowers.

6 Neanderthal DNA is found in about 2.5 per cent of modern humans from Europe and Asia, but Africans have no Neanderthal DNA.

7 *H. floresiensis* was fully bipedal, had small teeth and jaws, had stone tools.

8 *H. floresiensis* had a tiny brain about 380 cm^3, was only about one metre high.

9 *H. floresiensis* may have evolved from *H. erectus*, developing its dwarf-like features in isolation from other populations. Since Flores is surrounded by deep water, it must have been an island even during the ice ages, so they must have got there by boat.

10 Studies of Denisovan DNA from bone fragments show that they diverged from the line leading to modern humans about one million years ago. About 4–6 per cent of nuclear DNA of modern people in New Guinea, Fiji, New Caledonia and Vanuatu is Denisovan.

11 They were far more varied (e.g. chisels, points, blades), suggesting greater specialisation for particular uses. They used the Levallois technique, resulting in much finer, thinner, cutting edges. Far more cutting edge could be produced from a single stone.

Unit 6 The first modern humans

1

	Biological evolution	Cultural evolution
Comparative speed of change	Relatively slow	Can be extremely rapid
Underlying causes of change	Random genetic mutation and recombination	Imagination, creativity and problem-solving, usually in purposeful ways
How information is stored	In DNA	In brain, on paper, and (recently) electronically
Transmission	Via gametes and fertilisation	By language, art, writing
Examples of this kind of change in humans	Evolution of lactose tolerance in Europeans; evolution of malaria resistance by sickle cell allele	Development of religions and cultures; changes in musical tastes; any technological change; any language development

2 Huge numbers of bones at bottom of cliffs suggest herds of animals were stampeded over cliffs. The extinction of many species of large animals coincided with the arrival of modern humans in Europe, North America, Australia, and New Zealand.

3 'Modern' means skeletally modern.

4 *H. sapiens* found how to start fire by striking sparks off 'firestones', and could create much higher temperatures by the use of ducted air channels in the earth.

5 A = *H. erectus*; B = *H. neanderthalensis*; C = *H. sapiens*; D = *P. boisei*.

6 Q = Acheulean; R = Oldowan; S = Mousterian; T = Neolithic.

7

Broad category	Name of 'age'	Who?	First when? (approx. ya)	Short descriptions/ names of main cultural/technological development(s)
Industrial Revolution		Worldwide *H. sapiens*	300	Fossil fuels become cheap, abundant sources of energy
Settled agriculture		Worldwide *H. sapiens*	10–7 kya	Farming. First permanent buildings. First writing 6 kya

(Table continued over)

Broad category	Name of 'age'	Who?	First when? (approx. ya)	Short descriptions/ names of main cultural/technological development(s)
'Metal ages': first bronze, then iron		Worldwide *H. sapiens*	10 kya	Metal tools and weapons
'Stone ages'	Neolithic	*H. sapiens*	12 kya	Composite tools
	Upper Palaeolithic	*H. sapiens*	50 kya	Great diversity of stone and bone tools
	Mesolithic	*H. neanderthalensis*	300 kya	Mousterian culture, Levallois technique
	Lower Palaeolithic	*H. erectus*	1.9 mya	Acheulean
		H. habilis	2.6 mya	Oldowan, simple pebble tools
	(none)	*Australopithecus*	4 mya	(none?)

Unit 7 The spread of *Homo sapiens*

1 a The 'Out of Africa' hypothesis holds that modern humans left Africa relatively recently and replaced pre-existing populations of *H. erectus*. The 'Multiregional' hypothesis holds that modern humans have evolved independently in various parts of the world from local *H. erectus* populations.
  b First: the oldest fossils of modern humans in Africa are much older (195 kya) than the oldest modern human fossils outside Africa (120 kya). Second: mtDNA of African populations is far more varied than that of populations in the rest of the world, as would be expected if a small sample of an African population moved out of Africa and replaced *H. erectus* populations.

2 a They walked from Siberia to Alaska, across land exposed by fall in sea level during the Pleistocene ice ages, some time before 15 kya.
  b During the Pleistocene ice ages, sea levels were lower. Australia and New Guinea were one land mass, but there was still deep water separating this from Indonesia. This must have been crossed by boat or rafting, before 45 kya.

3 UV radiation is necessary for vitamin D being made in the skin, but is also carcinogenic. Further from the equator, UV radiation is less intense, so the need to produce vitamin D is more important than the slight risk of skin cancer. In these conditions, pale skin (with reduced melanin) is (or was) favoured by natural selection.

4 In the tropics, dark skin provides protection from the intense UV light and its ability to cause cancer. Under these conditions, skin cancer is a threat, and vitamin D deficiency is very unlikely. For these reasons, natural selection favours individuals with dark skin.

5 At some stage after diverging from the chimpanzee line, the population of human ancestors was reduced to a very small number, creating a genetic bottleneck. Second likely reason: *H. sapiens* has existed around 200 kya; chimpanzees have existed for several million years.

6 Human mtDNA has been sequenced and compared for people in different populations. Knowing the mutation rate of mtDNA it is possible (with the aid of a computer) to work backwards to determine the approximate date of the most recent common ancestor ('Mitochondrial Eve'), who lived between 150 kya and 230 kya.

7 A cline is a gradient of a phenotypic characteristic through the area occupied by a population. It results from the combined effects of selection at each locality, combined with the effects of gene flow between neighbouring areas. There are no clear boundaries between human populations, so there is no justification for continuing the idea of distinct 'races'.

Unit 8 Neolithic revolutions

1 Nomads are groups that move from one place to another as food supplies dictate.

2 !Kung people are nomadic hunter-gatherers, 'gathering' foods such as wild fruits, berries, edible roots, small animals like lizards and insects.

3 Wheat, barley, rice, corn (maize), potatoes.

4 Goats (meat, milk, leather); sheep (meat, milk, wool); cattle (meat, milk, leather, pulling power); horses (transport); dogs (hunting companions); guinea pigs (meat); pigs (meat); cats (controlling rats and mice); llamas (meat, milk, leather, wool); camels (meat, leather, transport).

5 Turkey, Iraq, Egypt, India, China, Peru, New Guinea.

6 One million years minus 10,000 years' settled agriculture = 990,000 years as nomads = 99 per cent of a million years.

7 Farming called for new skills and occupations (such as making farm tools and storage vessels). Settled communities could afford to make tools that were too cumbersome or heavy for hunter-gatherers and nomads to carry, such as large earthenware vessels. Food surpluses enabled populations to increase. Food surpluses also enabled occupations not directly concerned with farming, and increased wealth seems to have resulted in more hierarchical societies.

8 More food, increased population size, settlements and towns, writing.

9 Iron is/was made from iron ore (rock) by heating it with charcoal. Iron's benefits: a hard metal, making it useful for axes, etc. Iron mineral sources are abundant. Iron can be made into steel, which is stronger and less brittle than iron. Problems: smelting iron ore led to massive need for charcoal, causing deforestation. Iron and steel soon used for weapons, making war more deadly.

3.7 Gene manipulation

Unit 1 Selective breeding

1 Selective breeding is a process of using individuals with desired phenotypes for breeding purposes, and not using those with less desired phenotypes.

2 Mutations are the ultimate source of new or different genes. New mutant animals and plants give breeders more material to select from.

3 a Mutations increase variety, but are comparatively uncommon.
  b Crossing over increases genetic variety, and means no two gametes are ever the same.
  c Random allocation of chromosomes to gametes greatly increases variety.

4 A monoculture is a large area with just one plant species and little genetic diversity. The risk is that a sudden change in conditions such as a new pest could destroy all the plants, since they are all genetically similar.

5 Apples have been used and farmed by people for thousands of years. In that time, many mutations have occurred, giving farmers the chance to select individual plants and create new cultivars. These cultivars in turn will have had mutations, creating even more possibilities.

6 Hares are quick, and few dogs can catch them. Any hunter noticing that one individual among his own dogs was faster and more successful than the others would use it for breeding purposes and keep the pups for breeding. Their descendants on average were probably faster than other dogs. If this process was kept up for generations, and the new breed kept separate from other dogs, then the breed would have consisted only of very fast individuals.

7 Selective breeding can involve inbreeding, with loss of vigour. Also, some alleles may vanish completely.

Unit 2 Cloning

1 A clone is all the individuals that are genetic copies of the original parent. A clone can be artificial or natural.

2 Tissue culture techniques involve growing plants from tiny pieces of leaf or stem or root tissue. Can also be used for some animal cells.

3 Cloning can have evolutionary negative consequences because it reduces the amount of genetic variety (diversity), which makes a population vulnerable to sudden changes in the environment, and less likely to meet changing conditions.

4 Advantages of cloning: probably faster; all plants ripen at the same time; produce an almost identical crop, which simplifies marketing.

5 When using grafting, a farmer can combine a ' root stock' with desirable qualities such as disease resistance, with a fruiting variety that has other desirable qualities.

6 Tissue culture is a quick way of producing thousands of plants with identical gene make-up. It can be done indoors, taking up very little space.

Unit 3 GMO technologies

1 Each restriction enzyme cuts DNA at a particular base sequence, which is different for each enzyme.

2 To cut DNA at pre-selected points.

3 a Annealing mixes the two kinds of fragment, allowing the 'sticky ends' to form loose, H-bonded links.
  b Using DNA ligase joins the polynucleotide backbones with covalent bonds.

4 In vivo: 'in life', in living cells. Example: using *Agrobacterium* to insert a gene into plant cells. In vitro: in glass/in a container. Example: microinjection, injecting DNA into cells.

5 a PCR: polymerase chain reaction.
  b Purpose: to produce large number of identical copies from a very small initial sample of DNA.

6 Gel electrophoresis separates DNA fragments according to their size.

7 In gel electrophoresis, bigger DNA fragments do not travel as far compared to smaller fragments because longer fragments encounter more resistance in moving through the gel.

8 The purpose of using plasmids in the making of GMOs is to insert donor DNA into bacteria in which they are then replicated alongside the rest of the bacterial DNA.

9 Five methods: microinjection, biolistics, using a virus as a carrier, electroporation, *Agrobacterium*.

10 Success rate is very low because only a tiny proportion of the bacteria takes up the plasmids.

11 Both processes aim at producing plant or animal varieties that are more useful in some way than the original varieties, or have better qualities.

12 Compared with traditional selective breeding, the production of genetically modified GMOs is potentially a lot faster; is potentially able to introduce a specific gene for a specific purpose; is more high-tech, needing highly specialised skills; has resulted in new gene combinations and seed varieties becoming owned and controlled by corporations, and not freely available.

ISBN: 9780170355582